presents

PARENTING AND TEACHING YOUNG CHILDREN

Let us introduce you to a totally new textbook! We are proud of this textbook, because we are convinced that it offers a truly exciting approach to child development, parenting, family life, and child-care courses. Here's why:

1. PARENTING AND TEACHING YOUNG CHILDREN ties together three key areas—child development, parenting, *and* child-care careers.

   • Child Development

   Child growth and development forms the outline of the textbook. The changes of childhood are traced from prenatal growth through the kindergarten years. This provides a logical, orderly sequence for your course. It builds the strongest possible foundation for understanding children.

   • Parenting

   "What is the role of the parent?" "Do I want to take on that role?" "When is a couple ready for parenthood?" These are the first important questions, and Part I of the text deals fully with them. Throughout each Part, the interactions between parent and child are explored. Needs and concerns that parents experience are also discussed. We show a realistic picture of parenting—its joys and responsibilities.

   • Child-care Careers

   Students learn about the care giver's role, care-giver skills, and career opportunities. This is crucial for those students with vocational goals, but equally important for future parents who will interact with care givers and teachers of all kinds. The text is especially appropriate for classes with child-care laboratories in the school or community.

2. "Special Features" are found in each Part of the text. They visually reinforce important concepts. For example, take a look at pages 240 and 322.

3. "Decisions, Decisions" are the thought-provokers in each chapter. They draw the student into a problem-solving role as a parent or as a care giver. Pages 249 and 251 illustrate how.

4. Each chapter provides solid educational features: "Objectives," "Terms to look for," and "Activities." Check Chapter 14 on page 132. Also, notice the manageable length of this and all other chapters.

5. A complete Glossary of key terms starts on page 422. The glossary defines each term and refers students to the page where it was first introduced.

6. Each of the sixteen units can stand alone. You can tailor units to fit an individual curriculum or class. The Scope and Sequence Chart on page 6 helps you plan.

7. The writing style and reading level of the text is appropriate for tenth- through twelfth-grade students as measured by the Dale-Chall formula.

8. The photos and illustrations are great! Thumb through PARENTING AND TEACHING YOUNG CHILDREN and look for yourself. You'll see a wide range of men and women in the role of parent or care giver.

9. The complete Teacher's Manual provides useful lesson summaries and discussion questions, as well as reproducible tests and activity sheets.

PARENTING AND TEACHING YOUNG CHILDREN

Other McGraw-Hill Titles from

The Home Ec Professionals

CHILD GROWTH AND DEVELOPMENT   Hurlock

CONCEPTS IN CLOTHING   Graef, Strom

FOCUS ON FOOD   Peck, Moragne, Sickler, Washington

GUIDE TO MODERN MEALS   Shank, Fitch, Chapman, Ohl, Duyff, Hasler

HOW YOU PLAN AND PREPARE MEALS   Carson, Ramee, Cobe

PERSONAL PERSPECTIVES   Paolucci, Faiola, Thompson

SURVIVAL: A GUIDE TO LIVING ON YOUR OWN   Kelly, Chamberlain

TEEN GUIDE TO HOMEMAKING   Brinkley, Chamberlain, Champion

THE HOME: ITS FURNISHINGS AND EQUIPMENT   Morton, Guthrie, Inman, Geuther

TODAY'S GUIDE TO MODERN CLOTHING   Faiola, Pullen

YOUR MARRIAGE AND FAMILY LIVING   Landis

Professional Resource:

CREATIVE HOME ECONOMICS INSTRUCTION   Chamberlain, Kelly

Parenting and Teaching Young Children

Verna Hildebrand, Ph.D.

Professor of Family and Child Sciences
Michigan State University

Webster Division
McGraw-Hill Book Company

New York   St. Louis   San Francisco   Auckland
Bogotá   Düsseldorf   Johannesburg   London
Madrid   Mexico   Montreal   New Delhi
Panama   Paris   São Paulo   Singapore   Sydney
Tokyo   Toronto

Editor in Chief: Carol Newman
Managing Editor: Alma Graham
Photo Supervisor: Rosemary O'Connell
Coordinating Editor: Sandra MacGowan
Designer: James Darby
Production Manager: Karen Romano

Photo Research: Freda Leinwand
Text Design: Caliber Design Planning, Inc.
Illustration: Educational Graphics, Inc.

This book was set in 11 point Caledonia by
Monotype Composition Company, Inc. The color
separation was done by Kwik International Color, Ltd.

Library of Congress Cataloging in Publication Data

Hildebrand, Verna.
    Parenting and teaching young children.
    Includes index.
    SUMMARY: A home economics textbook that discusses
aspects of child development including parenthood, child
care, and day care facilities.
    1. Parenting. 2. Child development. 3. Children—
Care and hygiene. [1. Child development. 2. Parenting.
3. Children—Care and hygiene.   I. Title.   II. Series:
Home ec professionals.
HQ755.8.H54   649'.1   80-11280
ISBN 0-07-028775-9

About the Author

Dr. Verna Hildebrand writes *Parenting and Teaching Young Children* with an understanding of children, students, and parents based on many years of practical personal experience combined with an excellent academic preparation. She has the distinction of having already achieved nationwide recognition as the author of two of the leading university textbooks in the field—*Introduction to Early Childhood Education* and *Guiding Young Children*. Also, she has been writing numerous professional articles, speaking at professional meetings, and engaging in professional consulting.

Dr. Hildebrand has learned much as a successful wife and mother of two children—a daughter, Carol, who is an attorney, and a son, Steve, who is now a university student. Her husband of over 30 years, Dr. John R. Hildebrand, is an economist, author, consultant, and farmer.

Interest in child development for Verna Hildebrand began when she was a high school student taking a child-care unit in a home economics class. That interest in child development has continued through a long period of university study at Kansas State University at Manhattan, the University of California at Berkeley, and at Texas Woman's University at Denton.

During her career, she has been a graduate teaching assistant in university early-childhood laboratories, a teacher in day-care centers and in public school kindergartens in California, a home economics teacher in a high school in Kansas, and head teacher in university early-childhood laboratory schools at Kansas State University, Oklahoma State University, Texas Tech University, and Michigan State University. During her years at these universities, Dr. Hildebrand has taught thousands of students in undergraduate and graduate courses related to child development, family life, and to parenting, teaching, and guiding young children. Dr. Hildebrand is currently Professor of Family and Child Sciences at Michigan State University in East Lansing.

ACKNOWLEDGMENTS

I wish to thank Lois Lund, Dean of Michigan State University's College of Human Ecology, and Eileen Earhart, Chairperson of the Department of Family and Child Sciences, for facilitating an All-University Research Grant supporting the initiation of this project and for granting a quarter's leave of absence without pay and a year's sabbatical leave for doing the research and writing. I wish to recognize the help of Barbara Gaylor, Michigan Department of Education, and the help of the 152 Michigan high school teachers of parenting and child development courses who returned lengthy questionnaires that greatly influenced the content and approach of *Parenting and Teaching Young Children*.

The following individuals also merit thanks for curriculum and content guidance through personal discussions, for allowing me to discuss issues with their high school students, for permitting me to visit and photograph in the child-development centers, or for reading portions of the manuscript and making helpful comments: Catherine Landreth, University of California—Berkeley; Sylvia Ann White, Lincoln High School, San Diego, California; Mary Ann Parthum and Jo Ann K. Dohe of the Denver Public Schools, Colorado; Kay Kummerow, Elgin High School, Illinois; Hazel Taylor Spitze, University of Illinois, Urbana, Illinois; Joan Aldous, University of Notre Dame, South Bend, Indiana; Irene Wells, Fowler High School, Kansas;

Mary Ann Presnal, Kansas State University, Manhattan, Kansas; Helen Frieze, Mary Helen Mastin, Diane Pepper, and Paula Weber of the Wichita High Schools, Kansas; Lynne Cromwell, Rockville High School, Maryland; Phyllis Klein, Bay-Arenac Skill Center, Bay City, Michigan; Janet Masi, Marygrove College, Detroit, Michigan; Vera Borosage, Dena Cedarquist, Lawrence Schiamberg, Vern Seefeldt, and Cheryl Coates, Michigan State University, East Lansing, Michigan; Dorothy Stout, Grand Rapids Public School, Michigan; Analei Koets, Kent Skill Center, Grand Rapids, Michigan; Linda Peet, Haslett High School Child Development Center, Michigan; Laura Cox, Jackson Vocational Technical Child Care Center, Michigan; Nancy Ingram and Edith Bradford of the Lansing High Schools, Michigan; Theda Connel, Southeast Oakland Vocational Technical Center Child-Care Center, Royal Oak Michigan; Elizabeth Jane Rowe, Eastfield Community College, Dallas, Texas; Jo Ann Scott, Edna High School, Texas; Don Longworth and Camille Bell, Texas Tech University, Lubbock, Texas; Rebecca Peña Hines, Parent-Child Development Center and Child Development Associate Consultant, Houston, Texas; Betty Larson, San Antonio College Child Care Center, Texas; and Dena Stoner, State Department of Education, Milwaukee, Wisconsin.

V.H.

Scope and Sequence

	Part 1 Parents and Care Givers	Part 2 A New Person	Part 3 The Infant	Part 4 The Toddler	Part 5 The Prekinder-gartner	Part 6 The Kindergartner
Parenting Skills	Chapters 1 and 2	Chapters 4, 5, 10, and 11	All chapters. Emphasis in Chapters 15 and 18.	All chapters. Emphasis in Chapters 25 and 26. Special feature p.322	All chapters. Emphasis in Chapters 34 and 35. Special feature p.322	All chapters. Emphasis in Chapters 43 and 44. Special feature p.376
Care Giver Skills (vocational)	Chapters 1 and 3 Special feature p. 34		Chapters 18, 19, and 20 Special feature p. 286	Chapters 25, 28, and 29 Special features p. 286 and 322	Chapters 34, 37, and 38 Special features p. 322 and 346	Chapters 43, 46, and 47 Special feature p.376
Child Growth and Development — Emotional and Social	Chapter 1		Chapter 13 Special feature p.130	Chapter 22	Chapter 31	Chapter 40
Child Growth and Development — Physical		Chapter 7 Special feature p. 78	Chapter 12 Special feature p. 130	Chapter 21	Chapter 30	Chapter 39
Child Growth and Development — Mental	Chapter 1		Chapters 14 and 20 Special features p. 130 and 286	Chapters 23 and 29 Special feature p. 286	Chapters 32 and 38	Chapters 41 and 47
Nutrition		Chapters 7, 8, and 10	Chapters 15 and 16	Chapter 27	Chapter 36	Chapter 45
Health and Safety		Chapters 7 and 9	Chapters 15 and 17 Special feature p. 240	Chapter 24 Special feature p. 240	Chapter 33	Chapter 42

Contents

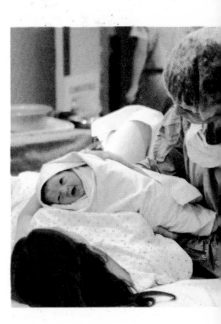

PART 5
The Prekindergartner 289

1

Parents and Care Givers

You will examine the role of parent and some reasons why people choose to become parents. You will also examine the role of care giver and learn what wage-earning careers are possible for care givers.

1

Children: A Part of Your Life?

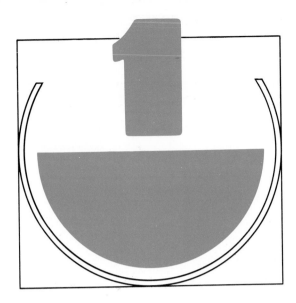

Looking Ahead

Objectives
To identify roles you might play as an adult.
To identify and explain a *time line*.
To explain the focus and benefits of this course.

Terms to look for   care giver • child-care career • parenting role •
time line • wage-earning role

Do you ever wonder what your life as an adult will be like? Many events in your future will be surprising. There is no way to predict what these events will be or when they will happen. But there is an orderly sequence to life, and you can make some predictions based on that fact.

What Is a Time Line?

A *time line* is a graph of how you will spend the years of your life. It will help you estimate the number of years you

will spend in each of life's stages. To make a time line, draw a line across a piece of paper or on the chalkboard. Divide the line into 10 segments—1 for every 10 years. That makes 100 years from birth to death. Then divide each 10-year segment into 1-year or 2-year units. Draw six parallel lines beneath this line. You can use the illustration on pages 16 and 17 as a sample.

The time line in this book shows six typical stages: student, worker, spouse, parent, retiree, and other. The "other" category allows you to fill in any long-range stage in your life that is different from the first five. Some other stages

Time line of Carlos Delgado

YEARS	0	5	10	15	20	25	30	35	40
Student		▓▓▓▓	▓▓▓	▓ x ▓	▓▓				
Worker					▓▓	▓▓▓	▓▓▓	▓▓▓	▓
Spouse						▓▓	▓▓▓	▓▓▓	▓
Parent							▓▓	▓▓▓	▓
Retiree									
Other (hold a political office)									

Time line of Eileen Simcox

YEARS	0	5	10	15	20	25	30	35	40
Student		▓▓▓	▓▓▓	x ▓					
Worker				▓	▓▓			▓▓	▓
Spouse							▓▓	▓▓▓	▓
Parent									
Retiree									
Other (live in another country)						▓▓			
Other (raise horses)									

may be military service, a second career, or a long-range ambition.

Put a small *x* on your present year. Then, fill in each column to show how many years you expect each stage of your life to last. Do not fill in a column if you plan to spend no time in that stage. For example, some people choose not to marry. Others marry but do not have children. Some people take early retirement, while others plan to work for most of their lives.

Estimating the Length of Each Stage

As a typical person receiving modern health care, you can now expect to have more than 70 years on your time line.

Some of you may live for about 100 years. Right now, you can probably look back on about 15 years. How many of those 15 years can you remember? You may remember some things that happened in your preschool years. But most of your memories are probably of your school-age years. You can now look ahead to spending more years in school, to launching a career, and perhaps to getting married and having a family.

By looking at your time line, you can get a sense of the stages that will make up the greatest part of your life. For another comparison, calculate the percentage of your life that you will spend in each stage. To make calculations easier, assume that you will live to be 100 years old. Then, if you are 15 years old,

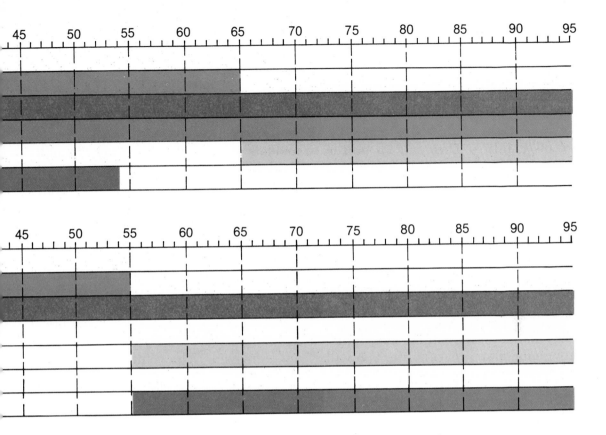

you can assume that you have lived 15/100, or 15 percent, of your life. If you plan to be a worker for 40 years, that is 40 percent of your life.

What percentage from your time line is highest? What percentage is lowest? Does estimating the length of your life stages give you any insights?

You may estimate your life span more realistically than our 100 years by using the life spans of some close relatives as a basis for calculation.

Doing Two or More Things at Once

At some points on your time line, stages may overlap. You will be playing more than one role. For example, you may be a student and a worker, or a spouse, parent, and worker. The more roles you try to combine, the more complicated life will become. Each role takes knowhow and requires repeated decision making. This overlap can be a great challenge. It makes a person's life full and active. But it also adds stress. When one role is going poorly, worry and frustration may result.

Think about the roles you play right now as part of your student stage. You might play the role of child, the role of sister or brother, and the role of worker or student. Each of these roles requires certain behaviors. How many roles do you need in order to develop your life? How many roles can you manage without being overloaded and ineffective?

Focus of This Course

In this course, you will focus on parenting roles and on wage-earning roles in various kinds of child-care careers. These roles are closely related. Both roles involve more than simply "taking care of" children. They call for nurturing, understanding, guiding, and giving of yourself. The word used in this book for a person who holds a job providing this kind of care for children is *care giver.*

In today's society, whether you choose to become a parent, a care giver, or neither, most of you will have some contact with children. In this course, you will learn about the ways children grow and develop from conception through the first 6 years of life. You will also learn effective ways to care for infants and young children. Soon, you will find that your understanding of the children in your family or in your neighborhood has expanded.

What you learn here will apply wherever you go. Human development occurs in the same sequences around the world. Human babies all learn to walk and talk in much the same way. Though there are differences in skin, eyes, hair coloring, language, and family styles, children all over the world are more alike than different.

A basic knowledge of human development and practice with child-care skills make you more likely to enjoy babies and young children. A person who does not understand a child's action may be bothered by it. For example, a newborn will cry loudly when its clothes are removed. The child's immature nervous system reacts to slight drops in

Nurturing children can be one of the most joyful, satisfying experiences a man or woman can have.

temperature. Knowing this, a parent or care giver will take steps to keep the infant covered during changes, instead of becoming worried or angry about the baby's crying. The adult also knows that this behavior will disappear as the baby's nervous system develops. Keeping the child covered during changes will not always be necessary.

This kind of simple know-how makes both child and adult feel more secure. Their experiences together will be more rewarding. As a result, they will build a stronger relationship.

Learning about children also teaches you about yourself. As you observe children, you will remember events and feelings from your own childhood. This leads to increased self-awareness and better understanding of your own values and reactions. You will discover ways of nurturing that are most easy and natural for you. You might also find that you gain insights into your own parents and the way your family interacts.

Using what you learn in this course, you can practice your skills on children in your family, neighborhood, or child-care center. This practice is important. It will let you see if the roles of parent and care giver are right for you.

Concluding Comments

This chapter discusses life's stages. You have been encouraged to draw your own time line and to think seriously about how you will spend your adult years. How much time will you take for each stage? How many roles might you take on at one time? Have you thought about which roles you would find easier to combine than others?

In this course, you will follow the development of children as they prog-

Learn about the roles of parent and care giver by seeking out, observing, and playing with children. Human development is most fascinating when it "comes to life" through a growing child.

ress through the first 6 years of life. You will become acquainted with parents and begin to understand the serious obligations and responsibilities of parenthood. You will learn and use information and skills needed to serve as a care giver to young children.

Finally, your new knowledge about human development and your experience with children should add to your self-awareness and help you make the best choices for your future.

? Decisions, Decisions

Imagine that you were to receive a million dollars a year for the rest of your life? How would your time line change?

19

1. Draw one time line showing your mother's activities and stages of life. Draw another time line showing your father's activities and stages. Now draw your time line showing the activities and stages of life you expect to have in your lifetime.

2. Compare the three time lines. How many years do your mother, your father, and you spend in the following stages: school, marriage, child-rearing, being employed, being retired?

3. How do your family's three time lines differ from one another? How much overlapping of stages do you see in your mother's and your father's lives? How much do you see in yours? Write a paragraph discussing the differences and similarities in the three time lines.

4. Write a paragraph discussing the time in your life when you think you will be handling the most stressful combination of roles. For example, do you think it would be difficult to work fulltime if you were the parent of one or more preschoolers? Would it be difficult to work while you were in college? Would it be difficult to hold a job with lots of travel while you were married? How would you cope with your respon-sibilities? Describe a typically busy day in your life at that time.

5. Make a poster or collage showing roles you expect to try. Use magazine pictures or draw your own pictures freehand.

6. During this course, you will need to be in contact with children and their parents. Identify three children from your family or neighborhood. Each child should be from a different age group.

   The age groups are:
   Infant—newborn to age one
   Toddler—one- and two-year-olds
   Prekindergarten—three-
   and four-year-olds
   School age—five-
   and six-year-olds.

Talk to the parent or parents of each child. Ask them if you may occasionally observe, play with, or help care for their child during this course. Find out if you may ask them questions about being a parent. These parents will be your "resource parents" for the rest of this course. As a starter, ask them if parenting is their only role at this stage in their lives. If not, what other roles are they handling? Do they find their current "stage" in life easy or difficult to handle?

The Role of Parent

Objectives

To identify reasons why people choose to have or not to
  have children.
To identify the joys and problems of parenthood.
To recognize a parent's mixed feelings about her or his child.
To explain why parenting requires a long-term commitment.
To recognize the cost of raising children.
To consider your own views on becoming a parent.

Terms to look for   ambivalence • conditioning

To Have or Not to Have

An old proverb says a person should do three memorable things in a lifetime: plant a tree, write a book, and have a child. Most people never write a book, and few people plant trees, but almost anyone can have a baby.

People decide to have children for many reasons. Probably the most important reason is the desire of people to recreate themselves. What are some other reasons why people have children?

Conditioning. Everyone first experiences life as a child. It is a role each of you has played. A past or present experience can condition, or affect, your attitudes and actions for a lifetime. Your feelings about parenthood are already conditioned by your experiences as a child. Although you can block out childhood memories, if you stop and think a moment, pictures from the past come flooding back. You remember the first time you were left behind with a babysitter. You taste again the joy of getting exactly what you wanted for your birthday. You relive a large holiday party with a lot of food, someone playing the piano, songs, and games. If your feelings about your childhood are mostly positive, you probably have positive feelings about parenthood.

Society also conditions our decision about becoming a parent. Adults, particularly married adults, have traditionally been expected to produce children. This expectation is as old as the history of human beings. Humans needed to reproduce in order for their species to survive. Furthermore, until recent times, there was no way to prevent reproduction. Today, adults who choose not to have children find that society pressures them in subtle and not-so-subtle ways to meet its expectations.

Identification with family. Often, people want to continue the family experience that began when their parents had them. They may want to present their own parents with grandchildren. Some families have a strong drive to continue the family line. They desire new members of the family to serve as representatives to the future and to carry on the family names and traditions.

Your feelings about parenthood probably come from memories of your childhood. These same memories influence many of the decisions that a parent makes.

For other families, the joy of day-to-day family experience is essential to their lives. They are most happy filling the house with relatives for important celebrations, such as Christmas or Passover. They enjoy watching the children play, taking the family to the zoo, seeing the children laugh at the local amusement park.

Adult love. The desire to have children comes from a basic, powerful, natural urge: love between adults. At its best, adult love is a combination of physical desire and friendship. It is a feeling that produces extraordinary closeness between men and women. An infant is the living, permanent expression of this love.

Appeal of children. Babies are very appealing. Have you ever noticed how much attention they command in a room full of adults? The parents become part of that limelight, too.

Most adults act spontaneously with babies and children. They feel free to laugh, act silly, and express the childlike parts of their personality. They experience the warmth of their caring and nurturing selves, too. The trust and affection that children give adults touches nearly everyone. Many people want this joy to be a part of their lives.

Curiosity. Some adults have children out of sheer curiosity. They know what it is like to be sons or daughters. But they question whether or not they can conceive. They think about what a child of theirs might be like. They are concerned about their parental roles. Will they be playmates, disciplinarians, protectors, or a combination of all three?

Taking all that life has to offer. Finally, people are afraid that if they do not have children, they will be sorry. Many peo-

Some couples are happy with their lives as they are. They choose not to have children.

ple feel that being a parent is a central experience in life. They fear that they will feel robbed if they miss this experience.

But there are other viewpoints. Young adults today are taking a harder look at the long-term commitment that having children implies. Some feel their lives would be better without children. Some people may be concerned that children will interfere with their careers—with what they want to accomplish in life. Or they may like to travel and do things on the spur of the moment and do not want to be tied down. Many adults get great satisfaction from developing their own physical and mental abilities. These young adults have good one-to-one relationships and are content with their lives as they are. As one such couple said, "We are our own family."

Some women fear the physical changes of pregnancy and the pain of delivery. Both men and women worry about caring for and supporting a child. Do they have enough patience to deal with a baby? Can they combine parenting with other careers? Will they have enough money? And the couple think about how a child will change their relationship with each other.

Some adults cannot imagine themselves tied to a long-term relationship. They have never had one and do not think such relationships work. Others have not had good experiences as children and are afraid they will inflict the same bad experiences on their own youngsters. And some just do not want the hassle. They cannot picture themselves as parents.

The thrill of being a parent is always mixed with the time-consuming demands of caring for a new baby.

Joys versus Problems

If you have ever had a bad experience baby-sitting or taking care of a younger brother or sister, you may have wondered why adults keep having children. The reason is that, most of the time, being a parent is satisfying.

Babies and children make their parents feel an overwhelming tenderness that few other experiences equal. There is the thrill of watching a human being develop. The first smile or step or word from a baby brings happiness and pride. As children mature, parents influence their youngsters' progress and help them explore the world.

Parents learn, too. One of the benefits of parenthood is the richness and growth that the adult experiences. Parents learn all sorts of things: how to furnish a child's room so it will be safe, evaluate a school, fix a balanced meal, buy a bicycle, say "no" and handle the period of anger that results.

When children grow up, many of them follow new paths—such as becoming a police officer or joining the Peace Corps—from which a parent can learn a lot. And if children become productive and happy adults, parents feel a great sense of accomplishment and pride.

But these joys are not achieved without problems. A new baby turns life upside down. New parents lose freedom and privacy. At the beginning, a baby requires so much time that the parents might feel isolated, staying at home rather than going to work or being with friends. If the baby cries too much or becomes sick, parents may feel a stronger anxiety than they have ever known.

Infants also require a lot of equipment. Suddenly, parents find themselves bumping into the crib or playpen that now clutters a small apartment. And babies cost money. If one parent has stopped working, a drop in income can keep the parents feeling "broke" all the time. If both continue to work, they must usually pay for child care. A parent may resent having to give up a career or change a job outside the home to a less demanding one. And men and women may dislike the responsibility and time-consuming demands of caring for a new baby.

? Decisions, Decisions

Marcia likes to babysit for children in her neighborhood. But sometimes they get on her nerves. She's glad to hand them back to their parents again. Secretly, Marcia worries that she might not like children. She wonders if she will be a poor parent. What do you think?

Mixed feelings

If you reread the last section and review all the joys and problems of parenting, you will find about an equal number of each. A good word to describe this situation is *ambivalence,* which means that a person is both drawn toward and away from something. This explains why parents have mixed feelings about their children. Because parenthood is a long-term commitment, parents' emotions about their children are not constant. A father may adore his baby daughter giggling happily in the tub. But he may dislike her intensely when she talks back at age 13. A mother may glow when her son gets an *A* in history and be horrified when he is caught breaking streetlights.

Parents love children, while hating the demands they make. One father enjoyed buying his 9-year-old son a bright yellow bicycle for his birthday. The boy was happy and proud of his "wheels." But during the first week he had the bike, he left it overnight in the schoolyard, and it was promptly stolen. His father was furious.

Another set of parents willingly gave up a house they had wanted to buy for a decade. They used the money to send their child to college. So they were hurt and angry when that child dropped out of school, saying, fliply, "I never asked to be born."

Some parents resent it when they make elaborate plans for a trip to see another part of the country and find their children sulking because they would rather be at home with their friends.

Parents learn to live with ambivalence, just as everyone else does. Discipline probably causes more mixed feelings than anything else. For example, if a mother does not set limits and stick to them, her child will walk all over her. If she does set up rules to which her child objects, she will worry about keeping the child's love. This happens because most people confuse love with liking and respect. If a parent is mature, she will probably always love her children, but there will be times when she does not like them. Her children certainly will not always like her. But if she is consistent and fair, she will probably always have their love and respect.

For this reason, it is important for people who become parents to know how they feel about a great many issues, from bedtime to pajama parties, chores, friends, homework, television, drugs and liquor, sex, driving, movies, community service, books, and travel. These are just some of the things you will have to make decisions about if you have children.

If adults are ready to be parents, they will be able to accept some of their negative feelings about children as a kind of payment for the joys.

Once a Parent, Always a Parent

Many people think that, once a child is old enough for school, their task as a parent is more than half over. Others recognize that their duties continue until the children are mature and can take care of themselves. Few understand that parenting is a lifetime occupation. Talk to any grandparent and underneath you will find a parent, concerned about an adult child.

Good parenting encourages the habit of responsibility, which changes as the stages of a child's life go by. In infancy, a parent or parent substitute is on duty all the time. The baby, a daughter for example, needs food, clothing, and cleanliness. She must be put to sleep, turned over, and carried from place to place. Without someone to care for her, she would die. A toddler can climb into her high chair and feed herself, but she needs someone to prepare the food and clean up after she has spilled it all over herself and the kitchen. Someone must dress her and take her out of her crib. Her parents must also do something else: protect her from the outside world while they teach her how to handle it, whether that means going downstairs or crossing a busy street. A preschooler can dress herself and go to the bathroom,

Parenting doesn't stop when children are grown. People are parents for life.

26

but her parents are still her primary teachers. She will get lost if her father drops her hand in the supermarket. She will burn herself if her mother has not warned her that the stove can be hot.

Even after formal schooling starts, parents have to stretch their children's minds, enrich their children's experience, and build their children's characters. And young adults, ready to go out on their own, still need advice, guidance, and financial aid. As a parent, you cannot be like 4-year-old Ricky, who wanted to "baby-sit" an infant cousin one day. After some minutes of cooing at the baby, Ricky turned to the mother and said, "Aunt Bea, I'm through with her," and went off to play on his own. Parents are not "through with" their children for many years—if ever.

Cost of Raising Children

The first four sections of this chapter deal with the pleasures and drawbacks of having children. But when it comes to costs, there are no pros and cons. Children are very expensive people.

The Department of Agriculture has done recent studies of how much money is needed to raise a child to age 18 in the United States. The researchers divided the country into four regions— north central, northeast, south, and west. The figures that follow are based on the cost of living in the north central region because that area is the most typical. These figures are for average children who are neither rich nor poor. The statistics are based on how much money people actually spent rather than on family incomes. They have been adjusted to the amount that money was worth in 1978. When you read this book in the 1980s, you will have to change

Being a good parent does not depend on money. But parents need to be financially prepared to provide the necessary food, housing, clothing, and medical attention for their children.

the amounts according to how much inflation has occurred since 1978. You can do this by calling the Bureau of Labor Statistics (listed under U.S. Government) in your area and asking for the yearly rate of inflation.

You should understand that these are average figures. They are probably too high for someone who is now 18, since prices were much lower when that person was 5 years old. They are also too low for a 1-year-old, because we do not know what inflation will do to the value of money 5 years from now. These statistics can only give you a very general idea of the expense of rearing a child from the moment the baby is born. You would have to add the cost of prenatal care and delivery if you wanted a more accurate picture.

The government found that the cost of raising an urban child in the north central region of the United States was $55,672 compared to $51,870 for a rural youngster. The following table shows you how these figures break down.

	Urban	Rural
food at home	$12,936	$11,992
food away	1,382	1,274
clothing	4,826	4,496
housing	17,718	16,630
medical care	2,952	2,686
education	840	840
transportation	8,440	8,114
miscellaneous	6,578	5,838
Total	$55,672	$51,870

Center for Educational Statistics, Washington, D.C.

If you decide to send a child to college, you would have to add more than $25,000 for tuition, room, and board at private universities, and $10,000 at public universities.

Looking at these numbers, you can understand why, in more households, both parents are working outside the home. The traditional working father and homemaker mother exists today in only 25 percent of all two-parent families.

What Do You Think?

You have had a lot of information and opinion filtered through your mind about the pros and cons of parenthood. Now it is your turn to think over this question. So far, your experience in life has only been on one side of the parent-child equation. Here are some questions designed to make you think about the other side.

1. Do you plan to have children? If so, how old do you think you should be when you have them?

2. Do you plan to work outside the home? Do you plan to work in business, or at a trade or a profession?

3. Would you be willing to give up an outside job to take care of a child? If not, do you think your spouse should, or would, take care of the family?

4. Perhaps you plan to be part of a two-paycheck marriage. If so, who will take care of your children? Will you share the responsibility? Will you hire someone, call on a willing grandparent, or look for a child-care center?

5. Think about all the parents you know—your own, those of your friends, your aunts and uncles. Pick out some who you think are good at parenting. Think about the characteristics they have that most impress you.

6. What are three things that you would want for your own children?

7. Think of three things your parents do that you think are good ways to handle disputes within the family, disciplinary problems, or just plain differences of opinion.

8. Have you spent much time baby-sitting? If so, are you good at it? If not, do you intend to get experience taking care of children?

9. Do you have a lot of patience? Can you play games with young children? Can you answer their questions?

10. Have you ever had to handle an emergency involving a young child? If so, how did you manage? If not, imagine such a situation and your response.

11. Do you think your own parents exercise too much discipline or too little? Will you be a tough disciplinarian with your children, or will you be permissive?

12. Do you like to be alone? Do you get along well with people? Do you like doing things for people you love?

13. If you had a limited amount of money, would it be hard for you to give up something you wanted and, instead, get something for your spouse or your child?

14. What are some of the experiences you have had with your own family that have been good for building close relationships (for example, trips, sports, shared hobbies)?

Concluding Comments

The decision to have a child is usually an emotional one. It is bound to be, since reasons for having children are rooted in people's past, in their relationship to their own parents, in their love for their partners, in their need to live up to expectations, and in the touching appeal of babies and children.

Even so, many young couples are weighing these emotionally heavy issues against their own life plans and goals. For some of these couples, having a child makes no sense. For many reasons, they do not choose to take on the role of parent.

Parents like to look for themselves in their children. Why?

Living with children presents joys and problems. Children are dependent, exciting, self-centered, and unpredictable. A parent can feel both love and annoyance. These mixed, or ambivalent, feelings are normal. Parents must learn to deal with them in a way that is helpful to their children and themselves.

The commitment to being a parent is a long-term one. Most parents are parents, in one way or another, for the rest of their lives. The role of parent is also an expensive commitment.

Today, it costs about $50,000 to $55,000 to provide basic needs for a child during the first 18 years of the child's life.

Given all these facts, most people who marry decide also to take on the role of parent. The desire to recreate oneself and to nurture offspring is a very powerful force.

Activities

1. Write a story about a couple who want to have children and a couple who do not. Allow the characters in your story to express their reasons and feelings. These may or may not reflect your own views.

2. Do you agree or disagree with this statement: "A couple is not a family until they have had a child"?

3. Design a poster. Either attempt to convince adults to have more children (pretend the birthrate in the U.S. has dropped alarmingly), or show people why they should *not* have children. As background, review the "Joys versus Problems" section of this chapter.

4. Interview your own parents or your resource parents (see chapter 1, activity 6). Ask them:

   a. Did their lives change after the birth of their child? If so, what kinds of changes took place?

   b. Was there anything about having a child that surprised them?

   c. Do they ever feel ambivalent (have both good and bad feelings) toward their child?

   d. What about the costs of raising a child? If both mothers and fathers are in your "resource" homes, is one staying home to care for the children? If not, is it because they both want to work? Or, is it because they must have two incomes to support their family? (Both reasons could be true.)

5. A national association for people who decide not to be parents:

   National Association for Non-Parents
   2010 Massachusetts Avenue N.W.
   Washington, DC 20036

   Write to this organization and ask for information.

The Role of Care Giver

Objectives

To identify careers involving work with children.

To identify parttime jobs and volunteer activities related to children.

To identify the qualities of a capable child-care aide.

To identify ways you can help in a child-care center.

To identify ways to relate to the lead teacher.

Terms to look for   child-care aide • child-care center • child-care teacher • lead teacher • parent helper

"What do you really enjoy doing?" asks your counselor. "What electives are you taking?" asks your mother. "What do you think you will major in?" asks your dad. From questions like these, it does not take long to get the message that the adult world is guiding you— perhaps rushing you—toward the world of work, toward finding the right career.

Looking back at the time line you drew in the first chapter, you will note that the career stage of life could cover 50 years or more. Choosing a career

requires planning and some tough decision making. Actually, most people make career decisions a little at a time. They start with some general experience and become more specialized as their years of experience build up.

In today's rapidly changing society, a person's life work may change several times during the working years. Therefore, do not panic if you cannot decide right now how to spend the next 50 years. Just try a lot of experiences, to learn what you really like and do well.

If you like what you are doing, you will feel happy about getting up and going to work most mornings. For the majority of people, that feeling of satisfaction is as important as the paycheck.

Care givers are people who earn a wage by caring for children. Their job uses the same nurturing and guiding skills that parents use.

A Career as a Care Giver

In Chapter 1, the word *care giver* was used to describe a person who earns a wage by caring for children. The role of care giver calls for nurturing, understanding, guiding, and giving of yourself. There are many types of jobs for care givers. The educational requirements for these jobs range from no formal training to a bachelor's or master's degree. A complete list of child-related occupations begins on page 41. Of these many occupations, two will be explored most frequently in this book. They are: teacher in a child-care center and aide in a child-care center. A child-care-center aide assists the teacher in carrying out day-to-day programs and activities that help children grow and develop.

Being a teacher or a child-care aide calls for many of the same skills as parenting. In fact, acting as a parent substitute is an important part of caregiving jobs with young children. One big difference between being a parent and being a teacher or a child-care aide is that, at the end of the work day, the teacher and child-care aide can go home. They can take a break from children—unless they have children of their own at home. Teachers and aides also get paid in dollars, while parents must get rewards through enjoyment of their children.

Teachers and child-care aides may also help parents care for their children more effectively. Many of these substitute care givers feel that the help they give to families is one of the most satisfying parts of their job. They can give parents the benefit of their experience and training. They can provide insights they have gained from working with large numbers of children and parents. But teachers and child-care aides do not expect to take on the total parenting job. Instead, they are supportive of parents.

Trying Out the Role of Care Giver

Many parttime jobs and volunteer activities allow you to try out a career. They test your interest and add to your skill in an area that you may eventually choose for your life work. Volunteering to work with children, parents, and care givers will help you decide how close to children and children's services you will want to be. These work experiences give a firm basis for career decisions about parenting and related child-care occupations. The following ideas for gaining experience with children may be possible in your community.

1. Play with a child in a park or a neighborhood while the parent is nearby.
2. Play with or read to children whenever an opportunity arises.
3. Volunteer to help in a children's library, or recreation program, or in a pediatric ward of a hospital.
4. Become a teacher of young children in your church or synagogue. Tend to the church nursery during services.
5. Volunteer to help an elementary or nursery school teacher after school, or during school.
6. Volunteer to supervise children who accompany their mothers to a well-baby clinic. Mothers busy with other children appreciate this help.
7. Baby-sit with children of friends and neighbors.
8. Tutor a child who needs special help in physical skills or in academic subjects.
9. Work in the toy department or in the children's clothing section of a store.

As you work with children, take every opportunity to learn more about them. Ask parents and care givers questions. Learn about the sponsoring organizations when you are helping with children. Each agency or organization offers a future career opportunity to work with children.

? **Decisions, Decisions**

Three-year-old Linda is telling you something about her new crayon drawing. You are listening carefully but cannot understand a word she says. What do you do?

Ways You Can Help in the Child-Care Center

Many of you will observe and assist in child-care centers as part of your course work—especially if you are in an occupational, vocational, or wage-earning child-care course. On the following pages are some brief suggestions telling how you can be helpful early in the school term, when you first enter the child-care center. For those who are dealing with one or two children in a home, these hints are easily adapted. Keep these ideas in mind as you study about each stage of child development. They are intended to help you get started. You will gain in understanding throughout the school term.

How to Help in the Child-care Center

Arrive on time. Follow the direction of both the teacher of your course and the children's teacher or parent.

In the Locker Room

1 Speak to each child quietly by name.
2 Help children locate lockers and hang up belongings.
3 Talk to children while they take off and put on outdoor clothing. Start a zipper or tug a boot part way. But let the children complete a task when they can.
4 Tell them, "That's a good job!" when they get a garment on.

In the Bathroom

1 Hurry with a child who needs to go to the bathroom. Children often cannot wait very long.
2 Assist with zippers and buttons when necessary. Praise self-help.
3 Encourage a child to flush the toilet but do not insist. Do make sure the child washes and dries hands.
4 Never shame a child who has an accident. Just help clean up the child. Put the soiled clothing in a sack, and report the incident to the teacher quietly.

34

In the Art Area

1 Get out materials needed.

2 Help the children put on aprons, if these are needed.

3 Let children draw their own designs. *Never* draw or make clay models for children or tell them what to draw or model.

4 Arrange a place for paintings to dry, and help children hang up their wet paintings.

5 Supervise the children when they wash their hands after art projects. Clean up the sink. Put away materials.

In the Block Area

1 Encourage orderly removal of blocks from shelves.

2 Allow children to topple their *own* blocks, not those of friends.

3 Help children replace blocks on the shelf when clean-up time comes. Do not do this before clean-up time.

In the Lunchroom and Snackroom

1 Help arrange the eating spaces. Let children take turns helping to set the table.

2 Check to see that all children have gone to the toilet and washed their hands before going to eat.

3 Plan a quiet time with children before mealtime. They will eat better if they have calmed down.

4 Serve *very* small servings of food. Don't force children to taste the food or pressure them to clean their plates.

5 Allow children to serve themselves seconds in food.

6 Help clean up the lunchroom or snackroom.

At Rest Time

1 Help arrange cots or mats for nap time. Darken the room and speak very quietly.

2 Be sure the children urinate after lunch. Some will need to have a bowel movement, so do not hurry them.

3 Help children remove their shoes and put them beside the mat.

4 Allow children to have stuffed animals or dolls on their cot or mat.

5 Hum or sing a quiet song to the children. Say, "I'm ready to sing to Jimmy, because he's a quiet rester." Stoop down and sing quietly to him.

6 Some children may not need to sleep. Ask them to remain quietly on their cots until the others have gone to sleep.

7 After the nap period, send children to the bathroom. Help them get dressed.

8 Help restore the room for the next activity.

36

At Story Time

1 Encourage quiet voices by using a quiet voice, yourself.
2 Divide the large group into several small story groups. Let the children select the books to read.

At Outdoor Time

1 Set out the equipment ahead of time. Make interesting arrangements.
2 Go out with the first children dressed for outdoor play. Or stay in and help the slower children dress while the teacher goes out first. Children should not have to wait with their heavy clothing on in a warm room while slower children dress.
3 Run with children to get them active and warmed up.
4 Get close to them to speak to them and give guidance.
5 Stay off children's equipment. Stop dangerous activity and redirect the children into doing something safe.

6 If children seem to be playing very well on their own, do not interfere with their play.
7 Try to help children who seem to be left out or unable to find something to do.
8 Provide drinks on hot days.
9 Put all equipment away, and lock it up where necessary.

ABCs of a Capable Care Giver

When you work with children, you often see yourself grow, as you help guide their growth and development. The role of care giver requires a positive and thoughtful way of working with others. Many of the personality characteristics listed below are ones you already own. You may find that others are strengthened as you put your best foot forward each day in a care giver role.

A. **Alert** to all children for whom you are responsible and to the tasks needing to be done.

B. **Bright,** being a fast thinker and a sound reasoner.

C. **Calm,** not easily flustered, when conflicts or competing tasks arise.

D. **Dependable** in following rules and directions.

E. **Enthusiastic** about working with children and parents.

F. **Fun-loving,** enjoying children and laughing easily with them.

G. **Generous** with your love, ideas, and energy, sharing these readily with parents, children, and co-workers.

H. **Healthy** in both mind and body, having the energy to carry on the work for the hours required.

I. **Initiating** activities that need to be done and doing them happily, without prodding or pressure.

J. **Just** and fair to all children, parents, and coworkers, regardless of sex, race, religion, income level, age, size, or disability.

K. **Knowledgeable** about children, families, and child-care centers.

L. **Loving** to children in your care.

M. **Mature** for your age and experience.

N. **Neat** and clean in appearance.

O. **Organized** on the job and at home so needed work gets done with a minimum of strain and confusion.

P. **Punctual** in arriving for the job and in keeping activities on schedule as required.

Q. **Quick** to respond to the needs of children, parents, and staff.

R. **Resourceful,** being able to figure out solutions to new problems and to find creative uses for materials.

S. **Strong** in body, having stamina for the required work.

T. **Thoughtful** of others, seeing the children's point of view and responding to their feelings and needs.

U. **Upstanding** in citizenship.

V. **Venturesome** in new ideas and new approaches to working with children.

W. **Witty,** using humor in dealing with children and others.

X. **(E)xcited** about the future and optimistically looking ahead.

Y. **Yearning** to be helpful to others.

Z. **Zealous** for children's rights and causes.

Relating to the Lead Teacher

The lead teacher is the professionally trained person in charge of the group of children. As the child-care aide, you follow the teacher's instructions in working with the children. The lead teacher needs the aide's help in planning the program and in conferring with parents. Aides are hired in order to extend the time and energy of the lead teacher. At one time or another, the lead teacher has done all the tasks you will be asked to do. You make a valuable contribution in helping the center deliver high-quality service to children and their families.

Always feel free to ask directions of your lead teacher. Discuss how things should be done until you understand and are in agreement. Feel free to make suggestions for activities and ways to deal with problems. Observe carefully, and tell the teacher things of interest you have seen children do. Volunteer to bring to the children an activity that you would like to do. This is one way of letting the teacher know that you are ready for more responsibility. For example, say, "I've made some puppets for an animal story. When could I use them in my small group?" Most teachers will be pleased with your interest and initiative and will give you permission to tell the story with your puppets.

Baby-sitting is one way you can learn about care giving now.

Baby-sitters or Parent Helpers

If you work as a baby-sitter or parent helper, with one or a few children, you can still follow some of the above suggestions in the way you relate to the children. In these jobs, you should try to do things the way parents want them done.

When you take care of children in their home, make sure you ask the parent or parents to provide the following written information:

1. The telephone number or numbers where a parent can be reached.
2. The approximate time the parent or parents expect to be home.
3. The number of the doctor or hospital to be called in case of an emergency. Also, a note from a parent giving permission for a child to receive emergency medical care in the parent's absence.
4. The telephone number of a close relative or friend, in case a parent cannot be reached.
5. The routine the parent would like you to follow with the children at feeding or mealtimes, bathtime, and bedtime.
6. Whether the children are allowed to watch television, how long they may watch, and what their favorite stories and games are. This information may differ if there is more than one child.

Try to get to know the children ahead of time. Ask the parents if you can come to their home once or twice while they are there. Or try to arrive a half hour or so ahead of time the first few times you care for the children. Also, get to know the parents as well as possible. And understand and respect their ideas about child rearing.

Keeping Records

Keep track of time you spend in volunteer work and class work. Write down dates, places, what you do, the hours you work, and the names and addresses of supervisors. First-hand experiences are valuable in career building. They give you the feel of a job much better than merely reading or hearing about it. This recorded information may help you apply for a job or a scholarship later on. Use cards and a recipe file box as a starter for your records.

Read and Study on Your Own

If you are serious about a career in children's services, you should enjoy reading about children on your own. School and public libraries are obvious places to visit. Bookstores sell many inexpensive paperback books about children, child care, psychology, and education. Popular magazines and newspapers are convenient sources of articles on children. Discuss ideas from reading with your friends, parents, teachers, and supervisors and with parents of young children.

Concluding Comments

This course can be a beginning step toward a future career of parenting, teaching, or providing other services to young children. This life work can be done in your own home, in centers outside the home, or as a dual career in which you combine the two. Career opportunities working with children in public and private child-care centers are expanding rapidly.

This chapter discussed the meaning of the word *care giver* and listed the many occupations that involve caring for children. The benefits of trying out a career as a care giver were explained, with suggestions for parttime or volunteer activities.

To help you prepare for class-related practical experience early in the school term, the qualities of a capable child-care aide were listed. These qualities are equally applicable to a helper in a family setting with one or two children.

Many ways for helping a teacher in a child-care program were suggested under various headings relating to activities in a child-care center. Some of these suggestions could be used in baby-sitting. Also included were some hints for relating to the teacher and to parents.

Activities

1. Spend at least two hours working and playing with children in one of the situations described on page 33, "Trying out the Role of Care Giver." Report your experiences, either orally or in writing.
2. Spend at least two hours in a child-care center. Divide your time among three or four of the different areas described in the section titled, "Ways You Can Help in the Child-Care Center." Describe some of the characteristics listed in the "ABCs of a Capable Care Giver" that you saw demonstrated by a teacher or an aide at the center.
3. For one of the above assignments, follow some of the suggestions given for helping in a child-care center.
4. Start a notebook or card file in which you list the time you spend working with children, where you do the work, what you do during this time, and what your reactions are.

Career Possibilities in Children's Services

Education-related

Aide or assistant in:
   Child-care centers
   Infant-care centers
   Elementary schools
   Recreation centers
   YWCAs and YMCAs
   Public libraries
   Church schools or synagogues

Infant care giver
Baby-sitter
Nursery school teacher
Child-care-center teacher
Kindergarten teacher
Special education teacher
Elementary school teacher
Religious education director
Librarian in school or children's library
Children's storyteller or puppeteer
Home economics agent or teacher
4-H agent
4-H junior leader or troop leader
Scout patrol leader or troop leader
Children's art instructor
Children's ski instructor
Children's swimming instructor
Children's gymnastics or dance teacher
Recreation coach
Recreation center director
Superintendent of schools
Principal of elementary school
College teacher of child development or child psychology
College teacher of elementary education, secondary education, home economics education, or special education
Researcher in child development, psychology, or education

Health-related

Volunteer in hospital or clinic
Receptionist in hospital, clinic, or doctor's office
Nurse's aide in pediatrics
Physical therapist
Registered pediatric nurse
Maternity nurse or nurse-midwife
Medical technician
Family physician
Pediatrician
Dentist
Dental assistant

Art- and Design-related

Children's book artist
Children's photographer
Children's clothing designer
Children's toy designer

Designer of child-care centers
Designer of schools
Designer of equipment for schools and children's centers
Designer of playgrounds and recreation centers
Home designer
Children's music teacher
Production worker, writer, consultant for children's television programming
Children's theater worker
Singer or writer of songs for children

Mental Health-related

Camp counselor
Recreation center assistant
Family or children's camp counselor
Aide with physically or mentally impaired
Big Brother or Big Sister volunteer
Foster parent
Probation officer
School social worker
Child-care licensing officer
Friend-of-the-court counselor
House parent in halfway house or institution
Family day-care care giver
Occupational therapist
Mental health aide
Psychologist or psychiatrist

Business-related

Salesperson in toy store
Salesperson in children's clothing store or department
Salesperson in children's book department
Children's party caterer
Toy builder
Toy designer
Maker of children's clothing
Designer of children's clothing
Children's television director or producer
Toy repairer
Entertainer for children's parties
Children's barber or hair stylist

Food-related

Restaurant helper
Cook's aide
Assistant cook
Camp cook
Child-care-center cook
Caterer for children's parties
School lunchroom worker
School dietitian
Pediatric dietitian

SUGGESTED READINGS FOR PART 1

Parenting

Education Development Center, *Starting a Healthy Family: Choosing Parenthood.* Newton, Massachusetts: EDC School and Society Programs, 1978.

Gordon, Sol and Mina Wollin, *Parenting: A Guide for Young People.* New York: Oxford Book Co., 1975.

Salk, Lee, *Preparing for Parenthood.* New York: David McKay, 1975.

Levine, James A., *Who Will Raise the Children? New Options for Fathers and Mothers.* NY: Bantam Books, 1976.

Whelan, Elizabeth, *A Baby, Maybe.* Indianapolis, Indiana: Bobbs-Merrill, 1975.

These magazines will have articles about parenting:

Children Today. Published by the Children's Bureau. U.S. Government Printing Office, Washington, DC 20402

Family Health. Published by the American Medical Association, 535 N. Dearborn St., Chicago, IL 60610

Forecast for Home Economics and *Co-Ed.*

Both published by Scholastic Magazines, Inc., 50 W. 44 St., New York, NY 10036

Parents' Magazine. 52 Vanderbilt Avenue, New York, NY 10017.

Psychology Today. One Park Avenue, New York, NY 10016

Care Giver Careers

Hymes, James L., Jr., *Early Childhood Education: An Introduction to the Profession.* Washington, DC: National Association for the Education of Young Children, 1976.

McFarland, Marilyn K. and Marialyce Knoll, *Exploring Careers in Child Care.* Bloomington, Illinois: McKnight Publishing Co., 1974.

Child-Care-Aide Skills

In addition to the readings listed, the following professional journals contain articles about care givers. These journals also list professional workshops or meetings that might be held in your area.

Childhood Education. Published by the Association for Childhood Education International, 3615 Wisconsin Avenue, N.W., Washington, DC 20013.

Day Care and Early Education. 72 Fifth Avenue, New York, NY 10011.

Educating Children. Published by the Department of Elementary, Kindergarten, and Nursery Educators of the National Education Association, 1201 Sixteenth St., N.W., Washington, DC 20036.

2

A New Person

You will identify what it means to be physically and emotionally ready to bring a new person into the world and to nurture that child's growth. Then you will learn how prenatal care, health practices, and health hazards affect prenatal growth and development. Finally, you will understand the last days of pregnancy and the birth process.

unit
2
Becoming
Parents

Ready for Parenthood

Objectives

To recognize the importance of being ready for parenthood.
To understand the advantages of planning for parenthood.
To recognize the changes a child makes in the marriage relationship.
To identify a good time to have children.

Terms to look for   conception • "custodian concept" • maturity

"Guess what! Flora and John are having a baby."

"Darling, I have news! You're going to be a father."

"What? You're pregnant! How can that be?"

Excited comments like these often follow the doctor's confirmation that a woman is pregnant. Depending on the circumstances, these comments may be said with pleasure, with anger, or with desperation.

Why would the news that a baby is on the way cause such strong feelings?

The reason is that creating a new life is one of the most exciting and rewarding experiences a woman and a man can have. It means that two adults are ready to accept a long-term responsibility that will alter the way they live.

The fetus begins to grow as soon as conception has taken place. *Conception* is the union of the male and female sex cells within the woman's body. The growth of the fetus continues for nine months, the period called *pregnancy*. Under normal circumstances, pregnancy continues until a baby is born.

When Are You Ready for Parenthood?

The checklist of parental readiness includes some important questions:

- Do the parents-to-be have mature personalities?
- Do the parents have a stable relationship?
- What are the parents' life plans, and how will the baby fit in with those plans?
- Are both parents physically and psychologically healthy?
- Do the parents have enough money to support a child?
- Do the parents have a place where they can care for the child?

Maturity

Is there one correct age to have a baby? Of course not. The right time for parenthood varies from person to person. A good measure of how ready someone is to be a parent is the person's level of maturity.

Maturity does not depend on the number of years since birth. It refers to that time in life when a person can think and act in a way that is reasonable, responsible, reliable, and independent. Mature women and men can take care of themselves. They have good judgment, and they stick with a job or a problem when

Mature love is when caring for another person is more important to you than how much that person cares for you. Good parenting requires mature love.

it becomes difficult. When necessary, they are able to inconvenience themselves for the sake of another person.

Take Martha, for example. She thinks she wants to have a baby. But she also likes to go out every night. Her friends and their social activities are really important to her. She is probably not ready to be a mother because she will resent staying home with her child. Or consider Hal. He does not handle responsibilities well. It is hard for him to hold the same job for more than a year or to remember such details as getting his car serviced. He would probably be overwhelmed with the responsibility and constant care that a baby requires.

Both Martha and Hal should put off being parents until they are ready to accept the "custodian concept." This idea suggests that parents are caretakers of another life and will create an atmosphere that nourishes that life from the beginning. For Martha, the "custodian concept" has special meaning since she will be the one who carries the fetus inside her. She will have to eat the right foods to provide enough nutrients for the developing fetus. She will have to be mature enough to give up certain things for the good of her future child. Liquor, drugs, and cigarettes are examples of three things that can harm a fetus.

Even mature young people find it frightening to take on major responsibility. Perhaps this fear is a sign that the person fully understands the responsibility involved:

"I signed a three-year lease on my apartment and the next day signed a long-term purchase agreement on furniture. I was scared out of my mind!"

When a child is born, the parents "sign" an 18-year contract. This contract, full of advantages and disadvantages, cannot be cancelled. A mature parent would not want it to be.

The birth of a first child changes a marriage. Having a baby too early in a marriage can strain the relationship.

Stable Relationships

Caring for babies and young children is a job that requires two sets of hands, two heads, and two hearts. When babies need attention, they will not wait patiently. They want to be fed, diapered, cuddled, and burped NOW! That is why a partner is vital. There is a helper when things get tough. Another person will often have ideas that make the job of parenting easier. Working together is fun, while working alone can be exhausting.

Couples are ready to have children when they feel secure in their relationship. The ingredients of that security are love, friendship, respect, trust, and the ability to communicate openly.

A stable relationship implies a balanced partnership, an important factor in raising a family. Twenty years ago it was accepted that the mother would rear the children. Today, fathers are also expected to take an active role in parenting.

The birth of a first child changes a marriage. Several years ago, a research study of 46 couples found that 83 percent of the couples had a crisis in adjusting to their first child. This crisis was greater for couples who had been married a very short time (less than a year) or a long time (more than 10 years) before the birth of the child.

Many new parents experience an "uneasy" feeling after their first child is born. For example:

"I was worried about the baby all the time. I kept thinking that she would die. If she died, it would be my fault, not Rich's. So I felt this huge responsibility was all mine and he couldn't help me. I was always mad at him, but at the time I wasn't sure why."

"Our life kind of collapsed when the baby came. We couldn't even go out to the movies anymore because Cheryl was breastfeeding him and he ate all the time. He cried a lot, too. Cheryl always felt tired, and she slept all the time. It seemed as though everything we enjoyed had disappeared forever."

"All we talked about was the baby. We loved her so much. Sometimes we would just sit and stare at her. One day Sue said, 'We never look at each other anymore.' And she was right. Even our eye contact had dropped off."

These couples do not have "troubled" marriages. Their reactions are fairly typical of the changes between a husband and a wife as they take on the new roles of father and mother. Most couples endure this period of stress. They adjust their relationship to include the busy role of parent along with the role of partner. But it often takes time. And it always takes mature insights and decisions. As one mother pointed out:

"It's not just a matter of 'How are the two of us going to adjust to the baby?' It's a whole new ball game. It's more like, 'How are these three people going to relate to each other?' "

At a time when 4 out of every 10 marriages end in divorce, couples need to be sure of their commitment before they have children. The chance of staying together is increased if a couple make the effort to build a stable relationship before their children are born.

Life Plans

You probably used to dislike having your relatives ask you, "What do you want to be when you grow up?" Yet everyone thinks about this question, because the work you choose is central to your life plans. Whether you want to be an engineer, a hair stylist, a lawyer, or a computer operator, you must find out what education and training are needed. Then you can set about achieving your goals.

When you have only yourself to think about, deciding what you want to do may be relatively easy. If you decide to marry, you have to integrate two lives

A baby complicates and sometimes changes the life plans of parents. Parents must decide how to achieve life goals and also meet the needs of their children.

and two careers. But a baby truly complicates matters, since a newborn requires fulltime attention from someone. Therefore, it is important to answer some of the following questions before deciding when to have a child.

Have I given myself enough education? Do I want or need to work at a job outside the home? Does my husband or wife want or need to work? Can we both work, or go to school, and hire someone to take care of our child? Is day care available? Can we leave our child with a willing grandparent? Do we *want* someone else taking care of our baby during the early years? Can we take turns caring for our child? How important are our careers? Can we each find parttime jobs and share child care? Can one of us quit working for a while and go back to work after our child is in school? Or will it be hard to find a job if we have been out of the work force for a few years?

? Decisions, Decisions

Ernest and Nina have two sons. Ernest is pleased with their family as it is. Nina wants to have another child because she wants to have a daughter. Each of them feels very strongly about the issue. How might they resolve their conflict?

A Number of Solutions

Couples find different answers to these questions. For Tony and Clara, who both work at the tire factory in their town, keeping their jobs was not a problem. Clara's mother volunteered to care for their daughter when she was born.

Helga and Jim both wanted children soon after marriage. Helga decided that Jim was making enough money as a sales agent to allow her to quit her job at the bank and be a fulltime mother. Helga, who is twenty-two, feels she has plenty of time to resume her career after their two small children are in school.

Sarah returned to work as an editor when her first baby was four months old. Her husband, Don, is an artist who works at home. He takes care of their son.

To be psychologically ready for parenthood, a couple must be realistic about a baby's ability to fill their emotional needs.

Sal and Angela are both serious about their work. Sal is a police sergeant. Angela teaches third grade. She took one semester off to have their daughter, Karen. When September rolled around, Angela went back to school. Sal arranged his schedule so that he could take care of Karen in the morning. On his way to work, he drops her at the day-care center. Angela calls for Karen after school.

David is a lawyer, Wendy is studying medicine. They want two children, but they have decided to wait until Wendy has finished her medical training. While their children are small, Wendy plans to work parttime to keep up with developments in her field. When they are older, she will devote more time to her profession.

Delaying Pregnancy

About 10 percent of the young married couples in the United States who are planning to have children are delaying pregnancy until their late twenties or early thirties. This new trend is allowing women and men to complete their educations and establish their careers before they have children. They often decide to have a baby when the woman is eligible for maternity leave. A few couples are each taking parttime jobs so that they can share the work of raising their families.

Physical and Psychological Health

To be physically ready for motherhood, a woman's reproductive system should have reached its mature growth. It should provide enough room for the developing infant and have a strong enough bone structure to carry the child safely. A mother-to-be must be well-nourished and healthy to produce a healthy baby. She should be free of venereal disease. She should also avoid other communicable diseases, especially German measles. German measles can deform the fetus if it is contracted during the first three months of pregnancy.

Fathers should also be in good health and free of venereal disease.

To be psychologically ready, both parents should want to have the child.

Wanting a child is an essential ingredient in making parenthood a joyful experience. But even the most wanted and planned pregnancy has its moments of doubt. Anxiety is natural. First-time parents do not know what they are getting into. They sometimes feel trapped, since they cannot easily change their minds. Couples who are psychologically healthy can express these fears. They discover that fears are as natural as the process of birth, itself.

Realism is another aspect of psychological health. A baby is never a doll. A baby is never everything its parents might wish it to be. Also, babies grow up. They do not remain cuddly little infants for long. A couple who are psychologically ready for parenthood recognize that a child can be sick, dirty, slow, or naughty, just as it can be healthy, clean, brilliant, and well-behaved. Predicting what your baby will be like is impossible. Generally, babies will be a mixture of the delightful and the difficult. To deal with both, parents need to be psychologically well-adjusted.

Some parents do not have a realistic idea about what the baby can do for them. They feel an emotional need for a baby, a need that calls for unconditional love. A baby is *not* able to fulfill this need. Having a child cannot give parents permanent feelings of self-worth. That is something parents must secure for themselves—before the birth of a child.

Money, Space, and Children

Romantics may believe that "two can live as cheaply as one." But the truth is that each person added to a family increases the dollar drain. The more children in a family, the more money the family needs for food, clothing, shelter, medical care, and education. In our society, children cannot make a financial contribution to the family because we have strong laws that prohibit child labor. These laws require children to stay in school until they are sixteen.

The costs of raising a family continue to grow with inflation. It is becoming increasingly necessary for both parents to hold a paying job. The large influx of women into the labor force in the last 10 years is proof of this.

Children are expensive people. How much do you think it would cost to set up an adequate home for a couple and their child?

Even if a person thinks she or he wants to be a fulltime homemaker and parent, that person is well-advised to learn some money-making skill before deciding to have children. Social security payments are rarely enough to take care of an individual with dependent children, should the main family wage earner die. If a couple divorce, alimony and child-support payments are often not enough. And many spouses fail to make these support payments, even when ordered to do so by the courts.

Financial readiness for children includes having an adequate home or apartment. Although babies do not take up much space, their equipment does. Couples who have enough room for their child have an easier time adjusting to the constant demands of parenthood. If there is some place that the baby can call its own, both parents can keep some of their privacy.

A Good Time to Have Children

When is a good time to have children? A couple are ready for children when they

- are sure of each other.
- have finished their educations and started to work toward long-range goals.
- are physically mature and healthy.
- have an adequate income to support themselves and their child.
- have an adequate home.

Planning for parenthood, and having children at a good time, gives both parent and child the best chance for a happy future.

"We went through all the hassle during the first three months. We had waited to have Erin, so we were surprised at the tension we felt. I guess nothing can really prepare you for it. Then when she was, say, six months old, things began to change. She could sit up, and she smiled. She played with toys. Best of all, she knew us. She saved her biggest smiles for Phil and me. You could see this little person emerging. She's still a hassle at times, but she has brought us such joy. We were ready to have a child—to share our life. Next month I'll be 26. And I am thinking that my life is pretty good. The things I really wanted, I got."

"Lyssa and I have two children now. Max was born when we were 30, and Andy was born when we were 33. We're both the same age. Looking back, it seems that we made pretty good choices. I met Lyssa when we were 24. We each had lived by ourselves and had already had a chance to 'sow our wild oats.' That seems really important now. I was working and going to college at night. Lyssa already had her degree.

We got married when we were 25. Since we were both working, we had money to do things. We could afford beach weekends and going out to dinner. We saved some money, too. But we always knew we would have kids. We were looking for the 'perfect time.'

First I got a promotion and had to relocate, so Lyssa changed jobs. Lyssa didn't want to get pregnant right after relocating. Then our car blew up and we had to buy another one, which cost us a lot. So we thought, 'Not now.' Then Lyssa got a promotion and wanted to concentrate on her job. Our parents started saying, 'I guess we'll never have any grandchildren.'

One night we talked for six straight hours about our life, about what we wanted for the future. We decided that we didn't want to go through life without children. We decided to have a kid when we were 30—no matter what. And we did.

Looking back, I can see all the experiences and head starts we had before Max came. Our marriage was good when Max was born. We had a lot to give him. We had a lot for Andy, too. I have a friend who got married when he was 20 and had a kid right away. He loves his kids, but he's always talking about feeling tied down and not getting what he wanted. I don't know. It's not the same for him. Lyssa and I are lucky, I think."

Concluding Comments

Next to deciding whether or not to have children, deciding when to have them is a major step. Planning for the birth of a child allows the parents to prepare a comfortable and stable environment for their baby. This preparation adds in an important way to the future well-being of the child and the parents.

Readiness for parenthood cannot be measured. However, there are some factors that a couple might consider to determine readiness. These are discussed at length in the chapter. They include: mature personality, stable relationship, life plans, physical and psychological health, level of income, and living environment.

The birth of a child has a strong effect on a couple's relationship, particularly during the months just following the birth of the first child. Adjusting to new roles and responsibilities can be overwhelming at first, even for parents who have planned and prepared. Mature couples with a settled relationship are best able to handle the emotional changes that a baby brings.

Couples who plan for parenthood are more likely to plan for other goals they hope to achieve. Children then are viewed as an addition to a positive future that is unfolding.

Prepared parents are free to offer love and security to their child and to each other. All the members of this family are thriving.

Activities

1. Look at the time line you drew in Chapter 1. How would having a child affect some of your plans? Would your plans change if you had your first child 5 years sooner or 5 years later?

2. Ask your resource parents (see Activity 6, p. 20) if their lives would have changed had their first child been born 5 years sooner or later.

3. Reread the excerpt on p. 50. What did the parent mean when she said, "It's more like, 'How are these three people going to relate to each other?'"

4. "Babies need lots of love and care from a mother. It's the father's job to earn enough to maintain the family. That's how fathers show they care." Why do you agree or disagree with this viewpoint?

5. This chapter has concentrated on readiness and planning for a cou-

ple's first child. Readiness and planning also apply to children born after the first child.

   a. Choose one classmate to research and report the latest studies about birth order. (Hint: magazines like *Psychology Today* often carry updated findings.) Do you agree or disagree with these findings, based on your own experience?

   b. Choose one classmate to research and report the views of three child psychologists on the matter of spacing children. Do these doctors agree on the best age for the first child to be before the next child is born? Do you agree or disagree with these findings, based on your own experiences?

Teenage Parenthood

Objectives
To describe the health risks of teenage pregnancy.
To understand the choices available to pregnant teenagers.
To describe the problems of teenage parenthood.

Terms to look for   low birth weight • premature

Do you know how many teenagers there are in the United States? Take a mental guess before you read the next sentence. The answer is 36 million. About 18 million, or half of them, are females. In 1977, more than 1 million girls under the age of 19 became pregnant. About 25,000 of these were under 15.

Not all of them had their babies. But almost 600,000 did give birth. During that year, 1 out of every 5 births in the United States was to a teenage mother.

It is difficult to talk about teenage parenthood in any positive way. Some teenagers think textbooks, parents, and other adults are exaggerating the hardships of being a teenage parent. These young people may feel parenthood is another adult privilege that is being withheld by the adults in their life.

However, adults are generally against early parenthood for good reasons. They know what being a parent demands of your personality, time, and money. No matter how mature a teenager is physically, he or she is almost never psychologically prepared for parenthood. Our society discourages early parenthood and does not prepare young people to become parents in their teens. The social and economic systems of most communities make teenage parenthood difficult. Low income, lost educational opportunities, social criticism and little child-care assistance are realities.

Health Risks

A girl can become pregnant even before she has started to have menstrual periods. The average age for menstruation is 12.8 years. However, when pregnancy occurs in a mother under 17 years of age, there is a sharp increase in the health risks for mother and child.

Adolescent girls younger than 17 have not finished their own growth. The demands placed on their still-growing bodies may wear down resistance to disease. If a teenager's bone structure is not mature, it may be physically unsafe for her to have a child. Young mothers can suffer prolonged, dangerous labor.

The baby is also exposed to risks. The most harzardous risk is *low birth weight.* Many babies of teenage mothers are small at birth because of inadequate nutrition during pregnancy. A *premature* baby is one who is born before the 9 months of pregnancy are over. These infants frequently have breathing problems and get sick more easily than larger, full-term babies. They also have a greater risk of being retarded, blind, deaf, or having other birth defects. The death rate for babies born to teenage mothers is double the rate for babies born to mothers aged 20 to 29.

For all these reasons, pregnant teens need good prenatal care from the earliest months of their pregnancy. Yet half of all teenagers who eventually give birth do not receive this care during the first 4 months. Some do not see a doctor during these months because they are frightened and unsure of what to do. Others may be trying to deny or not think about the fact that they are pregnant.

Difficult Choices

Once a teenager has determined that she is pregnant, she and her partner have difficult choices to make about the future. She may decide that she will give birth to her baby, but that since she and her partner are not ready to take on the duties of parenthood, they will give the baby up for adoption. Sometimes they make this decision before the birth. Sometimes they decide after the baby is born.

It is very difficult to give up a baby, knowing that you will probably not see your own child again. Parents who make this decision usually have thought long and hard about their own present and future needs. They also have imagined what life will be like for their baby. They decide on adoption for their own well-being and to give their child a better start in life. Most of these parents plan to have children again at a better time for both them and their future children.

Adoption agencies have lists of couples who cannot have children and would like to adopt one. It is well known that these couples are very carefully screened. Only those couples who have the potential to be good parents are eligible to receive an adopted child. Teenagers who place their baby with an adoption agency are sure that the child will get the loving, capable care the child needs.

Secondly, teenagers may decide that they want to raise the child, themselves. Today, 9 out of 10 teenage mothers keep their babies. What are some of the problems that these teenage parents must face?

Teenage Marriage

When teenagers find themselves pregnant, their first reaction may be to marry quickly. Often the couple had already talked of getting married some day. Sometimes parents push for marriage so the pregnancy will be less embarrassing. Of the teenagers who give birth before the age of 18, 40 percent are married at the time of the birth, while 60 percent are not.

These marriages do not have a good chance for long-term success.

The feelings of caring and romance that teenagers found so exciting when they were becoming partners seem to disappear. The freedom they expected as a married person actually turns out to be less freedom than before. Why? They are taking on the strain of a new set of problems. These problems are difficult even for more mature people who have a stronger sense of who they are and what they want for their lives: Where will the couple live? Who will pay for the delivery? Who will pay for the couple's expenses? What will both teenagers do about finishing school? How will they relate to social criticism, to their in-laws, and to their old friends? How will they react to 24-hour-a-day responsibilities? How will they live with a partner who is not as totally wonderful as they thought?

A few couples can "grow into" these demands. For many, it is just too soon to accept the responsibility of being married and of having a child. As a result, 3 out of 5 teenage couples who marry because of pregnancy are divorced within 6 years. It is not uncommon for the couple to be planning divorce even before their child has been born.

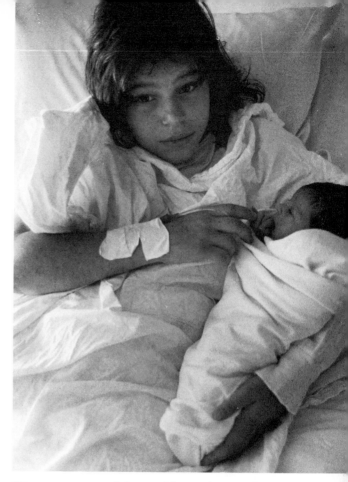

What are some of the problems this mother might face—both now and later?

Single Parenthood

A teenage parent, usually the mother, may raise a child without marrying. She often lives at home with her parents. Her parents or another relative help to raise the baby. Frequently, however, a teenager's parents cannot or will not help.

While money problems play a large part in teenage marriage, they are an even greater drawback for the single parent. Most teens simply have not had enough time to develop skills necessary for landing a good job. Teenage workers are twice as likely to be unemployed as

Some teenagers have a baby because they feel a strong need for someone to love. What do you think of this reason?

other workers. Furthermore, in order to go to work or to enroll in a career training program, the single parent must find someone to care for the child. Unless free child care is available, the parent usually cannot afford to pay for the care that would let her hold a job. This is often the initial problem that sinks a young person into the despair of poverty at the very time in life when she or he could learn to become a young wage-earner with a good future.

Also, the loss of friends, dates, and social fun is particularly hard to take. Melanie was 16 when she had her daughter. Her experience is similar to that of many single teenage mothers:

"When I first learned I was pregnant, I thought I wanted to die.

"I'd never be able to tell my parents. Well, finally, I did tell my parents, with the help of my guidance counselor. They helped me a lot. They found a special school for me to go to where I continued my regular classes. I learned about pregnancy and infant care, too.

"After Shelly was born, she and I lived with my parents. My mother was really a help with the baby in the beginning. And I'm glad I was able to finish high school. But now I just can't stay home. Shelly thinks my mother is her mother. And my mother and I fight about Shelly and everything else.

"When I got pregnant, Shelly's father didn't want to get married. But he said he'd help us and give me money when we needed it. Well, he gave me $200 when she was born and visited us about 4 times. I haven't seen him or gotten any help since she was 6 months old. His parents say they don't know where he is. I think he wanted to help, but he just couldn't.

"I want a place of my own, but I just don't know how it's going to happen. I don't have any money. If I get a job, who will watch Shelly? When she's 3, I can put her in the day-care center while I go to work. But between now and then, I have to find something else. A baby-sitter would cost as much as I would make. That's the biggest surprise of all. Everything costs more than I thought. I can't believe that I'm not able to at least provide for myself and a baby.

"Another thing that really upsets me is that I don't have any fun. I don't have friends now. My high school friends are doing other things, and I hardly see them. I don't have a chance to meet any new people, either. I used to go out all the time, so I had a lot of fun then. I haven't had a single date in over a year.

"I get really depressed. Sometimes I imagine what it would be like to run away. But I wouldn't leave Shelly. I really wonder how my life is going to turn out."

Teenage Fathers

The pregnant girl bears the major responsibility for a teenage pregnancy. But there is always a partner involved. Often, he is a teenager, too.

The reaction of teenage fathers ranges from not caring to feeling very guilty. Feelings of disbelief, anger, and helplessness are common.

Often, a teenage father will not talk about his feelings, particularly if he and the mother do not stay together throughout the pregnancy. He may not feel comfortable confiding in friends his age. He expects disapproval from adults.

Many fathers want to help. But, as one teenager put it, they don't want to "pay for one mistake for the rest of my life." They may provide the mother with moral support and money. It is much easier for the mother if the father helps make the decision to keep the baby or to put the baby up for adoption.

While many teenage fathers are as upset as mothers about the pregnancy, they receive little support. Friends and family tend to look on the mother's plight. Very little research has been done on the long-range results of being a teenage father.

Concluding Comments

One in 5 births in the United States is to a teenager. Most teenagers are not prepared to be parents. They must make difficult choices about their future and the future of their child.

There are health risks for a teenage mother under 17 and even greater risks for her baby. These risks are made worse by her not getting prenatal care in the early months of pregnancy.

Is fathering children a symbol of manhood? A symbol of maturity? What does becoming a father mean?

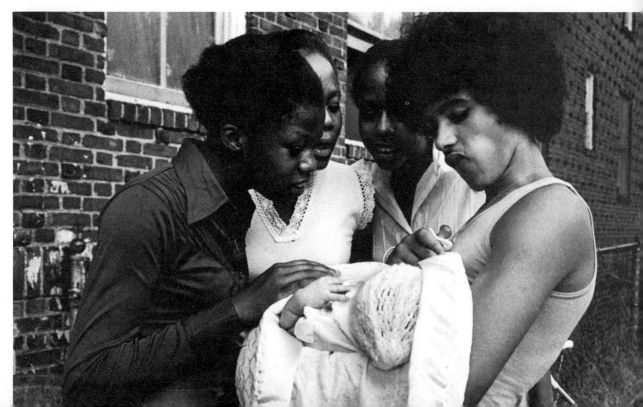

Both teenage marriage and single parenthood pose difficult problems. Three out of 5 teenagers who marry because of pregnancy are divorced in 6 years. Single parenthood is an economic hardship for a teenager.

Pregnancy and parenthood are exciting times for a couple when both are ready to take on this expensive, full-time responsibility. For most teenagers, pregnancy and parenthood have arrived too soon.

Activities

1. For more information on teenage pregnancy, write to the National Foundation March of Dimes, P.O. Box 2000, White Plains, New York 10602.

2. Make a list of services available in your community to assist pregnant teenagers. Call to find out the details of their services. Compile a notebook of this information to be available to students in your school.

3. Invite adolescent parents to your class to tell about their experiences with parenthood. Ask them what advice they would give to high school students about being a teenage parent.

4. Think through the problem of becoming a teenage parent. What decisions would you probably make? You do not need to discuss this with your class.

Heredity

Objectives
To explain how traits are inherited.
To identify inheritance-linked differences.

Terms to look for   amniocentesis • chromosomes •
   dominant genes • fraternal twins • genetics •
   identical twins • inheritance • random • recessive genes •
   X and Y chromosomes

"Mom, do you think I'll be 6 feet tall?" asks 15-year-old Steve.

"Everyone in my family has blue eyes," reports 7-year-old Carla.

"My, you're looking more like your mother every time I see you," says Kim's Aunt Esther.

Steve, Carla, and Aunt Esther are all interested in features that were inherited at the moment sex cells were joined.

This chapter examines the subject of your inherited characteristics. *Genetics*, the study of heredity, is a science that can help you understand something about your own unique features.

Inheritance Begins

Inherited traits are established the moment the sex cells combine. Located in the female egg cell, or ovum (plural: ova), and the male sperm cell is the biological blueprint—an instruction code guiding the development of a new human being. In modern computer language it is called "the program." Alone, each sex cell is only a cell. Together, the sex cells can become a human being.

Because of the "program" in each cell, the new person will be similar to other people around the world. He or she will walk upright, talk, think, and be able to reproduce other human beings. The person will have unique features, too, for the "program" also determines the child's sex, eye color, hair color, body type, and many other features.

The Inheriting Mechanism

The inheriting mechanism is already present in the plan within each of the two joined sex cells. The sperm is so tiny that a microscope is required to see it. An ovum is somewhat larger, about the size of a tiny speck of dust. Yet there are 23 *chromosomes* in each ovum and in each sperm. When the two cells combine, there are 46 chromosomes. Chromosomes are threadlike particles contained in the cell nucleus. The chromosomes in the cell nucleus carry

Genes work in pairs to develop physical characteristics. Each parent supplies one gene. Sometimes the two genes do not "agree" on what the characteristic will be. Then the physical feature is decided by the dominant, or stronger, gene.

the *genes*. Genes determine the inherited traits or features that make each individual somewhat different from all others. Genes determine what you have inherited from your parents, grandparents, and all other ancestors. These genes came out of a large collection that were contributed by your parents and their ancestors. Parents-to-be will find their offspring the product of selection by chance from this large collection of genes. According to one scientific estimate, the number of unique heredity arrangements could reach 64 trillion.

Random Selection

When the ovum is maturing and getting ready to be released by the ovary, the genes for determining each inherited trait are distributed in a random way to each ovum. *Random* means unplanned. For example, the way a deck of cards is arranged after you shuffle and cut them is a random arrangement. Genes determine a person's unique features. Into one ovum might go the gene for red hair; into another ovum, the gene for black hair; into a third, the gene for blonde hair, and so on for all the hair-coloring genes carried in the mother's gene pool. The same process takes place for the sperm in distributing the father's collection of genes for hair color. Genes for other features are also distributed to sperm and ova in a random fashion.

Dominant and Recessive Genes

One gene may be stronger than, or *dominant* over, another gene. The stronger gene carrying brunette hair is known by scientists to be dominant over the *recessive* gene for blonde hair. When a brunette-carrying gene and a blonde-

Females have sex chromosomes *XX*. Males have sex chromosomes *XY*. A baby inherits one chromosome from each parent. The baby always inherits an *X* chromosome from the mother. But the baby inherits either an *X* chromosome or a *Y* chromosome from the father.

carrying gene are paired, the brunette wins out. However, if the brunette-haired parent has any ancestors with blonde hair, he or she might carry a gene for blonde hair. Thus, if this sperm and ovum unite, a blonde-haired child occurs. This is how two brunette-haired parents, both carrying recessive genes for blonde hair, can produce the "surprise" of a blonde-haired child.

Sex Determination

Scientists tell us that special chromosomes, called *X* and *Y*, determine the sex of the child. The Y chromosome is needed for producing males. In contrast to the ovum, the sperm will have an X chromosome (female) or a Y chromosome (male). We know the ovum has only Xs, so if the male's X chromosome unites with the egg, the baby will be a girl. If the male's Y chromosome fertilizes the egg, the baby will be a boy. It is the presence or absence of the Y chromosome from the sperm that determines the sex of the fetus.

Scientists tell us that parents will soon be able to decide before conception whether their baby will be a girl or a boy. What do you think could be some results of this kind of choice?

Genetic Decisions

It has been discovered that defects can be passed on from generation to generation through abnormal chromosomes. There are now genetic counselors, or specialists who are called geneticists, who can calculate the odds of a couple's producing healthy children. When couples have one or more defects in their background, they can consult with these geneticists to learn the chances of having healthy children. If you know a baby of your own would probably not be healthy, would you prefer to adopt a healthy child needing a good home?

A new technique called *amniocentesis* enables doctors to perform prenatal tests to check for abnormal chromosomes in the fetus that could cause crippling diseases and mental retardation. Most doctors recommend the test to pregnant women who are older than 35 or who have a family history of birth defects.

Amniocentesis is done after the fourteenth week of pregnancy. A small amount of amniotic fluid surrounding the fetus in the uterus is removed with a special needle that is placed through the walls of the mother's abdomen and uterus. The amniotic fluid has cells from the fetus. The fetal cells are stained to make the chromosomes visible, and the chromosomes are checked for defects. If such defective chromosomes are found, some doctors may recommend aborting the pregnancy. A couple may then be able to conceive a normal child later. However, many people believe that aborting a fetus is morally wrong, whether the fetus is impaired or not.

Multiple Births

Multiple births are not common. However, the fertilized ovum sometimes splits into two identical cells. *Identical twins* will then be born. These babies are of the same sex and are very much alike, having inherited the same genetic makeup.

At times, a woman may release two or more ova at one time from the ovaries—especially if she has been taking drugs to increase her fertility. When two ova are fertilized, *fraternal twins* are born. Fraternal twins can be of the same sex or of different sexes. They will usually look different. They may not look any more alike than brothers and sisters who are years apart. Each fraternal twin has its own individual genetic makeup. This occurs because each child comes from a separate sperm and ovum. Multiple births of as many as eight babies have been reported.

What is the possibility of multiple births?

twins:	1 in 90 births
triplets:	1 in 8,000 births
quadruplets:	1 in 500,000 births
quintuplets:	1 in 54 million births

Concluding Comments

Separately, the ovum and sperm are only sex cells. But when they join, they form a new human being. Within each cell are chromosomes, which are threadlike particles. The 23 chromosomes of the ovum unite with the 23 chromosomes of the sperm, making 46 in all.

The chromosomes carry the genes, which determine the inherited characteristics that make each person unique.

In heredity, a random selection process takes place. Thus, chance determines what characteristics you inherit from the collection of genes contributed by your parents and other ancestors.

The ova contain only female, or X, sex chromosomes, while the sperm have both X (female) and Y (male) sex chromosomes. If the sperm that unites with the ovum has an X chromosome, the baby will be a girl. If the sperm has a Y chromosome, the baby will be a boy.

? ● **Decisions, Decisions**

Ed and Debbie have just found out that their first "child" is twins, due in two months. They are feeling frightened and upset. Why might they feel this way? What do they need to consider now?

Twins are twice of everything, which adds up to a tremendous amount of both work and fun. How can parents give each child a separate sense of identity?

1. Draw and complete the following chart on a separate piece of paper. *Do not* write in this book.
2. Based on the information in your chart, discuss your physical characteristics from the standpoint of random selection. Include a definition of the term *random selection* as it applies to genetics.
3. Write a paragraph discussing the characteristics you have that you would like to pass on to your child. Are these characteristics genetically determined?
4. Call the Public Health Department to ask, "Where can couples go for genetic counseling?" Get names and phone numbers. Call one or more of the numbers to learn what services are available. Make a written report and discuss your findings with the class.

	Hair Color	Straight or Curly	Eye Color	Skin Color	Height
You					
Mother					
Father					
Maternal Grandmother					
Maternal Grandfather					
Paternal Grandmother					
Paternal Grandfather					

3

A Healthy Pregnancy

Prenatal Care

Objectives

To describe the early signs of pregnancy.

To describe quality medical care for a pregnant woman.

To describe the needs of a mother-to-be.

Terms to look for Braxton-Hicks contractions • complications • fetus • general practitioners • gynecologist • nurse-midwife • obstetrician • Pap smear • pelvic examination • prenatal care • speculum

"Who was your doctor?" Maria asks a friend who has recently had a baby.

"Should we have an obstetrician or a general practitioner?" Joe asks his wife, Lettie.

These questions and many more are asked by a couple when they first begin to suspect that the woman is pregnant. They realize that there is something special about the medical science related to pregnancy. Couples will find out the fact that there are many different competent doctors in related medical specialities.

Medical Advice to Pregnant Women

The *gynecologist* is a doctor whose specialty is the health of the female reproductive organs. For example, this doctor can give women expert advice when they are having menstrual problems. Gynecologists perform the routine pelvic and breast examinations that all women should have at least once a year to check for breast and uterine cancer.

The *obstetrician* is a doctor who specializes in delivering babies and giving pregnant women appropriate care before, during, and after childbirth. Either the gynecologist or the obstetrician can answer a woman's questions, if she suspects she is pregnant.

General practitioners handle many questions and deliver lots of babies, too. They may call on gynecologists or obstetricians for assistance or for consultation, if problems arise. Most city and county health clinics offer medical advice and consultations for pregnant women.

Certified *nurse-midwives* are registered nurses who are specially trained in obstetrics and *prenatal* (before birth) care. They are able to perform normal deliveries of babies. Some hospitals have nurse-midwife delivery programs for women who desire such services. In addition, there are special childbirth centers where nurse-midwives take care of normal deliveries. This relatively new type of medical care will be discussed in more detail later in this chapter.

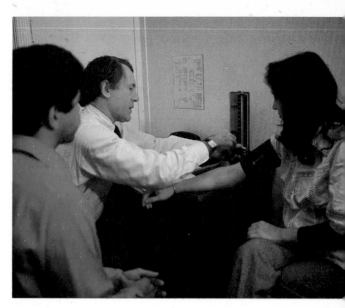

There are several kinds of medical specialists that a couple can choose from: gynecologist, general practitioner, or nurse-midwife. Couples should choose the kind of medical care they will feel comfortable with and trust.

Early Signs of Pregnancy

A woman's body gives several signs that tell her she may be pregnant.

Missing a Menstrual Period

Missing a menstrual period is one of the first signs of pregnancy that a woman notices. This sign is a most reliable indicator of pregnancy for women who have regular menstrual periods. Those whose menstrual periods do not come at regular intervals may miss two or more periods before suspecting that they are pregnant.

During the first 2 or 3 months of pregnancy, some women have a slight show of menstrual blood during the usual time for their period. They may feel a slight menstrual cramp when their period is due. These exceptions can cause confusion about whether or not a woman is pregnant.

After the second menstrual period has been missed, the doctor can probably determine whether a woman is pregnant without performing laboratory tests. The increase in the size of the uterus with a 2-month-old fetus will be an important clue.

Other Indications of Pregnancy

Another indication of pregnancy is that the breasts begin to enlarge and may feel tender. They are starting to develop in order to serve the needs of the infant after birth.

Some women who are pregnant have nausea. This nausea is commonly called "morning sickness," because it seems worst early in the day. The nausea makes some women think they have the flu or food poisoning. Usually, "morning sickness" disappears after the third month of pregnancy. However, this nausea is a problem to discuss with the doctor.

Eating a few dry crackers before getting up in the morning can help the nausea, as can waiting a while before drinking any liquids. Small, frequent meals throughout the day are usually better than large meals. With some women, the nausea can reach the point of vomiting. This is a problem, because proper nutrition during pregnancy is very important, even in the first few months. If a woman is so nauseated that she cannot eat, she and her doctor should try to find a way to relieve the sickness.

Increased need to urinate is another early sign of pregnancy. The uterus and bladder are close together. As the uterus expands, it puts pressure on the bladder. So the bladder needs to be emptied more often than before pregnancy.

Pregnancy Tests

A woman who thinks she is pregnant can have a test done through her doctor or through the Board of Health. Usually, the woman is asked to collect a urine sample as soon as she gets up in the morning. She then takes the sample to the doctor's office, laboratory, or to the Board of Health. There, the sample is tested for hormones that will be present if the woman is pregnant. A woman can usually learn the results of the test within 24 hours and sometimes even on the same day.

Several in-home pregnancy tests are now available in drugstores. A woman can conduct this test, herself, following the instructions that come with the test. The in-home test is almost as reliable and accurate as a laboratory test and is less expensive. However, women who suspect they might be pregnant should still see a physician.

Medical Care During Pregnancy

After a woman misses two menstrual periods, or has a positive pregnancy test, she should make an appointment to see the doctor. A woman with any medical problems, such as diabetes, should see a doctor after missing her first period. Doctors are sometimes reluctant to accept a woman in the later stages of pregnancy. By then, the woman may have developed physical illnesses that could have been prevented had she been examined and treated earlier.

Selecting Medical Care

The type of medical care a couple select during pregnancy for the delivery of their baby will depend upon finances and upon personal feelings about childbirth. A local hospital or medical society will give them information about obstetricians who are licensed and who are accepting cases. County health departments have information on the location and hours of public health clinics. In addition, the couple should talk to friends or relatives who are pregnant or who have recently given birth. These people can give information about the care they are receiving or have received.

Public health clinics, available for low-income patients, are often staffed with medical interns who are learning obstetrics. Interns will be supervised by licensed obstetricians.

Private doctors may practice alone or may be in partnership with one or more obstetricians. In some partnerships, the partner delivers the baby only if the woman's regular doctor is on vacation or is busy with another delivery. In other partnerships, another doctor delivers the baby if the woman's regular doctor is off duty for a weekend or holiday. Still other private clinics require that every woman get to know every doctor. Which doctor delivers the baby is completely a matter of chance.

If a woman is accepted into a nurse-midwife delivery program at a hospital, she will probably see and get to know all the nurse-midwives connected with the program. Such programs usually require an initial examination by an obstetrician to determine whether the woman is in a low-risk pregnancy category. This means that, in the opinion of the obstetrician, the woman is unlikely to experience any *complications* in childbirth, that is, any danger to her life or to the fetus's life during the delivery. Thus, a competent nurse-midwife will be capable of handling the birth. Of course, because the program is located at a hospital, qualified obstetricians will

Nurse-midwives are registered nurses who are specially trained in prenatal (before birth) care. Deliveries that are not expected to have complications can be handled by the nurse-midwife.

be available should any complication in the birth occur.

In some places, childbirth centers are becoming available to women. These centers are not hospitals. They exist solely for childbirth. They are usually staffed by nurse-midwives, under supervision of several obstetricians. Women must be in low-risk categories to use the centers, which are close enough to back-up hospitals to allow women who develop complications to get to the hospital within minutes. These centers cost far less than doctor-hospital care. The woman who has her baby at a childbirth center usually returns home within a day after giving birth.

Any pregnant woman deserves to feel comfortable with her obstetrician. If she decides to use a private clinic or partnership, she should feel comfortable with all the doctors connected with it. If a woman feels nervous or uneasy around one of the partners, she should tell her own doctor. Her doctor may honor her feelings and try to deliver her baby, even if she or he is not officially on duty at her delivery time.

A couple should try to gain all possible information about different childbirth methods before selecting an obstetrician. If the woman wants her husband or friend to be present during labor or delivery, she should be sure that her doctor and hospital permit this. If the couple want "rooming-in", in which the baby stays with the mother most of the time rather than in the hospital nursery, they should find a hospital that permits this.

The couple should also try to find out as much as possible about drugs used during labor and delivery. They should discuss these drugs with the doctor and get the doctor's opinions about them.

Another question a couple should ask is whether the doctor will be present during most of the woman's labor. Many women assume that the doctor will be there. They are shocked, and often upset, to find that their labor is managed by hospital residents and nurses and that the doctor comes in only to deliver the baby.

A good obstetrician will take plenty of time with each patient and will answer all questions. Such a doctor will not act rushed or impatient or treat any questions as trivial or self-evident.

Costs of Medical Care and Hospitalization

The costs of medical care and hospitalization are substantial. One can learn what the doctor's fees are by simply asking the doctor. These doctor's fees generally cover all care during the pregnancy, plus delivery of the baby and postnatal (after birth) examination.

It is wise and economical to begin seeing the doctor early in the pregnancy. Because costs of office visits are included in the general fee, and because the best and least expensive care is preventive care, there is no good reason for delay.

Hospital charges are climbing steadily. You can obtain current rates by calling the accounting department at the hospital. Besides the daily hospital room cost, there is a charge for the delivery room, for the nursery, and for medication, including anesthesia. An *anesthetist* is a person who is trained to administer anesthesia. An *anesthesiologist* is a medical doctor who specializes in administering anesthesia. Most hospitals require that one of these specialists be present in the delivery room. Even if anesthesia is not needed, the patient is charged a standby fee. Some saving is made if the mother stays in rooms with one or more roommates. The hospital chosen must be one where the woman's doctor is practicing. The doctor's fees are separate from hospital fees.

First Medical Examination

The doctor first takes a complete medical history. The dates of the woman's last menstrual period are important. From this information, the doctor can calculate approximately when the baby is likely to be born. The number of times the woman has been pregnant before and the outcome of each pregnancy are also important information for the doctor. The doctor inquires about any chronic health problems, any medica-

During pregnancy, a woman must learn to "listen" to her body. The need for rest and nutritious food is important. The need for emotional support is real, too.

tion the woman has been taking, and the general level of activity she engages in.

After the woman has been weighed and measured, a complete head-to-toe physical examination follows. The doctor has an analysis made of a urine sample. A technician draws blood for various blood tests. These tests are very important in caring for the pregnant woman and the fetus. A cancer test, called a *Pap smear,* is also done. This is a test every woman should have at least once a year.

The *pelvic examination* is one part of a complete physical examination. The woman dresses in a hospital gown. The nurse drapes her with a sheet. Then, lying on the examining table, the woman places her feet in the stirrups. The knees swing wide apart to enable the doctor to feel and check the uterus and the birth canal with a special instrument

called a *speculum,* which moves apart the walls of the vagina. The doctor is checking for evidence of an increase in the size of the uterus. The doctor often uses a flashlight for this part of the examination. Some doctors have a mirror placed at the appropriate angle to allow the woman to view portions of this examination.

From all this questioning, examining, and testing, the doctor is able to determine whether the woman is pregnant. If so, a regular schedule of visits is planned. Usually one visit per month is planned until the eighth month. Then, more frequent visits are scheduled, as the doctor thinks necessary. Doctors differ in some details. However, all doctors are interested in preventing complications and in getting enough information to be able to manage the pregnancy and delivery for the benefit of both mother and baby.

The doctor should answer any questions the woman has. Most doctors also answer questions on the telephone between office visits. The doctor may suggest a clinic where a public health nurse who can answer many questions is on duty. Advice on food and nutrition during pregnancy is very important. The expectant father should also be welcome at the doctor's office during each prenatal visit. He can talk to the doctor and have a better understanding of the pregnancy. Most fathers want to be included from the beginning in the birth of their child.

Healthy women can continue their normal activities for most of the pregnancy. Exercise of some type is recommended.

Body Changes during Pregnancy

The drawings on pages 78 and 79 show how rapidly a woman's body must grow to accommodate the developing fetus. It is truly remarkable that the skin and muscles can be so elastic.

Because of pressures felt today on women and men to be physically thin, some women may feel, or think of themselves as, "fat" while they are pregnant. This is a false and unhealthy attitude toward being pregnant. Pregnancy is a normal physical event that should not be confused with being overweight.

Most healthy women feel good throughout their pregnancies, with proper diet, rest, and exercise.

As the pregnancy progresses, many women feel occasional, irregular contractions. The uterus becomes very hard, but the contractions are not painful. These are called *Braxton-Hicks contractions*. They do not mean that labor has started, so they will not alarm the woman who has learned about them in advance for the birth of the baby. When real labor occurs, women will recognize the difference immediately.

The movements of the fetus are first felt as light flutters during the fourth or fifth month. These movements become stronger and stronger as the pregnancy progresses. The father can feel the movements by placing a hand on the enlarged uterus. Most women enjoy feeling the vigorous new life move around inside.

Activity and Rest During Pregnancy

Most healthy women will be able to continue their normal activities for most of the pregnancy. Exercise of some type is recommended for almost all pregnant women. Walking, swimming, tennis, jogging, and cross-country skiing can all be beneficial to women who are accustomed to these activities. Most doctors recommend that women do not take up a new sport during pregnancy. A pregnant woman should pay attention to her body's signals during exercise. If she becomes very tired or feels any unusual pain (other than normal muscle soreness), she should stop. Doctors will also advise women when they think less activity is desirable.

Many women who work outside the home continue their jobs until the day their babies are born. Others may feel the need to begin their maternity leave a few weeks earlier.

While activity continues, an increase in the amount of sleep and rest may be needed during pregnancy. Fatigue is common in the early months of pregnancy, as the body shifts into more complicated work. The need for sleep varies. Some women may require 8 hours, while others may need more. Many women find that a daytime nap—even if it is only for a half hour—refreshes them more than extra nighttime sleep.

Feelings during Pregnancy

Women who have planned their pregnancies, and who are happy to be pregnant, will usually feel positive most of the time. However, all women experience mixed feelings about the new role they are taking on. They wonder how much their lives will change after the baby is born. They may even feel occasionally that they have made a mistake. Sometimes, even though her husband is happy and excited about the pregnancy, a woman will feel lonely. Women may also not be able to over-

come feelings of ugliness as their bodies grow bigger. Some may fear that they will never be slim again.

Men as well as women wonder about the changes about to take place in their lives. A man may worry, as well as be excited, about his role as a father. He may feel inadequate and not ready to assume responsibility for a child. Most men experience great curiosity about the physical sensations of pregnancy. Some often feel a little resentful of the

Most women expect to stay on the job through all or most of the pregnancy. New laws allow women to return to their job and their seniority after maternity leave.

? Decisions, Decisions

When Jan and Robbie found out they were going to have a baby, they had totally different reactions. Jan didn't want anyone to know. Robbie was eager to tell the world. What happens now?

The Months before Birth

After the sperm and ovum unite, growth and development begin. Within hours, the fertilized egg splits into two cells. After 4 days, there are 90 cells. These cells move down the fallopian tube and attach to the lining of the uterus.

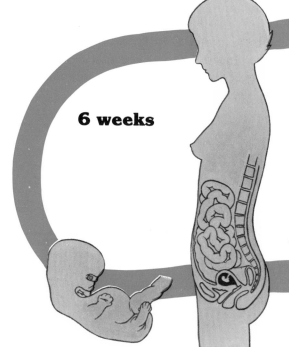

6 weeks

The *embryo* is the name of the fertilized ovum from the second to the eighth week of pregnancy. The embryo is enclosed in the *amniotic sac*, which contains fluid. From now on, it literally floats through the prenatal period. By 6 weeks, the embryo develops a simple heart and blood vessels. At 8 weeks, it begins to resemble a human being. From 8 weeks until birth, the embryo is called a *fetus*.

3 months

At 12 weeks, the heartbeat of the fetus may be heard, using an electronic stethoscope. Most internal organs are formed, and the sex of the fetus is evident. The fetus may suck its thumb.

The *placenta* is attached both to the mother and to the fetus. Nutrients and oxygen carried in the bloodstream pass from the mother to the fetus through the placenta. Waste products are returned to the mother through the placenta and discharged through her body. The *umbilical cord* connects the placenta to the fetus at the navel.

The fetus is only 3½ inches (about 8 cm) long and weighs less than 1 ounce (about 30 gm). Even so, the mother's body is slowly changing. Her breasts have enlarged and her abdomen has expanded slightly.

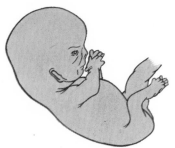

6 months

The fetus is now 12 inches (30 cm) long and weighs about 1½ pounds (about 1 kg). Muscles in the arms and legs of the fetus are strong. The mother may feel the movement of the fetus. The eyes of the fetus open and close. A fine covering of hair grows on the scalp, brows, back, and limbs.

The mother's uterus and abdomen enlarge to hold the growing fetus. The intestines are pushed aside to make room for the growth.

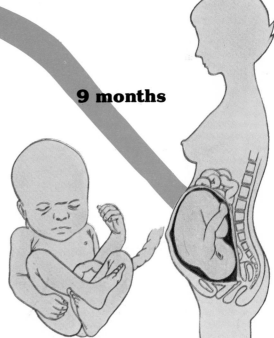

9 months

The fetus is now "full-term," or ready to be born. Its average weight is 7 pounds (3 kg) and its average length is 20 inches (.5 m). However, normal fetuses can range in weight from 5½ pounds to 10 pounds (2.5 to 4 kg). The body of the fetus is covered with a white, greasy material called *vernix* that keeps the skin from getting waterlogged.

Most babies are born about 280 days after the first day of the woman's last normal menstrual period. To calculate the approximate birth date, count ahead about 9 months from the first day of the last menstrual period and add 7 days.

special attention the woman receives. They are both fascinated and afraid of the changes taking place within the woman's body and within their marriage relationship.

All these feelings are normal. Instead of feeling guilty about such thoughts, men and women should talk about them—to their wives, husbands, friends, doctors, mothers, and to other pregnant women. Just finding out that others have the same feelings often helps.

Concluding Comments

The woman who misses a menstrual period, or who has several other symptoms of pregnancy, should go to a doctor for an examination and confirmation of her pregnancy. She may choose a private physician, private clinic, public health clinic, or midwife delivery service for her prenatal care and delivery. Good prenatal care means making regular visits to the doctor or clinic in order to prevent problems from arising. Plans will be made for delivery. Advice will be given regarding activity, clothing, food, and the growth of the fetus.

The process of growth and development begins immediately after conception. There is a rapid growth, with new features being added to the fetus almost daily. The pregnant woman's body grows and changes rapidly, too.

Women experience many different feelings during their pregnancies. Talking with others helps women realize that such feelings are not uncommon.

Activities

1. List at least three places in your community where a woman can go for a pregnancy test.
2. Talk with five women who have given birth in the past three years. Ask each woman:
   a. What signs made you first think you were pregnant?
   b. How early in your pregnancy did you first see your obstetrician?
3. Call or write to your local March of Dimes chapter. Ask for copies of their prenatal care pamphlets. Give either a written or an oral report on any differences you discover in prenatal care recommended for a 16-year-old versus a woman who is 24.
4. Find out whether any hospitals in your area have midwife delivery programs. Learn the details of such programs.
5. What folklore have you heard about pregnancy? Was this folklore once based on facts that were available at that time?

Prenatal Nutrition

Objectives

To identify nutritional needs of pregnant women.
To explain how the mother's diet is related to the health of
 the fetus.
To name the Basic Four food groups and the essential
 nutrients.

Terms to look for anemia • Basic Four • carbohydrates •
 fats • folic acid • malnourished • minerals • proteins •
 vitamins • well-nourished

You have probably heard the saying, "You are what you eat." In a very real sense, a fetus is what its mother eats. At no other time is one life as dependent on another as the developing fetus is dependent on its mother during the prenatal period. Healthy, robust babies are usually born to healthy, robust mothers. Poorly nourished mothers may produce ill, weak, or even mentally retarded babies.

Woman's Diet and Pregnancy

A woman should be healthy and well-nourished before deciding to become pregnant. She should have normal weight for her build and height. There is a great risk for both mother and baby when the woman is malnourished and underweight at the time she becomes pregnant. When a woman is undernourished, the placenta does not transfer essential nutrients to the fetus. Fetal growth can be retarded or fetal death can occur in malnourished mothers. A healthy fetus is more certain to develop when the mother has an adequate dietary intake.

Many women in less developed countries are malnourished. They do not have the appropriate foods available to provide a balanced diet. Even in the United States, there are women who cannot afford a well-balanced diet. Other groups are also malnourished. Often these are women who do not know what good nutrition is, women who diet unwisely to stay slender, and women who consume too many empty calories that do not provide the essential nutrients. A diet that is made up of French Fries, potato chips, sandwiches, and soft

Doctors used to think that pregnant women should strictly control their weight gain. Now, studies have shown that higher weight gain during pregnancy produces healthier babies.

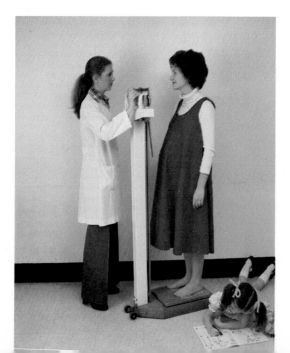

drinks lacks many of the vitamins and minerals necessary for good health. Women on such diets may feel "full" but may still be malnourished.

Weight Gain

Until the last 5 years or so, doctors in this country followed a policy of severely restricting the weight gain of pregnant women. The general rule was that women should not gain more than 20 pounds. Doctors believed that if the woman kept her weight down, the baby would be kept small, making delivery easier for the woman and the baby.

More recently, studies have shown that babies who weigh at least 7 pounds at birth are healthier and stronger and have a far better chance of survival than do smaller babies. In addition, nutritionists and doctors have discovered that inadequate diets can actually cause problems in pregnancy, labor, and delivery. Today, although the average recommended weight gain is 10 to 12 kilograms, or 22 to 26 pounds, most doctors agree that weight gains of as much as 40 pounds are not dangerous. However, they stress that weight gain should be from eating healthy, nutritious foods, not foods that are high in sugars or fats but low in nutritional value.

Extremely high weight gains do not benefit either mother or baby. Too much weight may place strain on the woman's circulatory system (especially if she is overweight to begin with). In addition, a woman who finds herself 10 or 20 pounds overweight after the baby is born may feel depressed.

You will remember that a calorie is a unit of measure indicating the amount of heat and energy in foods. During pregnancy, the average woman probably

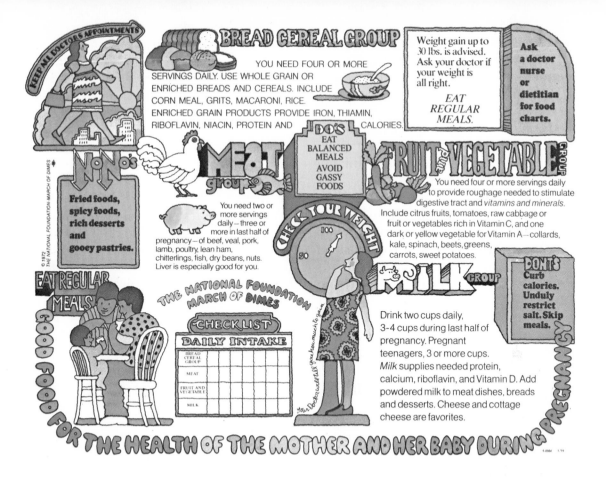

needs between 1800 and 2200 calories each day to feed herself and her growing fetus. A woman who finds herself gaining weight too rapidly may want to use a calorie chart to estimate her daily intake. Often, she may be eating more than she thinks she is.

Basic Four Food Groups

The *Basic Four food groups* contain essential nutrients called *carbohydrates, fats, proteins, minerals, vitamins, water,* and *salt.* The groups are listed here, with the number of servings required each day during pregnancy.

Group I: milk and milk products: 1 quart of milk, or its equivalent, each day

Group II: meat, fish, poultry, eggs, and beans: 2 servings (approximately 100 grams, or 3½ ounces) daily

Group III: fruits and vegetables: 4 servings daily (Be sure to include 1 serving of citrus fruit or juice each day.)

Group IV: bread and cereals: 4 servings daily, preferably whole grain

Carbohydrates and Fats. Carbohydrates are found in fruits, milk, bread and cereals, and to a lesser extent, in vegetables. So a pregnant woman will increase her carbohydrate intake somewhat. However, carbohydrates are also found in the "empty-calorie" foods, such as candy, soft drinks, and heavily sweetened desserts. Increasing the consumption of these foods is not desirable.

Although some fat in the diet is necessary, eating a lot of fat is not recommended. Fat adds extra calories, and many nutritionists now agree that it may be harmful in other ways. Greasy fried foods, such as French fries and potato chips, should be avoided as much as possible. These foods are also difficult to digest.

Proteins. Protein is the essential nutrient found in meat, poultry, fish, eggs, and beans. Milk also contains a lot of protein—about 9 grams in a glass of whole milk. A pregnant woman needs between 75 and 100 grams of protein daily to feed herself and her fetus. At least two servings of protein food, in addition to the quart of milk, should be eaten daily.

Minerals. During pregnancy, a woman's red blood cells increase in volume up to 45 percent. Also, during the last 3 months of pregnancy, the fetus stores enough iron in its body to last for the first 6 months of its life. Thus, a woman needs a high level of iron during pregnancy. A woman who does not have enough iron in her blood has a condition called *anemia,* which causes her to feel tired and listless. Iron is found in red

Milk is the best source of calcium, the mineral needed for developing strong bones and teeth in the fetus. A pregnant woman needs 4 servings of milk or milk products each day.

meats, liver, eggs, whole grain cereals, some green vegetables, dried fruits, and such natural supplements as brewer's yeast and blackstrap molasses. Foods are generally the best source of digestible iron. However, some women continue to have a low iron level despite an iron-rich diet. In such cases, a doctor will usually prescribe iron tablets or capsules.

Calcium is the mineral required for developing strong bones and teeth in the fetus. Milk is the best source of calcium. Therefore, a high intake of the milk group of foods is essential during pregnancy. Skim milk has all the essential nutrients and fewer calories than whole milk. However, many nutritionists believe that small amounts of fat are necessary for calcium absorption. Therefore, it may be advisable to drink some whole milk, or to drink milk containing 1 percent or 2 percent fat. Even if a woman does not enjoy the flavor of milk, she should include enough milk in her diet. She can cook with it as well as drink it to fill the needed quota of 1 quart a day. A few drops of vanilla will help disguise the flavor of milk. An egg nog can be made, which further enriches the milk with the protein of the egg. Most people enjoy milk more if it is served cold. Milk products, such as yogurt, cheese, and, occasionally, ice cream, can be used to make up part of the daily requirement. Cottage cheese, although very high in protein, contains only about half the calcium as the same amount of milk. A doctor who determines that the intake of calcium is too low will prescribe calcium tablets.

Vitamins. Although a well-balanced diet of foods from the Basic Four food groups is the best source of essential vitamins, most doctors also prescribe a prenatal vitamin supplement. *Folic acid,* a substance necessary for proper bone development, is difficult to obtain from food. Doctors and nutritionists believe pregnant women should have 1 milligram of folic acid a day. This is the amount found in most prenatal vitamins. There are other minerals, such as zinc, believed to be beneficial but difficult to get from foods. Supplemental vitamins should be taken only as directed by the doctor. Certain vitamins can be harmful if taken in large amounts.

Water. Water is important in the pregnant woman's diet. Water helps remove the wastes from the body. Drinking lots of water, juices, and other liquids is essential to good health.

Salt. Women were once told routinely to limit salt intake during pregnancy. This is no longer considered necessary, and women are generally allowed to use salt in moderation. Some swelling of the ankles is normal, especially during the last 3 months of pregnancy. However, if a woman's hands or feet become swollen, she should consult her doctor. The doctor may recommend reducing salt intake. If so, food can be cooked without salt, and other family members can add salt at the table. Many canned, frozen, and processed foods contain salt, so a woman on a low-salt diet should read labels carefully. Removing all salt is rarely required.

? Decisions, Decisions

Greta loves being pregnant. Now she can eat as much as she wants. Do you agree?

The father can directly affect the health of the baby by joining the mother in choosing and eating nutritious foods.

The Father's Part in Proper Nutrition

The father can play an active role in good nutrition for the mother and the fetus. Expectant parents can work together in planning interesting and varied meals that meet the woman's diet requirements. A husband might draw up and post calorie charts to keep track of the couple's food intake. Doing a little more than his share of shopping and food preparation would be especially helpful at this time. Most important, the husband understands and encourages his wife in her diet, sharing with her his involvement in this state of preparation for the baby.

Concluding Comments

The health of a fetus is dependent on what its mother eats. Healthy, robust babies are usually born to healthy, robust mothers. Malnourished mothers may produce ill, weak, or even mentally retarded babies.

A pregnant woman should not think about "eating for two" in the sense of doubling the amount of food she eats. The fetus is very tiny for a long time. Only about 300 more calories per day are needed to do the work of producing the new life.

A pregnant woman should eat between 1800 and 2200 calories per day. These calories should be obtained primarily from the Basic Four food groups. Protein, iron, and calcium are especially important. Most doctors prescribe special prenatal vitamins.

Doctors no longer insist that women strictly limit their weight gain, although gaining between 22 and 26 pounds is probably sufficient to nourish the baby. More harm is done when a woman gains too little weight than if she gains more than 26 pounds. However, excessive weight gain may be difficult to take off after the baby is born.

The intake of water and other beverages is essential to eliminate waste from the mother's and fetus's bodies. Although some swelling in pregnancy is normal, a sudden, rapid weight gain, or an extreme swelling of hands and feet, indicates the need to see a doctor immediately.

Draw the chart below on a separate piece of paper. *Do not* write in this book.

1. Write down everything you eat and drink for two days. For each serving of food and drink you consume, place a check in the appropriate place in the Basic Four food groups chart.

	Day 1	Day 2
Milk, milk products		
Bread, cereal		
Fruits, vegetables		
Meat, fish, poultry, eggs, beans		
Other		

Analyze your diet. If you were pregnant, would your diet be adequate? If not, what changes would you need to make?

2. Plan a day's menus suitable for a pregnant woman who does not like to drink much plain milk. Be sure to include foods containing enough calcium, protein, and iron. Try to choose foods *you* like.

3. Research the special need for enough protein in a pregnant woman's diet. What does protein intake during pregnancy have to do with the baby's brain cell development? (March of Dimes literature is a good resource.)

4. Obtain a list of the vitamins in a prenatal vitamin supplement. (You might copy these from a vitamin supplement available in the local drugstore.) What are natural food sources for each of the vitamins and minerals?

5. What additional nutrients are needed in the prenatal diet of a 16-year-old woman versus one who is pregnant at 24 years of age?

6. Talk to four women who were pregnant 25 or more years ago. How much weight did each gain during pregnancy? How much weight did the doctor tell each she *should* gain? Also talk to four women who have had a baby within the past three years. How much weight did each gain? How much weight gain did their doctors recommend? Using one color for actual weight gain and another for doctor's recommended gain during pregnancy, make a two-color bar graph illustrating your statistics. Has there been a change over the years in either recommended or actual weight gain among the women you interviewed?

Prenatal Health Hazards

Objectives
To identify some prenatal health hazards.
To identify some causes of prenatal problems and their possible solutions.

Terms to look for   fetal alcohol syndrome (FAS) • rubella • miscarriage • premature • prenatal health hazard • Rh factor • Rhogam • toxemia

What Can Harm the Fetus?

Pregnancy is normal and natural. Millions of women become pregnant each year. The 9 months of pregnancy can be healthy for both mother and fetus, if health hazards are properly avoided. Because the fetus is completely dependent on the mother, it can be disturbed by problems, both physical and mental, that affect the mother. Knowing about possible problems beforehand can help prospective parents avoid such problems.

Emotional Hazards

There is some evidence that severe strain on a mother's emotional health can affect the fetus. A woman who is under constant stress—from marriage, job, or other personal problems—may have physical imbalances that can affect the fetus. Thus, for a woman to feel generally happy, calm, and positive during pregnancy may be very important to the health of her baby.

This does not mean that a woman must be smiling cheerfully for 9 months. As stated in Chapter 7, all women have emotional ups and downs during pregnancy. But if a woman is always depressed, nervous, or upset, she may need some type of counseling to help her through pregnancy and the weeks and months that follow the birth of the baby. A woman's doctor may recommend a private counseling service for her to go to. Or the woman may visit a community mental health center, herself.

Smoking

Researchers now have concrete evidence that women who smoke during pregnancy deliver babies with a lower birth weight. These women also increase the risk that their babies may be born prematurely. This may be because the mother who smokes deprives her fetus of vital oxygen. Small babies and premature babies do not have the same high chances of survival as larger babies and full-term babies. For this reason, women who wish to become pregnant

A woman under unusual stress during pregnancy may develop physical problems that could affect the fetus. Couples usually find that the changes taking place during pregnancy cause some stress. It helps to stay active and in tune with each other's feelings.

WHY START A LIFE UNDER A CLOUD?

Smoking is harmful to your baby's health. Quit for both of you. For help call your American Cancer Society.

should stop smoking before conceiving. If they are already pregnant, they should stop smoking immediately.

Drugs

Any drug that a pregnant woman takes passes the placenta and gets into the bloodstream of the fetus. A woman who is addicted to hard drugs, such as heroin, is likely to give birth to a baby who is also a drug addict. No drug—including marijuana—has been proven safe to the fetus. Aspirin, antacids, laxatives, and other over-the-counter drugs should never be taken without a doctor's advice. Doctors generally prescribe drugs only if the pregnant woman's health would be endangered without them.

Alcohol

Alcohol is a poison that can harm growing tissues. Alcohol is absorbed into the blood and can pass through the woman's body and into the body of the fetus. A pregnant woman who regularly drinks a large amount of alcohol or who gets drunk from time to time runs a high risk of harming the fetus. Research has found a very serious birth defect called *fetal alcohol syndrome* (FAS). Babies suffering from FAS show many defects, or facial and other outer deformities.

Babies of heavy drinkers also have other, more common health problems. These include low birth weight, crankiness, and sometimes alcohol addiction, along with withdrawal symptoms.

Research has not determined how much alcohol is too much. At this writing, doctors are recommending that pregnant women never have more than two drinks in a day. Liquor bottles may soon be required to carry warnings to pregnant women about possible damage to the fetus. It may be safest not to drink alcohol at all, especially during the first 3 months of pregnancy. It is in these early months that the fetus is most vulnerable.

Fetal alcohol syndrome is a very serious birth defect caused by alcohol poisoning. The pregnant woman who regularly drinks alcohol or gets drunk from time to time during the pregnancy may harm the health of her baby.

Caffeine

Caffeine is also a drug and is now suspected of being harmful to the fetus. Pregnant women may want to eliminate or reduce the amount of coffee or tea they drink each day, especially during the first 3 months. There are many herbal teas and decaffeinated coffees available that do not contain caffeine.

? Decisions, Decisions

"I don't smoke," says Mary Ann. "My husband, Alan, smokes like a chimney, but I'm the one who's pregnant, not him." Do you think Mary Ann has a problem?

Venereal Disease

Venereal diseases, such as syphilis and gonorrhea, can cause harm to the fetus. If a mother has gonorrhea, her baby may be born blind, even though doctors try to prevent this by putting drops of silver nitrate in the baby's eyes at birth. If either parent has symptoms of venereal disease, he or she should be diagnosed and treated, preferably before conception.

German Measles

A woman who has not had German measles (rubella), or who cannot remember whether she has had this disease, should have a blood test to find out whether she is immune to it. If she is not immune, the doctor will usually give her an immunizing injection and advise that she wait at least 3 months before trying to become pregnant. A woman who has German measles during the first 3 months of pregnancy runs a very high risk of having a baby who is mentally retarded, blind, deaf, or crippled. Some doctors recommend abortion in such cases. This can be very upsetting to the parents who want a baby badly. It is far better to take precautions in advance.

Rh Factor

The *Rh factor* is a substance that is present in the blood of 85 percent of the population. These people are said to be Rh positive (Rh+). The 15 percent of the population whose blood does not contain this substance is said to be Rh negative (Rh−). These people are perfectly healthy, and the Rh factor only presents a problem for some pregnant women. If an Rh− mother gives birth to an Rh+ baby, the baby may be harmed, especially if it is the second Rh+ baby born to the mother. For this reason, obstetricians always test for this factor in pregnant women. A medication called *Rhogam* can now be given to Rh− mothers to prevent such complications.

Toxemia

The symptoms of *toxemia* range from badly swollen hands, face, and feet, and a rapid weight gain (3 to 7 pounds in 1 week), to severe headaches or blurred vision, convulsions, coma, and even death. A woman who has any of the early signs should see a doctor immediately. Toxemia occurs most frequently in the last 3 months of pregnancy.

Increasing evidence points to malnutrition as the most probable cause of toxemia. Therefore, it should be stressed again that all pregnant women should eat a diet high in protein and in calcium and other minerals. This diet should include foods from all Basic Four food groups.

Miscarriage

Bleeding or cramps during pregnancy can signal a *miscarriage*, which is a spontaneous abortion. Miscarriages are common, especially during the first three months of pregnancy. Often a miscarriage may be nature's way of stopping the development of a defective fetus. But this is not always the case. Some women may have physical problems that prevent them from carrying the fetus to term.

A woman who thinks she may be having a miscarriage should call her doctor immediately. She will usually be advised to go to bed and stay there until the bleeding stops. Often, with care, she will be able to carry the baby to term.

Bleeding accompanied by severe abdominal cramps almost always means that miscarriage will occur and that nothing can be done to stop it. The woman will probably have to go to the hospital so that the doctor can make sure no tissue is left in the uterus, which could cause infection.

Concluding Comments

Many problems during and after pregnancy can be prevented if both expectant parents prepare for the birth of their baby. The more knowledge a couple have, the greater will be their chance of having a successful pregnancy and birth experience. Preparation will be discussed fully in the following chapter.

Activities

1. Find out if you have had German measles or if you have been inoculated for German measles.
2. Research *herpes simplex II*, a venereal disease. Would this disease affect the fetus?
3. Write to the National March of Dimes for information on prenatal health hazards. Share your materials with the class.

National March of Dimes
1275 Mamaroneck Avenue
White Plains, NY 10605

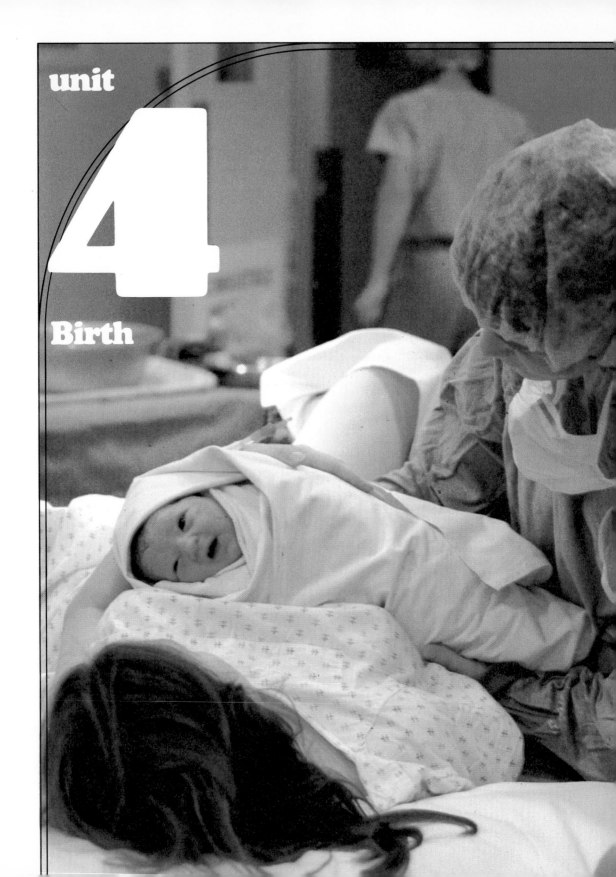

4

10

Preparing for Childbirth

Objectives

To identify the preparation the couple make to be ready for childbirth.

To identify the home preparation needed to be ready to feed, clothe, and bathe the baby and to put it to sleep.

Terms to look for   diaper service • LaMaze method of childbirth preparation • home preparation for baby's arrival • woman's personal preparation for childbirth

"My, you're big! Are you having twins?" "Have you got some names picked out?" "Is the layette all ready?"

These are a few of the questions that family and friends ask couples who are "expecting." The couple will have many significant questions of their own that will need answering.

The expectant parents will want to decide how to fix up the baby's room. They will have to decide what type of diapers to buy and to assess their laundry arrangements. They will decide on their preferred type of feeding for the baby. All along, they will be involved in classes or childbirth exercises that will make the actual birth easier.

Sharing Preparations for Childbirth

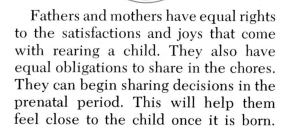

Fathers and mothers have equal rights to the satisfactions and joys that come with rearing a child. They also have equal obligations to share in the chores. They can begin sharing decisions in the prenatal period. This will help them feel close to the child once it is born.

Pregnancy can be an enjoyable time when couples share in the preparations for childbirth. This is a time to share ideas about the birth process and about child care.

Husbands can accompany their wives to the doctor's office during the pregnancy, at least part of the time. They will meet the doctor and gain confidence in her or him. Both parents-to-be can ask many questions and can talk over the myths and tales they have heard about pregnancy and childbirth. Getting straight scientific information will help alleviate many concerns they might have.

Pregnancy will be an easier and enjoyable experience if husband and wife share in the preparations for childbirth and for the baby's care once it is born. Some men are very interested in their wives' pregnancies from the beginning. Others—even though they want a baby very much—may pay little attention to the pregnancy period. This can be difficult for the pregnant woman, who needs someone with whom to share her feelings and ideas. Sometimes the doctor or clinic can help a husband become more interested. It is important for a couple to feel close to each other and to the fetus during this period.

Talking to each other, to other couples who have had babies, and, sometimes, to mothers and mothers-in-law and fathers and fathers-in-law can help expectant parents understand the pregnancy and the birth process. It can help them make decisions about how they will care for their baby. In addition, many books on pregnancy and on baby and child care are available. The names of some of these books are given in the "Suggested Readings" list at the end of Part 2 in this text. Some of these books can be very helpful. Others are confusing. Ideas about child rearing change rapidly, and a couple may find that two books give two entirely different philosophies. Rather than thinking that they have to choose a "best" way of childbearing or child rearing, couples should try to discover how *they* feel about child care. They should trust their own feelings. Parents who are confident will make a baby feel more secure than parents who nervously try to do everything "by the book" but who have not really examined their own feelings and opinions.

Classes, Exercises, and Breathing Practice

Many communities hold regular prenatal classes for couples. Here, couples meet other expectant parents and gain information from a professional nurse. The Red Cross, the Mental Health Association, the city or county public health offices, or a local hospital will have information about such classes.

Some couples prepare for childbirth by enrolling in *LaMaze* or other preparation classes. Dr. Frederick LaMaze was a French obstetrician who taught special breathing techniques to women. These techniques help them control the pain of contractions and take an active part in their labor and childbirth. Men are part of the course, too. Husbands learn to be helpful and to give encouragement and support to their wives. Later, when the wife enters the hospital, the husband will stay by her side during labor, supporting her during childbirth. Both will see their new baby born. Couples interested in this procedure must check with the doctor and the hospital to learn whether the participation of the father in the delivery room is permitted. If not, the couple may want to find another hospital that does permit this practice.

Prepared childbirth does not guaran-

Many couples take childbirth preparation classes. Hospitals allow trained husbands and wives to stay together through labor and delivery.

97

tee that pain-killing medication will not be needed. Women who receive La Maze training may still find medication necessary, especially for a first birth. New findings question whether medication during childbirth is always harmless to the fetus. Most couples who take childbirth classes hope to keep medication at a minimum. Couples must be realistic and flexible, however. There is no "failure" involved if medication is needed and used.

The LaMaze preparation method has been adapted and expanded since it was first introduced in the mid-1950s. Many hospitals and clinics now offer classes that go beyond the basic breathing techniques used in the LaMaze method. "Touch relaxation" classes are given in which husbands learn to use massage to help their wives relax. Other programs teach several kinds of relaxation techniques so that each couple can find the one that works best for them. Almost all preparation courses teach some form of "eye contact." The laboring woman is taught to look into the eyes of her husband or the childbirth coach. This helps her concentrate on following their suggestions during the labor. Nurses and nurse-midwives trained in this technique report that even unprepared women are able to give birth with little or no medication when a trained person establishes eye contact and gives them instructions.

Regular exercise will help a pregnant woman get into condition to deliver the baby. Specific exercise will help to relieve aches that come from the increased weight and strain on her back. Maintaining good muscle tone during pregnancy will speed a return to normal muscle tone after delivery. Thus, for both appearance and comfort, exercises

should be kept up. The woman should ask the doctor or childbirth instructor for advice about exercises. Her husband can participate in the exercises, too.

Preparing the Home

Babies take considerable room even though they are tiny. The house or apartment usually needs some special organization and preparation to welcome the new family member.

It is best to have a special room for the baby where the baby's bed and other belongings are kept. A baby needs a crib, with a firm mattress, that meets recommended standards of safety. A 54-inch crib usually can be used until the child is 3 years old. A bassinet, car bed, carriage, or wicker basket can serve as a temporary bed. The temporary bed should also have a firm mattress. The bassinet should be on legs or set on a table away from drafts. A pillowcase can be used for a bassinet sheet, or special bassinet sheets may be purchased. Several fitted sheets will be needed for the crib. There should be a waterproof cover on the mattress. A large towel can be placed on the mattress and under the sheet to absorb moisture. Special flannel-covered rubber sheets can be used

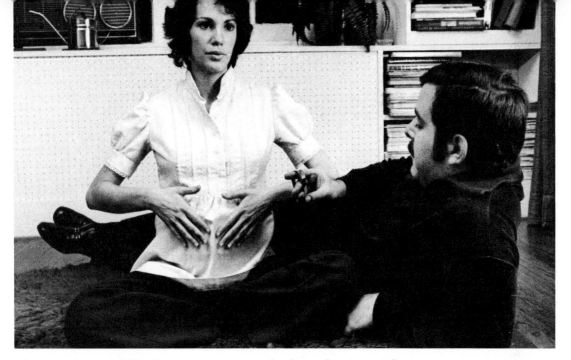

The LaMaze childbirth preparation method teaches special breathing techniques. These techniques help the woman control contractions and help the couple take an active part in labor and delivery. Fathers learn the techniques so they can stay beside mothers as supporters and coaches during childbirth.

for this purpose. These sheets can also be cut into squares and used to protect adult laps from overflowing diapers. A number of cotton blankets will be needed as well as a warm comforter or sleeping bag for cooler climates.

A chest of drawers is convenient for storing the baby's belongings. Open shelves close to the dressing table are handy for diapers. Diapers are often needed when both hands are busy holding and changing the baby, making it less convenient to reach into drawers for them. The top of the chest may be a convenient dressing table if it is the right height.

Bathing the baby in the kitchen sink will probably be fine in most homes. The sink is at a good height for the adult giving the bath. It leaves room for play-

ful kicking when the baby gets bigger. Other types of bathtubs will be discussed in Chapter 15, "Home Routines for Infants."

A tightly closed diaper pail to hold soiled diapers is desirable. A diaper service, if used, will give directions for storing soiled diapers. If you use disposable diapers, you should put them in a tightly closed container until you dispose of them. They cannot be flushed down the toilet without danger of clogging the drainage system.

Baby Clothing

A collection of baby clothing is called a *layette*. A small and simple layette is desirable. Most newborn babies sleep a lot during the first few months. They require mainly sleeping garments and diapers. The baby will grow very quickly, however. The layette of shirts and nightgowns that look gigantic when the baby is new will be getting small in weeks. For this reason, it is wise to buy only a few tiny shirts and gowns, size 3 months. Encourage friends to give some gifts in size 18 or 24 months, which will give the baby new garments once the tiny ones are outgrown.

How laundry is handled will help determine the number of each item needed. Trips to the laundromat become much harder with a new baby, who will need a great deal of attention. Most parents wash baby clothing several times a week. Even with the diaper service handling the major items, there are other garments and bedding that require laundering.

Now is the time to decide whether to use cloth diapers or disposables. The advantages and disadvantages of both are discussed in Chapter 15. Whatever the decision, stocking up on diapers in advance will make life easier when the baby comes home. Even if disposables are used, many parents find it convenient to have about a dozen cloth diapers on hand, also. They are handy to use for burping pads, for quick cleanups, and as pads to lay under the baby for a diaper change when you are away from home.

A useful layette consists of 3 or 4 undershirts, 2 or 3 gowns or one-piece stretch suits, 3 or 4 dozen diapers, 2 sweater sets, 2 waterproof pants (if cloth diapers are used), 3 or 4 receiving blankets, and a warm blanket or sleeping bag. Many one-piece stretch suits are so attractive and comfortable that parents

New babies do not need new clothes. They just need lots of clothes. Borrowing baby clothes or buying them from other parents makes sense.

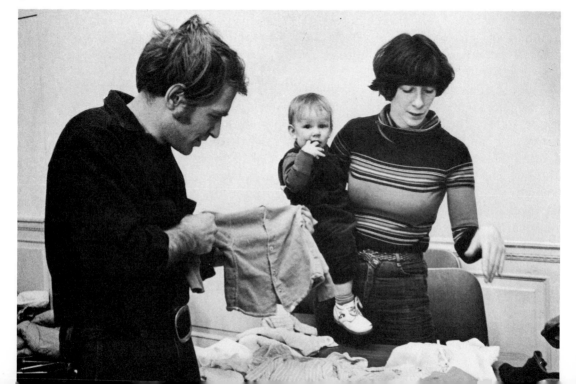

prefer to keep babies in them instead of dressing them up for outings. Therefore, dress-up clothing is seldom needed before age 1, and buying clothing in sizes 12, 18, or 24 months is more practical.

Having more clothes and blankets than this can be very helpful in saving laundry time. Many couples borrow from one another when they have babies a few months or a year apart in age. Since babies grow so quickly, borrowing is a good way to get a lot of wear out of baby clothes.

In preparing for the baby, couples should not feel they have to buy the most expensive cribs and furniture. Many couples enjoy finding old cribs and other items at garage sales or used-furniture stores. They then refinish or paint the furniture and make it safe, themselves, thus saving a lot of money. Old cribs should be carefully tested for safety, however. On some of them, the bars are far enough apart to allow a baby's head to get through. All of a baby's furnishings should meet the highest safety standards.

Whatever decisions parents make about the baby's needs, having everything ready at least a month in advance is a good idea. One couple's baby arrived a week earlier than expected. The night before the baby and mother were to come home, the father was up until 3 A.M. painting furniture.

Feeding Decisions

The couple should make decisions about how to feed their baby sometime before the baby is born. More mothers are nursing babies to give their infants the special benefits that mother's milk gives and to develop a closeness between them and their babies. Most mothers can breast-feed if they desire.

If the parents choose to feed their baby a milk formula by bottle, a method of mixing and sterilizing the formula and bottles will be needed. The usual equipment is a sterilizer or other container for boiling the bottles, about 9 Pyrex bottles, tongs for handling hot bottles, about 12 nipples, and a bottle brush and nipple brush. The doctor will advise parents about the type of formula to use for the baby. Feeding decisions will be discussed further in Chapter 15, "Home Routines for Infants."

? Decisions, Decisions

David's sister has offered her children's crib, highchair, playpen, and baby clothes to David and Eve. The items are out of date and not in good condition. She seems insistent that David and Eve use them. What can they do?

Concluding Comments

The final stages of pregnancy will be happy times for the woman and man who have wanted a baby for a long time and are sharing the final preparation for its birth. The process of giving birth and coming home with the new baby presents fewer problems for a couple who have prepared themselves well. If they have their home ready and the clothing, laundry, and feeding systems worked out, these first few weeks will be easier on all concerned. If the husband and wife have shared in preparations, they will be more capable and confident in their new parenting roles.

101

Activities

1. Interview a couple who recently had a baby by means of prepared childbirth. Did the father coach the mother throughout labor and delivery. How long was she in labor? Are their feelings about the birth mostly positive or negative? Describe their situation.

2. Interview a mother and father whose child was born at least 20 years ago. Was the father involved in the labor and delivery process? How long was the mother in labor? Are her memories of her delivery much different from the woman who was "prepared" for childbirth? How are the two fathers' feelings about childbirth alike or different?

3. Research the availability of prepared childbirth classes in your community. Report the results to your class.

4. Compare diaper use costs:
   a. Call a diaper service to learn the cost of using the service for two years.
   b. Figure the cost of using eight disposable diapers per day for two years.
   c. Calculate the cost of buying four dozen cloth diapers, plus doing two loads of washing each week for two years.
   d. Make a cost comparison chart. In addition, list factors that these figures do not include.

5. Interview the mother of an infant. Ask her about the number and usefulness of layette garments and equipment needed for an infant. Ask her about number of items, type and sizes, laundering, wearability, and so forth.

6. Visit the infant section of a department store or look in a mail-order catalog for price information for infants' clothing and equipment.

7. Based on the information you gathered in questions 5 and 6, make a chart or wall poster or design a bulletin board, showing layette garments and equipment needed for an infant. Include the costs of these items.

8. Select a classmate to call new and used furniture stores and ask about the price and safety features of a crib, a playpen, and a high chair. Check prices at neighborhood yard sales or garage sales. What conclusions can you draw about infant furniture?

A Baby Is Born

Objectives

To identify the final steps in preparation for childbirth.
To identify hospital procedures at childbirth.
To describe the stages of childbirth.

Terms to look for   breech position • cervix • cesarean section •
  contraction • dilation • episiotomy • fetal monitor •
  glucose • self-absorbing stitches • stages of labor • transition

"My water just broke, Doctor," says Janet Mayer to Dr. Snelling over the telephone.

"Have you had contractions yet?" asks the doctor.

"Yes, but not regularly." says Janet.

"Then wait until the contractions seem to be coming regularly—every 5 minutes or less—and call me back," requests the doctor.

Thus begins Janet's Saturday morning. She does not eat breakfast. Most doctors believe it is better not to have the stomach full during labor. *Labor* is the term that refers to the energy and effort used as the body prepares to push the baby out of the uterus through the cervix and out through the birth canal.

Janet showers and washes her hair, then checks to see that she has everything ready. After several more conversations with the nurse and doctor, she and her husband, Rod, are on their way to the hospital.

Hospitalization

Planning how to get to the hospital ahead of time and what is necessary to take will make the trip an easier one.

Transportation Planned

Janet and Rod had organized in advance several plans for getting Janet to the hospital. They wanted her to know what to do in case she needed to go to the hospital when Rod was away at work.

Suitcase Packed

Janet's suitcase has been packed for a week, waiting for this day. It contains a change of clothes for her, nursing brassieres, and an attractive housecoat. She has included two gowns that button in front. These had been recommended as most convenient for a nursing mother.

Janet has packed her cosmetics and other personal care items, including san-

The benefits of planning for childbirth become most real when labor begins. Couples know what will happen and what to do.

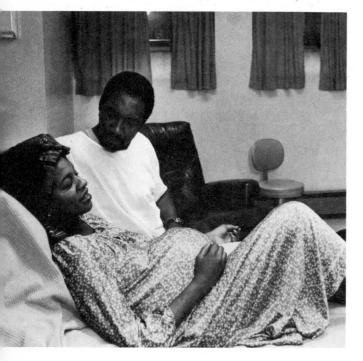

itary napkins. She learned that women usually have some minor bleeding that may continue for a week or more after the baby is born.

At the Hospital

Rod and Janet know just where to go in the hospital. They went to the hospital a few weeks earlier to visit a friend who had a new baby. They talked to the nurse about Janet's forthcoming hospitalization. They saw the nursery and the delivery room at that time, too.

Today, the nurse is waiting for them. The doctor sent the nurse to meet them after giving the go-ahead for Janet to come to the hospital.

Rod checks in at the business desk and fills out the required forms while the nurse leads Janet to the preparation room.

Preparation Room

Janet undresses and her clothing is checked in. She puts on a hospital gown. She gives Rod her watch and rings when he joins her later. This is a safety and sanitation measure.

The doctor, finding Janet in bed in the maternity wing, checks her blood pressure and gives her a pelvic examination similar to the one she had during her first visit. The doctor determines the position of the baby and the amount of *dilation*, or enlargement, of the *cervix*— the opening through which the baby will soon appear.

Many hospitals permit the husband to accompany his wife to the initial pelvic examination. Since this examination is often done by a doctor whom the woman has never seen, the husband's presence is reassuring.

Labor

Labor during childbirth is well named. The woman uses a lot of energy in labor and feels tired for several days afterward. The average length of labor for a first baby is about 12 to 14 hours. For most women, labor resembles severe menstrual cramps. Some women feel most of the pain in their lower back. This is called *back labor*. Following admission to the hospital and the initial preparation, the woman is usually in bed in the labor room. Here, the nursing staff can keep their attention focused on several women who are getting ready to deliver their babies. Some hospitals allow women to move around when they are still in the early stages of labor. Many hospitals have private labor rooms for each woman. Husbands can usually stay with their wives to help and support them. Expectant fathers no longer have to stay nervously alone in halls and waiting rooms. If they have had LaMaze or other training, they can participate fully during labor and delivery.

First Stage of Labor

The first stage of labor lasts an average of 10 to 12 hours, counting from the first contractions that come at regular intervals. A *contraction* is the tightening and relaxing of the muscles. The muscles surrounding the uterus are contracting and putting pressure on the fluids that surround the baby. The force is on the cervix, or opening, into the birth canal. The cervix dilates, or opens, a little at a time, until it finally measures about 10 centimeters, or 4 inches, across. This

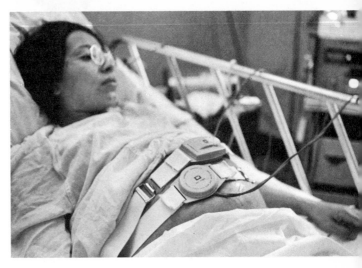

Many hospitals now use a fetal monitor. This device is shown here, wrapped around the woman's abdomen. It records contractions and the fetal heartbeat.

first stage of labor usually goes much more quickly for mothers who have already had a baby.

Janet learns the value of prenatal exercises and training for delivery in this first stage. Janet knows what is happening. She knows how to breathe and how to relax her muscles as needed. Perhaps most important, she is not afraid. Fear of pain causes more muscle tension, which adds to the actual pain. Fear may even prolong labor.

During all stages of labor, the mother's blood pressure and other vital signs are closely watched by persons responsible for this particular assignment. These people also listen to the fetus's heartbeat. Many hospitals today routinely use the *fetal monitor*. This device, which looks somewhat like a loose girdle, is wrapped around the woman's abdomen and connected by wires to a machine. The machine records the contractions and fetal heartbeat. Sometimes an *internal monitor* is

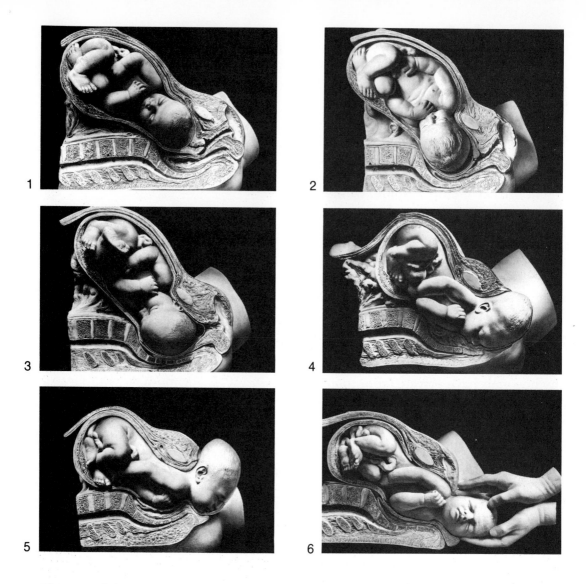

These models were made to show some of the key stages in the
human birth process. In the first model (1), made to show the
baby's position before labor begins, note the position of the head
and the normal width of the cervix. In the second model (2), the
baby's head has dropped into the birth position and the cervix
is starting to widen. In the third model (3), the cervix has
widened and the muscles of the uterus are beginning to force
the baby's head through the birth canal. Labor contractions are
now strong and frequent. In the fourth and fifth models (4 and
5), the head emerges and turns upward. The next step is the
birth of the shoulders (6), which is helped by the turning of the
baby's head. The baby's complete exist is rapid after the shoulders
are out.

106

used. A wire is inserted in the vagina to record fetal responses.

Many hospitals also give the laboring woman intravenous feedings of *glucose* (sugar water) to keep her blood-sugar level high and give her energy. If she has not eaten, and if her labor is fairly long, the glucose prevents fatigue.

During the first stage of labor, the husband can help his wife change positions when necessary, propping her up with pillows if she prefers a sitting or semisitting position. Some women are more comfortable lying on their sides part of the time. Women who are experiencing back labor may find that getting on their hands and knees relieves pressure. Husbands can also help their wives concentrate on breathing and on relaxing muscles, and they can massage tight arms, legs, or backs.

Toward the end of the first stage of labor, usually when the woman's cervix is about 8 centimeters dilated, *transition* occurs. This is usually a period of rapid, irregular contractions. Most women report that it is the most uncomfortable part of labor. Some women become nauseated or chilled. Many women become irritated and may speak sharply to their husbands, the doctor, or the hospital staff. Husbands who have had training will know that this is normal, and they will try to be as comforting and supportive as possible, as will doctors and nurses. Painkilling medication is most likely to be given during transition.

Second Stage of Labor

The second stage of labor begins when the cervix is fully dilated and the woman is instructed to push. It ends when the baby has been pushed out through the cervix, down the birth canal, and through the vagina into the doctor's gloved hands. This pushing stage lasts an average of 45 minutes for a woman having her first baby.

The training Janet had during her childbirth classes helps her know when to push and when to relax. Most women report that the pushing stage is more satisfying than it is painful. If they have

This is one of life's most joyful and memorable moments. After 9 months, parents see their child for the first time.

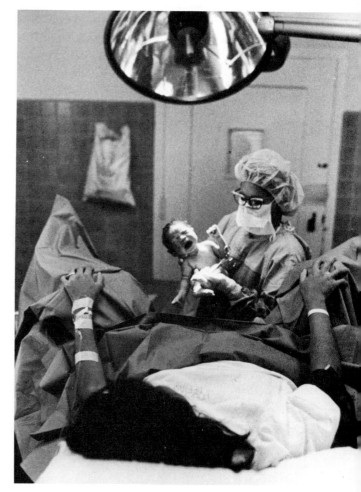

not had any medication up to this point, they will probably not need it now.

Rod is participating actively now. He stands by Janet's bed, looks into her eyes, and helps her interpret the clues from her body and from the doctor. She breathes, bears down, and relaxes as needed. Between contractions, she may feel completely relaxed and may even laugh and joke with Rod, the doctor, and the nurse. The doctor tells her that the baby's head can now be seen and that the baby has dark hair. She knows it will not be long now before she sees her baby.

Janet is moved to the delivery room when the baby is about to be born. Her lower abdomen and vaginal area are scrubbed and painted with an antiseptic solution. Her legs are covered with white, sterile, "cloth boots," and her feet are placed in stirrups connected to the delivery table. Her body is covered with a "sterile drape," or cloth. Some delivery tables now have slanted backs so that the woman can deliver in a semisitting position. If the delivery table is flat, the husband and nurse can use pillows to prop the woman. Or the husband can support his wife's back during the pushing contractions.

Rod has scrubbed well and wears a sterile gown and mask like the medical personnel. He stands near Janet's head where he can see and talk to her and prop her up if necessary. There may be a lot of people in the delivery room by now—the doctor, a nurse, a standby

Many hospitals allow mothers and fathers to hold their baby immediately after birth. This helps couples form a close relationship with their baby from the very beginning. The father, dressed in delivery room clothes, is supporting his wife's head.

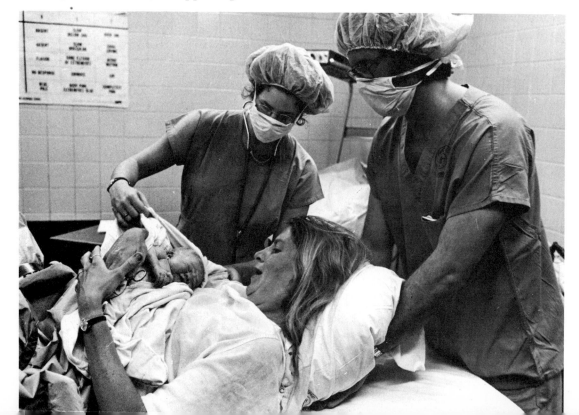

anesthetist or anesthesiologist, Rod, and possibly an intern or medical student. All of them will be encouraging Janet as she works to push the baby out.

An *episiotomy* is a small cut that is usually made in the opening of the mother's vagina to make it easier for the baby's head to come out. The doctor makes this cut rather than risk tearing of the vaginal walls during birth. A tear would be ragged and harder to stitch and to heal. The stitches used will be *self-absorbing*, that is, they will not have to be pulled out later on.

Finally, the baby's head emerges and, after a few more contractions, the entire baby is born. The doctor holds the baby up feet first to let the mucus run out of its mouth. Janet and Rod can both see their first-born child—a girl! The baby cries. The doctor clamps, or ties, the umbilical cord and cuts it. The nurse gently holds the baby on Janet's stomach where she can see and feel her child. The nurse then gives the baby to Rod for a moment. Rod holds the baby carefully, looking relieved and proud.

The baby looks strange with its whitish covering and spots of blood, but Janet and Rod are delighted with their child. The nurse takes the baby to an electrically warmed bassinet, because Janet's attention is required for the third and final stage of labor.

Third Stage of Labor

In the third stage of labor, the placenta and other membranes now come down the birth canal and are expelled. The nurse massages the uterus as it contracts and expels its contents. This stage takes about 10 minutes.

Complications and Differences in Labor

The above story describes an average labor, or what is sometimes called a "textbook labor." Labor is different for every woman and for every pregnancy, and very few women will follow this pattern exactly. Some normal labors last 24 hours or more. Others may last only for 3 hours. Some women never feel regular contractions. Their contractions just keep getting stronger and stronger, but they have no consistent pattern.

The normal position for a baby to be in is head down. However, some babies are born buttocks first. This is called the *breech position* and requires more skill on the part of the doctor. Babies may also be born feet first.

Sometimes a woman is not able to push the baby out by herself. Then the doctor must use forceps, an instrument to reach into the birth canal to pull the baby out. Such babies are born with marks on the face and head. These marks disappear in a few days. Forceps are generally needed for breech births.

Cesarean Section

If the placenta had been attached to the uterus in the wrong place, or if the placenta had started to enter the birth canal ahead of the baby, the doctor might have decided to do an operation called a *cesarean*. (The procedure is named after Julius Caesar, the Roman emperor who was supposed to have been born this way.) In the operation, the doctor removes the baby from the uterus through a cut in the abdominal wall. Such an operation is also needed when the birth canal is too small, when it fails to open properly, or when the fetus shows signs of stress. One sign of stress would be a sudden slowing of the fetal heartbeat. More time is needed for a mother's recovery when she has a cesarean than when she has a normal childbirth.

Medication

Many different types of medication are used for relieving a woman's discomfort during labor. If Janet used a drug, it was probably an *analgesic* or *tranquilizer*. Both of these types of drugs help a woman relax without dulling her senses too much. Thus she remains fairly alert and able to participate in her baby's birth.

Anesthesia is of three types. Janet probably had an injection of *local anesthesia* before her doctor sewed her stitches. She may have had an injection before the episiotomy was done. But often the pressure of the baby's head causes numbness so that no injection is needed.

Regional anesthesia blocks sensation in nerves in a certain area. For childbirth, a doctor may use a *spinal block,* or *epidural.* All of these require injecting a substance into the spine so that the woman no longer feels sensation in the lower part of her body. Of these, the epidural is the safest. It is also the most expensive because of the skill required to administer it. A woman who has had regional anesthesia may have difficulty pushing the baby out, because she cannot feel her contractions. Often, forceps are needed. Regional anesthesia is often used for cesarean sections.

General anesthesia is given to a woman to put her to sleep. It is used most frequently for cesarean sections, particularly when they must be performed suddenly. Sometimes a little general anesthesia, or "gas," is administered in the final stages of labor if a woman is in severe pain.

Recovery

After the episiotomy is sewn up, Janet is wheeled into the recovery room. Here, she rests for an hour or so while a nurse checks her blood pressure and other life signs. Later on, she is taken to her room where she meets her roommate, another mother whose baby is already 1 day old.

Janet is still too excited to be tired. She is anxious to see her baby and Rod, who is calling all the friends and relatives to report the good news. Before long, the meal cart arrives, and Janet realizes she is very hungry.

Rooming-in Plan

Just as Janet completes her meal, another cart appears. This one carries a bassinet with her baby and supplies for taking care of a newborn. The nurse tells Janet that the baby weighs 7 pounds, 14 ounces. Janet is delighted. The nurse helps her hold the baby to her breast. The baby begins to suck. "She does know how!" exclaims Janet.

Of course, Janet's breast milk will not come in for about 3 days, but now the baby is stimulating milk production and is getting *colostrum,* or "first milk." Colostrum protects newborn babies from infections.

Janet smiles and pats her baby. She

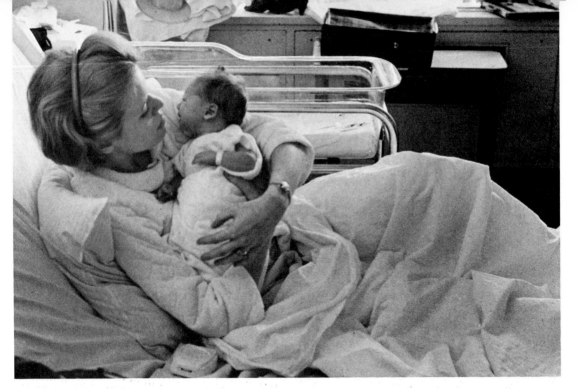

The rooming-in plan allows mothers and babies to be together during the hospital stay. This new plan is one of many fine changes being made in hospital childbirth procedures.

is delighted when Rod appears, and together they admire their child.

The rooming-in plan in this hospital enables Janet to keep her baby close to her during the day. That way, she can change the baby and learn to care for her. The rooming-in plan is more family-centered than other hospital plans. Rod asks for some advice from the experienced nurse who drops in to see how they are getting along.

Alternative Childbirth Arrangements

The childbirth procedure Janet and Rod used is probably the most common method of "natural childbirth" in today's hospitals. However, many women

and men, and an increasing number of doctors, are questioning whether it is the best method. Opponents claim that hospitals take the birth experience away from the family and make the family conform to "hospital procedure" for the convenience of the staff. Many people feel that spending most of her labor in bed, and then delivering on her back, makes a woman's labor and delivery more difficult.

Many families and child psychologists also question the practice of taking the baby away from the new parents for several hours or more. These people feel that mothers should hold and nurse their babies immediately and that the entire family should be together for a long period following the baby's birth.

Studies have shown that women who are allowed to keep their babies from the very beginning form close relationships easily and help the babies adjust to the world better.

Families and pediatricians are also questioning the almost routine use of drugs during labor and delivery. Although many childbirth classes lead women to believe that they will deliver their babies without drugs, the great majority of women are given some type of medication during their labor. No long-term effects of such medication on the baby have been proven. But fetuses whose mothers are medicated are known to be less responsive in the first hours of their lives. All medications pass the placenta and enter the fetus's bloodstream.

Almost no one would suggest that a woman should suffer during labor if her pain can be relieved with medication. However, many women can be helped through the more difficult periods of a normal labor if they have a supportive husband, doctor, or midwife to encourage them.

As a result of these complaints, the number of home births has risen sharply in the last several years. Alarmed by the increasing number of home births, many hospitals are changing their procedures to make the labor and delivery more homelike. Some hospitals have started the practice of having "birthing rooms" where a woman labors and delivers in the same room. She is allowed to wear her own clothes, if she desires to do so. She may walk around during labor as long as she feels comfortable doing so. Intravenous feedings and fetal monitors are used only if there is a real need for them.

Many women and doctors are also questioning the practice of routine episiotomies.

In birthing rooms and in some hospital recovery rooms, the baby is given to the mother right after birth, as long as all vital signs are normal. Mother and baby are wrapped in a blanket so that the mother's body keeps the baby warm. The staff members usually leave the parents alone with the baby for a while so that the family can get acquainted. Some hospitals even allow older brothers and sisters to come into the room to greet the new baby.

Midwife delivery clinics have the same sort of arrangements as hospital birthing rooms. Many obstetricians feel that such clinics are safe for normal births. Others feel that only hospitals, with their emergency facilities, offer adequate safety for mothers and babies.

Concluding Comments

Childbirth is a long-awaited event for a couple. Many of their hopes and fears are represented in the event. The labor and delivery period is tiring. It can sometimes be frightening for even the well-prepared woman. However, good doctors and hospital staffs are supporting and understanding. Many times a husband is allowed in the labor room. And, if he has been prepared in the expectant parent classes, he is admitted to the delivery room as well. Many hospitals are reevaluating their procedures and trying to make them more homelike.

The rooming-in plan is one family-centered plan. It helps the mother and baby get acquainted better while in the hospital. Also, the mother benefits from advice from experienced staff persons and roommates. After the baby is taken home, care rests on less experienced care givers—but care givers who are eagerly learning the important techniques.

The newborn baby sometimes has a distorted look, having been through a rather difficult process during birth. The baby looks better in a day or two, so parents need not worry.

Activities

1. Call local hospitals. Ask if fathers or other "coaches" are allowed in labor and delivery rooms. What requirements does each hospital have for childbirth coaches? Which hospitals permit "rooming-in" for mother and baby? Do they have "birthing" rooms? (These rooms may be called Alternative Birth Centers.)

2. Examine a model or pictures of a fetus in the birth canal. Label each body part and describe the three stages of labor.

3. Read about the Le Boyer method of childbirth. Then ask a doctor or nurse-midwife what he or she thinks professionally about this method of childbirth. Discuss your findings in class.

4. Read a personal account of the birth of a baby, such as the one by Sara Adams in *Children* by Mollie S. and Russell C. Smart, NY: Macmillan, 1977, pp. 38–39. Discuss the feelings of the mother and father during the birth.

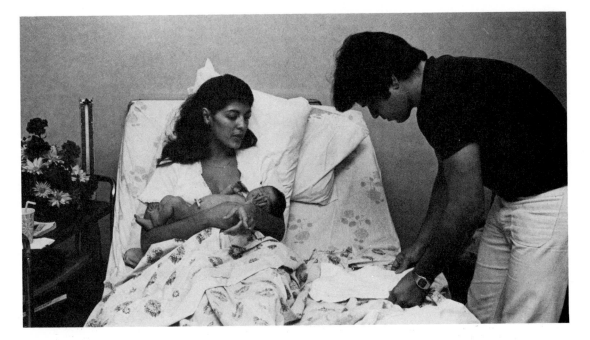

SUGGESTED READINGS FOR PART 2

Ams, Suzanne, *A Season to Be Born*. New York: Harper & Row, 1973.

Ashdown-Sharp, Patricia, *A Guide to Pregnancy and Parenthood for Women on Their Own*. New York: Random House, 1977.

Bing, Elizabeth, *Six Practical Lessons For an Easier Childbirth*. New York: Bantam Books, 1977.

Brenner, Erma, *A New Baby! A New Life!* New York: McGraw-Hill, 1973.

Colman, Arthur D. and Libby Colman, *Pregnancy: The Psychological Experience*. New York: Bantam Books, 1977.

11 Million Teenagers: What Can Be Done about the Epidemic of Adolescent Pregnancies in the United States. The Alan Guttmacher Institute, 515 Madison Avenue, New York, NY 10022.

Eshelman, Nancy, *Ready or Not*. From the "Let's Get It Together" series. Lexington, Massachusetts: Ginn and Company, 1974.

"Food and You—Partners in Growth During Pregnancy." Rosemont, Illinois 60018: National Dairy Council, 1977. (free leaflet)

Hall, Robert E., *Nine Months' Reading: A Medical Guide for Pregnant Women*. New York: Bantam Books, 1973.

Howard, Marion, *Only Human—Teenage Pregnancy and Parenthood*. New York: The Seabury Press, 1976.

Klein, Carole, *The Single Parent Experience*. New York: Avon Books, 1973.

Leboyer, Frederick, *Birth Without Violence*. New York: Alfred A. Knopf, 1975.

Marzollo, Jean, *9 Months/1 Day/1 Year*. New York: Harper & Row, 1976.

Nilsson, Lennart, *A Child is Born: The Drama of Life Before Birth*. New York: Dell Publishing/Seymour Lawrence, 1966.

"Nutrition and Pregnancy." White Plains, New York: 10602: The National Foundation March of Dimes. (free leaflet)

Nye, F. Ivan, *School-Age Parenthood: Consequences for Babies, Mothers, Fathers, Grandparents and Others*. Pullman, Washington 99164: Extension Bulletin 667, Cooperative Extension Service, 1976.

Pierce, Ruth I., *Single and Pregnant*. Boston: The Beacon Press, 1971.

Prenatal Care. U.S. Department of Health, Education, and Welfare, (OCD)73–17, Washington, DC: U.S. Government Printing Office, 1973.

Walton, Viki E., *Have It Your Way*. New York: McGraw-Hill, 1973.

3

The Infant

You will understand how infants grow and develop physically, mentally, socially, and emotionally during their first year. You will also learn principles of feeding, guiding, and teaching infants.

unit

5

The Growing and Developing Infant

The Infant Grows Physically

Objectives

To define growth and development.
To state four rules of physical development.
To give examples of head-to-toe development.
To give examples of ways to influence maturation.

Terms to look for   baby teeth • development • fontanel • grasp reflex • growth • head-to-toe direction • incisors • maturation • permanent teeth • sucking reflex

"Look how tiny his toes are! Will it take a long time for them to be as big as mine?" asks 5-year-old Shelly. She was admiring her new baby brother while her mother bathed him.

"That baby is already sitting up. I had forgotten how soon a baby learns to sit," remarks a visiting grandmother about her granddaughter. She admires 6-month-old Jackie as the infant's father encourages the baby to sit, reach, and to smile back at him.

Growth and Development

Big sister Shelly is asking about the physical growth of the baby. *Growth* means an increase in size and weight. Friends and family members frequently notice growth. Someone has probably told you recently how much you have grown. Such comments may annoy you

a little. You have probably noticed your own growth. Your shoes are tight, or your jeans too short. Growth usually stops between the ages of 16 and 18. About this time, the cartilage has filled in with calcium. This process makes hard bone at the ends of the long bones in the legs, feet, arms, and hands.

Baby Jackie's grandmother is noticing Jackie's development. *Development* refers to the baby's increased skill in using various body parts. The *first development rule* is that babies develop in the head region first, then the trunk, and last in the legs and feet. So, we say that babies develop in a head-to-toe direction. That is, they hold up their heads before grasping objects with their hands. They feed themselves before walking.

The *second development rule* is that children develop from the midline toward the fingers and toes. That is, they can grasp a big ball in their arms before they can catch a baseball in their hands. They can kick a ball before they can roller-skate. The fine skills of hands and feet are the last to develop.

The *third development rule* is that, as the brain develops, children respond to more and more sights and sounds in the environment. They can also respond to finer and finer details.

The *fourth development rule* is that development is a lifetime process, while growth stops about age 16 to 18. For example, someone who learns to type or to paint at age 70 is still developing.

Size and Weight

Growth in infancy, like prenatal growth, follows a predictable pattern. The pattern is very similar among all children around the world.

The average baby is 20 inches long at birth, or 50.8 centimeters. Of course, not all babies are 20 inches. Some are shorter and some are longer. They typically range from 18 to 21½ inches, or 45.7 to 54.6 centimeters.

Babies grow and develop at an exciting rate during the first year of life. They command their parents' attention. The more parents observe their baby, the better they can meet the baby's changing needs.

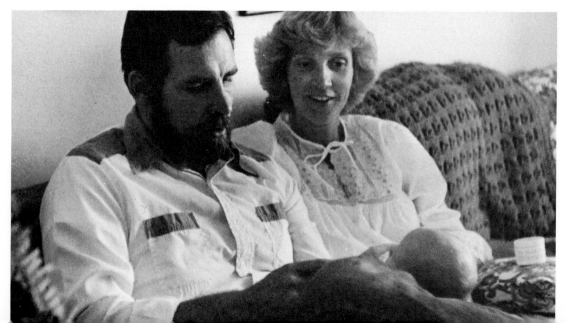

The average baby weighs 7½ pounds at birth, or 3.4 kilograms. Typically, the range is from 5¾ pounds to 10 pounds, or from 2.6 kilograms to 4.5 kilograms.

A 1-year-old baby will measure about 30 inches, or 76 centimeters, and weigh about 21 pounds, or 9.5 kilograms. A general rule is that the baby increases in height by 50 percent and triples its birth weight in the first year. That is, a baby 20 inches long at birth grows 10 inches during the first year. A baby who weighs 7½ pounds at birth will be 15 pounds at 6 months and 22½ pounds at 12 months. This is a very rapid rate of increase. If you are 60 inches tall now and were to add 50 percent, or 30 inches, to your height you would be 90 inches, or 7½ feet, tall. Clearly, the rate of growth slows down after infancy.

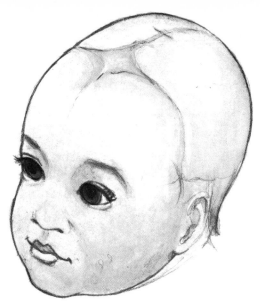

The "soft spot," or fontanel, on the top of an infant's head is covered with tough skin. There is no danger of damaging it with normal handling. Since the baby has little hair, a pulse may sometimes be seen beating under the fontanel.

? Decisions, Decisions

Brenda is 6 months old but cannot yet sit up without support. Everyday, her parents try to get her to sit unassisted. They are worried she is not developing properly. Their neighbors' child could sit alone at 5 months. What advice would you give them?

New Baby's Body

Many interesting observations can be made about body parts and body proportions of new babies.

The Head

The head of the newborn baby is very large. Compared to the baby's total length of about 20 inches, or 50.8 cen-

timeters, the length of the head measures 5 inches, or 12.7 centimeters—one-fourth of the total length. The head of an adult is about one-eighth of the total height.

A newborn's head usually looks elongated or peaked. But it becomes more rounded several days after birth. There are four pieces of bone that make up the skull. These are flexible and move slightly as the baby is forced down through the birth canal. This makes the head temporarily misshapened. The four skull bones will not join until the baby is about 18 months old. The area between them, at the top of the baby's head, is called the *fontanel*, or "soft spot." It is covered with tough, canvas-like skin. You may have been warned not to touch the baby's head because of this soft spot. In fact, this covering is very strong. You cannot hurt a baby by touching the head gently. The flexibility of the skull gives a baby protection from concussion caused by bumps or falls.

Newborns can turn their heads from side to side when lying down. They turn their face to the side when touched on the cheek. The head is very wobbly, so parents and care givers must put a supporting hand behind the head each time they handle the baby. Parents and care givers can encourage strengthening of the muscles that support the head by letting babies lie on their stomachs frequently. This gives the infants the opportunity to practice "head rearing."

? Decisions, Decisions

"Our new baby seems so tiny and fragile," said George. "I'm really not comfortable handling him. I'm afraid I'll hurt him." How can George overcome this common reaction?

Brain

The brain is large at birth, but brain development is incomplete. The part of the brain controlling posture and balance develops rapidly during the first year of life.

Hair

Some babies have lots of hair at birth while others are nearly bald. Some lose their first hair. The new hair that grows in is sometimes a different color than the first hair.

Mouth

The baby's automatic sucking action is important at birth. This is called a *sucking reflex.* When the mouth area is touched, the baby turns toward the touch and starts sucking automatically. This reflex helps the baby "know" how to eat from birth. Without it, a baby might not survive.

The inborn sucking reflex helps the baby "know" how to eat from birth. Some babies suck their fingers in the mother's womb before birth. Sucking is an important need and comfort throughout infancy.

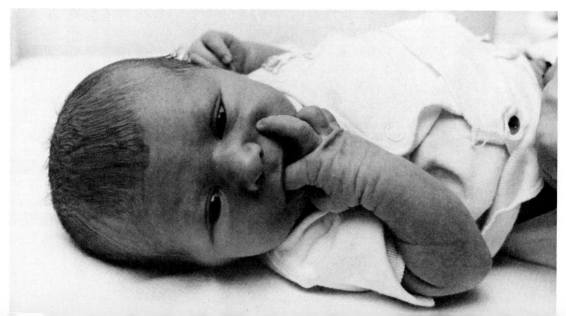

Teeth

The teeth buds are formed during the prenatal stage. For this reason, it is important for the pregnant woman to eat foods that contain calcium and phosphorous, such as milk. It is a rare baby that is born with a tooth, but this does happen once in a while. The average age for the first tooth to appear is about 6 months.

The first teeth are called *baby teeth*. The teeth are made up of calcium, which comes from the milk the baby drinks. Baby teeth last until age 5 or 6. Then, one by one they fall out and are replaced by *permanent teeth*. The teeth coming in at 6 to 8 months are usually the 2 lower middle teeth called *incisors*. The 4 upper front teeth, also incisors, come in between 8 and 12 months. Thus, the average baby has 6 teeth by about 1 year of age.

Eyes

Babies are able to see at birth. They notice movement. Dr. Burton L. White has done extensive research on children from birth to 3 years. He reports that newborn infants are best able to see an object that is between 5 and 18 inches away. Dr. White also states that the infant from birth to 6 weeks is extremely sensitive to bright lights. Newborns may open their eyes more in a dimly lighted room than in a brightly lighted one.

Ears

Babies have very good hearing. Newborns startle easily and will often cry when they hear loud noises. They like to have songs sung to them and usually become quiet when music starts. A baby who never startles at loud noises may have a hearing problem and should be checked by a doctor. Sometimes even tiny infants can wear hearing aids. Babies must be able to hear in order to develop language normally.

Arms and Hands

At birth, the baby has no control of arms and hands. The hands have a *grasp reflex*. The baby automatically grips tightly any object, such as a pencil or a finger, that touches the palm. This reflex fades out by 6 months, when voluntary grasping begins. Besides this grasp reflex, most babies tend to hold their hands in tight fists. Most babies are not able to open their hands freely until they are about 3 months old.

Babies first grasp objects in the palm of the hand with a whole-hand movement. It will be many months before they can pick up an object with the thumb and forefinger.

Legs and Feet

Legs and feet are the most helpless of the baby's body parts. First, the legs are drawn up in the prenatal position. The legs extend when the baby jumps with the *startle reflex*. In this reflex, both arms wave jerkily, the back is arched, and the head is thrown back. The baby usually cries following the startle. The startle reflex sometimes alarms new parents who are not aware of what it is.

Legs also make some automatic creeping or swimming motions. Legs and feet are the last body parts to be controlled at will. A baby sits alone and grasps objects with the hands long before learning to walk. Remember, the first rule of development is that the baby develops in a head-to-toe direction.

Trunk

The main part of the body is called the *trunk*. The trunk will double and redouble in size several times before the baby reaches adulthood.

In newborns, the control of the trunk must wait until the brain matures. After about 3 months, control of the head and spine begins. By 5 months, the baby can usually sit up with help. And, by 14 months, most babies are walking.

Parents and care givers can encourage play that builds body control. They cannot, however, "teach" this control, which comes only when the muscles are ready.

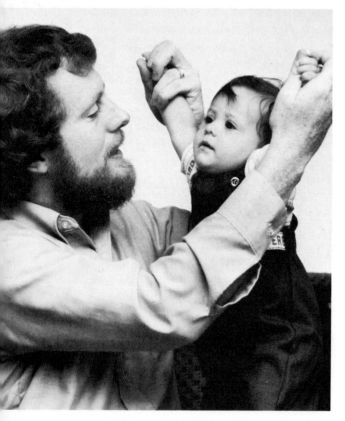

Maturation

The whole process of growth and development is called *maturation.* You have probably heard people say that a child is immature. Usually, this means that some part of the child's growth and development is not up to the typical level for a child of that age.

Most of the development and growth described in this chapter happen as the baby increases in age. Physical maturation cannot be taught to a child. A baby cannot be taught to sit or to stand before muscles develop. These skills can come only after the child's muscles mature. The biological clock seems to set the time for each child's muscles to mature, making it possible for that child to accomplish a skill. Each person's clock is different. However, through studying children around the world, researchers have discovered great uniformity in the ages at which a particular development occurs.

Helping Infants Develop Physically

Parents and care givers can encourage a child to practice body-control skills successfully as soon as muscles are mature enough. Adults should watch for signs of increased body control. They can also prepare for an approaching skill development by knowing what babies at each age level generally can do. Thus, parents can encourage children to practice new skills when the children are ready. (See page 130 for a timetable of physical development.)

When babies fail to develop according to the usual timetable, parents and care givers should seek medical advice. For example, a doctor discovered that one nonwalking 20-month-old had fluid in the inner ear. This prevented proper balance when the baby tried to walk. A minor operation drained the fluid, and the child walked soon after.

Because physical, social and emotional, and mental development are so closely related in infants, Chapter 20 will discuss specific ways for parents and care givers to influence development in all these areas.

Concluding Comments

Growth is the increase in weight and size that the baby experiences. *Development* refers to the increase in the skill of the baby's actions. *Maturation* refers to the combined processes of growth and development. Growth and development follow a predictable pattern.

A baby develops in the head region first and in the toes last. This shows the first rule of development—development proceeds from the head to the toes. The second rule states that development starts at a center line and moves outward toward the fingers and toes. The third rule is that as the brain develops the child notices more sights and sounds in the environment and can respond to increasingly fine details. The fourth rule is that development is a lifetime process, though the skeleton stops growing at about age 16 to 18.

Each baby matures according to his or her own biological clock. Yet, babies all around the world follow a similar rate of maturation, which varies only slightly.

Activities

1. Observe at least two babies under one year of age, one of whom is two or three months older than the other. Watch them as they eat, play, and are cared for. You will need to spend several hours with the babies.
2. From your observations, write a detailed illustration of the head-to-toe development concept. Compare the babies' physical development as you do so.
3. From your observations of these babies, describe how a child develops from the midline toward the fingers and toes. Give some examples of this development.
4. How do these two babies illustrate the development rule that, as the brain develops, the child responds to more and more stimuli and to finer and finer details? Be specific in your description.
5. How do *you* expect to continue *developing* after you stop *growing*? Give at least two examples of how you expect to do so.

The Infant Develops Emotionally and Socially

Objectives
To identify emotions and suggest ways of dealing with them in infants.
To identify social goals and suggest ways of fulfilling those goals for infants.

Terms to look for   attachment behavior • body language • communication • emotional development • emotions • positive self-concept • professional role • smiling to be sociable • social development

Amy, age 9 months, is sitting in the middle of the living room floor playing with her toys. She looks up as she hears footsteps outside. She listens, then drops her toy, and crawls quickly toward the door. She gurgles excitedly—knowing Daddy is coming. Somehow she knows his step and remembers the joy and happiness she feels when she sees her father. The story shows that she has already developed a feeling of trust. She expects something to happen, and it does. She trusts people and events.

Babies at birth show the beginnings of personalities all their own. Some babies cry a lot at first. Others seldom cry. Some seem to be often tense. Others are more relaxed. The baby's emotions those first days after birth are probably related to the birth process, to how well the baby adapts to life outside the womb, and to how well all the baby's body systems are operating. If all goes well, then the baby may be relaxed and happy. But if some problem arises, the baby may be tense and fretful.

Social Development

Social development refers to the baby's relationship with people. During infancy, a start is made on getting along with others, learning the expected social behavior, and learning to communicate. Much social development is closely related to emotional development. Therefore, the two are discussed together.

Amy, in the opening story, is developing socially as she communicates with her parents in their daily ritual.

Goals for Social and Emotional Development in Infancy

There are five important goals for infants that parents and care givers work toward during these early months.

1. *To develop a positive self-concept.* Parents and care givers want the baby to feel good about herself. They want her to feel that people love her. They want the baby to grow into a capable individual who can manage her affairs. They want her to feel "I am wanted," "I am loved," "I like myself," "I am in control of my world." Such a positive self-concept should bring more smiles than frowns, more laughter than tears, more confidence than fear, and more joy than anger.

2. *To develop a strong ability to give affection as well as to receive affection.* During the first months, the baby re-

During infancy, the babies are learning to trust people. They develop attachments to parents and care givers and learn about their self-worth from these adults. These lessons form the basis for all future social relationships.

ceives affection from parents, family, care givers, and others. Later, she will learn to give affection to others. Depending on the culture she lives in, she will learn various ways of giving affection.

3. *To develop an attachment to parents and care-giving people.* Between 3 and 6 months of age, the baby begins to recognize the persons who most frequently attend to her needs. She becomes excited when those persons appear. And she shows distress when they leave. This is called *attachment behavior.* This attachment gives the baby a secure base from which to reach out and

explore the surrounding environment. Evidence from research indicates that children who explore most are those who have had a firm attachment to a caring person during infancy. Therefore, it is important that at least one of the caring persons remains constant during the first year.

4. *To develop an interest in other people.* Being with people is important for young babies. Babies need enough experience with people to feel comfortable and nonfearful in family gatherings and in public places. Positive feelings toward people grow out of positive experiences. It is sensible for families to give their babies pleasant social experiences.

5. *To learn to communicate with others.* Communication is a two-way street. It means letting someone know what you think or feel and understanding what another person thinks or feels. Long before verbal language develops, the baby learns to interpret the actions of parents and care givers through *body language.* For instance, in the opening story, Amy seemed to know that the step at the door and the turning of the knob meant her father was coming. If the doorbell had rung, she might not have crawled to the door, for she has learned that the bell signals a stranger. You may have seen a parent put on a coat while a baby in the family watched. The baby would immediately want a coat on to go outside, too. When the care giver in the infant-care center brings in the bottles of milk, one baby lies down in the crib and reaches her hands up expectantly to receive her bottle. She understands that bottles mean feeding time. Actions communicate the intentions of others.

Long before verbal language develops, the baby learns to interpret the actions of parents and care givers.

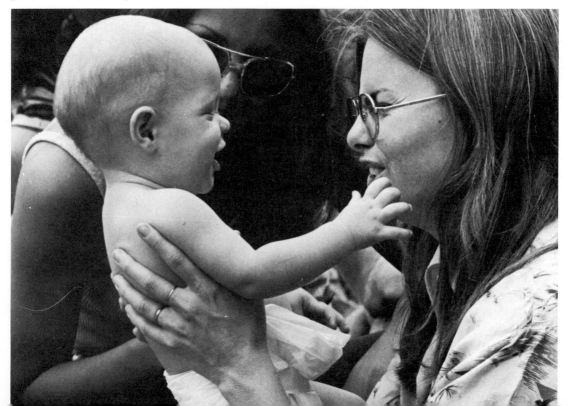

?
● **Decisions,**
        Decisions

"Just when I'm feeling frenzied and upset, when Chuck and I are snapping at each other, Melissa will start to fuss and cry. I don't know how, but she manages to make a bad moment that much worse." What's happening here?

The Family

The family is the baby's first social group. This group provides her emotional security. The emotional tone, or loving and caring that family members feel for each other, will be communicated to the baby. Babies are sensitive to tension. They often cry if conversations get loud and harsh, even when they do not understand the words that are being said.

When babies are in infant-care centers, they should be in small groups, somewhat like a family. The same care giver should be assigned to the same babies each day. This encourages the babies to develop some attachment for this person.

Dealing with Baby's Emotions

Emotions such as joy, happiness, and love can be encouraged by responding positively to the baby when she is expressing these feelings. *Positive response* means speaking to the baby, cuddling and kissing her, or playing a game with her when she is happy. These actions reward her for happy behavior.

Of course, responding to a baby's cries is also positive and essential. The baby whose needs are met promptly when he cries will develop a strong sense of security. However, if a parent or care giver gives attention only during crying, the baby learns to use crying to get attention. He may then develop a habit of being fretful.

Fear is an emotion that parents and care givers can help babies avoid by recognizing those situations that usually frighten the baby. Sudden actions may be frightening. Care givers who act smoothly and calmly may help keep the baby secure and unafraid. Strangers often frighten babies. So newcomers should approach a baby slowly or, better yet, let the baby approach them. Adults should never force a baby to pet an animal, go to a stranger—even a Santa Claus—or sleep in the dark if the baby is at all fearful. Even though the action may seem important to the adult at the moment, it may be inappropriate for the child. If you visit a department store during the holidays and observe the parents who force their infants to sit on Santa's lap for a picture, you will understand the truth of this statement.

Anger usually occurs when the baby does not get what he or she wants. A baby's angry outbursts do not usually last for a long time. Adults should never deliberately make a baby angry, but neither should they feel upset by occasional anger. Most infants are easily distracted from an object they desire. By distracting infants, adults can often avoid trouble.

A professional role is important when dealing with anger at home or at school. A *professional role* means that the adult remains objective and cool during a child's angry outburst. Never join the child in being angry, too. Do not give

127

attention in the form of either punishment or affection during or following angry outbursts. In fact, getting very busy in another room until the scene cools is often the best policy. In general, the less attention given to anger, the less anger will occur.

Encouraging Sociability

Newborn babies are never really sociable. They eat, they sleep, and they cry without paying very much attention to the people caring for them. Smiling to be sociable or smiling in response to another person usually begins between 6 weeks and 3 months, although an occasional baby will smile at a parent earlier than this. Parents and care givers can encourage a baby's responsiveness by smiling and by making frequent eye contact with the baby.

After about 3 months, babies become more alert to the people around them. Babies cannot be forced to be sociable or friendly. It is better to let them see people and decide how to respond to them. Once they can crawl, they may move toward a stranger. They may poke an inquiring finger into a neighbor's open-toed sandal. Or they may pull themselves up to stand on the insurance agent's knee. Then is the time for the stranger to say, "Hello." Babies often respond more readily to children than to adults. They may even play games, such as dropping a bottle or toy out of the crib or playpen so the older child will pick it up for them. Sociability begins in this way.

Concluding Comments

Emotional and social development in infancy go hand in hand. *Emotional development* refers to the expression of feelings. *Social development* refers to the baby's learning to like and to live with people.

Parents and care givers should keep in mind five goals for a baby's emotional and social development. These five goals are to help the baby develop:

1. a positive self-concept,
2. an ability to give and receive affection,
3. an attachment to parents and care-giving people,
4. an interest in other people, and
5. communication skills with others.

The family is usually the baby's first social group. A sense of family support is very important to help a child develop emotional security. In infant-care centers, babies should be kept in small groups. They should have the same care giver to foster attachment behavior and related emotional security.

When efforts to develop a positive self-concept are successful, babies smile more than frown, laugh more than cry, are confident more than afraid, and joyful more than angry. Because their personalities are in the formative stage, these first behaviors may be long-lasting.

The first sign of social response comes at about 6 weeks to 3 months when the baby smiles. Parents and care givers can encourage social response by smiling and making eye contact with the baby.

Activities

1. For several hours, observe a baby in the 8-12 month age range. Report specific examples of the baby's activities that illustrate progress toward the following five goals for emotional and social development:
    a. a positive self-concept.
    b. an ability to give and receive affection.
    c. an attachment to parents and other care-giving people.
    d. an interest in other people.
    e. communication skills with others.

2. Almost all babies experience fear at some time. Ask your parents about any fears that you might have had when you were a baby. How did your parents help you deal with these fears?

The First Year of Growth

Babies grow and develop at unpredictable rates. This chart shows what a "typical" baby might do at various times during the first year. Since there are no typical babies, expect in real life to see any size or activity earlier or later than this chart shows.

What can a 3-month-old baby do?

At 3 months, a baby is alert and responding to the world:
- When put on her tummy,
  she can hold her chest and head up for 10 seconds.
- She tries to swipe at toys hung over her crib.
- She cries less than she did as a newborn,
  and at 6 weeks she smiles.
- She turns her head toward an
  interesting sound or listens to voices.
- She loves to stare at people's faces
  and begins to recognize family members.
- She coos and gurgles.

Height: 23½ inches (59.4 cm)
Weight: 12½ pounds (5.46 kg)

What can a 6-month-old baby do?

At 6 months, he is developing control over his body:
- He can sit with support
  and may sit alone for short periods.
- He can roll over.
- He will hold out his arms to be lifted up
  or to reach and grab an object.
- He can hold his own bottle
  as well as his toys.
- He explores everything,
  by putting it in his mouth.
- He laughs out loud, babbles,
  "calls" for help,
  and screams when annoyed.

Height: 26 inches (66 cm)
Weight: 16 pounds, 12 ounces (7.58 kg)

3 months   **6 months**   **9 months**   **12 months**

What can a 9-month-old baby do?

At 9 months, she is exploring her environment:
- She can sit unassisted, crawl,
  pull to a stand, and side-step along furniture.
- She can use her fingers to point,
  poke, and grasp small objects.
- She feeds herself finger foods.
- She imitates simple actions and plays games
  like "peek-a-boo," "pat-a-cake," and "so-big."
- She knows her name and responds
  to simple commands, like "Wave bye-bye."
- She uses "jargon"—babbling in a pattern
  that sounds almost as if she is
  speaking a foreign language.

Height: 27½ inches (70 cm)
Weight: 19 pounds (8.60 kg)

What can a 12-month-old baby do?

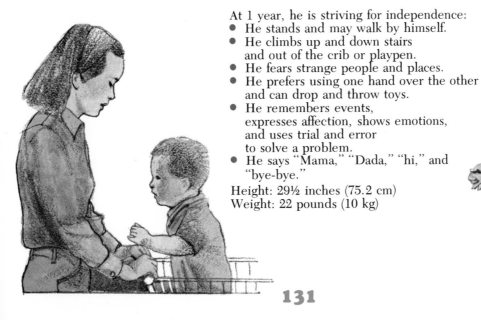

At 1 year, he is striving for independence:
- He stands and may walk by himself.
- He climbs up and down stairs
  and out of the crib or playpen.
- He fears strange people and places.
- He prefers using one hand over the other
  and can drop and throw toys.
- He remembers events,
  expresses affection, shows emotions,
  and uses trial and error
  to solve a problem.
- He says "Mama," "Dada," "hi," and
  "bye-bye."

Height: 29½ inches (75.2 cm)
Weight: 22 pounds (10 kg)

14

The Infant Develops Mentally

Objectives

To describe typical behaviors that show that babies are developing mentally.

To relate mental development to motor development and language development.

To give examples of infants learning through their five senses.

To identify parental and care-giver actions that encourage infants to develop mentally.

Terms to look for   babble • mental development • motor development • positive feedback • senses • sensory • stimulating environment

Becky, age 10 months, is getting ready for a bath. Her father, Reuben, unties her shoes and slips them part way off. Becky pulls them off and holds them up.

"Good!" exclaims Reuben.

While Becky watches, Reuben hides the shoes under a nearby toss pillow on the sofa. "Where did your shoes go, Becky?" asks Reuben.

Becky looks at her feet, looks up at her father's face, and then looks at the pillow. She laughs with delight as she lifts up the pillow and reveals the shoes.

Mental Ability

Becky's ability to remember for a brief moment where her shoes are hidden is evidence of her developing mental ability. A few weeks earlier, she only looked

confused and did not watch as her shoes went into the hiding place. Her father kept her interest by looking under several objects before showing her the shoes under the same pillow every night. He would say, "Are they here? No. Are they here? No. Here they are. Here are Becky's shoes." It was a game they both enjoyed.

Brain Development

An infant's mind cannot be tested in the ways we test mental ability in older children. We cannot give a paper-and-pencil test. We cannot even get verbal answers to questions, because the infant's language is only beginning to develop. We can only estimate how well an infant's mind is working by watching the infant's actions.

The brain develops first in those centers that control the spine and the arms and legs. Therefore, during infancy, the best clues about brain development and mental ability come from watching a child's motor development. *Motor development*, as you recall, refers to the ability to move and use the body, arms, and legs.

Studies show that infants love to stare at the human face. They will stare longer at a face, or even a sketch of a face, than at other forms.

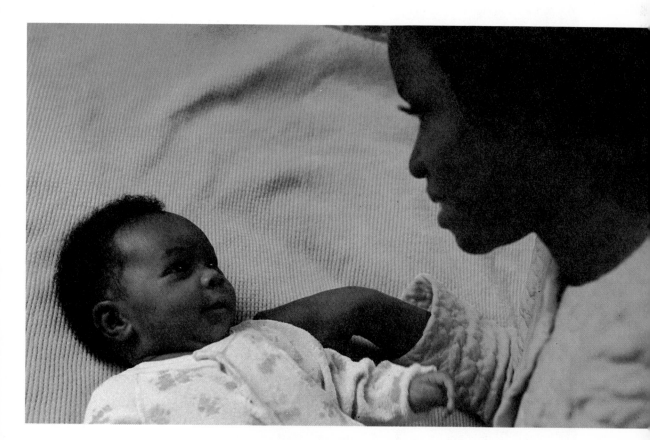

Early Clues to Mental Development

Dr. Nancy Bayley is a well-known psychologist who studied infants and watched them grow and develop over the years. Following are twelve clues that Dr. Bayley lists in her book *Studies in the Development of Young Children.* These clues alert adults to typical growth in mental ability for infants.

1. At 6 months, the baby turns in the direction of a spoon that drops out of the child's sight to the floor.

2. At 6.5 months, the baby makes sounds of satisfaction after securing something she or he wanted.

3. At 7.2 months, the baby smiles at his or her image in the mirror.

4. At 7.3 months, the baby looks for the fallen spoon.

Like many games babies play, "pat-a-cake" uses motor skill, social ability, and mental development. All these levels of development must be reached for the infant to play the game.

Brightly colored objects to look at, reach for, touch, and move help make a stimulating environment.

5. At 8.5 months, the baby cooperates in a game of peekaboo or pat-a-cake.
6. At 8.5 months, the baby listens to familiar words.
7. At 9.5 months, the baby pulls a string attached to a ring, in order to bring the ring closer.
8. At 9.8 months, the baby understands the meanings of several words.
9. At 10.4 months, the baby puts a block in a cup when shown how.
10. At 10.6 months, the baby unwraps a toy after seeing it being wrapped.
11. At 11.7 months, the baby imitates words.
12. At 12.9 months, the baby says 2 words.

You can try some similar activities with babies to make your own estimates of their mental growth. Dr. Bayley found that performance on tests given in infancy was not necessarily related to performance on later mental-ability tests. That is, the smartest babies did not always test the highest as preschoolers or as elementary-age children. The slower babies often caught up and passed their faster friends. Therefore, in your own observations, avoid making long-range predictions about babies.

? Decisions, Decisions

Jim finds it hard to talk to his new son. He feels silly talking to someone who does not understand, and he cannot think of anything to say. Should he try to change or not?

Learning through the Senses

You have five senses to aid your learning. These are the senses of 1) seeing, 2) hearing, 3) tasting, 4) smelling, and 5) touching. In the early months, a baby begins to learn about the world through the same five senses. Seeing is the least-developed sense at birth. You can check the items on Dr. Bayley's test that use one or more senses, especially seeing and hearing.

Babies gain information through their senses while they are playing, looking, listening, eating, bathing, and doing all their activities. All these sensations are stored in their brains. They listen, look, and touch. They taste (at certain stages everything seems to go into their mouths). It is a little harder to tell when babies are using their sense of smell. But if an odor is very strong, they will protest. Babies begin in infancy to learn about the world by using their senses. Not until about age 7 or so can children learn about the world by having someone tell them about it. Learning in the early years requires direct sensory experience if babies are to learn about people, places, and things.

For generations, people thought that a baby was born either intelligent or stupid and remained that way throughout life. Recent studies have shown that intelligence is not fixed but can be changed greatly by a *stimulating environment* at an early age. An environment is stimulating when it allows babies to use their five senses, by providing them with colorful objects to look at, interesting sounds to hear, and a variety of things to reach for and touch. This kind of environment, plus a great deal of interaction between infant and parents or care givers, can have lasting benefits

on an infant's intelligence. Chapter 20 outlines what surroundings and activities parents can provide.

? Decisions, Decisions

Betsy and Len are thinking of buying a special crib system with many detachable learning modules. The system, which is quite expensive, is supposed to develop a baby's mental abilities by stimulating the baby's senses. Should they buy it?

Language

With the development of language, we gain further information about how the child is learning. Babies around the world develop language in similar ways, even though the specific words may be in French, Swahili, English, or one of thousands of other dialects and languages. Language and mental abilities are closely related.

First, babies *babble*. This is a playful use of lips and vocal cords that all babies seem to enjoy. They repeat sounds over and over. They like parents and care givers to speak to them in words or in similar sounds. A conversation needs two people, even when one is an infant. Think how often parents and care givers can stop for a chat with a baby as they go back and forth with their daily routines at home and school.

Sounds resembling *mama* are used by babies all over the world. This word brings positive rewards in most families. That is, most mothers are very excited upon hearing *mama*. They kiss and hug the baby so that she or he repeats *mama* often. Pretty soon the baby says *dada* and *papa*. These words, too, become part of the vocabulary, as the father gives the baby positive feedback. *Positive feedback* means rewarding an action a baby performs. For instance, saying *papa* brings smiles and kisses from the father. In the infant-care center, the care

Parents and care givers should imitate the cooing sounds babies make to encourage language development. This imitation and response sets up a learning game that helps to form the basis for speech.

givers will help babies label their parents as *Mama* or *Mommy* and *Dada*, *Papa*, or *Daddy*. Babies will probably invent names, such as *Nannie* or *Mimi*, for their care givers. Care givers should respond to these names until babies learn to pronounce their real names.

Concluding Comments

Mental development moves rapidly in infancy. The brain develops the motor control areas first. Early motor ability gives us clues to the baby's current brain development and mental ability. Predicting later mental ability is not possible with these early tests.

The five senses are sources of information for the baby. A baby explores things through the mouth, hands, eyes, ears, and nose.

Language development and mental ability are closely related. Some items on mental tests are related to how the infant listens and responds to language. Babbling is a universal language of infants.

Activities

1. "Work" with a baby in the 6–12 month age range.
   a. Try the twelve activities from Dr. Nancy Bayley's test. Record the actions of the baby as you do so. Include the baby's exact age in your report.
   b. How many of these actions did the baby complete?
   c. Did the baby respond to the first few or more activities, but not to those described for older babies? Or did the baby respond unpredictably, ignoring some activities at both ends of the list?

2. Describe how this baby was learning through use of each of the five senses: seeing, hearing, tasting, smelling, and touching.

3. Make up some simple games you would enjoy playing with infants. These games should challenge their mental abilities. Discuss these games with your classmates.

Home Routines for Infants

Objectives
To describe home routines that provide for the infant's needs.
To describe home routines that support the new parent.

Terms to look for   antibodies • colic • cradle cap • formula • milk substitute • pacifier • postpartum depression • self-demand schedule • sterilization of formula

Maria, a mother of a new baby, was awakened from a nap she was taking on the sofa by the telephone ringing. It was a local charity asking if she would be responsible for collecting funds in her neighborhood during the following week. Maria had contributed to the charity for years and thought it was a worthwhile cause.

"I'm sorry. I'll be happy to contribute, but I won't be able to help you," Maria said. She talked briefly with the caller, then hung up and went back to her nap.

Resting Routine—A Must for Mother and Baby

Maria is correct in turning down the request. A routine allowing for afternoon rests is as important for a new mother like Maria as it is for her baby. Maria's body needs to rest and recuperate. She has to get back to prepregnancy condition, to nurse the baby, and to care for

the baby. Besides turning down new demands on her time and energy, Maria may also have to guide the visits of family and friends. They should not overtire her or the baby or interfere with home routines. The chart that follows is one example of a typical routine for a family with a new baby.

ONE HOME ROUTINE WITH BABY

6:00 A.M.　Baby awakens and cries. Mother changes diaper and gown.

6:05 A.M.　Mother nurses baby.

6:30 A.M.　Baby asleep and back in bed.
Mother returns to bed.

7:00 A.M.　Father gets up and makes breakfast for both.

7:20 A.M.　Mother and Father eat breakfast.

7:40 A.M.　Father leaves for work.
Mother finishes coffee and reads morning paper.
Mother prepares for baby's bath.

9:00 A.M.　Baby awakens needing diaper change.
Mother gives baby a bath.
Mother dresses baby in clean clothing.
Mother changes sheet on baby's crib.

9:30 A.M.　Mother nurses and talks to baby.

9:50 A.M.　Baby is asleep again in crib.
Mother reorganizes nursery.
Mother does household tasks.

12:00 P.M.　Mother fixes and eats her lunch.

12:30 P.M.　Baby awakens.
Mother changes diaper.

12:35 P.M.　Mother nurses baby.

1:00 P.M.　Baby goes to sleep.

1:15 P.M.　Mother takes a nap.

2:30 P.M.　Mother awakens.

3:30 P.M.　Baby awakens.
Mother changes diaper.
Baby is awake for 15 minutes, then frets as though hungry.

3:45 P.M.　Mother nurses baby.
Baby sleeps.
A neighbor visits briefly.

5:30 P.M.　Father returns home.

5:45 P.M.　Parents eat meal.

7:00 P.M.　Baby awakens.
Father changes diaper.
Parents hold and talk to baby awhile.

7:45 P.M.　Mother nurses baby.
Father puts clothes in the washer and later in the dryer.

8:15 P.M.　Baby is asleep.
Parents talk and watch television.

9:00 P.M.　Parents fold diapers.

11:00 P.M.　Baby awakens.
Father changes diaper.

11:15 P.M.　Mother nurses baby.

11:30 P.M.　Baby is asleep in crib.
Parents sleep.

3:00 A.M.　Baby awakens.
Father changes diaper.

3:05 A.M.　Mother nurses baby.

3:30 A.M.　Baby is asleep.
Parents are asleep again.

6:00 A.M.　Baby awakens and the day starts again.

This schedule is only an example of a home routine with a new baby. Because each baby is different, each schedule will be different. If parents are bottle-feeding, fathers may take turns at the morning, evening, and middle-of-the-night feedings. If mothers return to work outside the home soon after the birth of a baby, substitute care givers may come in to take care of the baby's needs.

At first, newborn babies cry when their clothes are removed for a bath. Soon they relax and enjoy a bath. The bath often becomes a special time for closeness between parent and child.

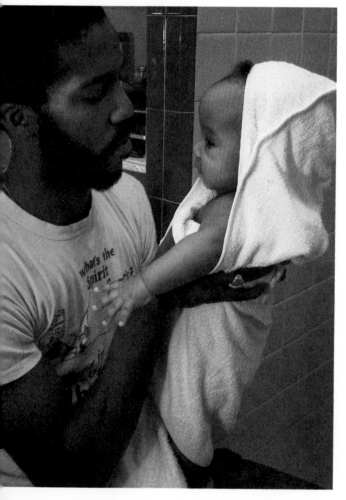

Also, many babies do not fall asleep so easily after each feeding. Some want to be fed constantly, leaving the mother little time to do anything else. Some cry more than others. All these problems will be discussed in this chapter.

Needs of the Baby

New babies need food and sleep. They need to be clean and warm. They need love. Parenting began with planning for parenthood. It expands with loving and caring for the baby. Early acts of caring for the baby assure the infant that its needs will be met. A sense of trust begins to develop.

Parenting applies to adoptive and foster parents as well as to biological parents. People who provide the loving and caring for children at home or in a child-care center are serving in parenting roles. Whether or not they are the biological parents is not important.

Food Needs

A baby's need for food is usually irregular at first. For this reason, most pediatricians now recommend that parents use "self-demand" feeding. This means that babies are fed when they seem to be hungry rather than according to a fixed schedule. The newborn's stomach will hold only 2 tablespoons of milk. This is why the infant may take only a little milk out of the breast or bottle, fall asleep, then awaken crying with hunger 2 hours later—or even earlier. Such frequent feedings can be exhausting to new parents. But this stage does not last

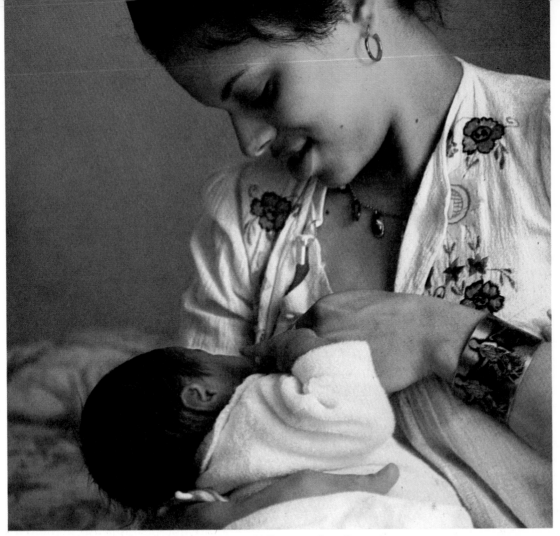

Breast-fed babies have fewer illnesses and allergies than formula-fed babies do. Breast-feeding also establishes a strong bond between mother and child.

long. Babies soon begin drinking larger amounts and going longer between feedings.

Breast or Bottle. Breast-feeding has definite advantages for both babies and mothers. Breast milk is a perfect food. It also contains substances called *anti-bodies* which protect a baby against infection. Colostrum, the yellow substance present in the breasts before the milk comes in, is especially rich in these antibodies. Studies have shown that breast-fed babies generally have fewer illnesses than formula-fed babies. There is also evidence that mothers who breast-feed are less prone to breast cancer in later life.

Breast-feeding also has the advantage of no preparation. In addition, the milk is always the right temperature. Some psychologists feel that breast-feeding also helps establish a strong bond between a baby and its mother. But some mothers feel that breast-feeding will tie them down or prevent them from going outside the home when they need or want to. This does not have to be true. Many breast-feeding mothers feed their babies in the morning and evening. Then, they have care givers give bottles during the day. Some mothers even "express," or squeeze out, their own milk into the bottles instead of using formula. This milk should be frozen if it is not to be used immediately.

Most mothers can nurse their babies if they keep trying and have patience until the milk supply is established. Usually, the more a baby nurses, the more milk the milk glands will produce. A baby can be nursed for as long as the mother wishes—a few months or as long as 2 years or more. Plenty of rest and as little stress as possible will make the mother's milk supply more reliable.

To make sure the milk is clean, the mother has only to keep her breasts clean through regular bathing and by wearing a clean brassiere. If her breasts tend to leak, she can put disposable nursing pads or tissues in the brassiere to absorb the milk.

The La Leche League (the milk league) is an organization of people who want to help mothers who desire to nurse their babies. The organization provides advice about breast-feeding and provides moral support. The La Leche League has branches throughout the United States. These branches are listed in telephone books in most cities.

Some mothers may have difficulty breast-feeding. Others may simply not want to breast-feed. A woman who is uncomfortable with the idea should not force herself to breast-feed. If she does, the baby will probably sense her tension and discomfort. Neither mother nor baby will enjoy the experience. Certainly, many healthy, well-adjusted children and adults were once bottle-fed babies.

One advantage of bottle-feeding is that fathers have more opportunity to share in the feeding process. Of course, they can also give the breast-fed baby an occasional relief bottle or a bottle of water.

Food is quickly related to attention and love in a baby's mind. Parents and care givers should always hold and cuddle the bottle-fed baby.

Cuddling and feeding go together. That is easy to see when we think about breast-feeding. It is also important during bottle-feeding to hold the baby in your arms and to smile and talk to the newborn while the milk disappears. An important part of the baby's security begins to develop during feedings. Some busy parents and care givers are tempted to prop up the baby's bottle. This should not be done on a regular basis. Even mothers of twins and triplets have found that it is important to take time to hold each baby during the feeding. In a pinch, they prop one baby while holding another. But they rotate so that the babies all get held daily.

Homemade Formulas. When parents decide to feed their baby by bottle, they choose a source of milk for the baby.

The word *formula* means the combination of milk, water, and sugar that is mixed for the infant. The formula could also be called the recipe for the baby's milk. An example of one of the many formulas is 13 ounces of evaporated milk

144

and 19 ounces of water, sweetened with 2 tablespoons of corn syrup. You may use sugar or syrup as a sweetner. Never use honey.

There are a number of prepared milk formulas developed especially for babies. These are dry powders or condensed liquids to which sterile water must be added. There are also types of formula that come ready to use in a can or in a baby bottle. The doctor makes a recommendation about which formula to buy and how to mix it. The cost of prepared formula is high. Consequently, many parents want to change to cow's milk from the grocery store as soon as possible.

Cow's Milk. The cow's milk found in stores and dairies in the United States is pasteurized. This means it has been heated to destroy any germs present. If unpasteurized milk from a farm is used,

One advantage of bottle-feeding is that fathers get a chance to share in feeding and cuddling the baby.

parents should boil it gently for 5 minutes to kill germs. When using cow's milk, it is best to use low-fat milk or to dilute whole milk with water.

According to Dr. Benjamin Spock, babies are less likely to develop eczema, a painful and unsightly skin rash, if they are given evaporated milk rather than fresh milk.

A new baby may be satisfied with only 2 ounces at a feeding—that is, 4 tablespoonfuls. When bottling the formula, fill each bottle with a maximum of 3 ounces at first. As the baby grows and wants more at each feeding, then fill the bottles to 4 or 5 ounces. It is important not to force the baby to take more milk than the baby wants. Overfeeding may cause the baby to have a stomachache. The baby may simply spit up and act hungry again before long. Also, overfeeding may make a baby too fat. There is some evidence that overweight infants becomes overweight children and adults.

Sterilization of Formula. *Sterilizing* means boiling the milk mixture to be sure no germs are present that might make the baby ill. As you might know, heat kills germs. Even though the milk, water, and utensils are thought to be clean, they must be sterilized anyway. You cannot see germs, of course, but bacteria grow rapidly in milk. Consequently, do not take any chances.

❓ Decisions, Decisions

"I hate to admit this," said Roger. "But I feel left out when Lena breast-feeds the baby. They seem to have this closeness that I can't be a part of." What could Roger do?

During the early weeks, the baby's digestive system is just beginning to function. Germs that might not affect an adult might make a baby sick. Clean hands, sterilized bottles and bottle nipples, and safe milk are very important. One microscopic germ is all that is needed to make a whole batch of formula dangerous for the baby.

There are two general methods of sterilizing formula. One way is to sterilize the formula and put it into sterile bottles. The other way is to mix the formula and to put it into clean bottles, with nipples upside down in the bottle and covered with the plastic disk and threaded cap. Next, put the bottles in a special sterilizer or in a big covered kettle. With several inches of water in the bottom of the sterilizer or kettle, boil the bottles for 25 minutes. Let the bottles cool, and then refrigerate them. Parents usually sterilize one or two small bottles of water at the same time. That way, the baby can be offered a drink of water from time to time.

Many parents prefer to use presterilized plastic inserts that can be filled and placed inside special nursing bottles. Once used, the plastic inserts can be thrown away. Even more convenient are plastic inserts that have already been filled with formula. Both of these methods are expensive. But they are convenient, are easy for traveling, and require sterilization of only nipples and bottle tops.

Allergies. Some babies are allergic to cow's milk. Substitutes are available that are made primarily from soybean powder. Mothers who do not want to breast-feed and who have allergic babies should consult their physicians about substitute formulas.

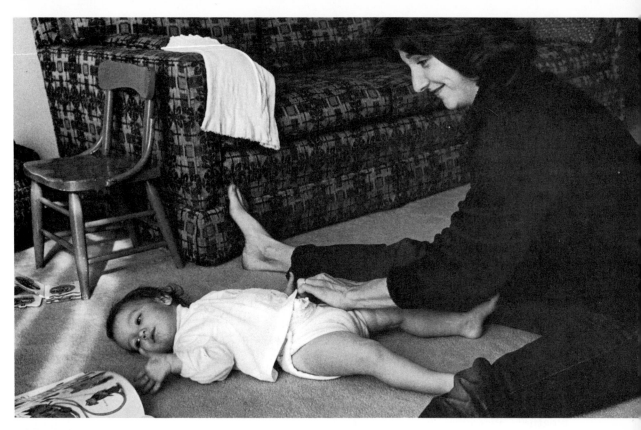

Older babies often squirm during changes. Offering a distraction is a good way to make the change quick and pleasant.

Clothing Needs

A baby's primary clothing need is for lots of clean, dry diapers. The great majority of families today use disposable diapers. These are far more convenient and less time consuming than cloth diapers, which must be washed. Also, most disposables come with a liner that draws moisture away from the baby's skin. In this way, the baby is kept drier with disposables than with cloth diapers and plastic pants. There are many different brands of disposable diapers. Some are more expensive than others, but they are thicker and more absorbent. Thus, the baby does not have to be changed as often. Disposable diapers come in sizes from "newborn" through "toddler." Most companies carry an "overnight" size, which is thicker and more absorbent than the daytime size.

There are two main drawbacks to using disposable diapers. One is that they are expensive. The second disadvantage of disposable diapers is that the paper and plastic used to make them are a drain on our valuable natural resources. Parents who are concerned about the environment may prefer to take the time and trouble to wash diapers.

Parents and care givers who use disposable diapers must dispose of them in a considerate way. Disposable diapers littered along the highway and in recreation areas caused the state of Oregon to ban their sale there.

In many areas, diaper service is still available. The service delivers the needed number of clean, sterilized diapers each week and takes the soiled ones away. This costs about the same as using disposable diapers. A disadvantage is that parents must keep the wet and soiled diapers in their home for a week.

Babies' other clothing needs depend on the weather. Newborns seem to like being wrapped up tightly. Perhaps this gives them the kind of security they felt in the womb. If the weather is warm, they can be dressed in just an undershirt and a diaper and wrapped in a lightweight receiving blanket. In cooler weather, warmer blankets and sleep sacks, which tie around the bottom, are useful.

Many adults tend to feel that babies need heavier clothing than adults do. According to most experts, this is not true. Overdressing a baby can make the baby perspire. This increases the likelihood that she or he will get chilled. Dr. Spock feels you should dress a baby only as warmly as you dress yourself.

Once a baby has grown large enough to be able to kick off blankets, parents may want to purchase footed sleepers, so that blankets are not needed. These sleepers keep the baby warm without restricting movement.

No matter how many clothes a baby has, it may not seem like enough. Babies wet, soil, and spit up on their clothes. Parents may feel as if they spend all their time doing laundry. Having plenty of undershirts, sheets, and small blankets helps save time in the long run.

Cleanliness

Babies should always be kept very clean. They need frequent diaper changes, both of wet and of soiled diapers. Cornstarch or baby powder can be used on the baby's bottom after a wet diaper is removed, but it is not necessary. If you use baby powder, be sure to put it in your hand first, then pat it on the baby. Baby powder contains *talc*, which can harm the baby's lungs if you shake it into the air.

After a bowel movement, the baby should be cleaned with baby lotion and a facial tissue, a damp washcloth, or one of the special premoistened towelettes now available for this purpose. Soiled cloth diapers should be rinsed well in the toilet and soaked with other diapers in a soapy solution in the covered diaper pail.

Most pediatricians recommend bathing babies every day. A sponge bath may be given the first few days until the navel heals. Special portable plastic bathtubs are available to bathe babies. One kind of inflatable tub is good for babies under 6 months. This tub is made so that the baby's head cannot slip under the water, thus leaving the parent's hands free while giving the bath. Parents who have space may want to purchase a *Bathinette*, a special bathing table that converts into a dressing table.

Bath time should be quiet, gentle, and pleasurable for the baby. Some babies enjoy their bath right from the start. Others take a few weeks or months to relax and enjoy it. Many newborns cry when their clothes are removed for a diaper change or a bath. Parents should be sure that the baby is not hungry at bath time. If hungry, the newborn may cry with dissatisfaction and associate bathing with unpleasantness.

Doctors also recommend washing the baby's scalp daily to prevent *cradle cap*, a dirty-looking, patchy scalp condition. A firm but gentle massage will not hurt the baby's head. If cradle cap does develop, you should consult the pediatrician or clinic.

Rest and Sleep

Most newborn babies sleep a lot. They are growing very fast and need a lot of rest. Where they sleep is less important than how long. They may sleep in a crib, a bassinet (a small baby bed), a carriage, an infant seat, or the car. Some parents like to put their babies in special infant carriers that strap onto the front of the parent. Then, the parent can carry the baby around while running errands and doing other tasks. The warmth and closeness the baby feels may help give the infant a sense of security in the early months.

Well-meaning friends or family may want to wake up the new baby. Parents should remind such visitors that the baby needs sleep but will probably be awake when they visit next time.

Years ago, parents were taught that baby's "schedules" were law. Parents were never supposed to interrupt naps. Most experts now agree that parents need not sacrifice all their plans for the baby's schedule. Babies are able to sleep in cars, in grocery carts, and in rooms full of people. In fact, some pediatricians believe that it is better *not* to try to be extremely quiet around a sleeping baby. That way, the baby gets used to sleeping in all kinds of circumstances. Some babies actually seem to enjoy the sound of a vacuum cleaner and will sleep peace-

Parents use mealtimes to stay in touch with each other . . . baby permitting.

fully while a parent vacuums in the same room.

Parents are thankful when the baby sleeps through the night. However, although the *average* baby may do so by 3 months, many babies awaken during the night for several months longer. Although parents do not have to jump up at the first whimper they hear, they should continue to attend to the baby's

Crying babies need comfort. They should not be left to "cry it out." Crying is not necessarily "good for the lungs."

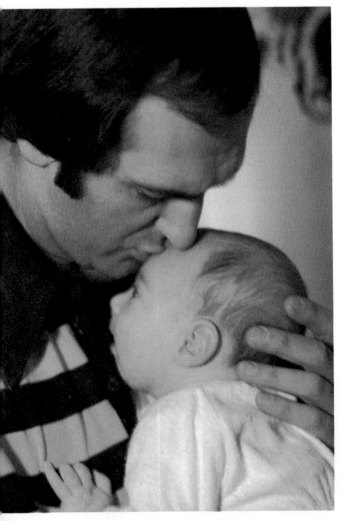

cries in the night. Sooner or later, the baby will sleep soundly throughout the night.

Crying

All babies cry—some more than others. Sometimes it is difficult to know why a baby is crying. Parents will first try to discover if the baby is hungry or needs to have a diaper changed. Perhaps the baby needs to be burped. Some babies have *colic,* or painful gas in the stomach. Such babies usually have a crying spell at the same time each day. Sometimes it may help if you give the baby a little water to drink. Or it may help if you hold a hot water bottle on the baby's stomach. Some babies are comforted by being carried in a front carrier. *Pacifiers,* or nipplelike sucking toys, may help. Many babies quiet down and fall asleep if taken for a ride in a car or in a baby carriage.

Many babies have a "fussy spell" at the same time each day. It is not necessarily colic—they may just feel fretful. Unfortunately, this fussy spell often happens just when the parents are trying to sit down to dinner. Many parents have found that a baby swing is a lifesaver at such times. Babies seem to enjoy the rocking motion. Some swings are large enough to hold the baby in an infant seat so that the back is supported properly. Other parents may want to use a cradle, which can be placed by the dinner table and rocked with the foot.

Most pediatricians invite parents to call at any time, if they have questions. Doctors or nurses may be able to suggest remedies for helping a baby stop crying. Prolonged crying is hard to tolerate, and parents often feel it will last forever.

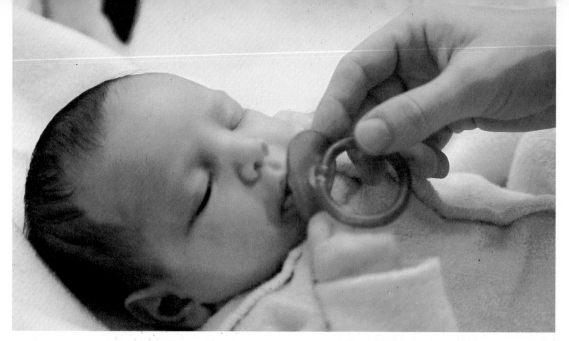

Sucking on fingers or pacifiers calms babies and makes them feel secure. Most babies who use pacifiers reject them at 5 or 6 months when they become more interested in exploring objects with their mouths. Even so, some parents think that pacifiers are "embarrassing" and a sign of poor parenting.

Parents need to try to keep calm and to help each other. They may also need help from friends, family, or neighbors.

Pacifiers and Thumb Sucking

The sucking reflex was discussed earlier, in Chapter 12. Breast-feeding may satisfy some babies. Bottle-fed babies may need to have very small holes in the nipples. This will make the bottle last longer and help to satisfy this sucking need. But many babies, both breast-fed and bottle-fed, need more sucking time. So parents may wish to use pacifiers. The back of the pacifier should be large enough that the baby cannot get the entire pacifier in the mouth and choke.

Other babies may learn how to get their thumbs in their mouths, even at a very young age. Some experts think that thumb sucking may be hereditary. Babies are known to suck their thumbs while they are still in the womb. Many adults are upset by thumb sucking. They may try to substitute the pacifier. Or they may simply keep pulling the baby's thumb out of the mouth. However, many child-care experts feel that thumb sucking is normal and healthy. One advantage is that, unlike the pacifier, a baby's thumb is completely under the infant's control. Dr. Spock observes that thumb-sucking babies and children are usually very secure.

There are still many adults who object to thumb sucking and to pacifiers. Some actually think a crying baby is preferable to one sucking a thumb or pacifier. Remember that a tiny newborn cannot

151

even open his or her fists. The only thing the infant really knows how to do is suck. Therefore, if sucking on the thumb or on a pacifier helps the infant feel more contented, there is no reason why the baby should not do so.

Needs of the Parents

No matter how well parents have prepared themselves for a new baby, the reality of having such a demanding little creature in the home 24 hours a day is a shock. Especially during the first few weeks, both parents may feel exhausted and disorganized until they adjust to new routines.

Some parents find that extra help in the home is necessary and welcome. One of the grandparents may come to help for a few days. Couples should discuss this need beforehand and should be sure they feel comfortable with the helping person. If grandparents or in-laws give too much advice or insist on doing things their way, parents will feel more nervous. The baby will probably sense this and cry more often. Such a couple may be better off on their own or with a close friend to help.

It is very important that both parents share the responsibilities of a new baby. Fathers can take their part in cooking, shopping, laundry, and housecleaning. Husbands should not look upon such chores as "helping" their wives, but as

Newborn babies are in the most "portable" stage of life. Getting out with the baby can offer new parents a breather and prevent feelings of being "housebound." Parents should make time for an evening by themselves occasionally, too.

"sharing" the parenting and household duties.

A mother who has had a difficult labor, a cesarean section, or twins may need help for a few weeks after her delivery, until she is feeling physically strong enough to get along on her own. If husbands are able to take off this much time from work outside the home, no additional help may be necessary. But this is difficult for most people who work outside the home.

Once the family has settled into a "normal" routine, parents should take time out for themselves and for each other. It is a good idea to try to find baby-sitters before the baby is born, when parents have time for interviewing. Once a couple feels ready, they may invite the baby-sitter to come in and get acquainted with the baby before they actually leave the baby with the sitter.

Parents often find that they are nervous the first time or two they are away from their babies, even if a relative is the care giver. Often they will go out for dinner and spend the whole time talking about the baby. This is normal. Gradually, parents will begin to feel comfortable leaving for a few hours, knowing that the baby is in good hands and will not suffer from their absence.

? Decisions, Decisions

"Don't worry about a thing," said Nancy's mother. "I'll stay with you and Bill after the baby comes. I've raised three children, so I can be a real help." Why might Nancy and Bill accept her mother's offer? Why might they turn the offer down?

Postpartum Depression

Some women—even third- and fourth-time mothers—feel sad and depressed after the baby is born. They may cry a lot for no apparent reason or feel completely unable to cope with the demands of the new baby. Such feelings are called *postpartum* (afterbirth) *depression*.

No one is sure what causes such feelings, but they are common enough that both husbands and wives should recognize and try to deal with them. Some women may feel isolated if they are staying home with a new baby after several years of working outside the home. Some may feel that the new baby is getting all the attention from relatives and friends—which is often true. Many women feel unattractive for several weeks after delivery. Add to these feelings the fatigue that is a normal part of having a baby, and you can see why a woman might feel depressed.

Above all, women should not be made to feel guilty for such feelings. They should try to talk with their friends, their husbands, and their doctors. Finding out that other women have had the same feelings often helps. Denying the existence of the depression is unwise and may make it worse. Some women may find that getting out of the house for a morning or a day each week will help. Others may discover that they would truly be happier going back to work outside the home, part time or full time, as soon as they are physically able. If so, they will need substitute care for the baby. This topic will be covered in Chapter 19.

In some cases, postpartum depression is so severe that the mother is actually

Postpartum depression is common. Supportive family and friends can be a great help. Most women quickly regain a more positive emotional state.

unable to care for her baby or refuses to relate to the newborn at all. A husband, friend, or relative who recognizes such symptoms should alert the woman's doctor so that she can get help immediately.

Concluding Comments

After the new baby comes home, routines change to accommodate the baby, the parents, and the physical condition of the mother. The parenting roles begin with planning for parenthood and expand with caring for and loving the new baby.

A new baby has many needs—food, cleanliness, warmth, and affection. Parents will try to meet all these needs to make the baby feel as secure as possible in the first months.

One decision new parents need to make is whether their baby will be breast-fed or bottle-fed. It is also possible to work out a satisfactory combination of the two methods. Whichever method is used, the baby should always be held and cuddled during the feeding.

Some couples' ability to foresee and plan for the changes required in home routines may make them so well prepared that they will not feel the need for extra help. For other new parents, relatives or friends may be very important in helping them make the adjustment to the responsibilities of the baby. It is very important for husbands and wives to share these responsibilities. It is also important for new fathers and mothers to take time for themselves and for each other.

After giving birth, some women experience postpartum depression, which may require special attention from their husbands, families, or doctors.

Activities

1. Develop a household schedule showing a "before-baby" home, and compare it to the "after-baby" schedule in this chapter. Figure out the total hours needed for infant care.

2. Interview a woman who has breastfed her baby.

a. Ask her why she decided to breastfeed rather than bottle feed her child.

b. How long did she breastfeed the baby?

c. Did she feel breast-feeding "tied her down" so that she could not do other things she wanted to do? Or did she feel breast-feeding saved time?

d. How much did breast-feeding interfere with her "normal" life as the mother of a young baby?

3. Interview a father whose wife breastfed their baby. Ask him his opinions on the above questions.

4. Talk to at least five parents of children under three years of age.

a. Did they use disposable diapers for the baby most of the time?

b. If they used cloth diapers, did they use a diaper service, or did they wash the diapers themselves?

c. In class, make a chart showing the results of all class members' surveys.

d. What percentage of all the parents questioned used disposable diapers? What percentage used diaper service? What percentage washed the baby's diapers themselves?

5. Talk to the father of a baby not yet one year old. (He could be the same father you interviewed in question #3.) How has he shared in caring for his baby?

a. Does he help feed the baby?

b. Does he bathe the baby?

c. How often does he play with the baby?

d. Does he feel he is getting as much out of parenting as is the baby's mother?

6. Ask a woman who recently gave birth if she felt depressed and unhappy occasionally after her baby was born. If so, what did she do about it?

Feeding Infants

Objectives
To identify basic guides for feeding infants.
To identify nutrients essential for infants.
To relate essential nutrients to common foods.
To identify actions of parents and care givers that are
  essential for infants' good nutrition and health.

Terms to look for carbohydrate foods • diarrhea • "finger foods" •
minerals in milk • nutrient • protein foods • "solids" • vitamin foods

"How has the baby's feeding been going?" the doctor asks Karl's mother as he checks over 5-month-old Karl. "Have you started feeding him solids yet?"

"I'm getting along fine nursing him," answers Berta, Karl's mother. "I've tried cereal and fruit, but he eats only a little bit of each. He takes a little orange juice every day and also some water from a bottle. I've been thinking of starting him on egg this week," says Berta, completing her parenting report to the doctor.

Nutrients

Nutrients are found in foods. They are the chemical substances needed for building muscles, tissue, bones, teeth, and blood. Nutrients help a baby's body grow, develop, and repair itself. There are six basic nutrients that parents and care givers must be sure babies have. These are minerals, protein, vitamins, carbohydrates, water, and roughage. As the six basic nutrients are discussed, refer to the Basic Four food groups covered in Chapter 8, "Prenatal Nutrition." Then relate this new information to that discussion.

Minerals

Calcium and phosphorus are two minerals that are needed to build strong bones and teeth. Milk is the only food babies take that is very rich in these minerals. Therefore, it is very important for a baby to get sufficient milk.

The mineral iron is needed primarily for building blood. Milk is not a source of iron. However, babies are born with iron-rich blood derived from their mothers. This prepares them for a prolonged milk diet. Meat and eggs are good sources of iron. Egg yolk is given to babies first. Many pediatricians do not like to give babies egg white until they are at least 1 year old. The reason is that many babies develop an allergy to egg white. An egg can be boiled softly and the yolk fed to the baby with a spoon. Or the egg yolk can be mixed with a little milk and scrambled gently. A baby of 6 months or older, a girl for example, will be able to pick up little pieces of hard-boiled egg yolk and feed herself.

During early infancy, family life revolves around the baby's feeding schedule, since newborns feed 8 to 10 times a day. By 3 to 6 months, the baby eats every 4 hours. Between 6 and 12 months, the baby can learn to adapt to the family's 3-meal schedule, with perhaps a bottle between meals.

Protein

Milk provides much of this important nutrient. Later on, when the baby eats meat, eggs, fish, and poultry, additional protein will be supplied. Some cereals are also rich in protein. Protein is needed to make muscles, tissues, and cells throughout the body.

Vitamins

As mentioned earlier, babies need Vitamin C, which is found in citrus fruits. If a mother is breast-feeding and has a diet rich in citrus fruits and other foods containing Vitamin C, the baby will not need any additional Vitamin C. Otherwise, the pediatrician may wish to give the baby vitamin drops. These should be given exactly as directed. Overdosing with vitamins can be dangerous.

Vitamin D is essential to make calcium and phosphorus build bones and teeth effectively. Vitamin D is manufactured by the body when the sun shines on the skin. However, since clothing usually keeps the sun's rays off the skin, other sources of Vitamin D may be needed. Again, the doctor may suggest vitamin drops. Cow's milk usually has enough Vitamin D for a baby's needs. This vitamin is added by milk-processing companies.

Vitamin A is essential for good eyesight. This vitamin is found in egg yolk and in all green and yellow vegetables, for example, spinach and carrots.

The Vitamin B complex consists of thiamin, riboflavin, and niacin. These are also essential vitamins. They are contained in cereals, meats, and dairy products.

Carbohydrates

Carbohydrates are the sugars and starches found in many foods. These are primary sources of energy for the baby. But diet experts caution parents not to regularly give a baby foods sweetened with sugar. These sweetened foods tend to satisfy appetite quickly, so the baby will not eat the foods needed to get other nutrients. By eating or drinking too many sweetened foods, the baby also will develop a taste for sugar that will last into adulthood.

Water

Water in the diet is essential for the digestive and elimination systems to work properly. Of course, milk contains a lot of water, so the baby gets plenty of water in the early months. However, a baby will like a sip of water from a bottle or a spoon occasionally.

Roughage

Cereals and fruits that the baby eats provide roughage. This element is also necessary for good digestion.

Elimination

Elimination, especially the bowel movement, is related to the baby's diet. Parents and care givers will become experienced in noting any unusual changes in the bowel movement. Some foods cause the baby to have *diarrhea*. Adults should immediately stop giving the baby a particular food if this food is causing diarrhea. Diarrhea is a severe looseness of the bowels that may also be caused by an infection. In the case of diarrhea, the parent or care giver should contact the doctor. Babies who only take breast milk normally have loose bowel movements.

Certain foods will cause changes in color in the bowel movement. For example, a baby who eats beets may have bright red bowel movements. Parents who do not know this may be greatly alarmed, thinking that there is blood in the stool. However, after beets, this red color is normal. Also, babies with their still-developing digestive systems may have bowel movements that contain bits of carrot or other foods the babies have swallowed whole. Again, there is no reason to be alarmed about this.

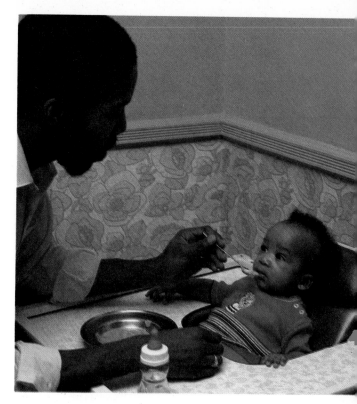

Babies can start eating solid foods any time between 2 and 6 months of age.

? Decisions, Decisions

Five-month-old Jill eats cereal, fruit, and milk. She refuses to eat vegetables, however, unless they are sweetened a little. Which is better—sweetened vegetables or no vegetables?

Foods for Infants

Babies need a variety of foods in order to get all the nutrients they need for healthy physical and mental growth.

Milk

Milk is a complete food for a young baby. It is all most babies get or need for several months. Milk supplies the baby with almost all the nutrients discussed above.

A mother who is breast-feeding should be sure to eat a diet rich in all the important nutrients. She should drink plenty of water, milk, and juices. Many pediatricians now feel that babies who are breast-fed do not need any vitamin supplements. Most do give vitamin supplements to bottle-fed babies.

Solids

Babies used to be given "solid" food—strained cereal or fruit—as early as 1 month of age. Most pediatricians

159

and nutritionists now agree that this is not necessary. They even feel it may be harmful. Studies have shown that babies who are started on solid food too early often tend to be overweight.

Breast-fed babies are often given no solid foods until they are 5 or even 6 months of age. One advantage of waiting this long is that a baby of this age will be able to eat tiny bits of "finger foods." The whole stage of feeding strained foods can be eliminated.

Bottle-fed babies and others who begin solids at 3 or 4 months of age usually start with either cereal or fruit. These foods are called "solid," but actually they are thinned. They have all the lumps strained or blended out so that the baby will not gag. Baby foods can be made at home with the blender or strainer. There are also special baby-food grinders. Parents can use these to grind small amounts of food right at the table. This way, the baby can eat some of the same foods the rest of the family eats.

Many parents feel homemade baby foods are healthier, because they are fresh and have no additives. Responding to this, baby-food manufacturers have begun to make their canned baby foods with no salt or sugar, and no preservatives.

? Decisions, Decisions

Ben grabs at the spoon as he is being fed. Food flies all over. If he gets hold of the spoon, he tries to put it in his mouth and bite it. How would you handle Ben's mealtime behavior?

New Texture

When solid foods are introduced, the baby will be puzzled by the new texture and taste. The child will probably roll the food back out of the mouth about as fast as you spoon it in. It is wise to mix only a small amount, for much of it will be wasted at first. You can try the new food using a rounded spoon with a small amount on the tip. Give the baby, a boy for example, plenty of time to explore this new taste and feel in his mouth. If the baby frets and fumes and spits the food out, do not force him. Just offer it again tomorrow. A baby who is forced to eat may grow to dislike the food and to dread mealtime. Wait a few days and try the food again—perhaps at a different time of day, or before the baby has had milk, or when he seems especially hungry. Remember, too, that even though it looks as if the baby has spit most of the food out onto the bib, he is tasting and swallowing some. Probably the baby will soon learn to like the new food.

Only one new food should be offered at a time or in a day. This way, you know which food is probably causing a problem, for example, a rash or an upset stomach. If you have served two new foods, you will have to eliminate both of them and start over to see which one agrees with the baby and which one does not.

After the baby is taking the cereal well and likes a variety of strained fruits, you can begin to offer vegetables and, a little later, some strained meats. There is no need to be in a hurry with solid foods if the baby is happy with milk. Solid food is expensive. And a lot of costly food is wasted when the baby is

Older babies enjoy eating finger foods. But these foods should not be used frequently as pacifiers. Babies who learn to depend on food for comfort tend to become overweight as children and adults.

very young. Mothers with their second babies tend to wait until the baby is older to begin solid foods.

The baby who is old enough to sit up and enjoy the family's company can have a taste of the family food from the table without any harm. Mashed potatoes, mashed banana, and applesauce are family foods the baby might like. Like nearly everyone else, babies generally enjoy ice cream. However, they usually prefer it mushy after the cold chill gets out of it.

"Finger Foods"

Giving 6- to 12-month-old babies "finger foods" is a way to help them begin to feed themselves. A toast stick that is quite dry or a cracker can be grasped in little hands and put into the mouth. A lot of the toast or cracker will get soggy and fall on the feeding table. But a little will find its way into the baby's digestive system. Do not give a baby raw, crisp fruits or vegetables, nuts, or candy. These foods are hard for the baby to chew, and they may cause choking. A fresh carrot stick can be dangerous. But a cooked or canned carrot, whole or sliced, is a colorful, nutritious "finger food." Soft fruits, such as bananas or avocados, are fine, too. Be sure to be close by to help if the baby does choke. Choking can be relieved by turning the baby upside down and patting the back.

A Nourishing Diet Is the Goal

The main parenting goal in feeding is to make sure the baby eats a safe, nourishing diet. It is very important to remember this goal as you feed the baby.

Feeding problems are often a result of parents' urging food on their child. Parents who adopt a flexible attitude prevent mealtime from becoming a battle of wills.

A nourishing diet can consist of a variety of foods. Babies' tastes vary in the same way other people's tastes do. One baby relishes spinach, while another likes green beans. With a variety being offered, babies learn to eat lots of different foods. Thus, they are likely to get the many nutrients that are needed for healthy growth and development.

Attitudes of Adults

Parents and care givers have personal attitudes about foods. They may feed babies as they, themselves, were fed— a practice that is not always the best. Parents and care givers should examine their attitudes toward food carefully. One old attitude is the "clean plate" rule. Some people put a lot of food on the baby's plate and expect a clean plate, even though the amount is too much for the baby's stomach. Even at this early age, it is best to let the baby decide how much is "enough." Parents and care givers should first start by placing a tiny taste of a food on a plate and trying that much with the baby. If the baby likes it, the parent should put a little more on the plate. If the baby does not seem to like the food, the parent or care giver should wait and try again in a few days. If no fuss is made, the baby probably will be eagerly eating the new food in a few weeks.

Many people cannot stand the mess babies make when they begin eating solid foods, especially when they feed themselves while sitting in the high chair. One teenage boy visited a family where the baby had spilled food all over the high chair and the floor around it. After the visit, he asked, "Mom, you didn't let me do that, did you?" The high schooler had a lot to learn before he would be ready to accept the mess that any children he might have would make while eating.

Babies and young children do make a mess while they are eating with their fingers or with a spoon. Though they may want to hold the spoon and try to feed themselves, they will often turn the spoon over just when the food gets near the mouth. That is to be expected. They have to practice just as a basketball player practices hitting the basket. Skill in eating will come in time, if the parents and care givers have patience and encourage the baby to try.

Concluding Comments

Good nutrition for the baby should begin before birth and continue throughout infancy. The six nutrients essential to body growth, development, and repair are minerals, protein, vitamins, carbohydrates, water, and rough-age. For several months, the baby is able to get most of these nutrients through breast milk or formula. Many pediatricians recommend supplementary vitamin drops.

Foods for the baby should always be clean. Infants are susceptible to germs, especially in the early months, when their digestive systems are just beginning to function.

The age at which solid foods are given varies. Most pediatricians now believe that solid foods are not necessary until the baby is 4 months old or older. Solids should be introduced one at a time, to see if the baby has any allergies.

Feeding takes a lot of time, and the attitudes of the parents and care givers are important. From them, the baby learns whether the feeding activity is going to be pleasant or unpleasant. Most babies look forward to being fed. In addition to filling their stomachs, feeding is a time for personal attention and cuddling. It is also a time for babies to play with new textures and to learn to feed themselves.

Activities

1. Plan a day's menus for a family consisting of mother, father, children aged 16, 10, 7, and a 7-month-old baby.
2. Explain how you would adapt the family's meals to suit the baby.
   a. Which foods would you mash or strain?
   b. Are there any foods on the menus which you would *not* feed the baby?
3. Look at a baby food cookbook, such as *Feed Me—I'm Yours* by Vicki Lansky (Meadowbrook Press; Bantam Books, Inc.). Try at least two of the recipes for strained or chopped foods, teething biscuits, and so forth. Report the results to the class.
4. Make a poster or create a bulletin board display illustrating the Basic Four food groups as they relate to the food needs of infants.

Health and Safety for Infants

Objectives
To identify recommended health protection for infants.
To identify recommended safety protection for infants.

Terms to look for   babyproofing • bonding • circumcision • foreskin • health protections • infant automobile safety seats • inoculations • pediatrician • safety hazards in homes

"Maggie has grown 2 inches and gained 1½ pounds since last month," Dr. Carroll tells the Nelsons, parents of 3-month-old Maggie. "She's doing very well."

Except for weighing and measuring, Dr. Carroll was able to carry out her whole examination while Maggie was on her father's lap. Maggie gurgles and smiles at the doctor, who took plenty of time so that the baby felt comfortable.

"Do you have any questions?" asks Dr. Carroll. Maggie's mother takes a list from her pocketbook. She asks several questions about diet, crying, and spit-ting up. Dr. Carroll takes plenty of time answering the questions. When the Nelsons get ready to leave, Dr. Carroll reminds them, "Remember to call me or talk to the nurse any time you have any questions."

Baby's Health Protection

Health protection for the baby begins at birth with a checkup by the baby's doctor or the hospital pediatrician. A

164

pediatrician is a doctor who specializes in the care of infants and children. It is a good idea for parents to decide in advance whom they would like for their baby's doctor. Parents should find a pediatrician with whom they feel comfortable. They should feel free to ask questions, even if they feel their questions might sound silly. An understanding doctor knows that many parents feel unsure of themselves. Most pediatricians will never laugh at parents' questions.

A good pediatrician will take plenty of time with a baby and will try to develop a relationship with the infant. Parents should always be present during the examination. They should be allowed to hold and comfort their babies, if necessary.

Parents will also want to find out how a doctor feels about such issues as feeding or pacifiers. A mother who wants to breast-feed should have a pediatrician who supports this decision. Parents who wish to bottle-feed should not be pushed to breast-feed. They should not be made to feel that the doctor disapproves of this decision.

Some pediatricians make house calls. This is important if parents feel their baby is too sick to move or if they will have a difficult time getting the baby to the doctor's office.

Well-baby clinics are becoming more and more popular. These clinics are usually less expensive than private doctors and can be used in the same way, for routine checkups and advice on problems.

Parents should make sure that they have some regular, reliable source of medical care for their babies. Then, if emergencies arise, they can telephone

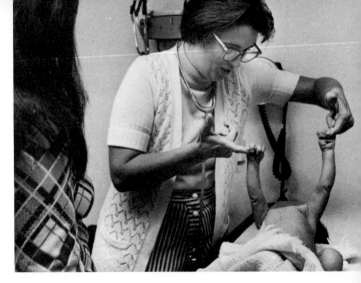

A good pediatrician takes the time to develop a comfortable relationship with both parents and baby. Parents should feel free to ask the doctor questions.

for assistance. The number for the doctor or clinic should be kept handy and should be left with baby-sitters.

Early Medical Care

As soon as the baby is born, the attending pediatrician puts drops of *silver nitrate* into the newborn's eyes. This is done to prevent possible infection from venereal disease that could cause blindness. Some doctors are now delaying this procedure for a half hour or so. They have learned that babies can establish eye contact with their parents at birth. This eye contact may be a very important part of the bonding that should take place between infants and parents. Bonding makes it possible for a healthy attachment to form between parent and child.

After the drops are given, the doctor checks the baby to see that it is normal. Then, the doctor weighs and measures the infant. Sometimes, all of these pro-

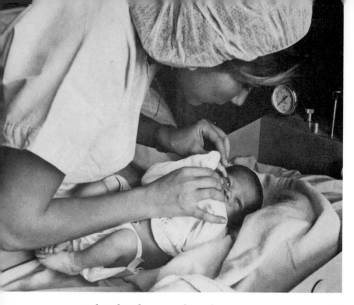

At birth, the newborn's eyes are protected against infection by silver nitrate drops.

cedures are delayed for a while until the mother has had a chance to hold her baby and breast-feed it for the first time.

Baby boys in the United States are often circumcised. *Circumcision* is a procedure in which a small portion of the *foreskin* that covers the head of the penis is cut away. In hospitals, this is usually done the second day after birth. However, many doctors now feel that the risk of infection is less if the procedure is delayed until the eighth day. Many doctors think that this operation makes it easier to clean the penis and prevent infections from occurring under the foreskin. The decision about circumcising a baby boy should be left to the parents.

Regular Checkups

Most pediatricians like to see the newborn immediately after birth, then again in about 3 weeks. After that, the baby usually has routine examinations once a month. These monthly checkups continue until the baby is a year old.

Calling the Doctor

As stated before, parents should feel free to call a doctor anytime they have a question about their baby. Some parents will call if the baby has a runny nose. Others will call only if they feel a serious illness is involved. However, there are some cases in which the doctor or clinic should always be contacted.

If the baby has a high fever, the parents should contact the doctor. All parents should keep a rectal thermometer on hand and learn to take the baby's temperature. Most doctors want to know immediately what the temperature is.

A baby who is screaming and pulling an ear may have an ear infection. Parents should take the baby's temperature and call the doctor.

If a baby has severe diarrhea—very thin and watery bowel movements—the parents should call the doctor. Allowing the baby to get severely dehydrated—as can happen when diarrhea occurs—is extremely dangerous.

Most doctors want to know about any unusual skin rash, vomiting, or loss of appetite.

Doctors and clinics can often advise parents by telephone. If they feel an illness is serious, they will want to see the baby and perhaps prescribe medicine. Babies cannot tell their parents what hurts. They sometimes have sore throats or other problems that parents cannot always determine. That is why a physician should personally check the baby.

Inoculations

Protection against a number of childhood diseases is available through *inoculations*. All of these are given in a physician's office or in a well-baby clinic. Each family should keep a careful record of shots the baby has received.

Babies may have reactions to some of these inoculations. They may be particularly fussy or even run a slight fever. Doctors usually advise parents that such reactions may occur. They may prescribe small amounts of liquid aspirin to make the baby more comfortable.

The following shots and oral vaccines are recommended:

1. DPT (Diphtheria, Pertussis-whooping cough, and tetanus) start at 2 months, with additional shots at 4 and 6 months. Booster shots are given at 15 to 18 months and at 4 to 6 years.
2. Sabin oral polio vaccine starts at 2 months, with additional oral vaccines at 4 months and at 12 to 16 months. An additional oral vaccine is given when children begin school.
3. Measles vaccine is given at 12 months.
4. Mumps vaccine is given at 12 months.
5. German measles vaccine is given at 12 months.
6. A smallpox vaccination is not needed in the United States anymore, but it is required for traveling in certain countries.

Medicine and Drugs

To avoid unnecessary risks, medicine prescribed by the doctor should be given as directed and for as long as directed. Some ailments may soon appear to be much improved. But the baby may still need additional medicine, as directed, to complete the cure. Never give any drugs that the doctor has not recommended. And never give larger doses of vitamins or medicine than those the doctor recommends.

Never store medicine bottles near the baby's bed. Even with the new baby-proof caps, babies may get the caps off and injure or kill themselves. An overdose of baby aspirin is the most common type of medicine poisoning. Children are familiar with the medicine and know that it tastes good.

Babies can be protected against dangerous disease and "common childhood illnesses." In many states, a record of inoculations is requried before the child is permitted to attend public school.

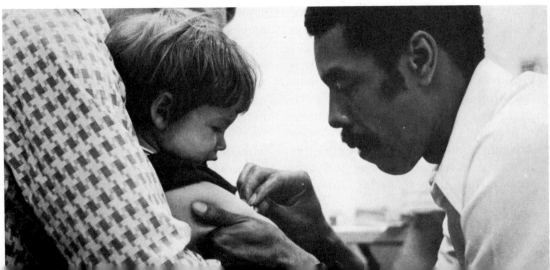

Baby's Safety Protection

There are many safety precautions that may be taken in the home to protect babies, including babyproofing rooms, protecting against falls, and protecting against accidents throughout the home.

Babyproofing Rooms

Taking safety measures in the home and in other places where babies spend a great deal of time is called *babyproofing*. Babyproofing means planning ahead to ensure the safety of the baby. (Look at the babyproofed house on pages 240 and 241.) As the baby develops, more and more places become dangerous. Babies do not have the experience to realize when serious dangers are present. Accidents cause more deaths among babies and young children than does any other cause of death.

Many psychologists today are op-posed to the use of playpens. They feel that keeping babies in these pens can slow their development by preventing them from exploring the environment. However, there are times when parents and care givers must give their attention to other tasks. At such times, a playpen can be very useful. A pen that folds or that is narrow enough to go through a door is most convenient. It can easily be moved from room to room or to a porch or terrace. Folding playpens can also be taken on trips where a safe sleeping and playing space will be needed.

An expandable gate used to close off doorways is useful to protect babies. It can be used to keep a baby from entering a stairwell with dangerous steps. It can keep a baby out of the kitchen when parents are preparing hot foods that might accidentally spill on the baby. A gate has the advantage of allowing a baby to see people on the other side. The baby is also free to move about a room while being kept away from dangerous areas.

Electric cords should be hidden from view as much as possible—perhaps with furniture. Some cords can be tacked or stapled along a floorboard or wall moulding. This gets cords out of the way and makes them less interesting to a baby who can crawl. Electric outlets should be covered with masking tape or special plastic covers.

Harmful cleaning supplies and tools should all be removed from low cupboards. Small objects that might be placed in the mouth and possibly swallowed should be removed from any area the baby can reach.

Unless safety measures are taken, there are real dangers in homes and centers for babies. Of course, adults in charge must always be alert to anticipate and give close attention to possibly dangerous surroundings and behavior.

Protection from Falls

Many babies fall off beds and bath tables, down stairs, and out of cribs. Many are badly hurt—even killed—from falls every year. Babies should never be trusted to stay on an adult bed. A baby is much safer in a crib or playpen. Crib and playpen sides should be kept pulled up for protection. Some eager babies pull themselves up at such a young age that a bassinet is unsafe for use for very long.

Some people think that nonwalking babies stay safely in place. This is far from true. They can dig their tiny toes into bed covers or carpet and inch along to an edge. They also soon learn to roll over and can move quickly after that.

Babies often fall down stairs, because parents have simply not realized how far their babies have learned to creep. Most babies survive such falls. Their bones are still soft and flexible, and their soft spots protect them from concussion. But such falls can obviously be very dangerous, and they are frightening for both babies and parents. So parents must anticipate babies' creeping and crawling before it happens. They should latch cellar doors or put gates in front of stairways.

Safety in Baths

Babies are easily scalded when water that is too hot is turned on in their baths. This is a needless danger. A parent or care giver must test the water for correct temperature. No hot water should be turned on in the tub or sink while the baby is in there.

Be sure to hold the baby securely at all times during bathing. If the phone or doorbell rings while you are bathing the baby, either ignore the ring or wrap the baby in a towel and carry the child with you to answer the ring. *Never* leave a baby or young child alone in the bath!

Also, never leave a baby alone in a bath with a young child. A recent study done in Hawaii found that many infant bath deaths took place with another child (age 2 to 5) in the bathtub. Parents assumed that the older child would recognize that the baby was in danger. The study also found that the median age of babies who died of bath accidents was nine months. Babies of nine months can sit unassisted and have good muscle control. Even so, they were still not able to save themselves from drowning in several inches of bath water.

Safety in Beds

A firm mattress and no pillow are recommended for a baby. Overly soft mattresses or pillows can smother babies if they get their noses covered just right. The mattress should also fit the crib, leaving no room for the baby to roll into a crack along the side. Padded crib bumpers should be used. These pads keep the baby from banging against the crib bars or from getting arms or legs stuck between bars. Newer cribs are required by law to have no more than 2¼ inches (6 cm) between bars so that babies cannot poke their heads through the bars. Parents who have an old or antique crib should check the width between bars. They may need to insert extra bars.

Toys left in the crib should be free of sharp edges that might cut the baby. There should be no small pieces that could be taken apart and swallowed. A common danger is the plastic eyes on stuffed toys. They can be pulled off and swallowed.

A baby should be protected from drafts with appropriate-weight sleeping bags or footed sleepers.

? Decisions, Decisions

You think that 6-month-old Spencer has just swallowed the safety pin he picked up less than a second ago. But you are not sure. What should you do?

Safety in Kitchens

A high chair may be dangerous when the baby becomes active enough to stand up in it. Many parents prefer the lower feeding tables. Seats should have safety straps for holding the baby securely. Be sure to keep the high chair or feeding table away from the stove. A baby who can reach the stove might grab a pot handle, overturn the contents, and get burned. Always keep an eye on the baby who is in the high chair or at the feeding table.

Tablecloths invite creeping babies to tug on them, bringing down the dishes, knives and forks, and hot food. Place

170

mats should be used until children are old enough to understand that they may not pull on tablecloths.

Ironing boards are unsteady if the baby pulls up while holding on to them. The iron cord is inviting to a curious baby, as are the dangling pieces of garments that are being ironed. While ironing, adults should keep the baby away from the ironing board. And they should put the ironing board away once they have finished with it.

Safety around Heaters

To protect against burns, parents should keep babies away from radiators, floor furnaces, and space heaters. Never use an unvented gas heater in the house or in the baby's room. Gas heaters should have a valve that cuts off the gas if the pilot light goes out. Without these protective devices, there is danger of death from lack of oxygen and from explosions. Do not use a gas oven to heat a room because of the same dangers.

Protection from Suffocation

One of the most dangerous household items for babies is the thin plastic bag from the dry cleaner. Babies enjoy pulling small blankets over their faces, to play peekaboo. Infants cannot tell the difference between blankets and plastic bags. In addition, the bags make attractive rustling noises. Babies who pull bags over their faces can suffocate within minutes. The best prevention is for parents to tie knots in plastic bags from the dry cleaner and discard them immediately. Other plastic bags, such as food and garbage bags, should be stored out of babies' reach.

Safety in Cars

From birth, babies riding in cars should be strapped into government-approved infant safety seats. The government safety standards were updated in 1976, so parents should be sure to buy a safety seat that meets these updated standards. Very young infants usually ride backwards, in a reclining position. Many safety seats can be converted to an upright position when the baby is older and able to sit.

Car seats are a must for infants. This type of seat meets government standards for babies weighing less than 20 pounds.

If car seats appear much too large for tiny infants, parents can pad the seats with rolled-up blankets. Car beds are not safe. They may be convenient, giving the baby a bed to sleep in when visiting. But these beds should be folded up and put in the trunk. Car beds should never be used to carry a baby in a car.

Parents should never hold a baby and drive. This is dangerous to parents, babies, and other motorists. Adult seats do not hold babies safely and can cause pelvic injury if the car makes a sudden stop.

? Decisions, Decisions

"Laura has a fever, but I've already called the doctor twice this week about one thing or another," said Laura's mother. "I'm afraid if I call again the doctor will think I'm a nuisance and a worrier." What should she do?

Crib Death

Occasionally, a seemingly healthy baby is put to bed at night and is found dead the next morning. No illness or accident can account for the death. This tragic event is called *crib death,* or in medical terms, *sudden infant death syndrome.*

Crib death occurs in babies older than 3 weeks and younger than 7 months. It strikes babies of the rich and poor alike. The baby of a "careless" parent is no more likely a victim than the baby of a "careful" parent. Crib death occurs in all parts of the world and has been recorded since ancient times. It was as common in the 1700s as it is today. Fortunately, it occurs only rarely.

Scientists have studied crib death at great length. As yet, there is no satisfactory explanation. It is not caused by suffocation, choking, bottle feeding, drugs, or cigarettes. It is not inherited. There is no increased risk of crib death for the couple's next child. Current studies point to the possibility of a sudden, overwhelming infection that the baby cannot resist. What kind of infection and how to prevent it are not known.

Crib death is shocking and heartbreaking for the parents. They often blame themselves or each other for things they did or did not do. Many couples can reach a better understanding of their reactions and feelings of grief by talking with a clergyman, a psychiatrist, or a counselor at a mental health agency.

Concluding Comments

A baby's health is of primary concern to parents and care givers. Health care begins at birth. Parents should continue it by selecting a regular pediatrician or well-baby clinic. Many diseases that were once common in childhood can now be prevented through inoculations. Parents should be sure to protect their babies by having them inoculated and by making sure the babies get regular checkups.

More babies die as the result of accidents than from any other cause. Babies do not have the experience that adults have to understand danger. So parents and care givers must make the environment babyproof to protect babies from harm. Infants riding in cars should always be strapped into approved safety seats.

1. Find out about well-baby clinics in your community.
   a. Call such a clinic and ask what services it provides and at what cost.
   b. Call several pediatricians and find out about their costs and services. How many of them make house calls?
2. Interview the parents of several children aged one to three years.
   a. Learn which immunizations their children have had and at what ages.
   b. Compare your results with the recommendations given on page 167.
3. *On your hands and knees,* check your home for infant safety. (That's the way the baby "checks" it!)
   a. List the things that could be dangerous to a crawling baby.
   b. Describe what you could do to make your home safe for a baby.
4. Research car seats for infants and toddlers.
   a. Why is it so important for a small child *always* to be in a well-made car seat while riding in an automobile?
   b. Which brands and models are recommended? (*Consumer's Guide* is a good resource.)
   c. Check costs of the recommended car seats. Compare department store and discount store prices.

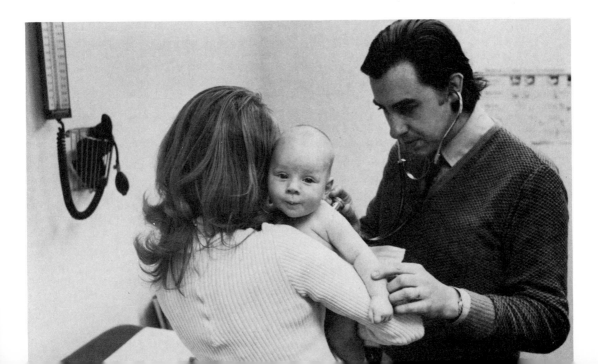

Guiding Infants

Objectives

To define guidance and goals for guidance.
To explain direct physical and verbal guidance for infants.
To explain indirect guidance and its uses in guiding infants.

Terms to look for   affective guidance • direct guidance • discipline • indirect guidance • physical guidance • positive reinforcement • punishment • socialization • verbal guidance

Dominic placed a graham cracker on the high-chair tray. He lifted Alonzo, his 7-month-old son, into the chair. Alonzo picked up the cracker in his fist and brought it to his mouth. He took a bite. He looked at the cracker, moved it back and forth from one hand to the other, then took another bite. After a while, the cracker became soggy from the saliva that it absorbed. Alonzo was toothless, but he seemed to be munching on the softened cracker. Some of the cracker fell to the tray. Alonzo was obviously enjoying the cracker and his experience with it.

Anticipating Behavior

Guiding infants begins with the parents' or care giver's understanding of what can be expected of the infant. Dominic knows that babies 7 months old are determined to put things into their mouths. Therefore, he puts objects such as crackers, dried toast, and banana chunks in front of Alonzo. He expects that the baby will put this food into his mouth and munch on it. Dominic hopes that Alonzo will soon become interested

174

in feeding himself. So his guidance has a plan based upon what he knows the baby is likely to do. Alonzo munches and entertains himself, allowing Dominic to put supper into the oven. Sometimes Dominic uses this technique to keep his baby happily occupied while he is preparing the baby's food.

Dominic also knows better than to lay objects near Alonzo that would be dangerous if put into the mouth. For example, if he were to lay a match down, it, too, would go into Alonzo's mouth. A fork, a tack, or a breakable glass object all might be interesting and go straight to Alonzo's mouth. Dominic wisely keeps such things out of Alonzo's reach.

Babies in the infant group range from quiet, immobile newborns to crawling, creeping, pulling-up 1-year-olds on the verge of walking. Adults who are guiding infants must take into consideration the amount of movement the infant can make on its own. Parents and care givers must expect that babies will move and that once they can move, they will "get into things." Thus, part of guidance is keeping valuable and dangerous things away from babies. Babies will not understand that they must not touch certain things until they are older.

Defining and Explaining Guidance

Guidance refers to the actions parents and care givers use to influence a baby's behavior. That is, adults will plan to influence babies to do things so that the babies will grow in ability to direct their own behavior. The behaviors adults teach infants are those needed for in-

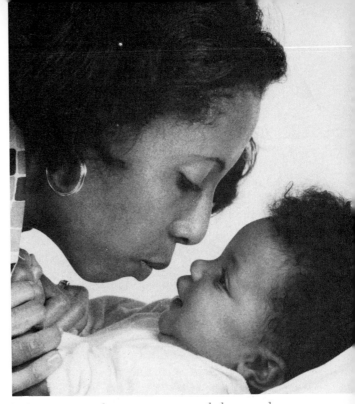

Infants cannot be given too much love and affection. Warm and loving care makes secure babies who are eager to please adults.

fants to be happy, to begin to take care of themselves, to learn, and to interact with others. Children need to learn these skills in order to be able to get along in society—a process we call *socialization*.

You have probably heard the word *discipline* used for getting a child to do what others think should be done. "He is a very well-disciplined little boy," is a pleasant comment for a parent to hear from the teacher. This comment usually means that the child follows the rules well. *Discipline* has another meaning. "That child should be disciplined" means "That child should be punished." Because the word *discipline* often has "punishment" as its meaning, we will use the word *guidance*. Guidance has

175

the goal of helping children learn behavior that will allow them to take over the task of self-guidance as quickly as they are ready. The goal of guidance is self-guidance. If you like the word *discipline* better, try to think of it, too, as being positive teaching for self-discipline rather than punishment. Guidance should be planned. Planning will make the learning process more effective.

Guidance Begins At Birth

Parents and care givers can lay the foundations for effective guidance when the baby is still a newborn. When parents and care givers respond quickly to babies' cries and meet their needs promptly, they help babies feel secure. These babies will learn to trust adults and will be more easily guided as they grow older.

For many years, Americans worried about "spoiling" their babies by giving them too much attention. Psychologists now agree that infants up to 1 year old cannot be spoiled by having their needs met. Sometimes these needs are for food, dryness, or warmth. Sometimes they are simply for physical closeness. Researchers have observed simpler societies and discovered that babies in these societies are often carried around on their parents' chests as the adults go about their daily work. A baby who begins to cry is promptly put to the mother's breast. If you asked one of these mothers about her feeding schedule, she would probably be very puzzled by your question. And yet, researchers report that they do not see "spoiled" babies in such cultures. Perhaps Americans can learn something about child rearing from these people.

Direct guidance helps babies learn what to do by showing or telling the right behavior.

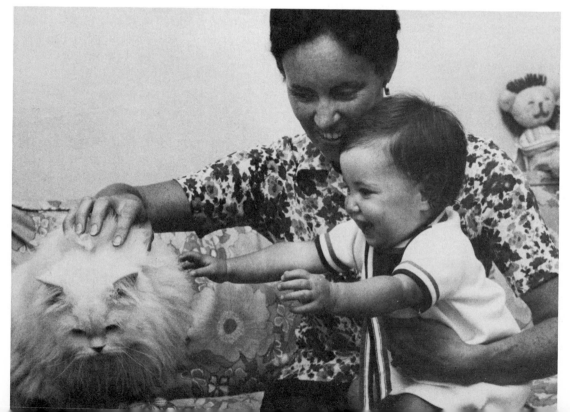

Many adults still feel that babies should "learn" to control themselves when they are still tiny. Babies who are left to cry learn nothing except that they are uncomfortable and that their needs are not being met. Such babies will have a difficult time developing the trust that is needed for later effective guidance.

As babies grow older, they can begin to learn something about the behaviors adults desire from them. The best way for them to learn such behaviors is through the following effective forms of guidance.

Direct Guidance

You use *direct guidance* when you go directly to infants, get down to their level on the floor, and help or lead them, showing or telling them what is to be done. Direct guidance means adult-to-child interaction that helps the infant begin to know what behavior is expected. Direct guidance can also be verbal guidance, where you tell the child what to do and how to do it.

Indirect Guidance

You use *indirect guidance* when you set the stage for infants to practice the behavior you prefer. That is, you arrange toys, equipment, food, and so on, so that the natural behavior of babies allows them to do what is right—to play happily, to protect themselves, and to get along with others. For example, a fenced-off room is a part of an adult's indirect guidance. Although babies like to be close to their parents and like to explore, if a gate is used occasionally on a kitchen door, a baby will learn eventually to accept this limit. However, no baby should be confined away from the

Praise for good behavior is called *positive reinforcement*. It is a powerful form of guidance.

parent for long periods of time—more than a half hour.

Dominic used indirect guidance when he laid the cracker on Alonzo's tray. He did not have to say or do anything else. Alonzo's natural interest took over from there.

Parents can avoid argument and difficulties with indirect guidance. They set the stage for desired behavior with it. Placing valuables and hazards out of reach (babyproofing) and having safe and interesting objects at hand are all parts of good indirect guidance.

Affective Guidance

You use *affective guidance* when you influence the infant's behavior through feelings. You show your pleasure over something a baby has done by smiling, hugging, talking, and the like. Babies learn to like to please the other people

177

Instead of a "No no," what kind of guidance could you use in these situations?

in their world—brothers, sisters, parents, and care givers. Affective guidance means showing pleasant feelings toward a baby who has done something of which you approve.

Punishment is also a form of affective guidance, used to let children know when adults do not like what they have done. However, punishment does not lead a baby to the goal of being a happy child. Physical punishment is not understood by a baby—all it does is hurt. Nor does it lead parents and teachers to the goal of teaching an infant what *to* do rather than what *not* to do.

Guidance Examples

Following are several examples of these three methods of guidance that you may be practicing with infants you know.

If you want a baby to crawl to you, you say, "Come here, Sasha." That is direct *verbal guidance.* When you accompany what you say with putting out your hands and helping the baby move toward you, that is direct *physical guidance.* You smile, nod your head in approval, and say, "Good girl! Hurrah!" That loving reward is direct *affective guidance.*

Here is another example. Eddie is on the diaper changing table. You give him a rattle to shake. "Shake it, Eddie," you say (verbal guidance). "Like this," you say, taking his hand and helping him get the feel of shaking the rattle (physical guidance). Eddie shakes the rattle. You smile, nod, and give him a quick kiss, saying, "You did it! Eddie, shake the rattle again" (affective guidance).

In the next example, you label the parts of the example that are verbal, physical, and affective.

Jimmy is in the high chair. You place the plastic cup, containing a small amount of juice, on the tray. "Drink your juice, Jimmy," you say. Then, you place your hand on Jimmy's and help lift the cup to his lips. He drinks a sip or two. "Orange juice," you say. "Jimmy, drink it." He drinks more juice. "Good! Jimmy. Very good." You smile and nod,

keeping your eyes on Jimmy's so he will know how pleased you are.

Sara, age 11 months and creeping, sees a paper on the floor. It is an unpaid bill that Sara's mother, Sue, needs to keep. Sara creeps toward the paper. Sue realizes Sara will probably crumple the paper or put it into her mouth. How can Sue prevent this, using the three forms of direct guidance? Think the solution through before reading further.

Sue could say, "Sara, come here." She could stoop low on the floor so Sara would turn toward her and away from the bill. She could say "Come get this rattle," as she shakes the rattle to get Sara's interest. Babies are easily distracted. Therefore, these two actions may distract Sara from the bill. However, suppose Sara keeps going toward the bill. Then Sue can go to her and physically help her change course and get involved with a toy or another object. She could say, for example, "Here Sara, see this dog? Listen to him bark. Woof! Woof!" Soon Sara will have forgotten the bill.

Avoid Too Many "No's"

Notice that it was not suggested that the words *No, no* be used. These words are often heard, especially in social gatherings when parents do not want to get up and properly distract their child. In guidance, the idea is to teach babies what they *can* do. Saying "No, no" tells them what they cannot do. Babies cannot reason that one thing is valuable or that something else is dangerous. They need to be busy, to handle things, and to explore. When they go where they should not or touch something they must not, it is best to offer them an interesting substitute to take its place. Saying "No, no," does get their attention. It may stop the undesirable behavior for a second. But it will not tell them what they can do the next second. It is better to redirect the baby verbally in the first place. Also, a better technique is to call the baby's name rather than say, "No, no."

Even with babyproofing, and using positive guidance as much as possible, parents and care givers sometimes must

179

say, "No." For example, suppose parents have a dishwasher. If a crawling and pulling-up baby continues to play with the controls (despite efforts at distraction), parents must say, "No" and follow it up with action. The first step would be to move the baby away from the dishwasher. But suppose the baby continues to return and play with the controls. The parent could then follow the "No" by setting the baby outside the kitchen and fastening a door gate. Of course, the baby should always be offered an alternative, such as a toy to play with. Most babies will soon learn that they may play in the kitchen only if they leave the dishwasher alone.

❓ Decisions, Decisions

Rita has an expensive stereo system and record collection. She wants to teach her daughter she must never touch them. Al thinks that the system should be covered up until the baby is older. "Unfair," says Rita, "the baby must learn some basic rules so she can fit into our lives." Who is right?

A Place To Be Messy

Parents can make it easy for a baby to stay out of trouble. This will keep people from getting upset about very natural baby behaviors. Since babies will be messy with their eating, adults should arrange the surrounding eating area for easy cleanup. A washable, rugless floor under the high chair or feeding table allows the food bits to be easily seen and mopped up. Or, put newspapers underneath. The newspapers can be rolled up and discarded after the meal. Gooey food should be kept away from babies when they are in the living room. Babies do not know that the couch is not washable. If they smear banana on the couch, it is really the adults' fault for letting them have food there.

Plastic pants or disposable diapers on babies keep clothes and furnishings dry. Babies are going to wet. Most people would rather not be wet on. Some would be very upset if a baby wet on them or on their furnishings. Using plastic pants or disposable diapers is just another example of how adults control the things in a baby's world.

Choose The Behavior To Reward

When you use affective guidance or positive rewards for infants, you should be sure you want the baby to repeat that kind of action. When you say, "Great!" and smile and then hug and kiss the baby, that should encourage the baby to do the same thing again. This is called positive reinforcement.

Sometimes a baby screams, and everyone comes running. A screaming baby who is picked up and played with learns that screaming brings rewards of attention. So it should not be surprising that the baby will scream again soon. If screaming bothers you, it would be far better to reward the baby with attention (affective guidance) during a period of happy, contented play. This will encourage that kind of behavior.

Avoid Scolding, Punishing, and Shaming

Some people reason that if rewards bring about desired behavior, so should punishments. They think that punishing, scolding, or shaming babies should

180

tell the babies what behavior you would like to have them stop. Guidance does not work that way. Surely, it is unpleasant for a baby to be scolded or punished. However, these techniques simply scare babies and leave them uncertain and insecure. For example, if a baby wets and cries, scolding will give one form of attention. The uncomfortable wet diaper will at least be changed. Thus, the baby's cries will be rewarded. But, scolding cannot stop a baby from wetting when the baby does not have control over the bladder muscles. Control over urination cannot be expected to come until the baby is more than 2 years old, and sometimes 3 years old. Scolding does not help the baby learn. It just teaches the child to fear the care giver or parent. For a while, adults should simply accept wetting.

? ● Decisions, Decisions

You tell Barry not to play with the electric outlet and you move him away. He crawls back. You move him away again and give him a toy to play with. He plays briefly and crawls back to the outlet. You carry him to another room. Before you realize it, he's back at the outlet. What now?

Concluding Comments

Guiding babies' behavior begins in infancy and continues throughout their younger years. They are learning to become self-guided people able to make decisions for themselves. Care givers and parents use three types of guidance—direct, indirect, and affective—to

This baby's parents have made sure that the bottom drawer holds only safe things that the baby can pull out and play with. What type of guidance have they used?

181

help the child learn the correct behaviors. Most guidance episodes use all three kinds of guidance.

Indirect guidance means setting the stage for the behavior desired. This type of guidance applies in arranging the setting for the baby to play, to eat, and to be bathed.

Punishment and saying "No" are ineffective methods parents and care givers should avoid. These techniques do not help the baby learn what to do.

Activities

1. Give an example of *indirect* guidance needed in your home, if you have a six- to twelve-month-old infant either living with or visiting you. Describe what you would do and the purpose of your actions.
2. Interact with a baby aged six to twelve months old.
   a. Report, either orally or in writing, on several examples of *direct* guidance that you use.
   b. Describe the verbal, physical, and affective aspect of each situation.
3. Observe several parents with their babies, either in their homes or in public places, such as a park or the grocery store. Report on the guidance techniques you see being used. Are many "No, nos" being used?
4. Write an essay. Describe what you can do, as the care giver for a baby, to avoid frequent use of "No, no" in your guidance of that baby. Include specific examples and reasons.

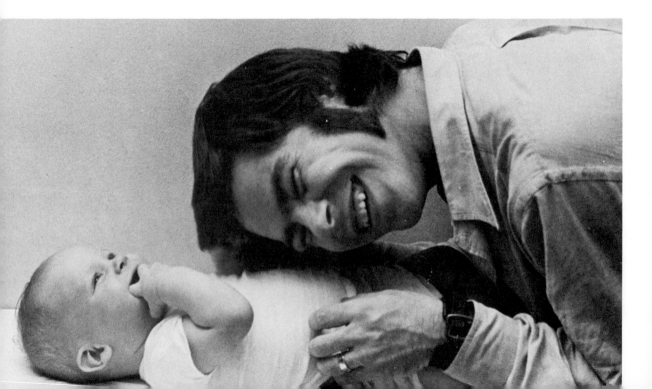

Substitute Care for Infants

Objectives

To discuss the need for substitute care for infants.

To describe characteristics of good infant care, in individual and group settings.

To discuss the importance of the parent-care giver relationship.

Terms to look for   family day-care home • infant-care center • paternity leave • primary attachment • staff-child ratio • staff development • substitute care giver

"See this, Juanita? See the ball? Whee! Where's the ball? Here it is! Look at the ball!" This conversation accompanies a simple game of hide-the-ball that Terry, an infant care giver, plays with Juanita, who is 5 months old. Terry uses a colorful sponge ball. She has played the game with Juanita for several days. Now Juanita has learned about this game and seems to anticipate the return of the ball. She gurgles happily when the ball reappears. Then the game of hide-the-ball begins all over again as Terry hides it a second time.

The First 5 Years Are Very Important.

A baby's education begins at birth. Parenting activities help the baby learn. Parenting activities include caring for, loving, and teaching the baby. The first 5 years are considered by many as more important than all other years for the child. In these years, children learn many facts, but they also learn how to learn. They learn about themselves and sense whether they are important to others or not.

With good care, babies and young children, whether at home or in group-care centers, learn, grow, and develop at a rapid rate. Everyone who contacts the child makes a contribution to the infant's development.

The Need for Substitute Care for Infants

Many, if not most, Americans have long believed that the best place for babies was in their own homes, with their mothers. And for many families, this is the ideal situation. However, other families have some present-day realities to consider. Many women today need to return to work outside the home after childbirth for economic reasons. Some are single parents. Some are primary or equal providers of the family income. Others must supplement their husbands' incomes in order to make ends meet.

More and more women are pursuing full-time careers outside the home. Taking 6 months to a year or more to stay home with their babies might prevent them from advancing professionally. Still others, although they love their babies as much as any other mothers do, find themselves restless and dissatisfied staying at home with an infant.

For all these parents, good substitute care for their infants is essential if the babies are to grow and develop properly.

The majority of parents who work outside the home leave their babies in the care of relatives or neighbors. In many cultures, older members of the family or community care for the youngest members. What are some advantages and disadvantages of this system?

At present, choices of substitute care are limited.

Sharing Parenting Responsibilities

Both parents may care for the baby on a full- or part-time basis. Although this type of care cannot properly be called *substitute*, since both people involved are parents, it is included in the discussion. Some couples decide that they would prefer for the wife to work outside the home full time, while the husband takes care of the baby. In some states, fathers have successfully gained the right to *paternity leave* from certain occupations. Other couples arrange for both mother and father to hold parttime positions. They try to arrange their schedules so that one parent is home with the baby most of the time. Although neither of these arrangements is common, both practices are growing and may offer an ideal solution to caring for infants.

Relatives and Neighbors

According to Dr. Dorothy Gross, Director of the Infant and Parent Development Program at Bank Street College of Education, the great majority of parents who work outside the home still leave their infants in the care of relatives and neighbors. Relatives may care for the babies in the babies' homes or in their own homes. In the case of neighbors, the infant is usually taken to the neighbor's home.

Dr. Gross goes on to say that the fact that few people use formal family day-care or group-care centers for their infants does not mean that many people would not prefer such professional care. The fact is that few child-care facilities exist. The field of infant care is very new. Many centers that do exist do not have licensing for infant care.

? Decisions, Decisions

"I want to stay home with the baby after it's born," said Louise. "But I've been getting negative reactions from people at my job. I have a responsible position, and my co-workers seem to think I'm foolish to quit. Now I'm beginning to wonder." How can Louise handle the situation?

Family Day Care

In family day care, an adult, usually a mother, cares for her own and other children in her home. In communities where family day-care homes are licensed, there are requirements about space, number of children, number of infants, safety, nutrition, and so forth. In an ideal family day-care arrangement, the care giver attends training sessions given by psychologists and educators. Training helps a care giver do as much as possible to help each child develop and learn.

Of course, there are also many informal arrangements, in which unlicensed people take care of babies and young children in their homes. These are also family day-care homes. Some of these care givers may be excellent. The important thing for parents to look for is a care giver who holds the same basic child-rearing philosophies as the parents do.

Private Care Givers

Parents who have enough income may prefer to have their babies cared for in their own home. Such parents will want to interview prospective care givers well in advance of the time when both parents will be working outside the home all day. The parent who is presently staying home should have the care giver spend at least a week getting to know the baby. Only when the parent feels that the baby is secure with the new care giver should he or she return to work outside the home.

Group Care for Infants

Group care for infants is a relatively new concept. There are not many centers that provide such care. Those that do vary widely. Many take infants and toddlers. Some have children as old as 4 years old in the same groups as the infants. Others may care only for infants, whom we have defined as babies up to 1 year old.

What Is a High-quality Infant Center?

The first factor to consider in group care for infants is *staff-child ratio.* Dr. Gross feels that no infant-care room should ever have one staff person alone. Therefore, it is best to ask how many infants there are per two adults. She feels that if there are both infants and toddlers in the group, there should be no more than two children under one year old, and no more than six or seven children all together, for two adults. If the children are all infants, there should be no more than five infants for two care givers.

Some parents can afford a private care giver. The care giver should spend time getting to know the baby and family before assuming fulltime care.

You can understand the need for keeping infant groups very small if you imagine some situations about infants. For example, suppose there are five infants and two adults. What happens when two 5-month-olds are hungry, one 7-month-old has a dirty diaper, and an 8-month-old is crying and needs to be comforted. Even if the fifth baby is playing contentedly, there is a lot for two people to handle.

Another reason for having two adult care givers is that the babies really do need to form attachments to both. In order for group care to be of high quality, staff members must have time off. If one care giver is on vacation or is ill, the babies need to feel completely secure with the other care giver.

Waiting until a baby is 6 months old to enroll in group care may not be realistic for some parents. Many employers refuse to grant maternity or paternity leaves for as long as 6 months. Parents may risk losing their jobs or their seniority if they wait 6 months before returning to work.

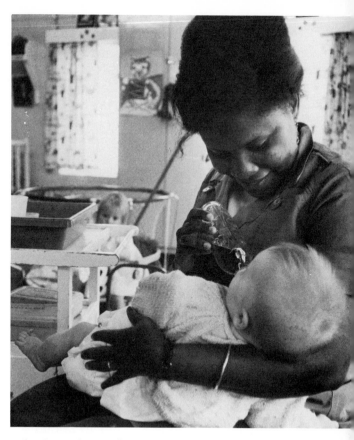

A high-quality infant care center has a low staff-child ratio. This allows care givers to pay special attention to the babies' needs and individual differences.

"Curriculum" in the Infant Center

Since increasing attention is being paid to the idea of early education, some companies have developed infant curriculum packages, which some centers purchase. Experts in the field of infant development would tend to support individualized programs for infants. Infants do not fit neatly into categories. Thus, no curriculum package could possibly meet the needs of all infants.

In fact, Dr. Gross states that when we think of infant centers, the model for what a high-quality center should be is not a good *school*, but a good *home*. Infants should get a good deal of individual attention. Care givers should pay attention to the individual differences of children and their need to eat and sleep at different times.

Guidance

A high-quality infant center uses the positive types of guidance discussed in Chapter 18. Crying babies should never be ignored. Good care givers know that babies cry for a reason. They are not concerned about "spoiling" infants under 1 year old.

Good infant care givers reward babies with smiles, pats, and praise. Babies in a high-quality center are never scolded, shamed, or punished. Positive commands, such as "Come here," "Eat the cereal," or "Put your arm here," will be favored over negative ones, such as "Don't throw food," and "No, no." Good care givers use distraction to keep babies out of trouble.

Flexibility

A good infant center is flexible in order to meet the needs of the families it serves. During the hours that the center is open, parents are able to bring their children in or pick them up at any time. If a parent happens to leave work early one day, the center does not frown upon the parent's picking the child up early. Instead, the center supports parents and encourages them to spend as much time with their babies as they can. Parents are also encouraged to spend time at the center whenever they want to and are able. For example, a breast-feeding mother may want to take a half hour to feed her baby as soon as she comes to pick the child up. Care givers will welcome her presence, because it will make the center seem even more like home.

Physical Needs

A good group-care center for infants meets all the physical needs that good parents meet at home. The center is always spotlessly clean. Food is refrigerated properly and conforms as much as possible to what parents have told the director about their babies' prefer-

ences. Of course, the food is also nutritious. (Refer to Chapter 16, "Feeding Infants.")

A good center is very careful about babies' health and safety needs. Most licensed centers have some affiliation with a local clinic or public health station.

High-quality centers try to get babies outdoors every day that the weather permits. Again, you can see the importance of a high ratio of staff to infants. Two strollers are about as many as one care giver can push.

A really high-quality infant care center has ongoing staff development. Care givers continually meet with one another and with their director to discuss the needs and progress of the babies they care for. They also learn new ways to help the babies develop.

Parent-Care Giver Relationship

Many parents feel guilty about leaving their infants to go to work outside the home. And some care givers may actually try to compete with parents for the babies' affection. Dr. Gross states that it is the responsibility of the center to be aware of such feelings and to support the most important relationship—the one between the baby and the parent. Parents should be asked what *they* want for their babies, and the center should try to do these things as much as possible.

High-quality centers are in contact with parents *daily*. Parents should try to allow 5 minutes each morning to let care givers know about such things as sleepless nights, teething, and other problems. Care givers and parents should have regular conferences to share in the development of the babies.

Dealing with Separation

A good infant-care center insists on a gradual, slow adjustment of the infant to the new care giver. Although the baby under 6 months might be easier to leave than the older baby, Dr. Gross feels it is better for an infant under 6 months not to be in group care for a full day. In order for babies to grow and to develop well, they need to form a *primary attachment*. This primary attachment should be to their parent or parents, not to an infant-center care giver.

❓ Decisions, Decisions

Marlene and Joe both need to work outside the home to meet their expenses. However, they have trouble leaving 3-month-old Joey with a baby-sitter. Both are afraid that Joey would come to love the baby-sitter more than he would love them. What do they need to consider?

Concluding Comments

Many parents need substitute care for their babies. This need is only beginning to be met. Most parents still use relatives or neighbors as substitute care givers. Many parents might prefer professional, high-quality group-care centers. But very few such centers are currently available.

A high-quality infant center should have the same characteristics as a good home. Infant care givers should not be thought of as *replacements* for parents, but as *supplements*, who support the parent-child relationship. A good infant-

care center should pay attention to the individual needs of babies. The staff-child ratio should be very high—no more than five infants for two care givers.

A good infant-care center should meet all the physical, emotional, health, and safety needs of babies. Guidance should be positive. Punishing, scolding, or shaming should never be used.

Infants must be allowed to form a "primary attachment" to their parents. Substitute care for infants supports this most important relationship. Even good care givers cannot replace loving parents.

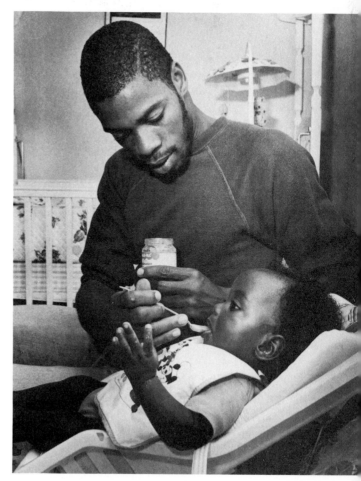

1. Is there an infant center for the group care of babies in your community? If so, visit the center. Then, write a report describing the center. Include answers to the following questions:
   a. How is the center licensed?
   b. What is the age range of the babies cared for in the center?
   c. How much are parents charged for the care of their babies?
   d. Are there any restrictions as to who may use the center? For example, is the center only for people who can afford to pay? Is it only for low-income parents?
   e. What is the ratio of babies to care givers?
   f. Does the center include male care givers? If so, what is the ratio of men to women? If not, why not?

2. Research family day care in your community. Based on what you learn, tell how you would respond to *one* of the following situations:
   a. You have a friend who is solely responsible for the care of his 9-month-old son. He wants to attend a trade school parttime and work parttime. Where, in your community, can he find satisfactory day care for his child?
   b. The single mother of an 8-month-old child dropped out of high school when she was in the eleventh grade. She realizes she now cannot get a good job without at least a high school diploma, but she has no one at home to care for her baby. What do you suggest she do?

3. Interview the parents of a baby under one year of age. Choose a family in which both the mother and father work at least parttime away from home.
   a. Who cares for their child when both parents are at work?
   b. How do they share in the at-home care of their child?
   c. Are both parents satisfied with their child-care arrangements, both at home and while they are working?

Activities for Infant Learning

Objectives

To emphasize the importance of development in the first year.

To give ways parents and care givers can help infants develop mentally, physically, socially, and emotionally.

To make some learning activities and games for infants.

Terms to look for   emotional development in infancy • mental development in infancy • physical development in infancy • social development in infancy

"Where's your nose, Jamie? Show me your nose. Put your finger on your nose. Yes, that's right, there's your nose. Jamie's nose." Mary used effective teaching techniques as she played the "Where's-your-nose?" game with 10-month-old Jamie. Mary held Jamie on her knees as she played this learning game with him.

This game was also a learning activity for Mary. She was learning to talk with the baby. She changed the question to try to help Jamie understand. She kept her eyes on Jamie's to keep the baby's

attention. Mary encouraged Jamie by nodding and smiling at him. She enjoyed the game with Jamie, because she knew from Jamie's response that the baby was enjoying the learning game.

Activities Enhance Development

Healthy babies are constantly learning. Parents and care givers must spend many hours in lessons and games, such as the one above. These activities help the baby grow in four developmental areas—mental, physical, social, and emotional. Can you identify these four kinds of learning in the story about Mary and Jamie?

A baby's *mental development* goes on constantly. The thought process is always working, since the brain controls all functions. All body movement stimulates motor control and *physical development*. *Social development*—liking and responding to people—is stimulated through all the friendliness, love, and encouragement other people show the baby. When a baby can begin to be sure of relationships and surroundings and react in an outgoing way, the baby is developing trust. As the baby feels safe enough to explore and try new things, *emotional development* is fostered.

Many experts agree that the first 3 years are the most important learning time of a person's life. Harvard psychologist Burton L. White expresses this view in his book, *The First Three Years of Life*. Obviously, this does not mean that children do not continue to learn and develop after they are 3 years old. As stated before, development can continue throughout life.

But a good foundation in the early years can give children the tools they will need to become competent and confident. Parents and care givers can begin laying this foundation when children are tiny infants.

Provide Eye Stimulation

When the baby is still a newborn, adults can provide eye interest by using printed sheets on the crib, changing the prints from time to time. When babies are able to open their hands, they may pull at the sheets, as if they are trying to pull off the printed figures.

Crib bumpers can also be gaily printed. Or plain white or clear bumpers can be purchased and then decorated with small cutouts of felt or colored poster board on the bumpers. Dr. White reported that babies respond most to the human face. So care givers can draw simple features on cut-out circles. Some babies will stare at these faces for long periods of time.

Provide Sound Stimulation

Since babies hear well, parents and care givers should talk and sing to them often.

You may remember lullabies you heard as a child. You may enjoy making

193

a list of all these quiet, restful songs that you and other classmates can think of. Quiet songs often come in handy in caring for babies. Changes of voice, tone, or tempo are excellent ways to get the attention of or to soothe a fussy baby.

After you have listed the old lullabies, try listing current popular songs that have a tune which might be useful with babies. Sometimes a peppy tune can be adapted to the splash of the bath water, for example. Make up your own baby-care songs, either with original tunes or by adapting tunes you know. Be creative. The babies will love it, and your care giver friends will soon be joining in.

Provide Movement Stimulation

Parents and care givers should encourage movement of the trunk, arms, and legs by frequently changing the baby's position in the bed or reclining seat. A baby who has gained head and neck control will enjoy being rolled over and playing leg and arm games. For instance, you can do pretend peddling with the baby's legs. And you can stretch the baby's arms out and back in a hugging motion. Such games should last only a few minutes. These activities can be done on the diapering table, in the bath, or on the floor. Most parents and care givers are comfortable getting down on the floor with a baby and letting the baby roll and tumble over them. A toy on the floor will attract the baby's attention and will encourage the baby to reach for and wriggle toward it.

Change the Scenery

Instead of leaving infants in their cribs most of the time, parents and care givers can move the babies from room to room, either in reclining infant seats or in chest carriers. This gives babies a change of scenery and more opportunity to be around adults. All four develop-

It doesn't matter whether you are musical or not, a baby will love to hear you sing.

mental areas—mental, physical, social, emotional—are stimulated when adults move babies from place to place.

Later, when babies are creeping and crawling, parents and care givers should follow all the babyproofing suggestions given previously. That will make it safe for babies to spend as much time as possible exploring. Babies who spend a lot of time in playpens do not have the opportunity to develop their curiosity.

Toys and Activities for Learning

As a baby-sitter or helper in an infant-care center, you can use the ideas mentioned above. Following are more suggestions of toys to make and activities to do with babies to stimulate their learning. You can try several activities. Compare notes with your classmates who try other activities. Also, see pages 286 and 287, "Making Toys for Babies and Toddlers."

Rattles

Rattles are good for getting a baby's attention. Before babies have outgrown their grasp reflex, they seem to like to shake their rattle when it is placed in their hand. Later on, when they can bring things to the mouth, they may also massage their gums with the rattle as they begin teething.

Study the different kinds of rattles and then make one. Remember, rattles should never have pieces inside or outside that would be dangerous for the baby if the rattle should accidentally come apart. Some edible cereals would be good to use inside a rattle.

Trips out into the world are important learning experiences for a baby. The chest carrier lets the baby travel in security and lets the parent use both hands.

A rattle is a good toy for testing a baby's hearing. See if the baby turns toward the sound when you shake the rattle on various sides of the crib.

Mobiles

Mobiles turning about are good for giving babies something to watch and to follow with their eyes while lying in their cribs. A mobile is made by suspending a set of pictures or objects on strings in a balanced arrangement so that the objects move and turn. This creates an effect of movement when the mobile is hung over the baby's crib. Some purchased mobiles have a windup music box attached.

195

While babies need a stimulating environment, the most interesting crib is no substitute for parents or care givers. Babies learn most through interaction with people.

Look at mobiles in a catalog or baby shop. Then, design one for use in a nursery. Be sure the mobile is hung out of the baby's reach if it is constructed of wire, string, or other materials that could be dangerous to an infant.

Cradle Gym

A set of plastic bracelets and a wooden ball or two can be attached to a heavy belting across the crib in the baby's view. This cradle gym should be either unpainted or painted with nontoxic paint. The baby will then have some-thing safe to reach for, to pull, to kick, and to look at. Babies soon learn that they can make the objects move by kicking. If a bell is attached, babies learn that they can make it ring. Investigate cradle gyms in a catalog or store, and make one that would be suitable and safe for a baby. Remember that every piece of an item to be handled and "tasted" by the baby must have rounded edges, have lead-free paint, and be too large for the baby to swallow.

Crawling Practice

Crawling is a motor skill that frees babies from spending all their time in one spot in the crib or playpen or on the floor. You can stimulate a baby's desire to crawl by holding an attractive toy a short distance away from the baby. For example, a baby might crawl to you if you hold out a bright ball and say, "Come. Get the ball."

Parents often enjoy allowing the infant to crawl over them while they lie on the floor or bed. This is a favorite activity for babies as they gain stability and begin to pull up to a standing position. A baby's motivation can be increased if the adult shows the baby a favorite toy, hides it, and encourages the baby to crawl about to find it. Such a game not only gives the baby crawling practice but stimulates social and emotional learning as well.

Ball Game

A first-stage ball game can consist of rolling a large ball to the baby who is sitting on the floor with legs apart. Show the baby how to roll the ball toward another person, too.

Choo-choo Box

For babies who are just starting to step around, holding onto furniture or the sides of the crib or playpen, a "choo-choo" box is a good toy. Use a cardboard box about 18″ × 14″ × 14″, and put a heavy catalog or two inside. The baby can pull up to the box and then push it along the floor, using the sides for support. Perhaps the baby will also enjoy getting into the box and sitting in the snug place it offers. To start the game, stand in front of the baby who is holding on to the box. Say, "Come here. Push the choo-choo."

The choo-choo box provides good preparation for walking. Walking practice can also be encouraged by giving the baby a toy, such as a ball, and then saying, "Bring me the ball." At first, be sure to squat low in front of the baby, only a step or so away. The baby will enjoy bringing you the ball and using your hands to maintain balance.

Blocks

Infants enjoy small blocks they can grasp in their small hands. You can make 1-inch cubes by carefully sawing them from pieces of 1-inch wooden strips available at a lumber supply store. Sand the cubes until smooth. You can encourage the baby to pick up a block and release it into your hand or into a plastic cup. Hold out your hand expectantly as you say, "Give me the block, Karen."

Teach a baby one step at a time, starting with the easiest task. Minimize mistakes by showing the right way and by having the child try again. Praise both attempts and successes.

Encourage her to put the blocks into a container. Later on, when her muscle control is further developed, Karen can learn to build a tower and a bridge.

Ring Pull-toy

Tie a string around one of the baby's toys. Attach a bracelet or embroidery hoop to the other end of the string. This toy enables you to teach the baby that a desired object may be secured indirectly. Place the bracelet in the baby's hands. Then place the toy at a distance and direct the baby's attention to it. Wiggle the string several times to show that you want the baby to pull the string. Smile and praise the baby for success. If there is no success, put the toy away. Wait for another day when the baby may be mature enough to understand and use it.

Touching Book

A book with familiar objects to touch and play with is popular with babies. You can make such a book, using your own imagination. Make the pages with a firm muslin fabric. Put two thicknesses together for a page. Then sew several pages together on the sewing machine or by hand with heavy yarn. Sew on appliqués of different figures, such as a cat of fake fur, a ball or shoes of plastic material, a large zipper with a ring, and so forth. The book can have words or not, as you wish. A poem for each page would be nice.

As you and a baby "read" the book, you can say, "Pat the kitty." "Show me the ball," and so on. Keep the reading sessions short, adding more books with familiar pictures as the baby shows interest.

? Decisions, Decisions

Buffy, who is 5 months old, does not seem to have very good hand-eye coordination. She finds it hard to locate and grasp objects. If you were her care giver, how might you help her?

Horsey Ride

The baby of 9 to 12 months old whose back is strong and head stabilized may like to play a "horsey" game. Bounce the baby gently on your knee or lower leg as you hold the baby's hands securely. Perhaps you can match the jogging with a poem like

Trot, trot to Boston,
Trot, trot to Maine,
Trot, trot to Providence,
And b-a-c-k again.

A baby who is not fearful may like to lean way back when you say "back again." Another poem that goes well with this game is

This is the way the baby rides
A gallop a trot
A gallop a trot
This is the way the baby rides
Early in the morning.

Concluding Comments

An infant's learning activity is difficult to classify as only mental, or only physical, or only social, or only emotional. Each learning activity has aspects of two, three, or even four of these areas of development. Every baby needs other people to spend time with him or her,

Babies do not need expensive toys. This baby's rich environment
was created by his older sister—free of charge.

talking and doing interesting things that will stimulate the growth of the human potential that lies within. Watching babies convinces most observers that babies strive to grow and develop. They actively respond to attention. They smile, coo, reach, and curl their toes.

Many experts now believe that the first 3 years are the most important time for children to learn. Parents and care givers can foster this development by stimulating babies' senses and providing many different kinds of activities and experiences for them.

Activities

1. Play at least one game with a baby. Choose one of the activities described in this chapter, in another reference, or one you make up yourself. Report on the activity, either in writing or orally.

2. Make a toy for an infant. Again, choose from the toys described in this chapter, in another reference, or create your own. Describe how the toy will help the baby develop mentally, socially, physically, or emotionally. (Your toy may help the infant develop in several ways.)

3. Read about the first year of development in *The First Three Years of Life* by Burton L. White. Report on White's suggestions concerning appropriate toys for babies under one year of age.

SUGGESTED READINGS FOR PART 3

Brazelton, T. Berry, *Infants and Mothers: Differences in Development.* New York: Dell Publishing Company, 1969.

Comer, James P. and Alvin F. Poussaint, *Black Child Care.* New York: Pocket Books, 1976.

Dodson, Fitzhugh, *How to Parent.* New York: The New American Library, Inc., 1973.

Dodson, Fitzhugh, *How to Parent.* New York: The New American Library, Inc., 1970.

Keister, Mary Elizabeth, *"The Good Life" for Infants and Toddlers.* Washington, DC: National Association for the Education of Young Children, 1834 Connecticut Avenue, N.W., Washington, DC 20009, 1970.

Leach, Penelope, *Your Baby and Child from Birth to Age Five.* New York: Alfred A. Knopf, 1978.

Olness, Karen, M.D., *Raising Happy Healthy Children.* Wayzata, MN 55391: Meadowbrook Press, 1977.

Parents' Guide to Childhood Immunization. U.S. Department of Health, Education, and Welfare, No. (OS) 77-50058, U.S. Printing Office, Washington, DC 20402.

Rozdilsky, M.L., and Banet, B., *What Now? A Handbook for New Parents.* New York: Charles Scribner's Sons, 1975.

Spock, Benjamin, *Baby and Child Care.* New York: Pocket Books, 1976.

White, Burton L., *The First Three Years of Life.* Englewood Cliffs, New Jersey: Prentice-Hall, 1975.

Willis, Anne and Henry Ricciuti, *A Good Beginning for Babies: Guidelines for Group Care.* Washington, DC: National Association for the Education of Young Children, 1975. (Address of NAEYC above)

Your Child from 1 to 6. Children's Bureau Publication, No. 30-1962. U.S. Government Printing Office, Washington, DC 20402.

4

The Toddler

You will learn how toddlers grow and develop physically, mentally, emotionally, and socially. You will discover ways to care for, guide, and teach toddlers. You will also discover a variety of activities for toddlers that will aid the development of their physical, mental, emotional, and social skills.

unit

8

The Growing and Developing Toddler

The Toddler Grows Physically

Objectives

To explain the physical growth and development in toddlers during the first to third years.

To explain how physical growth and development affect the way parenting persons deal with toddlers as compared with infants.

Terms to look for   average • baby teeth • deciduous teeth • milk teeth • toilet training

"Mother, Ginny is walking now," Jay told his mother over long-distance telephone one Sunday night in December. "She's been pulling up to everything for quite a while. Nothing is safe now if it's within her reach. The other night, Glenda said to Ginny, 'Come to Mommy,' and Ginny took her very first steps alone toward Glenda. We were both very excited. After Ginny's first steps, Glenda turned her around, and she walked two more steps to me. Ginny had a great big smile. She knew she'd done something special. I'm so glad you can come here during the holidays so you and Dad can see her," concluded Jay.

Milestones to Remember

There are many milestones to record of a baby's physical development. The date a baby first walks is one of the most important.

Parents should encourage walking and be around to help. But they should not try to protect the child from every little spill.

Walking

The baby, a girl for example, becomes a toddler when she begins walking. For some weeks before the baby starts walking, you will notice that she uses the legs and feet to reach for the floor. She likes to be held so that she can put her weight on the floor. If she is sitting in a stroller, she may try to stand up in it. She pulls up to the side of her crib or playpen and cruises around the edge. She needs lots of courage to let go and to step out on her own. She may cruise around for a month or so. Usually, if she lets go, she just plops down on her diapered seat and does not really hurt herself. Parents and care givers can help the toddler laugh about these little falls rather than teach her to "be careful."

Recalling that babies develop in a head-to-toe direction, you will understand why the baby, a boy for example, must gain control of his head and trunk before he gains control of his feet. A baby's head is large relative to the size of the trunk, legs, and feet. It takes a year for control of legs and feet to develop.

Research done by Nancy Bayley shows that 88 of 100 babies begin walking alone between 11½ and 15½ months. Therefore, 88 percent become toddlers between 11½ and 15½ months.

Though most babies walk between 11½ and 15½ months, 12 out of 100, or 12 percent, walk either before 11½ months or after 15½ months. Some may walk as early as 9 or 10 months; others, as late as 18 months. You must remember how particular averages are calculated whenever you hear about the *average*, *normal*, or *typical* baby. Here is one example to help you understand a simple average. Suppose there are 3 babies in a neighborhood. One walks at 9 months, one at 14 months, and one at 13 months. The total number of months is 36. If you divide 36 months by 3 (the number of toddlers), you get 12 months, which is the average age of walking for the 3 toddlers. You will note that no child was exactly average. Yet to refer to the average age is often convenient and helpful.

Walking is a locomotor skill—one of several ways the child can move the body through space. A child learns to walk before learning to run, hop, skip, and so on. Parents and care givers should encourage walking practice so that these later skills will develop properly. In the opening story, Jay and Glenda were encouraging Ginny to walk.

Toddlers need room to practice walking. Some couples living in small apartments take their toddlers to shopping malls where the toddlers can practice walking in the long halls. Here, they are safe from cars, have interesting things to see, and do not have to have their hands held continuously. In toddler centers, large areas are kept uncluttered so toddlers can walk without help.

Climbing gives the toddler new vistas. The toddler can get up on sofas and chairs and go up and down stairs. Most 2- to 3-year-olds—and often children of 18 months or younger—can manage to climb out of their cribs. Parents and care givers must be alert to this possibility and protect the safety of the toddler. Toddler safety will be further discussed in Chapter 24.

Height and Weight

By 1 year old, the baby has grown from about 20 inches at birth to about 30 inches tall. At age 2, the toddler is about 32 to 34 inches tall; at age 3, about 35 to 37 inches tall. Growing 3 inches during a baby's third year is a much slower growth rate—about 10 percent—compared with a 50 percent increase during the baby's first year of life.

The year-old toddler has usually tripled birth weight, weighing about 21 pounds compared to about 7 pounds at birth. The toddler usually gains 3 to 5 pounds from ages 1 to 2, and 3 to 5 pounds from ages 2 to 3, reaching a weight of 27 to 31 pounds by age 3.

It is important for parents and care givers to understand and remember this slower growth rate. A toddler eats less often and in smaller amounts than when he or she was an infant. This often worries adults, who may start pushing the toddler to eat more. The fights that may erupt are unfortunate for both. Excessive pressure causes tensions, which disturb appetite and digestion.

Remember, when you compare infants or toddlers, a few months difference in age represents significant growth and development. Instead of comparing their toddler's growth with the growth of a neighbor's toddler, parents should view their toddler's growth in light of the child's own growth record. Such records should be kept by parents and doctors. The genetic factors that each child inherits will influence growth figures.

Growth of Head, Trunk, Arms, and Legs

Several physical growth changes take place that redistribute the toddler's weight. This gives the child more balance than before.

After birth, the head grows less than most other parts of the body. Compared with the changes that occur in the trunk, arms, and legs, changes in the head size are small during the toddler period. The toddler's trunk, arms, and legs all grow longer. This lengthening redistributes the child's weight and makes the toddler seem less top-heavy.

Hands and feet are short and stubby during the toddler period. Use of hands and fingers gradually increases for the

During the toddler period, trunk, arms, and legs grow longer. During this "into-everything stage," the toddler needs supervision much of the time.

toddler. First, a full-fist grasp is used. Later, the thumb and fingers become able to pick up toys or food—usually bringing the object to the mouth. Apparently, this is a learning technique during which the toddler needs some supervision for safety.

Toddlers should walk barefoot as much as possible. This helps strengthen their feet and arches. When floors are too cold, or when toddlers are outside in cold weather, they should wear shoes with flexible soles. They should not wear stiff-soled shoes. Stiff-soled shoes can actually hinder their walking efforts. Most pediatricians now agree that sneakers are fine for early walkers, as long as they do not make the child's feet perspire too much.

Teeth

The appearance of first teeth is another physical milestone. The baby usually has 4 to 6 teeth by age 1. During the toddler period, the set of 20 teeth will come in. Some of these tooth eruptions may mean much discomfort for the toddler. "He's cutting teeth" or "She's teething" are frequent explanations of a toddler's fussiness. Teething toddlers require more patience than usual from parents and care givers. Fever, digestive disturbances, and other ailments that might be blamed on "teething" should be discussed with the doctor.

The teeth of infants, toddlers, and preschoolers are called *baby teeth, milk teeth*, or *deciduous teeth*. They stay only a few years before they fall out and are replaced by permanent teeth. Although they are temporary, these baby teeth serve three important functions: 1) They promote good nutrition, helping the child move from a liquid to a solid diet. The child can now bite and can later chew. 2) Baby teeth help shape the jaw as they come in. The child needs matching upper and lower teeth for the best chewing and for a good appearance. 3) If they are properly placed, baby teeth help a child to pronounce words correctly. For these reasons, dentists attempt to save the baby teeth as often as possible, even when costly fillings are required.

Teething toddlers like to chew and to put things into their mouths. Parents and care givers should provide rubber teething rings. Then the toddler can do all the chewing needed.

Dentists recommend that toddlers begin brushing their teeth by age 2. This helps set the habit as an important one. Brushing cleans decay-causing food from the teeth. Nighttime brushing is particularly important. Children can and should be encouraged to play at brushing their teeth. But they will not be able to do it properly for a long time. Parents will have to brush the child's teeth for several years.

Baby teeth are important. Dentists recommend that toddlers begin brushing their teeth by age 2.

Thumb-sucking has long been believed to damage a child's tooth placement. But many doctors now disagree with this view. A child who is a thumb sucker at the toddler age probably began the habit as an infant. Trying to break a toddler of thumb sucking by shaming, punishing, or painting bad-tasting substances on the thumb probably will not work and can be emotionally damaging.

Parents should not rush toilet training. They should wait at least until the child can master walking. Then these two difficult muscular skills will not have to be mastered at the same time.

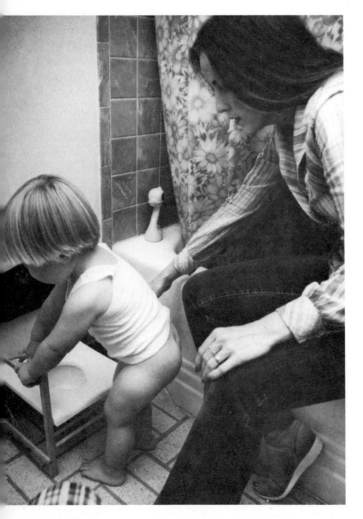

Toilet Training

Toilet training requires quite advanced physical development. Muscles in the bowel and bladder regions must be mature enough for the child to open and close them at will. This control does not come until after the child sits, stands, and walks well. Trying to toilet-train toddlers before they are mature enough often causes problems such as bedwetting later on.

Toilet training should start when the child begins to show an interest in toileting and in being dry—perhaps around 2 to 2½ years of age. A child should be able to walk into the bathroom and sit on a low toilet seat. Or the child should be able to climb a step stool to a special seat on the adult toilet. At this stage of physical development, the child will want to imitate parents and other children.

Some toddlers will prefer to use a little seat on an adult toilet, because it is more "grown-up." Other toddlers are more comfortable on a low toilet seat. Some children may even be afraid of falling into the adult toilet. A child's attitude may change from one day to the next. No toddler should ever be forced screaming onto an adult toilet. Some toddlers worry about the flushing noise of the toilet. Others do not like to see the feces disappear. When these things bother a child, a wise parent or care giver takes care of them later when the child is busy elsewhere.

Learning to control the bowel and bladder will take a year or more—to about age 2½ or 3. Therefore, parents and care givers must be prepared to help the toddler take many steps toward

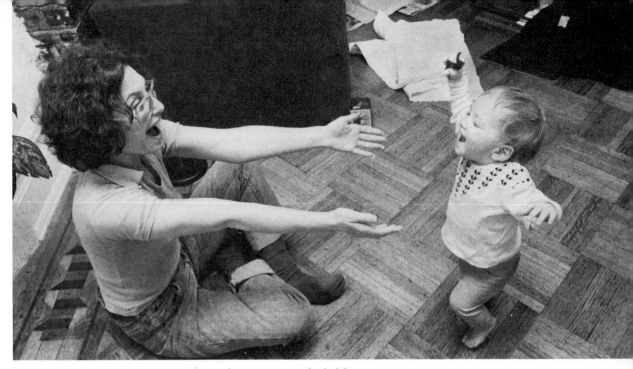

Becoming independent is exciting for parent and child.

this control. The toddler must want control. Toddlers will want it unless someone makes them very fearful and miserable. Parents and care givers should never punish, shame, or scold a child for failures. Warm approval and praise for success is far better in the long run.

Having the toddler wear training pants helps some children realize what is happening as they urinate. However, diapers should be used at bedtime and in public places, where wet pants on a child would be embarrassing and inconvenient for the parents.

Nighttime dryness generally takes longer to achieve than daytime training. Although most children are dry at night by age 3, many are not. Boys are frequently later than girls. Wetting at night should not be considered a problem unless the pediatrician feels it is. The best advice for parents is just to wait.

One morning, the child will wake up dry. Total dryness will come soon after, with an accident only from time to time.

? Decisions, Decisions

Craig started to walk at 12 months. About 1 week after his first unaided steps, he fell down hard and hit his head. He has not tried to walk again for several days. Should his parents and care giver try to get him walking again so he will not become afraid? Or should they do nothing?

Concluding Comments

The toddler period is an important one for physical growth and development. Several milestones are marked, such as first walking, many efforts at self-help, and increased movement in the environment. Physical development and growth are closely related to social, mental, and emotional development. Parents and care givers should let toddlers decide when they are ready for toilet training. In this way, toilet training will most likely succeed and will create the fewest problems for the child's future years.

? Decisions, Decisions

"I don't know what to do," said one mother. "Some pediatricians and books say to leave Page barefoot or let her wear sneakers. Others say that toddlers need shoes with good support. I want Page to have the best start. It seems that I can do something for her by buying those expensive walking shoes." What do you think?

Activities

1. Ask your parents the following questions, and then share their answers with the class:
   a. At what age did you first walk?
   b. What were your weight and height at one year of age?
   c. When did you get your first tooth?
2. Bring a picture of yourself to class taken when you were a toddler. Help create a bulletin board, using your picture and those of your classmates.
3. Talk to a parent of several small children. Get as much of the following information as possible:

   a. Age at which each child began to walk.
   b. Each child's weight and length at birth.
   c. Each child's weight and height at one year of age.
   d. Each child's weight and height at two years of age.
   e. Number of teeth each child had at one year of age.
4. Write a report in which you discuss this family's physical development. Did the children all develop at about the same rate? Or were they quite different, for example, with one being heavy and another thin?

22

The Toddler Develops Emotionally and Socially

Objectives

To explain the roles that emotions and social development play in personality development.

To explain how toddlers' emotions affect the way they view themselves.

To describe the social interactions of toddlers.

To explain what parenting persons can do to foster positive emotional and social development in toddlers.

Terms to look for   emotion • emotional problems • happiness • negative self-concept • parallel play • personality • positive self-concept • solitary play • social interaction • temper tantrum

"Good morning, Marty," smiles Dan, the care giver, as Marty's father brings him into the children's room. Marty, 2 years old, smiles back, but does not answer.

"Okay, Marty," says his father, as he takes off Marty's coat. "I'm going to meet Mom now. You can stay and play with the other kids until we come back for you." Although Marty has been coming to the children's room for several weeks, he bursts into tears, crying, "Don't go, Daddy." His father kisses him matter-of-factly and hands him over to Dan.

About 30 seconds after his father leaves, Marty is smiling again and chattering to Dan. Dan talks to him for a few moments, then puts him down. Marty races for the sandbox. When his parents come for him an hour later, he is busily pushing a truck around the room. He protests loudly when told it is time to go home. But when he sees the other children's parents coming to pick them up, he lets his mother help him with his coat. Then he waves good-bye and trots happily out the door.

Marty's behavior is typical of many toddlers. Although he does not want his parents to leave, he is obviously happy and comfortable in the care of another adult. This shows that he has been in many pleasant social situations. He is confident and independent with adults other than his own parents.

Children begin to have different personality traits as early as infancy. They learn many new patterns of emotional and social behavior during the toddler stage. This emotional and social growth adds to the uniqueness of each child's personality.

Happiness: A Goal of Parents

What would you say if you were asked, "What do you want most for your child?" Most parents would say, "I want my child to be happy."

Toddlers are no longer babies and not yet children. They can be a delight and they can be hard to handle.

Happiness is a feeling, or an emotion that includes joyful feelings. A happy child is one who expresses enthusiasm, yet is calm and self-confident. To be happy does not require bubbly laughter at all times. In fact, such behavior is clearly too tiring to be the whole of happiness.

What is desirable is an emotional balance. All children will feel unhappiness at times. The strength they feel from being loved and protected will help them recover from unhappy experiences and return to a state of happiness.

Positive Self-Concept

The goal of developing a positive self-concept continues into the toddler stage and on through life. During the toddler stage, many events help children decide that they are good, strong, capable, and loved. These feelings are typical of a child with a *positive self-concept*. If children's failures or shortcomings are stressed, they may decide they are bad, weak, incapable, and unloved. These are the feelings of a child with a *negative self-concept*.

Toddlers are in a tumbling, bungling age. These babies are just starting to reach out to people and things. They often bump into things and knock them around. Parents and care givers must clearly understand that children's bumping and breaking are not intentional but the result of immaturity. Toddlers are still too immature to understand the effects of what they do. Even if they could understand, they are too young to control themselves. Therefore, serious damage to children's self-concept results if they are punished for doing things that toddlers naturally do.

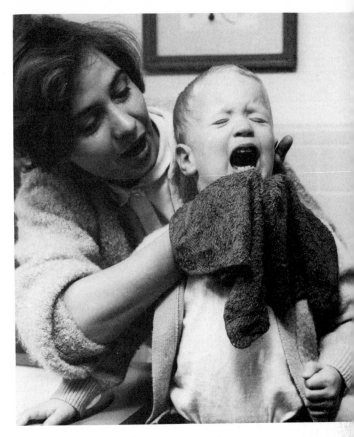

Toddlers want to do things on their own. They often dislike adult attempts to "help out."

Independence

Developing independence is a goal for toddlers, as it is for people throughout life. Toddlers gradually move away from being totally dependent on others as they were in infancy. Now they can put their own crackers into their mouths, climb into high chairs, pull off their socks, and do dozens of other tasks for themselves.

A toddler's drive toward independence may be strong one day and may cool the next. Parents and care givers

213

must be flexible. They should let toddlers help when they feel like it. They can reward the toddlers with smiles and words of praise for the positive efforts the children make. There is real joy for the child who feels successfully independent.

No is an early word toddlers use that signals their striving for independence. After they know the word *no*, they find they can control a little bit of the action. If parents ask, "Do you want to eat?" even a hungry toddler may answer, "No." This is part of the drive for independence. Parents and care givers

Having a tantrum is like blowing an emotional fuse. Parents can help by staying calm and holding the child until the anger drains away.

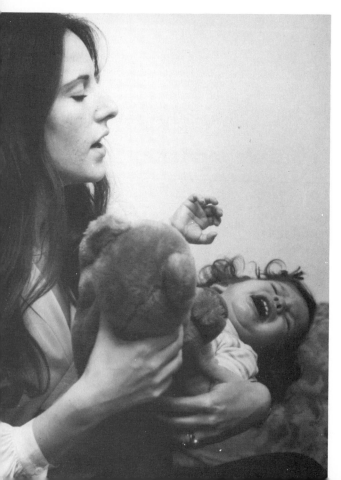

should be careful not to offer choices if there really are not any. "It's time for lunch now" will cause less conflict.

Parent Feelings

Parents often have mixed feelings about their toddlers' new striving for independence. Parents and care givers may be relieved at not having a helpless baby on their hands anymore. But sometimes they also feel some sadness at losing a little of the closeness they had with the baby. Also, living with someone who constantly says "no" can be very frustrating and tiring. This is a time when parents should try hard to have some time for themselves and for each other, away from the toddler.

Temper Tantrums

Temper tantrums may begin when children find they can say "no" or when they feel their wishes are not met. Adults need to be cool and objective to keep temper tantrums from growing in number and intensity. Generally, the best method is for parents and care givers simply to restate the decision, as calmly and quietly as possible. Say, "No, you can't play with the vase." Then put the vase away. The adult should keep busy at a distance until the child's noise begins to subside. Then the adult can say, "We'll find a toy to play with when you are ready." This helps the child know that the adult is not rejecting her or him but refuses to be part of the tantrum.

Some children may need to be held and comforted as the tantrum begins to wear down. Tantrums are hard on children, too, even though these tantrums sometimes help them let off steam. A

Things that are ordinary and harmless to you may seem strange and horrible to a toddler. These fears must be respected and gently changed over time.

child who has gone past the point of kicking and screaming and who is throwing toys or trying to damage things must be physically restrained. The adult should do this as gently as possible, perhaps continuing to talk to the child in a low, reassuring voice.

Some angry children will hold their breath until they actually turn blue in the face. This is a trait that has been observed in newborn infants. It does not mean the child is "bad." It is simply that child's way of expressing anger. No harm will result from the child's doing this. The adult should ignore it and follow the same steps as for dealing with other displays of temper.

Above all, adults should avoid losing their own tempers or shouting. This will

only make the tantrum worse. And it will teach children that they can, indeed, get attention by throwing tantrums.

Fear

As the toddler, a girl for instance, moves out into the world, she will meet people, animals, and things that may cause her to experience fear. Fears are a protective emotion—so the child will quickly seek her parents or the teacher. The adult should protect and comfort her when this occurs, rather than admonish her. For example, if fear of a cat persists, the parents can help their daughter overcome the fear through some pleasant associations. First the child can see cats at a distance, then closer and closer. She can see other people she knows petting cats. As the toddler realizes that most cats are harmless, she may agree to pet one. Liking a cat is not the most important goal here. It is overcoming unnecessary fear of strange objects or creatures that is important.

Many other fears may surface at this age. Some of them may seem totally unreasonable to the adult who does not understand toddlers' mental processes. For example, many toddlers develop a fear of the bathtub at this age. One night, they play happily in the bath. The next night, they scream and stiffen when the parent tries to bathe them.

Dr. Jean Piaget and others have discovered that children, at a certain point in the toddler stage (perhaps 18 to 27 months), do not understand *relative size*. That is, they truly believe they can go down the bathtub drain and disappear, just as the water does.

Sam, who is 18 months old, demonstrated such a fear. He suddenly became terrified of the bathtub. For several weeks, his parents gave him sponge baths. When his hair had to be washed, one parent would hold him so that the other could wash his hair. One night, he finally consented to be put in the bathtub. He seemed to enjoy his bath. But when his father said, "time to get out now," Sam quickly threw all his toys over the side of the tub. Then he jumped out as fast as he could. He was taking no chances!

Parents and care givers should understand that such fears are normal and are not "bad" behavior on a child's part. Understanding this, they can comfort children and help them get through this fearful stage.

Giving and Receiving Affection

During toddlerhood, children begin giving as well as receiving love and affection. Giving and receiving love and affection need to continue throughout each person's life.

Toddlers clearly respond to their parents and important care givers to whom they have become attached during infancy. The toddlers respond warmly and lovingly to the adults' love and affection. Then the adults reciprocate warmly and lovingly to the toddlers. The toddlers will have trouble if they have too many different care givers in their small world. Children need consistency to know whom to love.

Separation from a loved one is quite painful for toddlers. They do not yet understand that the parent, for example, still exists even though the parent is out of sight. The toddlers may cry bitterly. Teachers observe this sort of trauma in toddler centers many times each week. Distracting toddlers with a special toy or activity can help them get over being upset at separating from a parent.

Toddlers are learning to give affection. They need to form attachments to a few people who are a regular part of their lives.

Infants and toddlers can be taught to give and to receive affection. The amount of hugs and kisses that everyone uses in giving affection varies from family to family. Whatever the family custom might be, the toddlers can begin to learn the custom at this time. For example, parents can say, "Kiss the dolly," "Kiss Daddy," or "Give Mommy a big hug."

Emotional Problems

Emotional problems for a toddler are often caused by other people's unrealistic expectations of the child. Too often, something is expected that the toddler is not capable of—such as being quiet, not getting into things, or eating without making a mess. Also, some emotional problems are caused by inconsistent treatment from parents. For example, a parent may say it is all right for a toddler to play with Daddy's pipe one time, but reprimand the child for playing with it another time. Or a parent may smile at the toddler splashing bathwater one morning, but scold the child for splashing the next morning. This treatment leaves the child thoroughly confused. It can cause emotional difficulties. Some of these problems are the result of the home's being poorly arranged for the toddler. Perhaps there are too many things that the child is forbidden to touch or too few toys right for the child's age.

Tiredness and hunger are probably the two main causes of emotional outbursts. Parents and care givers who want children to be happy will try to keep them rested and well fed. Late bedtimes, late mealtimes, and long shopping trips can all add to emotional instability in young children.

Surprise or sudden action may trigger emotional outbursts in young children. It is good to move slowly and to bring in new people or things gradually, even leaving them at some distance while the toddler gets used to their presence.

Crying and occasional emotional outbursts do not mean that a child has emotional problems. Part of growing up is learning to deal with frustration. Crying is a normal, healthy way for a toddler (or an adult) to relieve feelings of frustration or sadness. Children's need to do this kind of crying varies with their temperaments. The child who seems to be unhappy much of the time is the one about whom adults should be concerned.

Alert and careful parents and care givers can set the stage for healthy emotional development. They can study the situation for clues when the child seems unhappy. Frequently, the problems can be lessened or removed through changes in the environment—either home or school—and changes in the people involved with the toddler.

? Decisions, Decisions

"I don't like to take Debbie anywhere now," said her father. "She's defiant at home, and we can handle that. But in a store or at a friend's house, she almost always acts terribly. She crys or refuses to walk. It's embarrassing." What might be happening? What would help?

Social Development

Social development refers to the child's ability to interact with people. Contact with people increases as the infant grows to be a toddler. More people and places are in the toddler's world. The child goes to see relatives, to visit the shopping center, and perhaps even to stay at a toddler center. All these places have people—strange faces and familiar faces. The social goal for the toddler is for the child to like and trust people and for people to like the child. Learning the give-and-take of social interaction is a goal during the toddler period as well as during school years and throughout life. For example, you, as a high school student, are making friends and learning new ways to deal with people in order to make your life more satisfying. The toddler is just getting started on this ladder of social development.

The family, and perhaps a toddler center, are the main social environments for the toddler. The home and family affect the toddler. And the toddler affects the home and family. The larger the family, the more social interactions the toddler will experience. Now the child notices people, toddles over to be near them, and coos and laughs when picked up or when jiggled on someone's knee.

Toddlers enjoy being around other toddlers. Their eyes light up when they see a friend coming. They play independently of each other, even though they obviously like to have others around. When children of several ages are in a room, the toddler will often watch another toddler.

Toddlers are aware of and sometimes afraid of strangers. When a relative arrives who has not seen the toddler recently, the relative is well advised to keep at a distance and let the toddler make the first move. Too fast an approach will send the toddler scurrying for a parent.

Toddlers are usually overwhelmed by large numbers of people. Groups should be kept small. Usually, one or two other toddlers is enough for a play group—or a birthday party. In toddler centers, specialists advise that groups be kept to four or five toddlers. One person should be the consistent care giver for each group.

Ability to talk helps form social relationships during the toddler period. You cannot ask someone to play, offer an idea for play, or disagree peacefully when you cannot talk.

Toddlers do not realize that their physical actions can hurt. Hitting, biting, and pushing may be the only way toddlers can show how they feel.

During the first year or so, the baby responds to some words of older people, for example, "Come here," "Put it down," "Give it to me." Next, the baby uses words for "mommy" and "daddy." Toddlers will use words for many familiar objects. They will also put combinations of two or three words together, such as, "Daddy go," or "Mary's cup." By age 3, most children can use sentences to express their needs. Remember, until word language develops, the only toddler language for saying "hello" to another toddler, for example, might be a push or snatching a toy.

Play time brings toddlers together with other children. A lot of social give-and-take is required in play situations.

Children watch each other, then imitate the behavior they see. They exchange toys and may quarrel over a single toy. At this stage, their play is not planned. One play episode does not last very long. *Solitary play* occurs when the child ignores others during play. *Parallel play* develops as toddlers move closer to other children, yet still play their own games.

Concluding Comments

Toddlers are growing and developing both emotionally and socially. The toddler stage can be difficult and frustrating for toddlers and parents alike. Toddlers try to gain independence. They often bump into people and things as they strive to control their environment. They can be grown-up and independent one minute and clinging babies the next. Effective parents and care givers will try to make positive, happy emotions outweigh negative, unhappy ones during the toddler years. At this age, the child is learning habits of responding that add to her or his unique personality.

Toddlers are reaching out socially. They enjoy the company of others, yet their lack of language skills prevents much social exchange. Solitary play is typical of the youngest toddlers. They begin parallel play as they notice other children and have opportunities to be with them.

Activities

1. Observe and, if possible, care for a toddler for an entire day. Keep a record of the child's behavior. (You may wish to combine this assignment with the first activity suggested at the end of the next chapter.)

   a. Does "your" toddler appear to be gaining a positive self-concept? Explain.

   b. "Toddlers are in a tumbling, bungling age." Describe several actions of the toddler that illustrate this sentence.

   c. Did the child have a temper tantrum while you were there? If so, how did you deal with it? If not, ask the parents if the child occasionally has tantrums and how they deal with such incidents.

   d. Does the toddler give and receive affection easily? How?

   e. Were you and any other care giver *consistent* in your interactions with the child? Explain your answer.

2. Interview the parents of the toddler:

   a. Ask them about their child's growth toward independence. Do they find the toddler quite independent one day, then very dependent the next? Give examples.

   b. Ask them about their child's fears and how they help deal with these fears.

3. Write an essay describing how a parent or care giver can help a toddler learn to be independent.

The Toddler Develops Mentally

Objectives

To explain how parents and teachers can know that toddlers are growing and developing mentally.

To explain how parents and teachers can foster mental development in toddlers.

To explain the relationship of mental development to sensory development.

Terms to look for   egocentric • object permanency • perceived and perception • positive feedback • productive language • recall • receptive language • sensorimotor stage • stimulus and stimulation • vocabulary

"Spoon. Ball. Milk. Shoes," says 2-year-old Becky, pointing to pictures in a book with cardboard pages. She cuddles against her mother's arm as they hold the picture book before them.

"That's right," says Marilyn, Becky's mother. "Yes. Good, Becky," she continues as they turn the pages and Becky labels each object. When a lamb appears, Becky does not seem to remember, so Marilyn says, "It's a lamb, Becky.

It says, 'Baa, baa.' " Becky looks up at Marilyn and says, "Ba."

Marilyn knows that Becky does not remember seeing a lamb. So she and her husband will take her to the zoo.

Labeling Is Evidence of Mental Ability

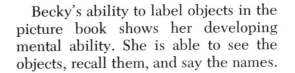

Becky's ability to label objects in the picture book shows her developing mental ability. She is able to see the objects, recall them, and say the names.

Marilyn and Jack have been reading to Becky for quite a while. Becky liked to look at the pictures when she was barely old enough to sit up. From that time on, Marilyn and Jack have pointed out the objects pictured, and they have labeled each object. Becky sometimes imitated the parents' pointing and babbled a sound in return. Now Becky has several books that she regularly brings to her parents to read.

Brain Development

Before birth and for 2 years after birth, the brain grows in size very rapidly. The portion of the brain controlling motor coordination and balance develops earlier and faster than other sections of the brain. A nutritious diet, stimulation of the mind and senses, and freedom from serious head injuries during and after birth are necessary for the brain to grow normally.

Functions of the Brain

Thinking and knowing are functions of the brain. The development and use of the brain are more highly advanced in human beings than in any other species. Mental development, intellectual development, and cognitive development are three phrases that mean the same thing. They are commonly used to refer to the growth of the thinking and knowing processes of the brain.

Brain Stimulation

From early infancy, Becky's brain has been bombarded with stimuli (the word *stimulus* is the singular form). These stimuli are received by one or more of her five sensory areas: eyes, ears, skin, tongue, and nose. The information received through sight, sound, touch, taste, and smell is recorded and stored in the brain. The brain is far more complex than the computers we have today.

The ability to see objects, remember them, and say their names is proof of developing mental ability.

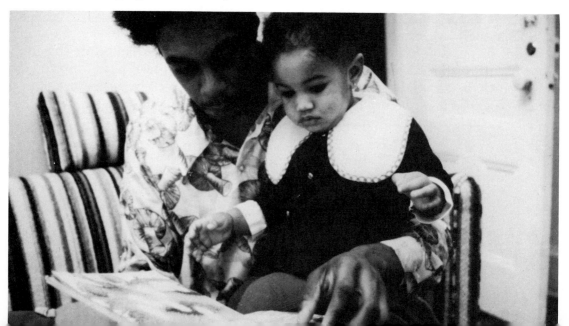

As Becky held the book, each picture served as a stimulus which her eyes perceived, or saw. Messages went automatically to her brain. Stored in her brain were words for the objects she saw. Through *recall*, Becky remembered the stored words. Through brain messages to the vocal cords, mouth, and tongue, she was able to say words to name the objects.

Becky's mother offered *stimulation* by showing Becky pictures and teaching her words that caused her to think, to know, and to learn. Becky perceived, or heard, her mother's words with her ears. Her ears sent messages to her brain.

Becky had had firsthand experience with most of the items pictured in the book. For example, she had seen, heard, held, tasted, and smelled various items. These sensory experiences had helped her to understand the objects far better than just seeing pictures would ever help her know them.

Sensorimotor Stage

Jean Piaget, a Swiss child psychologist, calls the child's ability to think during the first 2 years the *sensorimotor stage* of intellectual development. *Sensori-*, of course, refers to the five senses. *Motor* refers to the physical handling of objects. The toddler will move objects to the mouth, lift them, throw them, drop them, and so forth.

The child develops mental abilities by handling objects and by using all the senses to investigate things in the environment. These developing mental abilities help the child figure out new things to do with objects and new ways to think about them. Dr. Piaget developed these ideas by carefully watching his own children learn.

Children learn through all their senses. This child might smell the goat, feel its coat, and hear it make noise. These stimuli will help the child to recall the label "goat."

During these toddler years, children learn that objects continue to exist even when they are out of sight. This is called *object permanency*. For example, the toddler begins to understand that Father still exists, though he is not in the room or in the building. Toddlers also begin to realize that space exists beyond themselves. One 2-year-old toddler, whose two grandfathers attended her birthday dinner, revealed a dawning of object permanency when she said in awe, "I have two grandpas. I have two grandpas." Before this, she had dealt with each grandfather separately. Getting them together helped solve a riddle for her.

223

Enthusiasm for learning is catching. On nature walks, parents can introduce their children to the environment.

The toddler's thinking is very self-centered, or *egocentric*. That is, everything is learned and viewed in relation to the self. For example, 20-month-old Gene accidentally stepped on his mother's foot. When his mother exclaimed, "Ouch," Gene laughed delightedly. The accident had not hurt him, and he did not have the ability to understand his mother's pain. Therefore, the incident was funny to him because of the unexpected exclamation it brought from Mother.

Ways to Influence Mental Development

Parents like Marilyn and Jack, and care givers in infant and toddler centers, must give toddlers adequate stimulation if the brain is to develop normally. They can influence the mental development of toddlers in these four ways:

1. By providing proper play materials for toddlers.
2. By interacting with toddlers frequently during the day.
3. By responding verbally and emotionally to toddlers.
4. By setting the stage for toddlers to learn.

Providing Proper Play Materials

Experiences with many objects found in the home and with toys help children think about, know, and understand their world. A kitchen kettle and spoon to stir, a grocery box to sit in, or a newspaper or old magazine to tear all make good playthings. Plastic toys in the bath give experiences with floating, pouring, and moving. Large crayons provide first drawing and writing practice. Pull and push toys stimulate thinking and moving at the same time. Some pull toys have noisemakers that interest children as they walk. Books showing familiar objects will stimulate a child, as Becky was stimulated in the opening story.

Interacting with Toddlers

Both the parents and the care givers should find time to interact with children. They should talk to the toddlers, directing their attention to a variety of types of stimulation. An everchanging set of sights, sounds, smells, tastes, and things to touch will stimulate children to know more and to think more. To provide this stimulation, parents and care givers can take the toddlers out in the yard to look at nature. They can take the children on walks to see, hear, feel, and smell the sights and to experience the people in the environment. Parents and care givers should help children focus on objects by naming each object. Tapping an object, moving the object in front of the children, or making up games with an object will also get the toddlers' attention. The parents' and care givers' enthusiasm for learning will be contagious. Repeated interaction during the day is better than just one social session.

? Decisions, Decisions

"I eated bana," said 2-year-old Denise. "No, Denise," said her mother, "you ate your banana. Say, 'I ate my banana.'" Denise did not say anything but quickly turned to other interests. Is her mother right to correct her grammar? How else will Denise learn correct grammar?

Responding to Toddlers

Parents and care givers can encourage toddlers to learn by giving the children positive feedback for mental functioning. For example, they can praise toddlers for asking questions, for responding to questions, and for working with various learning activities. Recall that Marilyn said, "That's right. Yes. Good, Becky" each time Becky labeled an

object correctly. There was also enthusiastic feeling and love in her responses to her daughter's efforts. Both parents should be responsive. A high level of responsiveness in parents is related to excellence in the mental functioning of children. Care givers must also respond verbally and emotionally to every child every day. Positive feedback helps children know you value their efforts. Punishment and too many restrictions will hinder children's mental development.

Positive feedback encourages toddlers to talk. By responding verbally and emotionally, parents teach children to express themselves.

225

Setting the Stage

Parents and care givers should organize the children's living space so that there are many worthwhile mental activities. There should also be plenty of time to do them. Household and playroom orderliness are helpful to a child's learning. Certain toys may be kept in a special kitchen drawer for those times when the child wants to play near the parents as they work there. A special living-room shelf for "Becky's books" and "Becky's puzzles" helps Becky know these are special materials for her.

Setting aside regular parent times for the child will aid learning. For example, one father sets aside 10 minutes after

Toddlers must learn from their family that books are good and important.

How is this mother using indirect guidance? What problems and benefits can she expect?

breakfast to read to the child. At night before bedtime, the mother regularly reads to the child. Another mother puts a puzzle out for the child to work while waiting for lunch. These routines aid the mental development of the child.

Care givers, too, must plan arrangements in play equipment in playrooms to encourage the toddler's thinking, knowing, and understanding. Creative play equipment and activities should not be segregated according to sex.

Books Stimulate Mental Development

Books give toddlers opportunities to think and to express what they know as they point out and label objects in the book. Sharing books with loving family members and care givers stimulates a toddler. It gives the child an early impression that thinking about things in books is good and important. Suitable books for toddlers have only a few items per page and only a word or two per page. Cloth books are available that are more durable than paper books. Hard, cardboard pages are easier for the toddler to turn.

Language

The development of language gives parents and teachers clues regarding the child's mental development.

During infancy, the baby hears and experiments with sounds that are like vowels and consonants in our language.

When parents and care givers talk to the baby, there is a big increase in the number and volume of these early vocalizations. The baby will sometimes start these social conversations. The conversations grow increasingly lively if the adult responds with smiles, talk, and a nod of the head. However, if the adult fails to respond, studies show that babies react with obvious sadness and disappointment. In his work in pediatrics at Harvard University, Dr. T. Berry Brazelton shows this behavior in films he has developed for teaching and research.

Two Types of Language

Two types of language development take place during the toddler stage. One is *receptive language,* or understood language. The second is *productive language,* or speaking. Receptive language develops first. By age 1, the child responds to some language of the parents and care givers. For example, toddlers usually understand, "Eat your cracker," "Give it to me," and "Put it down."

At about age 18 to 20 months, the toddler begins producing language. The child builds a list of words to respond to and a list of words to say. By 20 months, the average toddler can use 50 words and 10 phrases.

One toddler excited his parents and his big sister when he began adding words rapidly. The parents and big sister recorded the words as they heard them. Here is their record. The boy was 16½ months old when their record began.

January 29 — tree, pat
January 30 — toes, teeth, Carol
January 31 — mine, nice, fly, funny, boy, cat, powder

February 1 — school, doggie
February 6 — apple, peach
February 7 — dirty
February 11 — but

He continued adding new words nearly every day. By March 2, he combined words—"I'm fine." By March 6, "I have book." By May 1, "I get down" and "Red shoes."

Productive language greatly increases communication between toddlers and family members. It also gives toddlers more power and control over their world. When the toddler above said "I get down," it meant he was through eating.

Imitation of family members' words is one way that language develops. However, grammatical forms are often started by the child. For example, in the record above, the parents and sister did not say, "I get down." The toddler arranged those words himself from his storehouse of words. This shows that language development is not all imitation. It depends on the child's creativity and on the motivation to talk. Interest and enthusiasm from others—parents, sisters and brothers, and care givers—is positive feedback. This feedback encourages the toddler to continue talking.

It should be emphasized that ages given here for speech development are *average.* Language development is very individual. One toddler may begin to speak by learning single words for many objects. Another may babble, making noises that sound like sentences but that cannot be understood. This toddler may suddenly begin talking in clear sentences, having never used isolated words.

The ability to use pronouns is also different from child to child. For example, one 2-year-old may continue to say, "Sara wants a cookie. Sara has a ball." Another may use the pronoun "I" much earlier.

Mental Retardation

By the ages of 1 or 2, some toddlers may show signs of mental retardation. If several of the normal developmental steps fail to occur—for example, if a child has not crawled by 1 year, does not respond to people, or has not attempted language at all—the child should be examined by a physician or others able to determine mental difficulties in children this age.

Retardation is usually heartbreaking for parents. Often they feel guilty, as if something they may have done has caused the problem. There are counselors and social workers who can help families deal with such feelings. These counselors and social workers may also be able to help parents make decisions about whether to keep the retarded child at home or to place the child in an institution. Although moderately retarded children will probably be better off at home, severely retarded children can cause serious problems with other siblings. Some parents feel able to cope with such problems. Others do not. All these are questions that trained social workers can help to answer.

The moderately retarded child who is teachable should receive remedial help immediately. The earlier the treatment, the better the chances of an improved status and normal life for the mentally retarded child.

Retarded children should receive help as early as possible. While parents have done nothing to cause retardation, they usually can do something to help it.

Concluding Comments

Mental development is dependent on brain development, which begins before birth and continues during the first 2 years of life. The brain needs adequate nutrition and stimulation to develop normally.

Sensorimotor is the state identified by psychologist Jean Piaget, describing the learning methods of a toddler. Toddlers

229

need things to handle, taste, see, hear, and smell to learn about their world. For a long time yet, they will need to explore their world with all their senses. This will enable them to think about and to understand their environment.

A love of books can begin during the toddler period. Parents and care givers should be sure there are suitable books available. And the child should have ample opportunity to use books with someone who cares about learning.

Activities

1. As you observe and care for a toddler, describe how you influenced the child's mental development in the following ways:
   a. *By providing proper play materials.* What did the child play with? What was the child learning as she or he played?
   b. *By interacting with the toddler frequently.* What did you show the child? What did you do together?
   c. *By responding verbally and emotionally.* What kind of feedback did you give the toddler for the activities? Describe in detail.
   d. *By setting the stage for the toddler to learn.* What toys and books were available for the child? Did you take the toddler for a walk?
2. "Read" to a toddler. This may mean showing the child the pictures in a picture book and letting him or her name the objects. Or the toddler may be ready to listen to a short story.
3. Pay close attention to the toddler's language development:
   a. Give examples of receptive language. What did you say that the child apparently understood?
   b. Describe the child's productive language.
4. Ask the child's parents to keep a record of productive language for a week. How many and which words did the toddler say? How many months old is the toddler?
5. Learn about the resources available in your community for families with mentally retarded children.
   a. Are social workers available who can help parents with problems they may have with their retarded child?
   b. Are there personnel who can work with retarded children and help parents to work with them at home?

Health and Safety for Toddlers

Objectives
To describe essential inoculations for toddlers.
To describe protective measures to ensure the safety of toddlers.

Terms to look for   diphtheria • infectious • oral poliovirus • pertussis, or whooping cough • tetanus

Lee is 18 months old. Today Frank, his father, has brought him to the well-baby clinic for a checkup. As they arrive, they see and hear the parents and babies. Some children are tearful. Frank hopes that Lee will not cry. After Frank registers Lee at the desk, he removes Lee's coat and brings a toy out of a bag, giving it to Lee. Frank speaks to a mother in the waiting room. "Does your baby have to have shots, too?" he asks.

The mother replies, "I don't want him to have them. They hurt and I hate to hear him scream."

"Well, Lee may scream," says Frank, "but it is better that he cry from the shots than die from the diseases. Any-

way, the nurse usually gives the children a balloon that helps them forget all about it."

Frank is a wise parent. He believes the old saying, "An ounce of prevention is worth a pound of cure." In the case of children's health, preventive measures are always simpler and less painful than the diseases.

Accidents

Toddlers are open to all the dangers that babies confront. These dangers were discussed in Chapter 17. In addition, children at the toddler stage walk into danger. Very soon, toddlers can also run and climb into danger. Parents and care givers must develop precautions. They can do this by removing dangerous objects and never leaving the toddler unsupervised. They must remember that the skill and speed in the toddler's legs far exceed the child's ability to think about the possible danger.

Accidents claim the lives of large numbers of toddlers every year. Home accidents are often the result of adult carelessness.

Burns

Children can be burned in the kitchen around the stove and by hot foods and liquids. Heaters can set children's cloth- ing afire, resulting in death to many youngsters. Fire-retardant chemicals were developed for children's garments. Some of these have been removed from the market because they may cause cancer. Perhaps new and safer methods of making clothing fire-retardant will be developed.

Children can fall on heaters and floor furnaces, suffering serious or fatal burns. Toddlers must be watched carefully to keep them a safe distance from these appliances.

Scalding in the bathtub is another cause of burning. Parents and care givers should always test the water before putting a child into a bath. They should stay close by to be sure that the child does not accidentally turn on the hot water.

Having touched something hot, this two-year-old is more surprised than hurt. Learning the concept of *hot* is one of the important lessons of the toddler years.

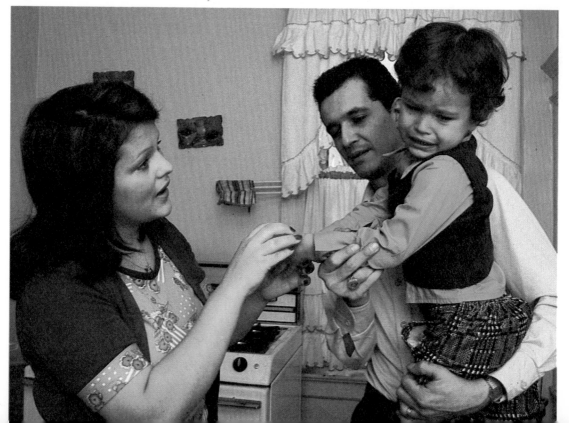

Like any true explorer, toddlers will climb stairs "because they are there." Supervision and a folding gate will prevent accidental falls.

Either at home or at school, fire is a frightening thought for people responsible for young children. Could children quickly be moved to safety? Plans and arrangements must be made so that the answer to that question is always "yes." Nursery schools and day-care centers must have fire inspections regularly. They must plan ways that children could be moved to safety in case of fire. Ask about fire precautions in centers close to you. A plan of action should be drawn up in case of fire in the home. Purchase of a smoke detector to give early warning of fire should be considered.

Hot is one of the first words children should learn. The best way to teach this is to let them touch something that is uncomfortably hot, but not hot enough to harm the child. For example, if the oven is on and the outside of the door is hot, a parent can say, "Hot!" as the toddler approaches it. When the toddler reaches out and touches the door, the parent should say, "Hot" again. The toddler will draw back and may cry a little bit. But if the parent distracts or snatches the child away, the child will not learn the idea of "hot." Later, the child may be seriously injured if she or he tries to touch something that is dangerously hot.

Drowning

Water is a serious hazard for toddlers. Any child living near a lake, ocean, creek, pond, tank, or swimming pool, or attending school near one, could become a victim of drowning. Very close supervision is required at all times. It takes only moments for a small child to fall into water and drown.

Falls

Toddlers can be hurt by falls down stairs. For toddlers, it is easy going up stairs and hard to get down. Parents often teach a toddler to crawl backwards down the stairs. Even then, parents should watch toddlers to be sure they use this technique rather than falling head first the whole distance. An extension gate is a good investment for families with an open stairway accessible to toddlers. Toddlers need and enjoy the practice of going up and down stairs. But parents may want to put a gate at

the top of the first three or four steps. That way, a fall will not be as dangerous. Firm latches on basement doors are also needed.

Toddlers can fall from furniture, too, as they become skilled enough to climb on chairs, beds, and low tables. Having rugs under such pieces of furniture will help to soften falls. Toddlers love to jump up and down in their cribs. Many are able to climb out by 18 months of age or earlier. Parents can lower the mattress to its lowest position and raise the railings to the highest to prevent falls. Crib extenders are available to make crib sides even higher. Or parents may prefer to lower the crib side so that the toddler can climb out easily and without falling. Climbing is good for large muscle development, and toddlers should have some opportunities to practice.

High chairs can be a source of falls. Some children are so active that they need a seat belt to keep them in. Many parents prefer the lower and broader feeding table. Toddlers can also fall from shopping carts, strollers, carriages, and automobiles. Parents can easily be distracted for a moment, and a child can quickly get into an unsafe position. Alertness at all times is essential.

No matter how alert adults are, toddlers will still fall hundreds of times as they practice walking and running. Sometimes they trip over their own feet and hit their heads on furniture or walls. Parents cannot turn their homes into padded cells. So they should help their toddlers learn to take a few falls with a sense of humor. Fortunately, nature has provided a certain amount of protection for the infant's and toddler's head. The soft spot, or fontanel (see Chapter 12),

234

does not fuse until 18 months. It provides a partial cushion against concussion. Of course, an unconscious child or one whose eyes are glazed after a fall should receive immediate medical attention.

Poisoning

Chemicals in the home are hazards to a toddler who eats, drinks, or inhales them. The medicine cabinet with its many bottles is very dangerous. Even the bottle of baby aspirin can cause death if the baby eats all the aspirins at once.

Cleaning agents are harmful if swallowed, breathed, or sprayed into eyes. They should be stored out of reach, preferably in locked cupboards. Knowing where toddlers are and keeping them away from such dangers is always wise.

Traffic

Auto accidents claim thousands of children's lives every year. Statistics show that toddlers who are securely strapped in approved safety seats are rarely killed or seriously injured in car accidents. Many toddlers go through a stage of screaming and resisting being strapped into seats. Parents should calmly and firmly ignore these protests. Having a special toy for distraction, singing a song, or perhaps offering a nutritious snack may help. Children will get used to safety seats. They will even crawl into them on their own after a while. Car seats that are raised so the toddler can see out the window will make the child happier. Children should use safety seats until they weigh 40 pounds. Then they are ready for adult seat belts.

Toddlers also run into the street and are seriously injured or even killed. Parents have even backed their cars over

Dangerous Household Products

- Air fresheners
- Ammonia
- Antidepressants and tranquilizers
- Antifreeze
- Aspirin
- Bleach
- Cleaners and disinfectants
- Deodorant
- Drain cleaner
- Floor wax
- Gasoline and oil
- Hair remover
- Kerosene
- Lighter fluid
- Lye
- Metal and furniture polishes
- Nail polish and remover
- Oven cleaner
- Paint and paint thinner
- Pesticide
- Putty
- Rubbing alcohol
- Spot remover
- Toilet cleaner
- Turpentine
- Varnish
- Weed-Killers

Toddlers are known to quickly dart away from adult hands. Hold a toddler's hand firmly while crossing the street. Always remain with a toddler while the child plays near a driveway or a street.

their own toddlers. The best solution is a close watch on toddlers playing near a driveway or near a street. When moving a car, parents should either take the toddler in the car with them or be sure the child is safe in another person's arms. In the moment it takes to start a car, a toddler can dart behind a wheel out of sight. The results are tragic.

? Decisions, Decisions

Eighteen-month-old Judy has figured out how to undo the buckle on her infant car seat. She can remove the safety strap on her stroller as well. What would you do if you were her care giver?

Illnesses

Children recover from most common illnesses within a few days. However, it is reassuring to parents to be able to call the doctor for advice. Parents should describe accurately how the child is acting if the doctor is to give sound advice without seeing the child. Make some notes before calling the doctor. Has the toddler had a prolonged cough? Does the toddler have diarrhea? Does the child eat? How high is the temperature? Do you know if the child has been exposed to any diseases?

Reading about diseases in a baby book can give parents clues about their child's illness. Dr. Benjamin Spock's *Baby and Child Care* is published in paperback by Pocket Books. It is available at a reasonable price in bookstores, newspaper outlets, and some grocery stores. Reading about diseases and their symptoms helps parents understand better when they talk to a doctor or nurse. The Spock book contains advice, too, in case parents cannot reach a doctor right away.

Trips to the Doctor

Toddlers will continue to see the pediatrician regularly, although less frequently than when they were infants. Most doctors will want to see them about every 3 months until age 18 months, then every 6 months until age 2½ or 3.

Many toddlers develop fears of the doctor during this stage. These fears may be due to memories of inoculations. Or the toddler may simply dislike being undressed and examined. Some children may hate to be put on the scale. Others may dislike the examining table. Still others may not be afraid but may be so active and wiggly that examining them is difficult.

A sensitive pediatrician will help calm the toddler by talking quietly, letting the parent hold the child during the examination, and taking plenty of time. In his book *Toddlers and Parents*, Dr. T. Berry Brazelton says that he often demonstrates his stethoscope and other examining tools on the child's stuffed animal or special security blanket.

Parents or care givers can also help keep toddlers calm through these examinations. They should try to remain relaxed and comforting—even if, despite all these methods, the child screams through the entire examination.

Most hospitals have an emergency room where parents can take children who have sudden illnesses or accidents.

For example, many toddlers have had their stomach pumped in an emergency room on a weekend when their own doctor was not available. The emergency room is only for emergencies. Also, because of the extra expense, adults should avoid using them whenever possible. Emergency rooms with accident victims can be very frightening to parents and children alike. It is far better for parents to keep a child protected than to be forced to go to the hospital emergency room.

? Decisions, Decisions

Two weeks ago, Wally cut his leg and needed stitches. Now, he is afraid of doctors and nurses. He seems to think they were the cause of his pain. Wally's parents are wondering whether or not they should cancel his regular check-up next week and wait until he gets over his fear. What should Wally's parents do?

In spite of all precautions, children will have accidents and may need emergency care. If this happens, the parent or care giver should remain calm. A good emergency facility will let the parent or care giver stay with the child through most emergency procedures— if the adult is calm. Having a familiar adult along will help keep the child from being too fearful.

Adults are bound to have some guilty feelings if an accident happens to a child who is in their care. This is normal, but it does not really help the child or the

237

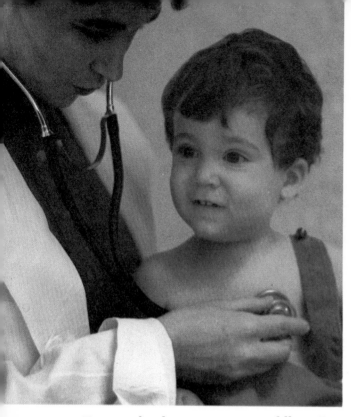

Trips to the doctor can upset toddlers. Parents should remain relaxed and should comfort the child during the examination. Talk quietly and reassure the child.

Chapter 17. Refer to that chapter for the recommended ages for the various shots. Parents should make sure toddlers get booster shots at age 18 months for inoculations for DPT (*diphtheria; pertussis, or whooping cough;* and *tetanus*) and for the *oral poliovirus* vaccine. Parents should save the record card for all shots and refer to it for the correct time for booster shots. Most infectious diseases could be controlled in the United States if every parent got the proper inoculations for their young children.

Childhood diseases can cause serious damage. For example, a toddler can have an extremely high fever with measles that can cause permanent brain or heart damage. Measles can be prevented with proper inoculations. Before the poliovirus vaccine was developed, crippling from polio frequently occurred. Why would parents fail to protect their child from this dread disease? Why would they take a chance that their child might never walk and run like other children?

adult. If you have taken every possible safety measure and an accident still occurs, concentrate on helping the child. A child who has developed language when an accident happens may need to talk about it for months. In such a case, the parent or other adult should be willing to listen and discuss it until the child has worked out all his or her feelings about it.

Inoculations

A detailed discussion of inoculations required for infants was presented in

Concluding Comments

Health and safety protections for toddlers call for major emphasis on the prevention of illnesses and accidents. Both parents and care givers should watch children every night and every day to keep children safe. Inoculations, or "shots," are essential to ensure prevention of a number of severe diseases. These diseases are most harmful to the youngest children. Therefore, the inoculations should never be delayed simply because the infant is small. It is precisely because infants are small that inoculations are most essential.

1. Make a toddler safety check of your house and garage. Describe the changes needed to make it safe for a toddler.
2. Interview parents who have both a toddler and a home swimming pool. What precautions do they take for the child's safety?
3. Visit a well-baby clinic and learn about its services and recommendations for inoculations. Write a report.
4. Call a day-care center.
   a. Ask about the inoculations required for children before they can enter the center.
   b. Ask how children would be evacuated if there were a fire at the center.
   c. Are there fire extinguishers available? If so, where?
   d. How often does the fire inspector come to the center?
   e. Write a report containing the information you have gathered.
5. Clip at least five news stories about tragic deaths that have occurred to infants and toddlers. Write a short report on preventive measures that could have been taken to protect these children.

Can you think of some general principles for keeping toddlers safe on special occasions or in new environments?

How to Babyproof Your Home

Accidents cause more deaths among babies, toddlers, and young children than does any illness. Here's how to prevent the accidents that happen around the home.

1 Use an expandable gate to keep children from stairwells and dangerous areas.

2 Cover electric outlets with special caps, and tape electric cords to the floor or wall moulding.

3 Keep fans and space heaters out-of-reach.

4 Turn pot handles toward the rear of the stove.

5 Slats on the crib or playpen should be no farther apart than 2¼ inches (6 cm). Keep crib sides at highest level for toddlers.

6 Lower the hot water temperature to 120°F or 130°F, to prevent scalding. It will still be hot enough.

7 Put all dangerous household products in a securely latched cabinet. (For a list of these products, see p. 235.)

8 Lock the medicine cabinet. Buy only those products with childproof caps. *Never* refer to medicine as "tasting good."

9 List the phone numbers of your doctor, nearest hospital, police, fire department, local emergency squad, and nearest poison center next to the telephone.

10 Fasten seat belts in high chairs, carriages, and shopping carts.

11 Stick rubber appliques on the bottom of the bathtub.

12 Install smoke detectors in your living room. Have a family plan of action for fire.

13 Use short tablecloths or placemats. Hanging tablecloths are an open invitation to pull. Hot, sharp, or heavy items can come down on the child.

14 Unplug cords from irons, coffee pots, blenders, and other appliances that can be pulled over.

15 Buy fire-retardant clothes and pajamas for children.

16 Protect your valuables and favorite things by putting them out of reach or by packing them away until the child gets older.

17 Paper or plastic cups are safest for kitchen and bathroom.

18 Lock up power tools and hobby supplies.

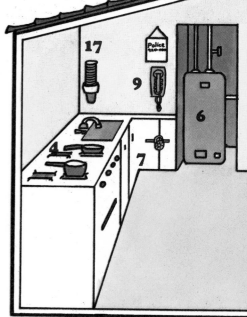

Guiding Toddlers

Objectives

To describe ways to use indirect guidance with toddlers.
To describe ways to use direct guidance with toddlers.
To explain the relationship between the toddler's striving
for independence and the methods of guidance.

Terms to look for   affective guidance • autonomy •
direct guidance • indirect guidance • negativism • physical guidance •
"terrible twos" • verbal guidance

Jana, her mother, Ruth, and her father, Sam, were relaxing in the living room after dinner. Jana threw a foam ball at her mother, who was sitting in an armchair, reading the paper. Ruth saw the ball coming, reached down, and rolled the ball back to her 15-month-old daughter. Jana was delighted with her mother's response and got the ball again. This time, she laid the ball in Ruth's lap, on top of her newspaper. Ruth took the hint and laid down the paper. She got down on the floor for a game of roll-the-ball. Jana's father put down his book and joined in the game.

Toddlers benefit when parents attend to them in the evening. When one parent spent the day with the toddler, this is a good time for that adult to be relieved by the other parent. Toddlers are busy people, and no one rests around them.

Independence: Goal of Toddler

By now, you are well aware that toddlers are striving for independence. They seem to have an inner drive to

243

On the way to the "terrible twos," parents and care givers need to stay calm and to keep their sense of humor.

During their negative period, toddlers especially need warm, loving, nurturing parents and care givers. Such adults can maintain their composure and sense of humor when toddlers revert to babyish or negative behavior. Becoming independent is a long uphill struggle from infancy to adulthood. Adults may find children difficult at this age. But they should remember that being a toddler is even more difficult than caring for one. Toddlers need all the help they can get.

Independence: Goal of Guidance

The other people in the child's family, neighborhood, and toddler center are also involved in the child's struggle for independence. To let the toddler grow in independence, the family and other care givers must gradually let go of their control over the child. They must give up their control little by little as the child shows responsibility and readiness to take over in particular areas. The best parenting requires that parents work themselves out of a job as their child moves toward self-guidance and maturity.

But parents and care givers must help children feel secure and loved, even as the children strain the bonds toward freedom. Toddlers must depend on parents and care givers to protect them at times when they forge ahead too quickly. They may try to reach beyond their strength or their ability to understand.

Guidance is the action that adults take to influence a child's behavior. This action can stop, teach, or redirect the

become free and self-directed. They want to get away from being as controlled and as protected by adults as they have been up to this point. Psychologists call this drive for freedom and independence the drive for *autonomy*. With this drive comes another trait that is described as *negativism*. Toddlers say "no" frequently. They often seem to want to do the opposite of what adults want them to do. This stage reaches its peak at the point which many parents call the "terrible twos." Negativism usually begins to subside between the ages of 2½ and 3.

child. Guidance must free a child to become her or his own boss and to become self-directed.

The challenge to parents and care givers is to decide, from moment to moment and day to day, what freedom each child is ready for and how best to guide development. Knowing how most children grow and develop helps adults make these judgments and plan guidance for the child.

Indirect Guidance: Space Arrangement

The environment or surrounding of home and yard and the toddler center must be *toddlerproofed*. This will ease the strain on toddlers and care givers as the children strive for independence. Toddlerproofing is a form of *indirect guidance*. The guidance is indirect because it does not deal with the toddler in person, yet it does influence the child's behavior. Indirect guidance involves arranging the home, yard, and toddler center so toddlers can play safely and have few places or things that are off limits. Toddlerproofing lets toddlers direct their own play and exploration without adults stepping in all the time.

Guiding indirectly means thinking about arranging and storing toys, furniture, furnishings, and personal effects so that toddlers can play, experiment, and learn freely. Toddlers need freedom

Guidance is the action parents take to stop, teach, or redirect the child. The goal of guidance is the child's ability to be self-directed.

Parents can aid mental development by setting aside regular times for reading or playing with their toddler.

to explore, move, and climb. They should not be stopped at every turn, either to protect themselves or to protect property. Following are five examples of indirect guidance, or toddlerproofing, which can be carried out at home.

1. Terry's mother put caps on all the open electric outlets. She also set furniture against every lamp cord. These two acts cut down on the number of "no, no's" Terry heard every day. He and his parents were more at ease after these simple safety steps were taken.

2. Beverly's father set the dirty garbage cans outside the yard fence. There, Beverly could not get to them. Her father realized that she had been pushing,

rubbing, and pounding the dirty cans. So he set out a clean tin bucket that Beverly could safely move about and pound with her stick. Bev is still too young to decide what is dirty, clean, or damageable. Removing the dirty cans and substituting a clean can for moving and pounding solved a problem easily.

3. Angela's mother removed the 100-year-old books from the lowest book shelves in the study. She replaced them with a few of Angela's stuffed toys, books, and blocks. The heirloom books, with their beautiful leather covers, were from Angela's great-grandfather's collection. Angela's mother realized that she would have to be on guard constantly to protect them. She decided,

instead, to move the books for the few years when Angela might harm them.

4.   Trev's father moved the household cleaning supplies to a locked cupboard high in a storage closet. He did this when Trev seemed to show a lot of curiosity about those bottles. Giving Trev several safe plastic bottles to play with while bathing helped satisfy his curiosity about bottles. Trev's father knew that cleaning solutions are very harmful to babies. He wanted to be sure Trev did not get into any harmful substances. He was taking no chances.

5.   Marjory built three sets of shelves— one each for the kitchen, living room, and Diana's room. On these shelves, she and her husband, Bill, stored Diana's toys. They also included other safe things for Diana to play with. The kitchen shelf contained a pair of sauce-pans, two cans of soup, and a wooden spoon. The living-room shelf held a teddy bear, a sponge ball, a puzzle, and some books. In Diana's room, the shelf contained toys that Diana was ready to use. The games with small pieces or those that were breakable were stored for use when Diana was older. Marjory kept the crayons out of sight in another cupboard in the house. Though Diana liked to draw, she was not old enough to know that drawing had to be done on paper and not on the walls. Therefore, Marjory wanted to limit Diana's use of crayons to the times when either she or Bill could supervise their use.

Indirect Guidance: Time Schedules

The previous examples of indirect guidance involve arranging the physical space or environment. Another kind of indirect guidance is organizing family schedules to influence a toddler's behavior. There are 10 important areas of time organization for parents to consider.

1.   Develop a household routine for shared daily and weekly chores. Plan where shortcuts can be made. Knowing when chores must be done and where everything is stored helps the parents and others—baby-sitter or visitor— know better how to help. A routine makes decision making easier. Habits develop that get tasks done more quickly.

2.   Cut down on some activities, especially if you both frequently feel overwhelmed or tired. For example, to leave time and energy for the toddler, you may need to curtail holiday preparations and entertaining. You may need to cut down your involvement with outside social activities.

3.   Plan ahead for shared shopping trips, or take turns. Shopping takes longer with a toddler. Therefore, if the toddler must go along, start earlier in the day while the child is still fresh. Allow plenty of time for interacting with the toddler as you go along. Go home before the child gets tired or hungry.

4.   If you have to leave for work or for an appointment early in the morning, set things in order the night before. Then get up earlier than usual. A parent who is rushing around nearly always overstimulates a toddler. This causes the child to be more demanding and harder to manage. Earlier bedtimes are also needed for parents to have enough sleep to cope well.

5.   Save time for an outing every day for you and the toddler. Parents, partic-

Even short outings take longer with a toddler. Toddlers get tired, hungry, and cranky. They wear out very quickly when their hands are held up straight.

toddler's behavior is likely to be most difficult. Resting at midday is far more important than completing household chores. Consider streamlining or eliminating many household chores if the only time to do them is when the child sleeps.

7. Encourage assistance from others— grandparents, friends, neighbors, and baby-sitters. These people can become important to the toddler and take some of the load off the parents. Others can and will help, and it is good insurance to let them do so. If an emergency arose, the parents would feel that others had enough experience with their child to provide proper care.

8. Be firm about an early bedtime for the toddler. Toddlers need a lot of sleep, although they do not know it. Parents also need time together for themselves. Being confident that an early bedtime is best for the child helps parents to be firm when toddlers begin trying to set their own bedtime. The toddler is not yet ready to make this decision. This will be discussed further in Chapter 26, "Home Routines for Toddlers."

ularly those who stay home every day, need to go where they can be with adults awhile. Or, if possible, arrange for a teenage babysitter to come after school 1 or more days a week. The baby-sitter can take the toddler to the park and give you some special time alone.

Some parents organize play groups of about three toddlers. The playmates' parents see each other daily. Each day, one parent stays at home, organizes activities, and keeps all three toddlers. This gives the other parents a break from child-care duties.

6. Rest, or relax in some way, while the toddler naps. A parent often is exhausted by evening—the time when a

9. Keep work done ahead of deadlines. Toddlers do not understand deadlines or outside pressures. When you have deadlines to meet, plan to be ready ahead of schedule. Then, if your toddler is sick or fussy, you can provide the needed care and will not have to worry. After all, you are already ahead of schedule. Student parents, especially, need to get term papers done early for this reason. Other adults can be especially helpful at such times.

10. Give the toddler first priority when you recognize that the child is hungry, lonesome, or tired. At such times, a

toddler's tolerance wears thin and independence vanishes into dependence. A quick decision to let other things go and attend to the toddler is wise. A quick bowl of cereal, a few minutes of rocking, or an early naptime may head off many explosions. For a time, the toddler will be like a baby. In such a state, the child can protest harshly and make a wreck of a room, a meal, or a person. This is a time for parents to maintain coolheadedness.

? Decisions, Decisions

Sonia has learned to take off her shoes and socks. Now, she takes them off anytime and anywhere. Sometimes it is not important for her to wear them, but sometimes she must keep them on, especially to keep warm. What guidance can her parents or care givers give?

Direct Guidance

Direct guidance means influencing the toddler's behavior through personal interaction with the child. There are three types of direct guidance: 1) physical guidance—helping, showing, and leading; 2) verbal guidance—using words to direct the toddler; and 3) affective guidance—letting the toddler know you are pleased or displeased with the child's behavior.

Physical Guidance. Toddlers are little mimics. Demonstrate how you want them to use a spoon, drink milk, pull off a coat, or toss a ball. They will probably follow your lead.

Toddlers often react negatively to having their hands held. Having your hand pulled straight up for a long period of time can be very uncomfortable. Therefore, reserve handholding for the times it is needed for the child's safety.

Verbal Guidance. Remember, the toddler's vocabulary is limited. Short, direct verbal guidance is required. Here are eight rules to follow:

1. Get the child's attention. Be sure the toddler sees and hears you. Stoop down. You should be close enough to be certain of eye-to-eye contact for verbal guidance to be effective.

2. Use positive statements to tell the toddler what you want done. Avoid negative statements telling the child what you do not want done. The "don't" commands stick in the mind, and the child cannot figure out the "do" part. For example, say, "Bring

Positive statements tell toddlers what they should do. "Don't" statements leave the child unsure of the right way to behave.

the magazine to me," rather than "Don't play with the magazine." Say, "Put the banana in your mouth," rather than "Don't drop the banana on the floor." Say, "Drink your milk," rather than "Don't blow bubbles in your milk." Getting over the "don't" habit will increase a parent's or care giver's effectiveness in guiding the toddler.

Give one direction at a time. Give the direction at the time and place you want the child to carry it out.

3. Put the action word first in the sentence. This helps the toddler concentrate on the important action part in the command.

4. Give choices only when you want the toddler to have a choice. Often people start with "Do you want to . . .?" If you use this form with toddlers, you can expect a frequent "no."

5. Simplify the toddler's choices to two alternatives when possible. Giving too many choices overloads the toddler's mind.

6. Give only one direction at a time. A toddler cannot remember both "shut the door" and "hold the railing when you go down the steps."

7. Give a direction at the time and place you want the child to carry it out. A toddler will forget if you say, "When you finish the puzzle, put it away." However, when the child is through with the puzzle, you can say, "Put the puzzle on the shelf. That's where we keep it."

8. Clearly state limits so that the toddler knows where to stop. For example, say, "Write on the paper, not on the table." Limits are many, even when families try to toddlerproof the home. Adults must first state limits and then follow through with enforcing them.

Affective Guidance. Affective guidance refers to the interactions that let toddlers know how you feel about behavior. Letting children know you love them will provide security and warmth. Children will respond warmly to "Good" and "Fine." Toddlers will like a hug, a pat on the head, a kiss, or just having you pay attention to them and talk to them.

These are examples of positive feedback, which encourages a child to repeat behavior that has just been carried out.

If you do not like behavior, such as a temper tantrum, one remedy is to ignore it completely. Either praise or punishment is attention. When a child's behavior fails to get your attention, the child will often stop. Ignoring a behavior is a form of negative feedback. Another form may be frowning or giving a firm verbal command. If these methods do not work, the adult must firmly stop a toddler who goes beyond a limit. For example, if the toddler in the example above continues to write on the table, the adult should simply take the crayon away. The child can then be offered another activity.

Physical punishment is also a form of negative feedback. Spanking and slapping a toddler are not as effective as other methods of guidance. And physical punishment may leave children with emotional problems that are serious or that may become serious later on. However, an occasional swat on a diapered bottom (and it is the rare parent who *never* does this) is less cruel than saying, "I don't love you," "I'm not your friend," or "You are bad."

Saying, "You are bad" can be especially damaging at this age. Children are beginning to form a self-image. If they are constantly told that they are bad, they will begin to believe it. They may feel so bad about themselves that their behavior will become worse. Besides, the statement "You are bad" is not accurate. What the child did may be bad. The action is bad. But the child is not bad. Breaking a rule does not make someone a bad *person*. Be specific. Say,

"Hitting hurts people. It is against the rules." This makes more sense to a toddler.

? Decisions, Decisions

When Alex gets angry he kicks. His father gets very upset when he is kicked by his young son. He thinks Alex is being a "brat." What might this parent do to stop the kicking? What should he not do?

Toddler Abuse

There is a growing awareness in the United States that some parents and other adults abuse their children. Children are beaten, burned, and psychologically damaged. Toddlers are very vulnerable to abuse, particularly by parents who have little understanding of what a toddler can be expected to do. Toddlers' striving for independence, their negativism, and their returning to babyish behavior are a strain for parents who do not understand that most toddlers behave this way.

Researchers have discovered that parents who abuse their children were usually abused as children, themselves. Such a parent may not be able to cope with the frustrating behavior of a toddler. The parent may automatically inflict on the child what the parent suffered in childhood. Such a reaction is similar to a temper tantrum. However,

"I can't stand this kid for one more minute!" Many parents have felt this way at one time or another. This feeling signals the need for immediate action. Find someone to give you a hand with the child. Find a way to cool off.

a temper tantrum that results in child abuse is an offense that society should not tolerate in adults.

The social services of the various states are attempting to help parents who are abusive. They have set up "crisis" or "hot line" telephone numbers. Parents can call these numbers for help when they feel they are in danger of abusing their children. Parents can call anonymously. They are often helped by being able to talk about their problems. In addition, there are parent self-help groups. In these groups, parents meet to discuss the problems, feelings, and frustrations that may cause them to harm their children.

Schools are required to report to authorities any unusual bruises, cuts, burns, or other injuries on children. Of course, schools and toddler centers should have the same responsibility to protect children, not to harm them.

Concluding Comments

Toddlers are striving for independence and straining the bonds of dependency that have held them to their parents. They may be very independent at times. Then they may go back to babylike, dependent behavior at a moment's notice. They often exhibit the difficult behavior that psychologists call negativism. If toddlers are tired, lonesome, or hungry, they may be very difficult to guide. At such times, giving their needs priority is the best solution.

Indirect guidance includes toddler-proofing the household and organizing time schedules to allow extra time for dealing with the toddler. This eases the strain on the parents and helps both parents and toddler. Using appropriate direct guidance—physical, verbal, and affective—encourages the toddler's independence. Direct guidance also enables adults to provide love and security for the child while teaching and learning take place. The important guidance principles discussed in this chapter can be used with all young children.

1. Describe the difference between:
   a. making a home *safe* for a toddler;
   b. toddlerproofing a home as a form of indirect guidance.
2. Describe three things you could do to toddlerproof a home. Explain how this toddlerproofing would be a form of indirect guidance.
3. With parents' permission, observe one or more toddlers for an hour or two.
   a. Describe a child's activity which shows a striving for *autonomy.*
   b. Does this toddler demonstrate negativism? If so, give at least one example.
4. With permission, observe a parent or caregiver with one or more toddlers:
   a. Using direct quotes, record three statements of direct verbal guidance.

   b. Analyze these statements according to the rules stated in the chapter.
   c. How effectively did the guidance influence the child's behavior?
5. Continue to observe the parent or care giver with the toddler(s):
   a. Describe three episodes of direct physical guidance.
   b. How effectively did the method influence the child's behavior?
6. From the same observation:
   a. Describe three episodes of affective guidance.
   b. How *effectively* did the *affective* guidance influence the child's behavior?
7. Find out the kinds of child-abuse prevention services available in your community. What kinds of help do they offer to parents and children?

26 Home Routines for Toddlers

Objectives

To describe toddlers and how parents cope with them at home.

To describe typical home routines for toddlers.

To describe the needs of the parent who stays at home to care for a toddler.

Vincent, a toddler of 14 months, fretted to get out of his stroller. Liz, his mother, lifted him out of the seat and let him walk beside the stroller. After a moment, he bent down and picked up a feather from the sidewalk. He held it up to Liz for approval. She said, "Feather, Vince. That's a feather. Nice."

After a few more steps, he walked up some stairs and sat on the top. He seemed happy with his excursion. After a time, Liz patted the stroller seat, saying, "Do you want to ride, Vince?" Vince came down the stairs and stood by the stroller, expecting Liz to pick him up. She did, and they continued toward the park.

A morning walk was a daily ritual for Vince and Liz. They were living in a small city apartment. Liz felt that both she and the toddler needed this daily outing, which was a pleasant change from the apartment.

While Vince explored the outdoors, Liz was able to socialize with some other parents who did not work outside the home and who usually brought their youngsters to the park. For Liz, this social contact played an important part in her daily schedule. It helped her cope with the heavy demands Vince placed upon her emotionally. The outing fulfilled the need to talk with other adults, while still caring for the toddler.

A daily outing lets toddlers practice their new independence.

One Home Routine with Toddler

6:30 A.M. Toddler awakes. Plays with toys parent has placed in crib. Talks to herself.

7:00 A.M. Alarm rings. Parent awakes.

7:05 A.M. Parent feeds child and self breakfast.

7:25 A.M. Parent washes and dresses child and self.

7:55 A.M. Parent finds child's lost hat. Collects material for work.

8:00 A.M. Parent and child leave their apartment and drive to the care giver's house.

8:15 A.M. Parent and care giver talk briefly. Parent hugs child, says good-bye.

8:25 A.M. Parent drives to work.

8:30 A.M. Child follows care giver from room-to-room as care giver goes about morning activities.

9:15 A.M. Child and care giver walk slowly to grocery store and return.

11:50 A.M. Care giver feeds child lunch.

12:15 P.M. Child plays with toys and listens to records, sitting on care giver's lap.

1:30 P.M. Afternoon nap.

2:50 P.M. Snack—apple juice and graham crackers.

3:00 P.M.	Child and care giver walk to nearby playground for a short outing.
4:10 P.M.	Child plays at taking canned goods out of low cupboard while care giver goes about tasks.
5:30 P.M.	Parent picks up child and talks with care giver.
5:45 P.M.	Parent and child shop for food and pick up laundry. Child is cranky and cries.
6:10 P.M.	Parent prepares dinner for both.
6:40 P.M.	Dinner.
7:20 P.M.	Parent and child play with blocks.
8:00 P.M.	Parent puts child in pajamas, reads story.
8:30 P.M.	Parent puts child to bed, begins household tasks or reads and relaxes.
11:00 P.M.	Parent goes to bed.

Shopping Routines

Shopping and other household errands may get easier as the baby becomes a toddler. Then, the child can sit up well and can more easily go along with the parents. Juggling the toddler and the laundry or groceries will be a problem for a couple of years yet. The child often needs attention just when the parent is burdened down with bundles or is driving. Shopping schedules that include the toddler must take into

By planning for a toddler's needs, parents can avoid "supermarket scenes."

account the child's need for food and rest. Parents should shop early in the day before the child gets hungry or tired. Short trips are best. Parents or care givers should bring along a bag of supplies—extra diapers, a few toys, crackers or teething biscuits, a bottle of juice—to help themselves and the toddlers get through the shopping trip peacefully. Many unpleasant scenes are played out in supermarkets when parents disregard this advice. Many parents prefer to have one parent stay home with the children while the other shops. They take toddlers shopping only on short trips.

Toddlers will give up their security devices when they no longer need them. It is a mistake for parents to push their child into giving them up.

❓ Decisions, Decisions

"I'm so discouraged," said Charlotte. "There are always dishes in the sink, toys on the floor, tears to dry, meals to fix, and laundry to do. I can't even get out to get my hair cut. Maybe Toby is an especially difficult child. Maybe I'm doing something wrong." What changes might Charlotte try to make? What cannot be changed?

Rest and Sleep Routines

Society has set up the idea of daytime naps and unbroken nighttime sleep for young children. To most parents, naps and unbroken nighttime sleep are desirable. But it is normal for children's sleep patterns to vary. The fact that some toddlers sleep less than others is not a sign of bad or abnormal behavior.

Naps

The need for a nap varies among toddlers. Some need more sleep than others. During the years from 1 to 3, though, the toddler usually gives up the morning nap.

Parents who are coping with the change from two naps a day to one may need to serve lunch earlier. Then they can put the toddler in bed for the afternoon nap around noon. Perhaps the toddler will sleep a little longer during the afternoon now. If the child does not sleep longer, bedtime at night may have to be earlier. The parents must take their cues from the toddler. A toddler who gets grouchy, rubs the eyes, or starts to fall asleep needs to put to bed earlier.

Bedtime Rituals

Nighttime rituals can be established during the toddler period. Most parents like a little time in the evening to play with a toddler. This is especially important when one or both parents may have been away all day. Fathers may change toddlers and dress them for bed, for example. If parents like a little rough-and-tumble play with the toddler, they should do it early in the play period. They should then gradually shift to quieter activities. This will get the toddler relaxed and ready for sleep. Overstimulation can cause the child to have problems with relaxing and going to sleep. Looking at books and listening to parents sing quiet, restful songs can be the final cues for the toddler that it is bedtime.

Pleasant Bedtime

Adults should make every effort to keep the bedtime and going-to-bed routine pleasant. Bedtime should be something to look forward to. Therefore, going to bed must never be used as punishment.

Leaving the light on or turning it off should be decided according to the toddler's preferences. Do not ask the child whether or not to leave the light on. Just try it different ways and see which works best. Some toddlers like the light on. They like to look around and even babble to themselves for a while before falling asleep.

Some toddlers like to take a security blanket to bed with them. Others have a stuffed animal or doll that comforts them as they fall asleep. Still others suck their thumbs or pacifiers.

Many toddlers are given a bottle at bedtime. With their stomachs comfortably full, they can more easily drift off to sleep. However, dentists warn against the condition they call "nursing-bottle mouth." Some children fall asleep with the nipple still in their mouths or with their mouths full of milk. This can cause serious tooth decay. If a toddler will accept water, it should be substituted. Otherwise, parents should make sure that the bottle is no longer in the toddler's mouth after the child has fallen asleep.

Trying to force toddlers to give up any of these security devices is a mistake. All of them are ways children use to deal with their environment on their own. The child who makes the decision to give up the bottle or security blanket will be more independent and secure than the one who is forced or shamed into giving it up. Dr. T. Berry Brazelton feels that blankets and stuffed animals should be allowed even when they have been worn to shreds.

Sometimes the toddler calls for attention after being tucked into bed. It is usually better to give that attention in the bedroom and near the crib. A rocker is useful in the toddler's room at bedtime. A toddler who reenters the family scene can become stimulated all over again.

The parents need to be confident in their decision that now is the toddler's bedtime. They will lovingly but firmly lay the baby down and cover the child. They may sit by the bed and sing quietly if their presence seems needed. They will not bring the toddler out to socialize more or to be with guests. The toddler will then want that attention tomorrow night and other nights.

Parents should not allow toddlers to prolong bedtime indefinitely. Almost all

Toddlers often feel as if they are being deserted at bedtime. Parents must be loving but firm. Toddlers need a full night of sleep and parents need to spend time with each other during the evening.

toddlers will go through a stage of trying to manipulate parents into sitting with them until they fall asleep. Sometimes this takes an hour or more. Parents who are certain that the child is tired and who have followed the usual bedtime routine should kiss the child good night and leave the room. Sensitive parents will feel bad when they hear the child's wailing. But they should recognize that this is part of growing up. The child will soon realize that the parents are firm in their decision and will stop resisting sleep.

Children should never be punished for not sleeping. Abusive parents have been known to slam toddlers into their beds and beat them when they have not gone to sleep easily. Such treatment will only make sleep problems worse and will cause severe emotional damage.

Parents should remember that hurried and impatient action will be felt by toddlers. Toddlers interpret body language before understanding verbal language. They may become more restless if they feel rushed out of people's presence without customary routines.

Awakening During the Night

Toddlers do sometimes wake in the night. Usually, changing the diaper and arranging the covers to keep the child warm will be enough to get the toddler back to sleep. Some children may want a drink of water or a sip of milk.

A double diaper is recommended at night from age 1 on. A double diaper absorbs enough to keep pajamas, sheets, and covers from getting wet during the night. Some parents change the toddler's diaper at the parents' bedtime. Most toddlers sleep soundly enough not to be bothered by this. And it prevents their waking up soaked later in the night.

Toddlers do wake up crying from bad dreams or nightmares. Since they have not developed language fully, it is hard to know what these nightmares are about. Usually, children need to be fully awakened so that they see the parent and can be reassured. Then, they can calm down and go to sleep again.

Awakening Early

Most toddlers awaken early—usually earlier than their parents prefer. Some toddlers will welcome a dry diaper and a warm bottle and may even go back to sleep for a while. Some may play contentedly in their cribs for a time after taking the bottle.

Sometimes, parents tuck the toddler in bed early in the evening. This lets them have the evening free for their pursuits. When they do this, though, a wide-awake toddler will probably be on their hands early in the morning, when they might like to sleep longer.

Toddlers who wake from bad dreams need comfort fast. They may become more frightened if they have the chance to hear their own voice crying. Arriving quickly lets the child return to sleep in a short time.

? Decisions, Decisions

Dean had a bedtime ritual. First a drink, then a kiss on his nose, then a kiss on teddy's nose, then turning on the nightlite. But the ritual is growing. Each week a new step is added. Dean will not go to sleep until the whole ritual is completed, and it is becoming a long chain of events. What can his parents do?

Bathing and Dressing

Diapering is still a major part of the toddler's dressing routine. Diapers will be needed through the toddler period and during nap- and bedtime until children are at least 3 years old. Diapering time may be a good time for parents to talk and smile with the toddler. However, many toddlers actively resist having their diapers changed. They squirm, wriggle, kick, and are amazingly strong for their size. One set of grandparents who kept their grandchild for the weekend reported that it took both of them to diaper her—one to hold her, and one to put the diaper on.

Adults might want to try allowing the child to stand up during the diaper change. Children who resist all efforts at changing may need to be laid on their stomachs, with an adult hand or arm firmly on their backs.

Laundry for the toddler still requires a good deal of time. Bed clothes and enough play clothes to keep the toddler reasonably clean require attention two or three times a week. Most parents find disposable diapers a blessing.

Diapering a toddler is diapering a constantly moving object.

Adults should not expect children to try to keep their clothes clean. Toddlers are very busy exploring, and they get very dirty doing it. Trying to change their clothes every time they are a little dirty only makes more work for the adults. It also interferes with the child's activity. Unless clothes are wet, it is easier to wait until the end of the day to bathe toddlers and put them into clean pajamas.

Many toddlers look forward to a bath. They enjoy playing in the water and floating a toy or two. Others may be afraid of a bath and may refuse to take one. Sensitive parents will respect these fears and will attempt to keep the toddler clean with sponge baths until the fearful stage is over.

Visitors

Toddlers usually enjoy visitors, though they may prefer not to be picked up by strangers. They may take their time warming up even to relatives they do not see often. Regardless of who is present, a toddler's needs for food, rest, and attention must be met. Otherwise, the child will become fussy and unsociable. At this stage, children often seem to resent parents' conversations with other adults. They will become clinging and demanding to distract the parent's attention. Parents may be able to divert the child to some activity for a short period of time. But they may simply have to accept the child's behavior as natural to toddlers. They may then try to see their adult friends at a time when no toddlers are present.

Toddlers are still inexperienced in cooperative play with other children. Therefore, when children visit, the adults should maintain supervision to keep things peaceful. Sometimes, though, parents should let toddlers try to handle problems for themselves—as long as they are not actually hurting one another. Parents who are overprotective may keep their children from learning valuable lessons about getting along with others.

Parents' Needs

Life with an active toddler is very tiring and demanding, although it can also be very rewarding. Parents must take time for their own needs or they will find themselves resenting their tod-dlers and being less than effective as parents. The needs of parents will vary according to family arrangements.

The Parent Who Stays Home

Traditionally, in our society, it was the mother who stayed home to raise the toddler. Now, however, an increasing number of fathers are more heavily involved in child care. Either parent will have special needs and problems. And when both parents work outside the home, there is also a greater reliance on child-care professionals or child-care centers.

Spending the whole day with a toddler is exhausting. Parents who work in the home may not have time to keep things as neat as they would like, especially since toddlers drop and spill things. Parents of toddlers should try to lower their housekeeping standards a little. The spouse who works outside the home can do many of the household chores in the evening to help the parent who has been with the toddler all day.

Parents who stay home to care for toddlers often feel that their minds are becoming dull, even though it takes a lot of thinking to keep ahead of a toddler. These parents may feel that they never talk about anything but their children. If possible, the care-giving parent should try to find someone else to take care of the child one morning or afternoon a week. This will give the parent time to pursue adult interests. In addition, both parents should try to leave time to spend alone with each other. This is such a busy time in a young couple's life that they often forget to make time for one another. This can put a strain on the marriage, and, in the long run, it is not good for the toddler.

Parents need time with each other, time away from their child, and time for socializing.

If parents have friends, relatives, or baby-sitters they can trust, they should try to take an occasional weekend away from their children. They should not feel guilty about this. If they have done all they can to make children secure, the children will not suffer. Children may "act up" for a few days when the parents return. But once the normal routine has been reestablished, the children will settle down.

Parents Who Work Outside the Home

When both parents work, either part time or full time, they may feel more fulfilled as individuals. But they must also recognize that their lives will be even busier and more hectic than when one stays at home.

Finding proper care for their children is a major concern of parents who work outside the home. Schools for toddlers will be discussed in Chapter 28. However, many parents prefer to have private care givers for their children.

Working parents of toddlers may now face a special problem. They may realize that the person who was a wonderful care giver for the baby is not the best person to take care of the growing toddler. For example, Anne's mother, Freda, had been working since Anne was 6 months old. Ms. Clifford, the baby-sitter, had been a warm and loving care giver. She devoted all her attention to Anne, smiled and sang to her, and took her out for walks. Sometimes, she even called Anne "my baby."

One day when Freda came home, Ms. Clifford greeted her with a frown. "Anne is getting to be such a bad girl," she said. "She refused to eat her lunch today. And she tries to pick up dirty things from the ground every time we go out." Anne, who was now 15 months old, was displaying normal toddler behavior. But this baby-sitter had definite ideas about what "good" behavior was and could not tolerate the toddler stage. After a few more episodes like this, Freda re-

Both parents work outside the home in 18.5 percent of all two-parent families in the United States.

alized that she would have to find someone else to take care of her child.

Another type of problem may be frustrating and exhausting to the parent who works outside the home. Many children will be on their best behavior for a baby-sitter or at a toddler center. Then, when they see their parents, they will revert to negativism, whining, and other babyish behavior. How many parents have heard a care giver say, "He never acts like this when he's with me"? The child sometimes seems to be punishing the parent for leaving.

Parents should realize that such behavior, although it is certainly not pleasant, is normal. Toddlers need to display such behavior at times. They may act this way with parents simply because they feel most secure with them. Well-adjusted toddlers know that parents will still love them, even when they are fussy and babyish. Tired as they are, parents should try to keep their sense of humor and remain calm.

The Single Parent

In a population survey taken in March 1978, the U.S. Census Bureau estimated that almost half of all children born today will spend a meaningful part of their childhood with only one parent. This survey indicates that there is a sharp rise in the number of single parents. Single parents experience more than the usual problems that face parents of toddlers. The single parent also may face loneliness. Single parents do not have wives or husbands to hand the child to when they need relief. They may feel that they have no one to talk to at the end of a long day. If they are single as a result of separation, divorce, or death, their toddlers may be having emotional problems. Children of this age are not verbal enough to talk about their feelings. So single parents will need to give them extra attention—at a time when the parent also needs extra attention.

Friends and relatives are especially important to the single parent. Having someone to take care of the toddler for a while can give the parent a needed break.

Single parents have formed groups in many localities. They get together to talk over their problems, to form baby-sitting pools or play groups, and to help set up toddler centers in their communities. Sometimes, simply being able to talk to other adults in the same situation helps the single parent feel less alone.

Baby-sitters

Parents who want to go out regularly should find several competent baby-sitters to call. Many high school students need and enjoy this kind of experience.

Parents should be sure that toddlers know the sitter well. Perhaps parents should ask the sitter to come an hour early the first time or two. The list of instructions and emergency numbers parents should leave is discussed in Chapter 15, "Home Routines for Infants."

Children may protest loudly when parents leave. If the parents have confidence in the baby-sitter, they should *never* let the child's screaming stop them from going out. It is best to kiss the child good-bye and leave quickly. Sometimes parents come back again and again to reassure the child. This only makes the child feel the parents are not sure of themselves, and the toddler will

Parents of toddlers should know of several capable babysitters.

cry even harder. If parents are really worried, they can call as soon as they have reached their destination. The sitter will usually say, "She stopped crying as soon as you got in the car."

Concluding Comments

Life with toddlers is both frustrating and rewarding. The life-style of parents must necessarily adjust to fit the toddlers' needs for food, rest, and activity. Toddlers demand to move about independently. Yet their ability to recognize and reason about danger is still undeveloped. House and yard arrangements must take this fact into consideration.

Parents must also remember to consider their own needs when living with a toddler. They should make time for each other and try to get out occasionally. Working parents and single parents may have special problems, but they can try to get help from each other and from other care-giving adults.

Activities

1. Ask your parents to describe any bedtime ritual you had when you were a toddler. Did you have a security object? What was it?
2. Ask three parents of toddlers about their child's sleeping habits.
   a. What is each toddler's nap schedule?
   b. At what time does each toddler go to bed at night?
   c. Describe each toddler's bedtime ritual.
   d. How early does each wake up in the morning?
3. Talk with a toddler's parent who does not work away from home. Does the parent make time for personal activities? Or does she or he feel constantly involved with the toddler?
4. Now talk with a toddler's parent who does work away from home. This may be either a single parent or a parent whose spouse also works away from home. What problems does this parent have in finding time for the toddler, for household tasks, and for personal interests and needs?
5. Picture yourself in one of the following situations:
   a. A parent and toddler are waiting on the checkout line in a supermarket. The toddler grabs a package from a low shelf and tries to open it. The parent takes the package away. The toddler starts to scream and cry.
   b. A parent has taken a toddler along to a self-service laundry. The parent is busy putting laundry and soap powder into the washers. Meanwhile, the child toddles away and tugs at the door of a dryer being used by someone else.
   c. A parent and toddler are shopping in a department store. While the parent is trying on a garment, the child starts to toddle out of the fitting room, back into the store.

After you play out one of the above scenes in your mind, write a report. In your report, answer the following questions. Consult the chapter for information. You might also ask some parents of young children for suggestions.
   a. As the parent, what would you do in the situation? How would you use direct and indirect guidance, as discussed in Chapter 25?
   b. What actions would you try to avoid?
   c. How would you keep the problem from happening again?
   d. Share your conclusions with your classmates.

Feeding Toddlers

Objectives

To explain why a toddler's need for food has decreased.
To explain how to encourage toddlers to feed themselves.
To explain the importance of nutritious foods for toddlers.

"Here's your cereal, Michelle," said Jim to his 2-year-old daughter. He set the cereal in front of her. It was warm oatmeal with milk and a few raisins.

Michelle began to eat the cereal. But she was distracted by her big brother, who was leaving for school. She watched Stan until he was gone, then turned her attention to the cereal.

Jim had already said, "Good-bye, have a good day, Stan" and closed the door. He poured himself a cup of coffee and sat back down at the breakfast table with Michelle. "You're doing fine, Michelle," he said with an approving smile.

Michelle liked to have her father stay with her while she ate. He fixed a piece of toast, gave her half, and ate the other half with his coffee.

Michelle said, "More milk." Jim poured a small amount into her cup. She handles herself pretty well, Jim thought proudly, remembering the mess Michelle used to make when she first started learning to eat.

Self-feeding

Learning to feed themselves is a major advance for toddlers. By the age of 12 months, many babies are able to hold a spoon. If they do not feed themselves, it is time for parents and care givers to hand them a spoon and to encourage them to use it. Most toddlers are usually eager to try.

These first few months of self-feeding are a messy time. The cereal gets all over the toddler's face. Fingers are covered with food. Milk frequently gets spilled. After a meal, a bath may be required to clean up the child who is just learning to manage a spoon and a cup alone. But parents survive the period, and toddlers thrive. By 15 to 16 months, toddlers who have had 4 months' practice feeding themselves are usually quite capable. If parents wait until 20 months to encourage self-feeding, the same mess usually results. Also, toddlers whose parents wait may begin to think that feeding themselves is not their job.

Parents must give 1-year-olds the freedom to feed themselves. At first, they take a lot of time and effort to eat even a little. Their skills improve with practice.

The toddler's high chair or feeding table can be set next to the family's dining table. The toddler will enjoy this sociable situation. Generally, toddlers eat the food the family eats. A plastic cloth or some newspapers can be placed under the child's chair to reduce the worry about the mess the child will make. A plastic feeding apron with a pocket along the bottom for catching food is some help in keeping food off the child's clothing. A washcloth kept nearby is essential for washing the toddler. This keeps the child presentable and keeps sticky fingerprints from getting on the house and furnishings. A toddler who is handed the washcloth and told, "Wash your face," will get some of the food off and will not mind the face washing so much.

Milk from a Cup

Toddlers will take most milk from a cup, though they may still want a bottle at naptime or bedtime. It is wise to fill the toddler's cup no more than one-quarter full at a time. Then, when a spill occurs, there is less to clean up. It is better to teach the child to ask for "More, please." This way, the decision of "how much" is left to the child.

Some parents worry that milk intake will drop when their child moves to the cup. This is true to some extent. However, most children are now eating other nutritious foods. The influence of parents and of sisters and brothers who drink milk may be important. The toddler will tend to notice others who drink milk and will imitate them. Milk is an important food for young children, since their teeth and bones are growing. A child should have 24 ounces of milk each day in order to have the calcium

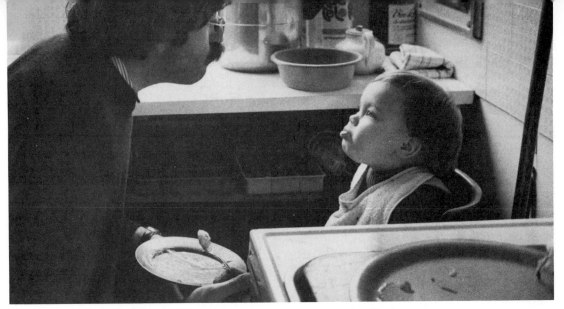

Toddlers become less interested in eating. Their need for food is not increasing as rapidly as it did during the first year. Parents often worry needlessly that their children are not getting enough to eat. Believe children when they say, "No more."

? Decisions, Decisions

Jake mixes his applesauce in his mashed potatoes, dips his cheese in the juice, and wants to eat his pudding and meat at the same time. His care giver is upset about these strange combinations. What should she do?

needed. Remember that milk is available in other nutritious forms. Cheese and yogurt are good substitutes. Many toddlers love a grilled cheese sandwich, cut into small, bite-sized pieces. If you give a child yogurt, offer the plain, un-flavored kind, not the heavily sugared kind. You may think the yogurt needs sugar or honey to taste good, but let the child decide. Many children love the tart flavor of plain yogurt.

Reduced Appetite

Growth occurs at a slower rate for the toddler than for the infant. This means that the amount a toddler eats is not increasing as rapidly as it did during infancy. This slower growth fact is hard for parents to remember, and sometimes parents play games to encourage a toddler to eat more. The games may turn into harsh battles, which the parents are sure to lose. Such battles should be avoided. Children may begin to think they are "eating for Mommy" or "eating for Daddy," when eating is something you do for yourself. There will be days when a child is only a little hungry. So after 10 to 15 minutes of having the food in front of the child, the parent should put it away. Then the child can be cleaned up. When children do not eat, parents should avoid filling them up on snacks. Otherwise, the children will learn that, if they do not eat at mealtime, there will be a snack to eat soon. This is a difficult habit to break if it gets started.

Eating preferences are very individual. Many nutritionists now feel that eating several small meals a day is healthier than eating three large meals. If a toddler likes to eat this way, parents should make sure that nutritious foods are provided, such as whole-grain crackers, cheese, fruit, and unsugared juices. Water should also be offered frequently. That way, the toddler gets plenty of fluids and does not overdo the juices. Toddlers who do not seem to like water will usually drink diluted juice. High-sugar foods are damaging to the teeth and may spoil the child's appetite for nutritious foods.

Some parents have the habit of moving around the kitchen while the toddler is supposed to be eating. A toddler may get distracted and want to get down when there is no one else at the table for company. Some parents find that sitting down with the toddler and relaxing with a glass of milk works better than leaving a toddler to eat alone. Also, this is a good time for socializing.

An important rule for parents and care givers is to let the toddler begin deciding how much to eat. It is best to put only a teaspoon-sized serving of appropriate foods on the child's plate to encourage tasting everything. A toddler will enjoy asking for more. Some toddlers will object to having certain foods on their plates. It is best for the parents not to make an issue of it.

Around age 2, toddlers begin to use a fork for bites of fruit, vegetable, or meat. Knives will not be used until children are 3 or more. A piece of toast used as a pusher is handy for a toddler who is learning to fill a spoon or fork.

Remember that toddlers are in a "no" stage, often saying "no" to any question. For example, to the question, "Do you want some carrots?" they will probably say, "No." Say instead, "Here are your carrots. See if your spoon can pick them up." Avoid giving toddlers a choice unless you are willing to accept the "no."

Eating is usually much more important to parents than it is to toddlers. Many parents may be replaying struggles they had with their own parents when they were children. Also, preparing food for someone who refuses to eat it can be very annoying. The parent actually feels rejected.

Jill, age 2, had a diet of yogurt, fruit, grilled-cheese sandwiches, peanut butter, and milk. Both parents fretted, and so did both sets of grandparents, although the pediatrician told them repeatedly to stop worrying. Whenever Jill ate with the family, her mother and father would say, "Do you want some broccoli, chicken, potatoes?" The answer was always a definite "No."

One day, Jill's parents were discussing her health. They realized Jill had had no illness more serious than a runny nose for a year. She was growing normally, her hair and skin were beautiful, and she had plenty of energy. Her parents resolved that day not to mention food to Jill again. They allowed her to continue her strange, but nutritious, diet and never tried to get her to eat any of their food. They had never made non-nutritious snacks available.

Jill seemed to know what was good for her, even if it did not please the adults around her. Her parents were wise not to force her to eat. Trying to force-feed children turns mealtime into an unpleasant battle. It ruins children's appetites. It may even cause vomiting.

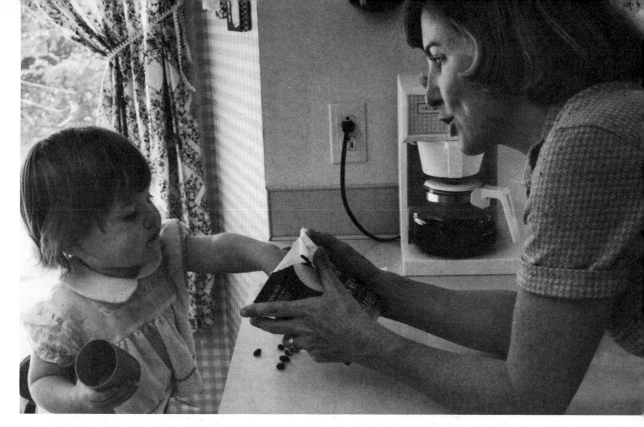

Toddlers will choose a nutritious diet if nutritious foods are offered.

In addition, making too big a fuss about food can be one cause of obesity in children. Insisting that a child "clean the plate" when the child is no longer hungry may cause a buildup of fat cells that will remain a problem through adulthood.

Nutritious Foods Available

Parents and care givers should provide only good, wholesome, and nutritious foods for toddlers. Adults should keep other foods away from toddlers entirely. It is very easy to get toddlers into the habit of wanting soft drinks and candy if these are around. But toddlers will not want these foods if they are not accustomed to them. They will choose a nutritious diet if the foods available are nutritious. The many young children with teeth full of cavities are evidence of poor diet resulting from too many sweets and too little milk. A child who drinks a soft drink will not have room for a glass of milk. Similarly, a child who eats a sweet doughnut or some candy will not have an appetite for an egg or some fruit.

Sweet foods should never be used as rewards. Saying, "You can't have your dessert until you finish your meat" makes children think dessert is more valuable. Then they will want sweets even more.

Toddlers like their food at room temperature, so serious efforts to keep it hot or cold are not needed. It is useless to argue with a child and say, "Eat your food while it's hot." The child very likely does not care if the food cools.

Concluding Comments

The toddler period can be one of turmoil when it comes to eating, but parents and care givers can avoid some of the pitfalls. It is the time to let children take over their own feeding. Believe the toddler when you hear, "No more." Avoid coaxing a child to eat, as this can create problems that may become serious. With a decrease in the rate of growth, the need for food is reduced. This is a fact that parents should try to understand and remember. If a child is growing normally and is healthy, parents should not worry too much about what the child eats, as long as available foods are nutritious.

Nutritious foods are very important for toddlers. High-sugar foods should be avoided or eliminated to protect teeth.

Activities

1. With parents' permission, observe a toddler at mealtime:
   a. Record the child's age in years and months.
   b. How is the child seated and prepared for the meal?
   c. What is the menu for the meal?
   d. What does the child do and say during the meal?
   e. Does the child seem to enjoy the meal?
   f. Does the child feed him- or herself most of the time?
2. Make a record of everything the toddler eats and drinks for 24 hours. If necessary, ask the parents to help you. Did the child get foods from each of the Basic Four food groups?
3. Why do you think Jill was healthy, even though she ate only yogurt, fruit, grilled-cheese sandwiches, peanut butter, and milk? How does this diet fit into the Basic Four food plan?
4. Make some toast pushers either at home or in the school kitchen.
   a. Ask the toddler whose eating habits you have been observing to taste-test your product.
   b. Report the child's verdict to the class.
5. Interview the toddler's parent:
   a. How does the parent feel about the child's progress in self-feeding?
   b. Describe any feeding problems with the child?
   c. What kinds of food does the child like? What does the child dislike?
   d. Write a report of your visit, then discuss it with your classmates.

Schools for Toddlers

Objectives
To describe three types of schools for toddlers.
To explain the need for schools for toddlers.
To describe high-quality schools for toddlers.
To describe the qualities of good care givers for toddlers.

Terms to look for   day care • family day-care home • play school • solitary play

"I need someone to help me take care of my son. He's 14 months old," said Mary Ann, a 19-year-old widow who was talking to the director of the day-care center. Her counselor at the adult education center had recommended that she look into this day-care center for help with her child so that she might continue her education. She explained. "My husband, Jeff, died last month in a motorcycle crash. There was no insurance and no social security. But I can get a grant to finish school. I dropped out of high school when I was 16 so I could marry Jeff. If I can complete my high school equivalency, then I think I'd like to go to technical school and learn computer programming. Now I have to plan how to support myself and my child."

Day-care directors hear variations of Mary Ann's story every week. The director explained the service to Mary Ann and showed her the rooms and playground where Jeffrey would spend his time during each day. Mary Ann was grateful for the warm and understanding response that the director gave her. She began to feel good about her decision to go on with her education. She felt that Jeffrey would be in good hands.

growing need for day care for toddlers. In most parts of the United States, day care for infants and toddlers has never been as common as day care for older preschool children. There is presently a lively debate over whether there "ought" to be day care for infants and toddlers. There are parents who now want and need such care for their toddlers. Mary Ann is one of a growing number of one-parent families requiring toddler care. The demand is so great and the spaces so few that the high-quality centers nearly all have waiting lists.

Play School

Play schools for toddlers are being organized around the country. These usually last about 2 hours in the morning for a few days each week. Many play schools include the parents in some helping activity around the centers. Some of the play schools for toddlers are cooperative groups organized by mothers and fathers who want some group play experience for their toddlers. The costs of these cooperative groups are low, because the parents do most of the work, themselves.

A group of parents can form a cooperative play school for their toddlers.

Toddler Programs

There are three types of programs that accept toddlers. They are day care, play schools, and family-care homes.

Day Care

Day care refers to 8 to 10 hours of care outside the home, with provisions for eating, sleeping, and playing and for health and safety protection. There is a

? Decisions, Decisions

Everything is happening at once! Alice finishes a puzzle and wants your praise. Sam starts crying because Janet pushed him over. Lewis spilled his milk and is now tracking it all over the floor. Ray just picked up the sharp scissors off the lead teacher's desk. What do you do first?

Family Day-Care Homes

Family day care refers to care by women and men who keep children in their homes for a fee. They may accept only toddlers. Or they may include a wide age range of young children. Some include after-school children as well. Many family day-care arrangements are made among friends and neighbors. In some states, these people are licensed, and in others they are not. Usually these adults care for four or five children in addition to their own.

Sometimes family day care is an excellent arrangement for toddlers. The atmosphere is homelike. And the presence of children of different ages may be beneficial. Parents should be sure that the care-giving mother or father shares most of their views about child rearing. Also, parents should be sure that television is not used as a substitute care giver.

What Is a High-quality Toddler Program?

An ideal toddler program provides both care and educational activities for children from ages 1 to 3. The basic routines of the home that were discussed at length in Chapter 26 must be carried out for the children. High-quality care means that the staff provides care and educational activities that are as good as or better than most children get at home. Routines of eating, sleeping, and playing are necessarily individualized. Careful attention is given to the health, comfort, and cleanliness of the toddlers.

If you dropped by a high-quality tod-dler-care center, you might see some toddlers playing with toys, others sleeping, and still others eating or being diapered. There is a relaxed spirit in the room of five or six children. The care givers know that high-pitched voices and too-fast activity can overstimulate and tire their charges.

There is color and beauty in the room, for toddlers need things to see, touch, and wonder about. There are things to climb over and under and to hide in and crawl through. It looks as if having fun would be easy.

There is a comfortable, friendly feeling among the care givers. They obviously love toddlers and have a great deal of patience and sensitivity. They show their enjoyment of children by talking with them and giving hugs freely. When the need arises, they calmly help to comfort what may seem like a very upset child.

There are strong links with the toddlers' homes. You will see care givers reporting on the day's happenings to parents. You will see parents sharing the pleasures and problems of the night or weekend with care givers, who are accepted as a part of an enlarged family.

What Activities Do Toddlers Like?

First, you may want to review some of the special characteristics of toddlers. Then, think about what sorts of activities toddler centers should offer. Remember that toddlers usually engage in solitary play—unconnected to the play of the children around them. Parallel play develops later.

Toddlers who have been around other children a good deal may be somewhat

A good day-care program for toddlers provides a homelike routine, including lots of individual attention and lots of things to do.

more social. They may pass an object back and forth, hug each other, or poke at each other briefly before going again to play on their own. Good care givers will encourage and praise such contacts.

Assisting in a School for Toddlers

In many study programs, you will be allowed to assist with toddlers. You are being entrusted with an important responsibility. You should prepare yourself in these 10 ways.

1. Spend some time with the teaching care giver—the person in charge of the small group of children. You should take time whenever possible to talk about what this care giver is doing—step-by-step—before you have to be responsible for any toddlers. Listen carefully, watch closely, and take notes. The opportunities for such discussion and demonstration may be few, but they will be very helpful.

2. Watch what the head care giver does with the toddlers, and follow

that example. Toddlers get very confused if they are handled in different ways by their care givers. Consistency is very important to the adjustment of the toddlers.

3. Use your creativity in interpreting toddlers' behavior and applying the facts you know about child development. Become skillful at encouraging toddlers to keep trying to do a task. You can think of new toys and new ways to use old ones as you get used to your role. In time, you will become a knowledgeable care giver like your teaching care giver. With this experience, you can become a teaching care giver, yourself.

4. Be alert, clean, and orderly so that you can keep the toddlers healthy, safe, and happy.

5. Get well acquainted with the toddlers, and enjoy their success and progress. You will have a front seat for watching young lives unfold. Each child is special and different from the others. For example, one day Amy will be helpless as a baby, wanting help with a jacket. The next day she will surprise you. She will put the jacket on and try to put the zipper together, too.

6. Give warm, affectionate hugs, and share your lap generously with the toddlers.

7. Be calm and professional when the going gets rough—when all at once one toddler throws a tantrum, another spills milk, and another needs a diaper change. A professional care giver, like a professional doctor, is cool in emergencies. This makes everyone feel confident.

8. Learn more about child develop-
ment and how it applies to "your" children. Learn also about play activities for toddlers and about talking to them. And learn about how to deal effectively with parents and your care-giver associates.

9. Be prepared to be tired and frustrated at times. Caring for toddlers is taxing. However, openly discuss difficulties with your care-giver associates. Probably, together, you can find the causes of some problems and some possible solutions.

Assisting in a school for toddlers is demanding. For most care givers, the enjoyment of watching daily progress is a warm reward.

10. Share with parents their toddler's successes and your interest and concern. Remember that many things care givers discuss with parents should be kept confidential.

Concluding Comments

Toddler care and schooling outside the home are unique and special, because the needs of toddlers differ from other age groups. Toddler-care centers are relatively new in the United States. Parents and child-care experts want to be sure that high-quality programs will be offered. An awesome responsibility falls on care givers who influence children in their most formative years, when ideas and habits are first being formed. Those who take part in these programs—parents and care givers alike—must be constantly alert to ensure that first-rate care is provided.

Activities

Research the away-from-home care available for toddlers in your community:

1. Call the nearest day-care center.
   a. How many children can be enrolled?
   b. What is the age range of the children in the center?
   c. How many men and how many women are on the staff?
   d. How much does it cost to have a toddler cared for in the center?
2. Learn about play schools in the community.
   a. How involved are parents in the play school?
   b. Who pays the expenses of the play school?
   c. What is the age range of the children?
3. If you have not already done so, find out about family day care in your area.
   a. Is there one telephone number you can call to get a list of family day-care centers in your area? What is the number?
   b. Have these centers been licensed by the state? If so, what are the requirements for licensing?
4. Visit one of the above facilities. Answer the following questions:
   a. How many children aged one to three are in one group?
   b. How many care givers are present?
   c. What are the children doing?
   d. How would you describe the emotional climate of this group—happy, chaotic, sad, stressful? Explain.
   e. How does the care given the group you visited compare with the kind of care that has been recommended in this chapter?

Learning Activities for Toddlers

Objectives

To describe qualities of good toys for toddlers.
To list toys for toddlers that will stimulate learning in several areas of development.

Terms to look for   dramatic play • hidden curriculum •
large motor-coordination toys • small motor-coordination toys

Sharon, who is 2 years old, was trying out a new puzzle. It was made of nine different shapes in three colors—yellow, red, and blue. Sharon sat at the table. With her left hand, she removed each piece on the left-hand side. She placed the pieces on the table, next to the puzzle edge, in the order of removal.

With the right hand, she removed the pieces from the right-hand side of the puzzle. She lined them up in order along the right side of the puzzle. Now, the center pieces presented a problem, but not for long. Sharon used her right hand to line the pieces in a row just above the puzzle. Now the puzzle board was empty.

Sharon began with her left hand and returned the pieces, one by one, to the left side of the puzzle. Now her right hand picked up the pieces along the right-hand side and returned each of those correctly. Again she used her right hand for the center row, returning the pieces to their proper places.

Sharon seemed to enjoy her new puzzle. She worked it several times. She organized her exploration in a careful way. Another child might have dumped all nine pieces in a heap and might have used a trial-and-error method to get them back. But Sharon kept the pieces in line in such a way that she was never confused as to where they belonged.

Who knows where Sharon's ability to handle this problem will lead her? It is of interest, too, that Sharon used both hands with skill.

Puzzles such as the one Sharon worked are just one type of learning activity that parents of young toddlers can provide. Puzzles are part of the "hidden curriculum" set up by parents who want their child to learn well.

Parents usually have the highest hopes for their child. They may not expect the child to be a "superkid." But most hope for average or above-average abilities in all developmental areas. Thus, concerned parents work to provide good educational toys for their child.

Learning as They Play

Learning occurs as the toddler plays and engages in eating, resting, bathing, and other personal activities. You have studied about physical, mental, social, and emotional development as though they were separate and distinct. Actually, all these areas are really coordinated or integrated within the child. The teaching you do and the toys you provide bring together activities that stimulate several types of development.

Some parents spend a great deal for toys. Parents could save a lot of money if they planned purchases more carefully. They need to consider the educational value of the toy as well as its enjoyment value. Some toys are cute or "gimmicky" but have little educational or enjoyment value. The dollars-per-year cost can be figured for each toy. If a toy for 1 child falls apart in 1 year, the cost-per-year-per-child is higher than if a toy lasts 2 children for 2 years. Remember, though, that a toy that falls apart from repeated use is far more valuable than the toy that is never used.

on, the wagon becomes a "car" in dramatic play and is parked in a block "garage" that the toddler builds. Such versatility makes the toy less costly than a toy that serves only one purpose and is then forgotten. A windup toy may be a single-purpose toy. Usually the parent winds it up, and the child watches. When the child finds that there is nothing else to do with the toy, the child loses interest.

Choosing Toys

Toys for toddlers should be durable and strong, safe to use, and usable in different ways and in different places.

1. *Durable and strong.* Toys will take a beating from the toddler and friends, so the toys must be tough enough to withstand this. Many toys have continued uses as the child matures. Thus, durability is important.
2. *Safe to use.* No matter how the toy is used, it must have no sharp corners that might cut. It must have no small parts that come off and that could be swallowed. And it must have no paints that are poisonous if chewed on, for example, lead-based paints. Lead-based paint is now illegal in commercially made children's toys.
3. *Usable in different ways and in different places.* A good toy stimulates the child to think of several ways to use it. For example, a toddler's small wagon is a pull toy today. Tomorrow, the child may load and unload it with other toys or may sit in it. Later

Large Motor-coordination Toys and Equipment

A climbing gym is popular in many toddler centers. It offers a toddler an opportunity to climb stairs, sit, and then slide down. In addition, the child can crawl under the slide and sit inside a hidden space.

Wooden planks may be added to the climbing gym. They can provide an elevated place for sitting, for climbing on and over, and for jumping up and down and off. Toddlers' leg skills and ability to balance are challenged. Climbing toys can be purchased for the home also.

Kiddie cars and kiddie wagons encourage walking skills. The toddler is not yet ready for pedaling. Pull toys also invite a child to walk around the playroom or yard.

Balls are important for stimulating motor activities. Toddlers' catching and throwing skills are only beginning. Toddlers enjoy rolling balls along the floor. Balls should be made of soft material—rubber, foam, plastic. Finger holes or spaces in the ball make it easier for little fingers to grasp.

Toddlers learn from everyday experiences as well as from toys. This child gets the family "junk mail" to work on and play with.

Small Motor-coordination Toys

Puzzles give small fingers coordination practice. For toddlers, select those with only six to nine pieces.

Large-sized crayons, chalks, and paint brushes are best for toddlers. They generally grasp with a fist and take large, whole-arm strokes.

Nesting cans or cubes that may be placed inside each other or stacked to build a tower are a challenge that toddlers enjoy. Toddlers also like stacking rings that require the placing of a ring over a spindle. Parents can collect different-sized tops from cottage cheese or yogurt containers, plastic milk jugs, and discarded medicine bottles. The toddler will enjoy sorting through them or putting all of them in a box or can, then dumping them all out again.

You can make toys from items around the home that will help toddlers with small, motor coordination. See page 286 for ideas.

Floating bath toys can make bath time more inviting. Items around the home, such as plastic dishes and bottles, may be used. A plastic sieve can be made by punching holes in the lower half of a plastic milk jug with an ice pick. This sieve is nonrusting and easily replaced. Toddlers like to watch the water run through the holes in the sieve.

Dramatic Play

Large cardboard blocks are versatile pieces of equipment that last 6 or 7 years. This makes the cost-per-year quite low. If they are purchased during the toddler period, they will be used in many ways for years to come. The blocks, about the size of a large shoe box, are reinforced inside. This makes them extra strong and durable. The toddler often carries a block around under the arm in the same way a football player carries a ball. Later on, the blocks will be "houses," "garages," and "roads" as the child develops imaginative play around them.

Dolls and stuffed toys should be washable. Toddlers may adopt one of the cuddly toys as a comfort toy. They often turn to some favored soft object or toy when feeling tired, ill, or lonesome.

A hat or scarf may be worn to imitate someone the toddler knows. It also may be used to play a hide-and-seek game by covering a favorite small toy.

"One more time, Mom." Records can bring children songs, stories, and dances. Here, a mother lets her toddler place the record on the turntable.

? Decisions, Decisions

You need to buy a birthday present for a 2-year-old. What can you buy for less than $2 that the toddler will enjoy and learn from?

Music

Music can enrich a toddler's life in many ways, for example, through songs, records, and rhythm instruments. Parents can begin with the songs of their own childhood. Children's music books are beautifully illustrated. They will stimulate both child and parents to break out in song.

Books

Books for the toddler should be simple, durable, and well illustrated. Parents should help toddlers enjoy books now, since books will enrich the child's whole life. If parents and teachers want to promote a child's success in school and later in life, they can hardly do better than to see that the child has books. Reading to a toddler can be fun for both adult and child.

Toys to Make

The diagrams that follow this chapter show toys that parents, care givers, and baby-sitters can make for toddlers. If you assist in a toddler center or if you baby-sit privately, you may want to pack a bag full of some of these toys. These suggestions may also give you some ideas of your own for toddler toys.

Concluding Comments

Parents and care givers should give careful consideration to purchasing toys and equipment for toddlers. Play is very educational for toddlers if enough thought is given to choosing toys and equipment. Good toys are not always the most expensive items. Many can be made of used household items.

Toys for toddlers must be durable and strong, safe to use, and usable in different ways and in different places. A toddler's playing with appropriate objects stimulates all areas of development—physical, social, mental, and emotional.

Activities

1. Visit a toy store:
   a. Choose three toys for toddlers that meet the three criteria for choosing toys, as described in this chapter.
   b. Describe each toy. Discuss what the toddler might do with each item. Also record the cost of each toy.
   c. Choose three toys that do not meet the three criteria for choosing toys.
   d. Describe them and tell why they would not be suitable toys for toddlers. Record the price of each toy.
   e. How do the prices of the acceptable and unacceptable toys compare?
2. Choose a book you think a toddler would enjoy.

   a. Record the title, author, and a description of the book.
   b. Read the book to a toddler.
   c. Describe the child's reactions to the story.
3. Make a "mail-slot" game for a toddler.
   a. Find a shortening or coffee can with a plastic lid.
   b. Cut out a slot about 3 inches by $3/8$ inches in the lid with a knife. Make the slot big enough so the plastic tops of orange juice cans go through.
   c. Secure a dozen pull-off lids from frozen orange juice concentrate containers. Do *not* use lids with sharp edges.)
   d. Use your "mail-slot" game with a toddler.
   e. Report what happens.

Making Toys for Babies and Toddlers

The playthings you make yourself are not only the least expensive, they are often a child's favorite. You can quickly make a toy to encourage a specific skill that a child is developing or to reflect the child's current interests.

large buttons

large metal jingle bells

dried peas

cornflakes   rice

Babies use rattles and shakers to learn that they can make noise happen. Toddlers love them for the pure joy of noise. Use margarine dishes, plastic juice cans, or film canisters with securely taped covers, pill containers with child-proof lids, or securely fastened, transparent plastic bottles and jars of assorted shapes. Fill with safe, nontoxic objects. Any nonedible filling should be too large to swallow.

Toddlers love to fill, carry, and dump. Homemade totes make excellent carriers.

Cut a large plastic bleach bottle in half.

Cover the cut edges with masking tape or colored tape. Make handles of ribbon or plastic. Decorate the outside. The bottom half is a tote.

The top half of the plastic bleach bottle makes a fine funnel.

Soda-bottle carriers make good totes. Line each section with adhesive paper, or put a container in each. Decorate.

Use actual photographs of the baby or toddler with parents or other significant adults. Mount on cards. Keep available in a book or hanging low on the wall. Cover with clear adhesive-backed paper. This is especially good for school and substitute-care situations.

A plastic sieve can be made by poking holes with an ice pick in the bottom of a plastic milk jug.

To make bath toys, partly fill clear plastic bottles with colored water and objects that rotate or float in the water. For example, use large wood beads, spools, keys, large buttons, and so forth, to fill the bottles. Tops must be fastened securely. Glue placed under the threaded top will help.

Dropping objects into a container is an ideal game for developing hand-eye coordination.

in here

Use a large bleach bottle. Cut an opening to catch dropped objects. Cover the edge with colored tape or masking tape.

comes out here

To make picture cards, use magazine pictures of simple objects, of people, or of food, and paste them on cardboard or large index cards. Cover with clear adhesive-backed paper.

Keep them in a shoe box or some other available container so that babies and toddlers can pick them up and look at them.

Use a 1- or 2-pound coffee can with a plastic lid, or use an oatmeal box. Cut a hole in the lid. Use clothes pins, poker chips, small blocks, and so forth, to drop in.

Cardboard dividers from supermarket egg-delivery cartons (or sheets of heavy cardboard) make sturdy books for the very young. Select pictures that are large, clear, simple, uncluttered. Pick a theme—babies, animals, mommies, daddies, food, toys, and so forth. Be sure to choose pictures that show all parts. For example, do not choose a picture of half of a person or part of a dog. Cover them with clear adhesive paper.

Or make a texture book. Use velvet, terry cloth, foil, or sandpaper to paste on dividers.

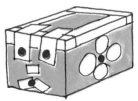

Milk cartons covered with colorful adhesive paper make fine blocks. They are sturdy and have a size relationship to one another. Use quarts, pints, half-pints.

Cardboard cartons, sealed with the dividers left inside, make sturdy, large blocks for lifting, sitting on, stacking, climbing on. Decorate with adhesive-backed paper, or leave as is.

287

SUGGESTED READINGS FOR PART 4

Brazelton, T. Berry, *Toddlers and Parents: A Declaration of Independence.* New York: Dell Publishing Co., 1974.

Briggs, Dorothy Corkille, *Your Child's Self-Esteem: The Key to Life.* Garden City, New York: Doubleday & Co. Inc., 1975.

Comer, James P. and Alvin F. Poussaint, *Black Child Care.* New York: Pocket Books, 1976.

Dodson, Fitzhugh, *How to Father.* New York: The New American Library, Inc., 1973.

Fraiberg, Selma, *The Magic Years: Understanding and Handling the Problems of Early Childhood.* New York: Charles Scribner's Sons, 1968.

Ginott, H. G., *Between Parent and Child.* New York: The Macmillan Co., 1965.

Highberger, Ruth and Carol Schramm, *Child Development for Day Care Workers.* Boston: Houghton Mifflin Co., 1976.

Hildebrand, Verna, *Guiding Young Children.* New York: The Macmillan Co., 1975.

Hope, Karol and Nancy Young, ed., *Momma, The Sourcebook for Single Mothers.* New York: New American Library, 1976.

Keister, Mary Elizabeth, *"The Good Life" for Infants and Toddlers.* Washington, DC: National Association for the Education of Young Children, 1970.

Leach, Penelope, *Your Baby and Child from Birth to Age Five.* New York: Alfred A. Knopf, 1978.

Segal, Marilyn and Don Adceock, *From One to Two Years.* Rolling Hills Estates, California 90274: The Nova University Play and Learn Program, 1976.

Smart, Mollie S. and Russel Smart, *Children Development and Relationships.* New York: The Macmillan Co., 1977.

Spock, Benjamin, *Baby and Child Care.* New York: Pocket Books, 1976.

Your Child from 1 to 6. Children's Bureau Publication No. 30-1962. U.S. Government Printing Office, Washington, DC 20402.

5

The Prekindergartner

You will learn how prekindergartners grow and develop physically, mentally, socially, and emotionally during ages 3 and 4. You will discover a variety of activities for prekindergartners that will aid their total growth and development.

unit

11

The Growing and Developing Prekindergartner

The Prekindergartner Grows Physically

Objectives

To explain the physical development that takes place during the 3- to 5-year period.

To explain how changes in physical development affect the way parenting persons interact with children 3 to 5 years old.

To describe activities that help 3- to 4-year-olds practice large and small motor skills.

To explain services available for disabled children.

Terms to look for large motor skills • mainstreaming • motor skills • small motor skills

"Hold my hand, teacher," begged Pat. He was starting to cross a foot-wide plank that was suspended between two sawhorses.

The teacher put out one finger, and Pat supported himself as he cautiously crossed. He smiled happily as he jumped off. Then he returned to the end of the line to await another turn. As he arrived at point "Go," the teacher again offered one finger. This time, though, Pat said, "I can do it *myself*." He did,

balancing his body with outstretched arms and jumping off the end with increased confidence. The next time around, Pat actually jumped on the board. He made himself spring in a rhythm that he had seen others enjoy.

Pat is typical of children at the prekindergarten ages of 3 and 4. Like others, Pat is making large and rapid progress in developing—physically, mentally, socially and emotionally. In this chapter, you will look at the physical development of prekindergartners.

Both girls and boys need motor-skill practice. Physical skills promote language practice and social contacts. They also add to a child's self-confidence.

Physical Development Relates to Total Development

The physical skills of the prekindergarten child influence other areas of development. For example, the 3- and 4-year-old who can run and climb can move with ease among other children. Generally, 3-year-olds walk well and can run and climb. They may hesitate, though, when other children are around. They sometimes fear that they will be pushed. By age 4, prekindergartners are usually full of self-confidence on the jungle gym or tricycle. They move fast. Sometimes, teachers or parents fear that

they will fall—but they seldom do. They know their own limitations.

At this stage, prekindergartners are making new social contacts with other children on the playground and in the park. These contacts are an important preparation for later life. Thus, physical motor skills are aiding social development. Further, increased social contact requires language for communicating. Language is also needed for solving problems of sharing and taking turns. Therefore, physical skills are indirectly aiding language skills.

As social contact and language exchange take place, emotional development occurs. A child feels more confident and moves away from the parent or care giver. Notice that Pat in the opening story was pleased to refuse the teacher's offer of support. Pat may cry easily or not at all if he is slightly hurt. He may confidently or hesitantly climb the jungle gym. These are examples of emotional development.

Pat shows increasing mental development as he remembers people, places, and events. He also grows in the ability to solve problems. He can decide how to get down from a high place or how to reach a ball that he threw.

Critical Years Are Before Age 5

The prekindergarten years are an important time for children to gain ability in motor skills. *Motor skills* refer to the ability to move the body through space—to walk, run, jump, hop, slide, gallop, and so on. Throwing and catching skills need practice at this time. These skills are basic to learning dances, games, and work-related skills of later years.

Most children practice motor skills naturally if given the space, the time, and the friends to play with. However, in many homes, the space is limited—outdoors as well as indoors. Some parents may want their children to sit quietly in front of the television. These parents do not realize that too little active movement will do permanent damage to their child's motor-skill development.

Unfortunately, some prekindergarten schools may limit children's active running and climbing. They may do so because of lack of space or fear of injury. Some teachers do not want to bother dressing children to go outdoors. Or they do not want to go outside, themselves, to supervise activities. Also, in some schools, some adults do not consider physical-development activities as important as mental-development activities. Thus, children may sit at tables doing learning games for long periods. Much of the same mental learning would result if the children ran, climbed, and investigated outdoors.

Motor-skill practice is vital for both girls and boys. Children of both sexes love and need to run and play, climb and jump.

Very often, adult attitudes shape the way children behave. A parent or care giver might feel that girls should not climb trees or play in an active, unrestrained way. Discouraging such activity may keep girls from developing strong, healthy bodies. It may prevent them from exploring and learning about their environment. Learning physical skills is important to the whole development of the child. Girls and boys both must learn to work with and control their bodies.

Large Motor Skill Practice

The following are some activities that will help children develop their large motor skills. Children can practice these activities at home with their parents or baby-sitters or in the prekindergarten setting. Children who live in small apartments may need to use the sidewalk or park for some activities.

1. Walking
   - forward, backward, sideways, zigzag, stooped low, stretched high.
   - on a balance beam, on a rope laid on the ground or on a piece of masking tape on the playroom floor.
   - like a giant, like a mouse, like a doll, like a dancer.
   - following signals from red and green lights.
   - on stepping stones (for example, on blocks arranged as stepping stones or on carpet squares).

2. Running
   - forward, backward (for older children)
   - with red and green light signals for stop and go.
   - an obstacle course in the yard, park, or gym.

3. Jumping
   - from a box or jumping board (child may want hand held at first).
   - on a jumping board: first up and down, and then off.
   - over a fishing pole raised at only one end, but held loosely in case the child hits the pole (child chooses how high to try jumping).
   - over a pillow placed on a mat or on the grass.
   - combined with running to touch a high object, such as a balloon.

4. Galloping
   - slow, fast.
   - right foot leading, left foot leading.
5. Hopping
   - forward, backward, sideways.
   - bending down to pick up a ball or a bean bag.
   - playing hopscotch.
6. Pedaling
   - forward and backward on a tricycle.

? Decisions,
  Decisions

Ricky is handicapped and walks with a limp. On the first day of the nursery school program, children followed him around imitating his limp. They were having great fun doing this. To your surprise, Ricky thought it was funny too! He seemed to enjoy the attention and was limping a little more than necessary. What would you do if you were the care giver in charge?

Small Motor Skills

Small motor skills continue to develop during the prekindergarten years. As toddlers, the children were just learning to feed themselves. Now, as prekindergartners, they begin to take off and put on clothes, to work large zippers and buttons, and to turn knobs. Large zippers and buttons on clothes encourage independent dressing. The prekindergartners have become more skillful at mealtime and usually eat with less mess.

Large crayons and fat pencils help children develop the muscles and coordination needed in writing. The child first uses a fist grip to scribble all over the paper. Gradually, the child learns to use a writing grip. At that time, smaller crayons and pencils become more appropriate.

Handedness is usually established around age 3 or 4. The hand a child uses reflects which side of the child's brain is dominant. Therefore, trying to force a left-handed child into right-handedness is a mistake. The child can become very confused. In addition, the child may have difficulty later in such skills as reading and writing. Also, forcing right-handedness may make left-handed children feel something is wrong with them, which can damage their self-image. Adults should try to help the left-handed child learn to use the left hand well.

All kinds of puzzles, small blocks, erector sets, lacing kits, small cars, and small dolls stimulate small-motor-skill practice. Many of these objects are more appropriate for 4-year-olds, because they demand greater skills than 3-year-olds have. Teachers and parents should watch the child use small things. If the child seems to be frustrated, adults should put the toys away for a while. Tying shoes is a difficult skill that most children will learn during kindergarten.

All children should practice small motor skills often during the preprimary years. These important skills are the basis for writing, drawing, cutting, and modeling that will be very useful during the later periods. Children need appropriate equipment to use. They also need encouragement and loving support to motivate them to continue their practicing.

Disabling Conditions

Many physical or mental disabilities can occur before, during, and after birth. Damage can result from illness or accident. Today, all states have medical and corrective services available for disabled children. Some states offer services to newborn infants, while others start such help at age 3. Parents or care givers who believe a child needs special help should contact local public health officials for advice on services available.

Mainstreaming

Until recently, disabled children were separated from children without disabilities. Often, disabled children did not attend preschool programs, because there were none available. Sometimes, even school-age children were kept out of school because of lack of funds for special programs.

The federal government has now recognized the right of disabled children to be educated, just like their nondisabled peers. In recent years, there has been a growing movement toward *mainstreaming*—placing disabled children in regular classrooms and thereby keeping those children in the mainstream of life. Educators agree that disabled children develop their potential more fully if they can learn with children who are not disabled.

Even though a child has a disability in one area—for example, blindness—he or she will be able to learn through the senses of hearing, touching, tasting, and smelling. Blind children without other disabilities can run, climb, swing, and ride tricycles like sighted children. Emphasis must always be on the things one *can* do rather than on what one cannot do.

A child confined to a wheelchair can still develop through the senses as other children do. Physical therapy and exercise may help such a child gain at least partial use of the legs. Often the child will develop very strong arms to compensate for the loss of leg strength.

Special teaching techniques may be required if disabled children are in the school in which you are assisting. Follow your teacher's advice closely. A question you might think about is: How would I want to be treated if I were considered to be disabled? With opportunities for education and training, many

Most disabled children can be mainstreamed into regular preschool programs. Both the disabled child and the other children benefit.

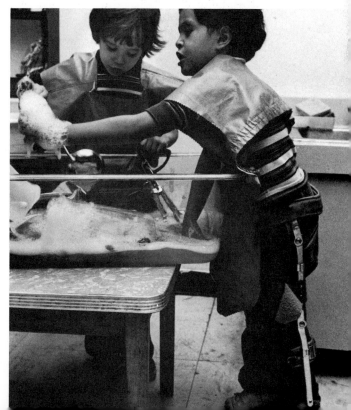

disabled children become able adults.

Several professions deal with education of disabled children. If these professions are of interest to you, talk with your teacher, guidance counselor, or specialists in the areas of disabilities. These people may help you choose the career most suited to your interests.

Concluding Comments

For proper physical development during the prekindergarten period, children need to practice and refine their motor skills. Active play, including running, climbing, jumping, throwing, and catch-ing, helps them develop important skills they need for games and work. The development of motor skills also contributes to social, mental, and emotional development. So prekindergarten children need a lot of physical exercise.

The federal and state governments are taking more responsibility for mainstreaming children with disabilities. Educators agree that disabled children develop their potential more fully in regular school classes. Their disabling conditions need not be handicaps to development and learning. Care givers should emphasize what disabled children *can* do, not what they cannot do.

Activities

With their parents' permission, spend two hours with several prekindergarten children. Include a boy and a girl. Record their ages in years and months.

1. Set up activities that will help them develop their large motor skills.
    a. Encourage them to walk in different ways—on a piece of masking tape laid on the floor; zig-zag; stooped low.
    b. Encourage running, jumping, and hopping.
    c. Play catch with each child. Describe the way each throws and catches the ball.
    d. Write a report of the children's activities. Did you see any difference in the way the children performed?
2. Observe these same children practicing small-motor skills.
    a. When coloring, do they use a fist or hand grasp?
    b. Offer each child a pair of safety scissors and a newspaper page. Ask them to practice cutting. Describe the results.
    c. Are the children right- or left-handed?
3. Ask the parents of the prekindergartners with whom you have been playing the following:
    a. Is the child quite active—running, jumping, generally practicing motor skills?
    b. Where does the child practice motor skills? What equipment does the child use?
    c. What activities do you play with your child? Are your activities quite active? Or do you and your child prefer quieter, indoor projects?
    d. What are your goals for your child so far as physical development is concerned?

31

The Prekindergartner Develops Emotionally and Socially

Objectives

To explain the value of play in promoting emotional and
social development.

To explain how 3- and 4-year olds differ from toddlers
emotionally and socially.

To explain sharing and taking turns.

To explain the value of dramatic play.

Terms to look for   cooperative play • dramatic play • jealousy •
parallel play • sex-role stereotyping • sharing • sibling rivalry •
taking turns

"Hello, fire fighters? Come quick! There's a fire at my house!" exclaimed Paul over the toy telephone in the housekeeping corner. Paul was calling two red-hatted fire fighters in the "firehouse" next door to the housekeeping corner in the prekindergarten room.

Cindy and Chris made siren noises as they ran to Paul's house. They pretended to have hoses in their hands. "Go outside, Paul," said Cindy. The fire fighters swished their hoses, making water sounds with their lips. "There, that's out!" exclaimed Chris and "sirened" out the door.

Imagination, knowledge, and cooperation combine as these 3- and 4-year-olds invent a scene of fire fighters saving a house. Their play is important for social, emotional, and educational growth.

Social and Emotional Goals

Prekindergarten children are working on five important social and emotional development goals.

1. Becoming more independent.
2. Learning to get along with others.
3. Understanding what it means to be a girl or a boy.
4. Learning to give and share affection.
5. Developing a positive self-concept.

Independence

The toddler spent a good deal of time struggling for independence. Yet the toddler still needed to cling to the parents and was often afraid of separation. At age 3, if development has proceeded fairly well, the same child will feel much more confident and independent. At age 3, children know that their parents love them, so they no longer fear separation. They know from experience and from increased mental maturity that their parents will always come back. In fact, 3-year-olds often will not even bother to say good-bye when a parent leaves them at preschool or with a grandparent.

Along with increased independence comes an increased desire to take responsibility. Most 3- and 4-year-olds love to help. And parents and teachers will find that children are able to do many simple tasks.

Fears

Prekindergartners may still have fears—of water, animals, the dark, and so forth. Parents may not understand the source of these fears, and children often cannot tell them. Often children generalize. A child who has been stung by a bee might become afraid of all insects and spiders for a while. Simply being told that most insects do not sting will not necessarily help. Probably the best way to deal with children's fears is to encourage the children to talk about them if they want to. Adults should also make the children feel as secure as possible. Children should never be rid-

iculed or be called babyish. Such tactics serve only to damage the children's self-concept and make them feel even more insecure.

Sociability

Just as prekindergartners are becoming more independent, they are also experiencing rapid social development. Their interests are expanding beyond home and parents. They increasingly seek out other children as playmates.

Play: A Medium for Social and Emotional Growth

Through play, children gain skills, knowledge, and experience that is useful to them as prekindergartners. In addition, this learning is the basis for the development that must take place in the next stage of life. Play makes a very large contribution to children's social and emotional development. Parents who enroll children in prekindergarten classes often say they want their child to learn to get along with other children. As a child moves from the self-centered stage of the toddler, parents recognize the fun and development that comes from being with other children. In this day of small families, a parent often cannot easily provide a consistent group of playmates. Such playmates are available if the child is enrolled in a prekindergarten group.

When prekindergartners do have the opportunity to be together, their play shows rapid growth. At age 3, children usually engage in *parallel play*. They play *next to* each other rather than with each other. There is little or no interaction or cooperation. For example, two 3-year-olds may each push a car along the sidewalk. They may not talk to each other but simply push the cars and make sound effects. Or they may appear to be having a conversation, but a listener may hear something like this:

Ellen: I have a great, big truck, and I'm taking it to the dump.

José: I'm a fire fighter, and I'm hurrying to put out a fire.

Ellen: My mommy made spaghetti for dinner.

José: I have a baby brother, and he can walk now.

Although these children probably enjoy each other's company, they are not really playing *together*.

By age 4, children have usually developed enough social maturity that they have begun *cooperative play*. Now they really play *with* each other. They may work together to build a garage for their cars. Or perhaps they will race their cars down a ramp. This stage of play requires exchanging ideas, using words, and planning activities.

The ages given here are averages. Since more and more toddlers are now in play groups and other group settings, parents and teachers often observe that 3-year-olds engage in cooperative play.

Social Skills of Sharing and Taking Turns

Play in the prekindergarten encourages social skills of sharing and taking turns. In a high-quality program, there is sufficient opportunity and equipment for

The parallel play of 3-year-olds leads to cooperative play in 4-year-olds. Parents and care givers can help children learn to share by making children feel good about themselves and the people around them.

children to interact socially. The children must share the equipment and take turns. Sharing is a social skill that prekindergartners learn. The idea of *sharing* denotes generosity as opposed to selfishness. It includes a feeling of concern and respect for another. This feeling makes one child care about letting another child have or use something the first child currently has or is using. Sharing is harder than taking turns. *Taking turns* refers more to getting an equal chance at something. For example, waiting in line at the slide is taking turns. But real sharing means that one child knows another child well and wants the other child to have some or all of what the first child has. Sharing is done voluntarily, by secure children who feel satisfied. Sharing requires sensitivity to the needs of another.

Often when adults say to children, "You've got to share," what they really mean is, "You've got to take turns."

To teach children to share, adults need to help them feel good about themselves. Then they are able to take pleasure in seeing another child feel pleased. At home, parents should let children make decisions about what toys they want to share and which ones they would rather not share. Suppose Diane is expecting Josh to visit. Diane's father can say, "You know, Josh will want to play with your toys when he comes." If Diane says, "He can play with my blocks, but not with my teddy bear," her father might say, "All right, then we'll put the teddy bear away until Josh goes home."

In a group setting, children will learn to share better if they are kept in small groups and get to know each other. When adults see sharing, they can say, "Bobby, I like the way you shared your ball with Jennifer." This gives Bobby a word for his act and an insight into Jennifer's feelings. Also, the adult encouragement makes him feel good about himself.

The equipment of a prekindergarten is for all children to use. Teachers often say, "It's yours while you're using it." This means that when one child is through using the equipment, then the equipment is available for someone else. This concept of community property is new for most children when they enter prekindergarten.

At home, toys usually belong specifically to one child. At home, each child controls and is responsible for personal belongings. Even in large families, parents usually like to make sure each child has some toys that are his or her own. Children may object when parents want to pass certain toys down to a younger child. Parents should treat such feelings with respect, and allow the child to make the decision about giving up the toy.

❓ Decisions, Decisions

Kenny's dramatic play is often about the violence he has seen on television. He shoots people, pushes them off buildings and zaps them with laser beams. Occasionally, he hurts another child. If you were Kenny's nursery school teacher, what would you do?

Dramatic Play

Dramatic play is spontaneous, imaginative, unrehearsed play. In dramatic play, children may pretend to be people or animals and to take part in events that they know about. The story that opened this chapter is an example of dramatic play. Children who engage in dramatic play are often also playing coopera-tively. Cooperative dramatic play involves several children in a unified theme.

The home is a popular theme for dramatic play. Children create scenes of home with fathers, mothers, babies, and other children who are eating, sleeping, and sometimes being fussy. A supply of blocks may also contribute to house-keeping play. Or blocks may encourage children to build roads, homes, airports, or shopping centers. Dramatic play also occurs outdoors on the jungle gym, in the sandbox, and among the wheel toys and packing boxes. Children label packing boxes "houses" one day, "corrals" another day, and "submarines" the next. Themes are limited only by how far the children's imaginations will stretch.

Four factors cause dramatic play to be so prominent at this age:

1. Children have well-developed language skills by this time.
2. They have broader experiences with people in the community. This gives them ideas for roles, conversation, and action.
3. They have learned to cooperate with others in the give-and-take of the social situation, and they have many ideas about resolving conflicts.
4. They are not self-conscious, so they feel free to express themselves.

Dramatic play benefits children in many ways.

1. It provides an outlet for the children's inner thoughts and feelings.
2. It helps a child solve personal problems. A child who feels left out in other activities may take a leader-ship role here and make contact with other children.
3. It teaches children about roles in society. A child can pretend to be a

letter carrier, a store keeper, a carpenter, a doctor, and so forth. Children can also try out various family roles.

4. It satisfies children. Dramatic play helps children expand their minds.
5. It provides practice for language skills. Children practice new words to express ideas.
6. It helps children learn and practice society's rules of courtesy, taking turns, sharing, and cooperating.

Adult's Role in Dramatic Play

Adults often ruin dramatic play when they get more than momentarily involved in it. Parents, teachers, and helpers should observe dramatic play quietly from a distance. They should hesitate before stepping in. Children can solve most of the conflicts that arise. They have ideas to act out, though at times it takes quite a while for a scene to develop fully. True-to-life dramas often develop, complete with verbal and social interaction. No parent or teacher could write or produce these dramas effectively. Parents and teachers can help most by providing a few props that will stimulate the spontaneous role playing that is at the heart of dramatic play.

Adults can also learn a lot about children by observing their dramatic play. In *The First Three Years of Life,* psychologist Burton White observes that a child's self-concept is often reflected in the roles that the child chooses in dramatic play. A child with a well-developed self-concept is likely to pretend to be an adult. A child who is not developing as well might repeatedly take the role of a baby or dog. While adults should not interfere with dramatic play, they should be aware of the child who is *always* the baby. They should watch this child in other areas of family and school life.

Dramatic play is a lovely thing to watch. Adults should stay behind the scenes, observing and enjoying. Often, they can gain insight into the children's development.

Sex-role Stereotyping

Through the third and fourth years, children are sorting out information about being a girl or a boy. Activities should be "children's" activities, rather than "boys'" or "girls'" activities. Parents and teachers should encourage children to participate in all activities. That way, children can find out what they like and do best. They can begin to develop their potential as human beings.

Even parents and teachers who believe in full equality of the sexes will often hear children playing in a very stereotyped way. Bill might say to Marie, "You can't be the doctor. Only boys can be doctors." Bill's own pediatrician may be a woman, but he may have seen only male doctors on television or in story books. Adults can say, "Of course, women can be doctors." But a more effective approach might be to look for books and pictures that show women and men engaged in all professions and activities—fathers and mothers holding babies, policewomen and policemen, men and women driving tractors and trucks, male and female ballet dancers, and so forth. Such pictures will teach children more effectively than will adults' lectures.

Jealousy and Sibling Rivalry

Jealousy is an emotion that combines anger, fear, insecurity, and anxiety. It stems from a real or imagined loss of love. Children are sometimes jealous of a parent, a sister or brother, or a close friend. Parents will almost always observe some jealousy when there is a new baby in the home.

The child who is confronted with a new sibling often fears that all the parents' love and attention will now go to the new baby. The 3- or 4-year-old may be open about these feelings, saying, "I don't like the baby. Why don't you take it back to the hospital?" Another child may feel guilty about such feelings and try to cover them up by constantly hugging and kissing the new baby.

When psychologists talk about *sibling rivalry,* they are referring to the way children compete for their parents' attention. A certain amount of sibling rivalry is normal in a family. If such rivalry is too intense, however, the family situation can become uncomfortable. The children and the parents will suffer.

How can parents cope with jealousy and sibling rivalry?

1. Wanting their children to grow up liking each other is an important goal for parents. Keeping this goal in mind will help parents deal with jealousy.

2. Being aware that jealousy will occur and accepting that fact will help parents cope with it.

3. Parents should prepare their child for the birth of a sibling. That way, the baby does not come as a shock. A 3- or 4-year-old will be better able to understand what parents explain than a younger child will. Saying, "You're going to have a new brother or sister to play with," is not a good idea. "The new baby won't be able to do anything but eat, sleep, and cry," is more realistic.

4. Some hospitals and childbirth centers now allow the mother to go home

Parents can help children talk about and work out jealous feelings. The older child needs extra praise and physical affection during this period.

very shortly after the birth of a new baby—sometimes the same day. Others allow the older child to visit the mother's hospital room. This shorter separation from the mother often helps relieve a child's feelings of jealousy.

5. Many 3- and 4-year-olds can help care for the new baby. They can push a carriage, hold the baby on their laps, assist in bathing it, and so forth. Helping gives the older child the idea that it is "our baby" instead of an intruder. However, a child who is forced to leave his or her activities to help with a baby will become more resentful.

6. Parents should accept children's expressions of jealousy. "You are feeling a little angry that Baby Jimmy takes so much of my time," is more effective than, "It's not nice to hate your little brother. You must love him." Children have a right to their feelings.

Sometimes these jealous feelings will appear in a child's dramatic play. Either at home or in the prekindergarten setting, a child might say, "This is a bad baby." Then the child might angrily throw a doll onto the floor or hit it. This is a healthy way to deal with jealous feelings. Parents should not worry that a child would treat the baby the same way. Most 3- and 4-year-olds are certainly aware of the difference between a baby and a doll.

Teachers who see children acting out their feelings this way may want to discuss the behavior in parent-teacher conferences. Sometimes, parents and teachers are able to work together to help children with their jealous feelings.

7. Comparing children with one another can foster more jealousy. Parents—and teachers—should not talk about one child's being slower, prettier, or smarter than another.

8. Encouraging competition between siblings can also cause more jealousy. Rather than saying, "Can you beat Sandy into the bathroom to wash your hands?" parents might say, "We'll be ready for dinner when both of you have washed your hands." Setting the stage for one sibling to "win" will not serve the goal of helping children like each other.

9. The older child should have the opportunity to continue or expand friendships and activities. Saying, "We have to stay home because of the baby" is sure to cause resentment. No older children want to spend their life waiting for a baby brother or sister.

10. The older child will need to be reassured about still being loved. The best way for parents to show this love is for each of them to make an effort to spend time with the older child. Pats, hugs, and kisses help, too. Saying, "I love you" is important. But the child will not believe it if the parents do not accompany words with actions.

11. Parents should remember that each child is an individual and that equal treatment is therefore impossible. Most parents are sensitive enough to recognize children's different emotional needs and to deal with them accordingly. Children are aware of their differences. And they appreciate adults who recognize their individuality.

Concluding Comments

Children ages 3 and 4 are in a period of rapid social and emotional growth. They are becoming increasingly independent. They are usually much less anxious about being separated from their parents. Prekindergartners may still have fears. Adults should treat these fears sympathetically.

Play makes an important contribution to children's emotional and social development. Through play, children learn to practice getting along with others. They learn to share and take turns and to give and share affection. They also learn to feel good about being a girl or a boy. And they begin to develop a positive self-concept.

Dramatic cooperative play is an advanced form of play. It requires several children to develop the ideas and carry out the various roles. Parents and teachers can foster social and emotional growth by encouraging children to participate in dramatic play.

Activities

1. Watch a group of three- and four-year-olds play, for several hours if necessary.
   a. Describe an example of parallel play that you observe.
   b. Describe a cooperative play situation in the group.
   c. Report a dramatic play incident that occurred.
2. In the activity above, did the children seem to understand what it means to be a boy or a girl?
3. Analyze the picture books either in a child's home or in a preschool.
   a. Find examples of sex-role stereotypes in at least three books. Discuss your findings with your class.
   b. Find at least three picture books that do not feature sex-role stereotypes. Describe them.
4. If you have a younger sister or brother, ask your parents if you had shown jealousy or sibling rivalry toward her or him. If you are the youngest, ask the same information about older brothers or sisters.

The Prekindergartner Develops Mentally

Objectives

To describe the behaviors that show growth of mental functioning in prekindergarten children.

To describe the thinking process typical of prekindergarten children.

To relate creativity and mental development.

Term to look for   preoperational thinker

"I'm going to go to the Ice Capades tonight. Are you?" 4-year-old Robb asks Jo, as the prekindergartners take off their coats following outdoor play.

"I already went. I went last night," responds Jo. "You should see those clowns! It was so funny when they crashed like this," she laughs, demonstrating a fall on the head. "One of them is so fat," she says, showing how fat with her arms. "The other one is so skinny, like this," she concludes, showing Robb how skinny she means by using her hands.

Jo and Robb have entered a stage of mental development where they can remember and think about things that happened on other days. Jo is able to describe an event. This is a higher level of mental ability than many younger children have.

Brain Development

During the prekindergarten years, children continue to use all five senses to experience the world around them. All their experiences contribute to their mental development. Actual brain growth has slowed, but development of the complex structures within the brain continues. Thought-provoking games, language, and active exploration are necessary to provide the brain with stimulation for development. Adequate nutrition continues to be important for brain development at the ages of 3 and 4.

Preoperational Stage

From the sensorimotor stage, the child grows and develops into a *preoperational* thinker, according to Dr. Jean Piaget, the Swiss psychologist mentioned earlier in this book. Piaget concluded from watching his own children carefully that this preoperational stage usually lasts from age 2 to age 7.

Once a child between the ages of 2 and 7 has decided about something, the child has difficulty putting evidence together to form new conclusions. A prekindergartner can give a cookie to every child at the snack table. But suppose the cookies are then taken back and all placed together on a tray. The child will probably be confused and think that there are not enough for the children. To the question, "Are there more children, more cookies, or the same number of each?" the child will answer, "More children." The prekindergartner thinks there are more children because the children are spread out over a larger area than the cookies are. The child is unable to reason logically that just moments before, the cookies were matched up with the children. He or she cannot reverse the thinking process and put things back as they were.

The preschool years are the time to learn how to learn. Learning takes place through play and new experiences. Some researchers believe that half of a person's intellectual ability is developed by age 4.

"Why are you reading, Daddy?" As soon as Daddy answers, there will be another question. It is important for him to answer that one, too.

Language Development

The language of 3- and 4-year-olds is becoming more complex. Many children of this age have large vocabularies. They can speak almost as well as adults, with only occasional errors in grammar and pronunciation. Adults can help children's language develop by listening and talking to them and by treating their thoughts and ideas with respect. Instead of correcting grammatical errors, adults will find teaching by example more effective. If a child says, "I goed to the circus yesterday," an adult might answer, "Oh, what did you see when you went to the circus?"

Prekindergartners enjoy rhyming words. Parents and teachers can play rhyming games, such as, "Tell me a word that rhymes with *rock*." If children cannot think of a word, the adult might say, "It's something you put on your foot before you put your shoe on," or "It's something that you use for building bridges."

Books are important for fostering mental development. Children who are read to regularly will often spend long periods of time "reading" their favorite stories to themselves.

? Decisions, Decisions

Scott tells "stories" about monsters, wild adventures, and celebrities. He claims they are all "for real." One day, he broke a glass and told an elaborate story about the robber who broke it. How would you handle Scott's imagination? What is the difference between imagination and lying?

Curiosity

If prekindergartners have had opportunity to explore in earlier years, they will still be very curious at this age. They notice tiny details that may escape adult eyes. They will ask questions about everything.

Around the third birthday, children may suddenly begin asking "Why?" about almost everything. Every answer they get can lead them to another question. "Why don't the trees have any leaves? Why do leaves come out in the spring? Why isn't it spring now? Why is it winter?" Sometimes these questions are almost impossible to answer. The adult may need to say, "Why do *you* think?" or simply, "I don't know."

Although these questions can drive adults crazy at times, the ability to ask questions is important to a child's early learning. Parents and teachers should try to answer children's questions as well and as truthfully as possible. The child whose questions are met with annoyance will eventually stop asking them. If curiosity is dampened, the child will become less enthusiastic about learning, and mental development will suffer.

Imagination and Creativity

The imagination children show in their dramatic play—alone or in groups—is evidence of increasing mental development. Parents may find that children are able to turn toys and "found" objects into many different things. For example, one little girl had a set of plastic nuts and bolts that she used for "dirt" in her dump truck. The nuts and bolts became "corn" when she put them in her wagon attached to a tractor. When she put them in her pocketbook, they were "money." Her pocketbook was an empty plastic bandage can. While she played, she talked or sang songs to describe what she was acting out. All these activities showed imagination, resourcefulness, and memory development.

Imaginary Playmates

Some children have imaginary playmates. These playmates usually have names, certain clothing, and definite characteristics. A child may carry on many conversations with the imaginary playmate. The child may say to a parent, "Watch out! You almost stepped on Molly." Some playmates go everywhere with the child. Others reside only in certain rooms. Studies show that imaginary playmates occur mostly among bright children who are only children or the oldest in families with several younger siblings. Sometimes the imaginary playmates disappear with the birth of a brother or sister. They almost always disappear when the child starts school. The child may explain, "Molly went to live in Chicago."

Make-believe adventures help children develop their own creativity and imagination.

Adults should be very careful to distinguish between imagination and lies. The child who says, "There's a lion in my room," or who makes up imaginary playmates is using creativity and imagination. Such imaginative stories are not lies. In fact, children should be encouraged to use their imaginations. The ability to imagine and create is a sign of mental development.

Concluding Comments

Prekindergarten children have an increasing ability to understand, remember, and discuss their experiences. This is evidence of their growing mental ability. Children of this age are usually curious. They will ask many questions to gain information about their surroundings. Their language becomes increasingly complex.

Prekindergartners also show increasing mental development in their imaginative and creative play. They are able to use toys and other objects in a variety of different ways. They are also able to act out familiar scenes, stories that have been read or told to them, or their own make-believe adventures. Sometimes they have imaginary playmates.

Parents and teachers can help stimulate children's mental development in many ways. They can show genuine interest in children's thoughts and ideas. They can encourage children's creativity and imagination. And they can answer children's questions as often and as truthfully as possible.

Books and stories are especially important in language and mental development. Not only do they help children increase their vocabularies, but they also provide the raw material for creative dramatic play.

Adults can also stimulate mental development by providing a wide variety of activities for children. Specific activities will be discussed in Chapter 38.

Activities

1. Enter into a conversation with a three- or four-year-old child.
   a. Record the child's age in years and months.
   b. Try to get the child to discuss what he or she is doing.
   c. Take notes, then write an anecdotal record of your conversation.
   d. Does the child appear to have an extensive vocabulary?
   e. Is the child's use of grammar fairly mature?
   f. Did the child seem to enjoy talking with you?
2. Ask the above child to show you his or her favorite books. Describe the choices.
3. Ask the parents if the child asks lots of questions. Do they think the child shows much imagination? Report their response.
4. Ask your parents if you or any of your brothers or sisters ever had an imaginary playmate. Or, perhaps you can remember this experience, yourself. Report orally or in writing to the class.

Health and Safety for Prekindergartners

Objectives

To explain safety measures needed for prekindergarten children.

To compare the needs for inoculations of prekindergarten children, infants, and toddlers.

To explain the need for care of the teeth for 3- and 4-year-olds.

"Here, Nathan, I'll use this needle and give your baby a shot," says 4-year-old Angie. "The doctor gave me this shot thing the other day when I got a shot. Now, when I give your baby a shot, you say 'Ouch' and pretend to cry, okay?"

Nathan, holding his "baby" tightly, seems fearful of Angie and her "shot thing." But, almost as though he were really in a doctor's office, he stands soberly while Angie gives the doll a shot.

Angie and Nathan are dramatizing a scene that is both familiar and scary to young children. Both children have parents who take care of providing their inoculations regularly.

The Prekindgergartner's Health—Inoculations

Refer to Chapter 17 for the list of inoculations required and when they should be given to a child. By ages 3 and 4, any inoculations that have not been given previously or that need boosters should be given immediately.

At ages 3 and 4, children may enter nursery school and day-care centers. They visit shopping centers and other public places. Chances for exposure to serious diseases increase. Therefore, all shots and boosters should be up-to-date.

Some states require that children have an up-to-date immunization record before they can be admitted to nursery schools and day-care centers. Parents should keep records in a safe place and update them with each booster.

Sanitation and Hygiene

For the most part, 3- and 4-year-old children are competent in the bathroom. But, they may need help cleaning themselves after using the toilet. Prekindergartners should be encouraged to wash their hands after going to the toilet and before mealtime.

Parents and teachers should teach children habits of cleanliness. Prekindergartners can help keep floors, tables, and chairs clean. They especially love using sponges. In fact, they will often thoroughly wash everything in sight if given a sponge and a bowl of water.

The prekindergarten years are the time for a first trip to the dentist. Dental treatment now might save much orthodontic work later.

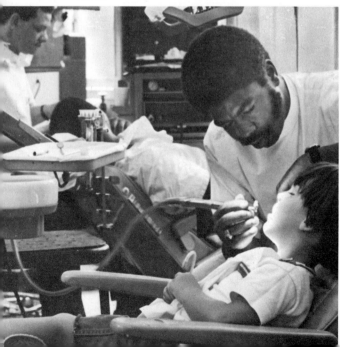

Tooth Care

Young children's teeth must receive attention during the prekindergarten years. Adults must teach children to brush their teeth well in the morning and evening and after meals. The high number of dental cavities among young children has caused day-care centers to require children to brush teeth while they are there at noon. At ages 3 and 4, it is now time to teach children to protect their teeth by avoiding too much candy.

When a child's tooth decays or is knocked out, dentists now may try to save the tooth. The dentist may drill out a decayed spot and fill the cavity. Teeth knocked out in an accident may be reset. Parents should keep the tooth and take it along with the child to the dentist immediately for resetting. Retaining the baby teeth in the mouth is important for proper spacing of permanent teeth and for proper speech development.

? Decisions, Decisions

Carlos, one of the children you are caring for, has a nosebleed. There is blood all over his hands, face, and clothes. He is sobbing with fright and the other children are getting frightened too. What do you do?

Accidents

Accidents injure and kill many young children each year. This is especially tragic because most accidents can be prevented. Children run and play along sidewalks. They can be hurt if they run between parked cars to get a ball. They ride tricycles fast and can be injured in driveways or streets.

Making sure that children are in a secure play area can prevent many such accidents. But 3- and 4-year-olds are also old enough to learn safety rules. Without making children overly fearful, adults should stress the danger of a moving car. Adults should teach children to stop at corners and driveways and to look both ways before crossing. Adults can help children practice both independence and safety by setting limits, such as, "You may run ahead now. Stop at the corner and wait for me."

Many deaths and serious injuries result from automobile accidents. Prekindergartners should travel in approved car safety seats. If children have reached a weight of 45 pounds or more, they should be strapped securely into seat belts. If parents know that the child is going on a class trip and will travel by car, they should emphasize to teachers that they want their child to wear a seat belt. Allowing children to bounce in the back of a station wagon is dangerous.

Young children are sometimes bitten when they play with or tease dogs they do not know. Adults should teach children not to approach strange dogs and to be gentle with dogs they do know.

Illnesses

If prekindergartners are in a nursery school or day-care center, they will probably be exposed to a lot of colds. Children this age often do not cover their coughs and sneezes. Fortunately, most colds are not especially serious, and they do not seem to bother young children much. A child who has a fever or a bad cough or one whose nose is running heavily should be kept home from school.

Contagious Diseases

Chicken pox is the most common contagious disease that 3- and 4-year-olds contract. If children are in a prekindergarten program, the disease will often strike most of the children in a group. Breaking out usually occurs 11 to 19 days after exposure. A number of red pimples will appear. Tiny blisters will form on top of them. These pox usually appear first on the chest and face.

Later, pox may cover the entire body. Children may feel well until they begin breaking out. That is why they expose so many of their friends. The itchy blisters can be very uncomfortable. A cool bath with baking soda dissolved in it can help relieve the itching. Permanent scarring can result from scratching the pox. Parents may want to clip the child's fingernails when the first pox appear. A child who has had chicken pox is usually immune for life. Some children have natural immunity and never contract the disease.

Scarlet fever is another contagious disease for which no inoculation presently exists. Before the discovery of antibiotics—drugs that kill disease-causing organisms—scarlet fever was extremely serious. Now, if diagnosed promptly, scarlet fever can be cleared up in less than a week. Scarlet fever usually begins with a severe sore throat and high fever. A child with these symptoms should see a doctor immediately. Although antibiotics work quickly on the disease, they must be begun as soon as possible. Left untreated, scarlet fever can develop into rheumatic fever, which can cause lifelong heart problems.

Care During Illness

When children are running high fevers, they usually sleep most of the time. However, once the fever is gone, 3- and 4-year-olds are very hard to keep in bed. A parent may have to invent games for the child to play to pass the time. Special crayons, cutting, and pasting may help. Children with chicken pox may enjoy looking at themselves in the mirror, then drawing pictures of what they see. Telephoning friends and relatives can also keep a bedridden child occupied. Allowing the child to watch a little more television than usual probably does not hurt. And it may help the parent.

In general, parents should avoid giving a sick child too much attention. The child may get the idea that being ill is a good idea. While being sympathetic toward a child who is really feeling miserable, adults can encourage recovering children to do a little more for themselves each day, until they are ready to get back to normal activities.

Hospitalization

Being in the hospital can be a very frightening experience for a young child. Many hospitals today recognize this and encourage parents to stay with their child. They may provide an extra bed for the parent in the child's room.

If parents know in advance that their child will have to be hospitalized—for instance, for a tonsillectomy—they should prepare the child. They can tell the child, in terms the child can understand, exactly what is going to happen, and why. "The doctor is going to take

Hospital stays are very frightening. Whenever possible, prepare the child well in advance. Several good childrens' books describe a child's stay in the hospital.

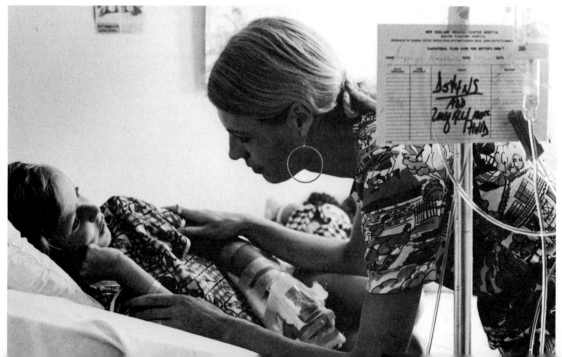

your tonsils out so that you will not get so many bad sore throats. Someone will give you a special shot to make you go to sleep while the doctor takes your tonsils out. When you wake up, Mommy or I will be with you. Your throat may hurt for a few days, but you will probably get to eat a lot of ice cream." Children are perfectly capable of understanding the truth. They will be much less afraid if they feel they can trust the adults who take care of them.

Concluding Comments

Parents of 3- and 4-year-olds should be sure that their children's inoculations are up-to-date.

Accidents continue to be a major cause of injury and death to children. Many of these accidents can be prevented with proper precautions.

Prekindergartners should be learning important hygiene practices, and they should learn to take care of their teeth.

Chicken pox and scarlet fever are two contagious diseases prekindergartners may contract. In addition, they may catch colds from one another. Sick children should be given special attention to keep them comfortable in bed, but they should also be encouraged to prefer health to illness.

Hospitalization can be very frightening to young children. Parents should try to find hospitals that allow a parent to stay with a child. Parents should also prepare a young child well in advance if the child must be hospitalized.

Activities

1. Poll five families with preschool and school-age children.
   a. How many children are in these five families?
   b. How many of these children had cavities in their baby teeth?
   c. Have any of the children had a tooth knocked out accidentally? Was the tooth reset?
2. Call several dentists in your community. (Each dentist should be called by only one student.) Ask the following questions, then write a report to share with your classmates:
   a. Do you find there has been an increase in dental cavities among 3- and 4-year-olds in recent years?
   b. What do you do if a 3- or 4-year-old has a cavity? Do you pull it or fill it?
   c. Can you reset a tooth if it gets knocked out?
3. Talk to the parents of a 3- or 4-year-old child who was recently hospitalized for at least one night. Ask them to describe how their child felt about the experience.
4. Telephone several hospitals.
   a. Ask them if a parent may stay with a child who is hospitalized at their facility.
   b. If so, is the parent encouraged to do so?
   c. Will the parent have a bed?
   d. Will the parent be charged extra if the parent stays?

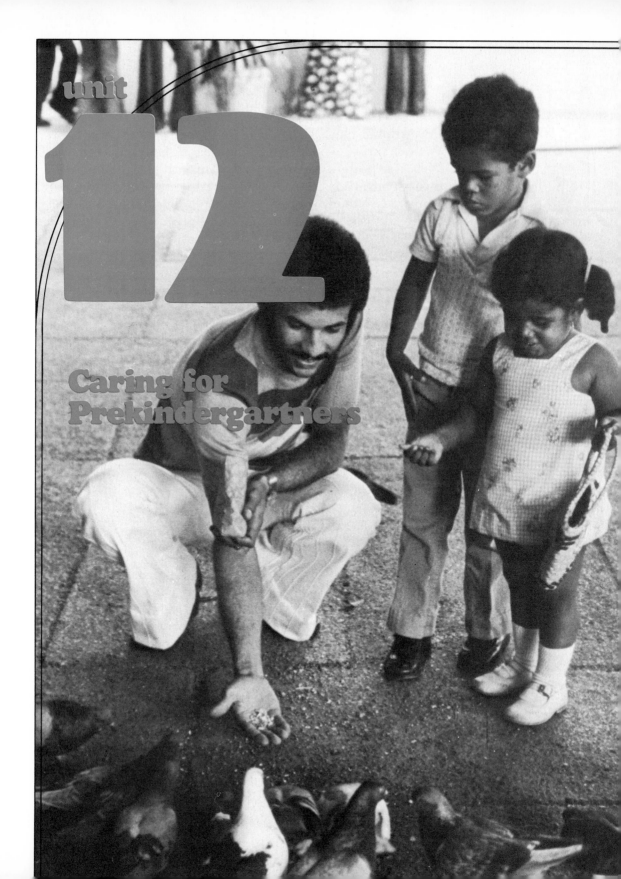

12

Caring for Prekindergartners

34

Guiding Prekindergartners

Objectives

To explain how guidance principles apply to prekindergartners.

To explain the need for limits on children's behavior.

To explain the guidance required after limits are stated.

To explain the relationship of guidance to the child's developing self-concept.

Terms to look for

affective guidance • limits • negative feedback • positive feedback

Maria exhanged greetings with the teacher as she entered the prekindergarten classroom with her mother. While her mother spoke to the teacher, Maria went directly to her locker near the door. The locker had her name printed clearly on it. She deposited her coat and hat. She returned to her mother's side. "Bye, Mommy," said Maria, as her mother left for work. Maria knew her father would be there to pick her up when the class was over.

"What are you going to do today, Maria?" asked Mr. Randall, the prekin-dergarten teacher. "I'm gonna' paint," said Maria. She proceeded to the easel, which was prepared with fresh paint, clean brushes, and large sheets of newsprint. Maria slipped her smock over her head and began to paint. She looked up as other children entered the classroom. But she immediately returned to her painting.

If you were to observe Maria, you would notice how easily she moves through this early morning routine. She knows what she is expected to do, what she is allowed to do, and where things are stored. Maria's teacher has set the stage so children can direct their own learning activities. The teacher sees his role as preparing the classroom well before the children arrive on the scene. Also, he lets the children know he is pleased to have them at school. The teacher's quick visit with the mother helps him learn facts about the child, the family, and the home. This might influence how the day goes for Maria.

Adapting Guidance Principles to Prekindergartners

The principles of direct and indirect guidance that you learned in Chapters 18 and 25 are useful to apply with prekindergartners. (See page 322 for a summary of those principles.)

Guidance has been defined as all the actions adults use to influence children's behavior. This definition means that guidance goes on whenever parents or teachers relate to children. Good guidance techniques help the children know what to do. The guiding actions are educational rather than simply reactions to children when the children do something "naughty." Remember that the goal of guidance is for each child to become self-guided or self-directed. Children need to be able to make correct decisions about behavior when parents and teachers are not there to enforce rules. By ages 3 and 4, children are becoming aware of right and wrong.

Limits

Some people may say: "Perhaps guidance should be largely positive. Adults should guide children indirectly and directly as to what to do. But how do

"Nobody goes beyond those trees." Adults must set limits to protect children and to help them achieve self-control.

you let children know what they cannot do?"

It is true that there are necessary limits that children must learn as they mature. For example:

1. *Limits must be set to protect the child's safety.* Safety in the home, on the streets, and at school are early lessons.
2. *Limits must be set to protect other people.* Adults guide the interaction of children to teach them the rules of social give-and-take.
3. *Limits must be set to protect the learning environment.* Another child's working space or learning environment is "hers while she is using it." A child is redirected or stopped from knocking down another child's blocks or from throwing someone else's puzzle off the table.
4. *Limits must be set to protect property.* Children are taught to take good care of their own things and the property of the home and school.

Following Through on Limits

A child must accept and adhere to many limits. The essential point about limits is to state them clearly and consistently to the child. It is equally important, though, to stress permissible things to do. Adults are responsible for following through after stating the limits. They should be sure that the child does not overstep the limits without receiving negative feedback. Otherwise, the child will probably break the rule again soon.

If a child's behavior receives negative feedback or response from the adult *every* time, the behavior will soon stop.

Parents and care givers who set limits must follow through to enforce them. A child must receive negative feedback *every* time the undesirable behavior occurs. The child must also be told what kind of behavior is desirable.

For example, if Billy is spitting on the children in the sandbox, the parent or teacher says, "Billy, stop spitting. If you need to spit, go spit in the toilet. Spitting is dirty." Here you notice that the limits and the consequences are stated.

Billy spits again, so the parent or teacher leads him to the bathroom saying, "Billy, you may spit in the toilet and no place else. When you are through spitting, you may come out." The parent or teacher leaves Billy alone in the bathroom to keep from giving him positive feedback in the form of attention.

Billy comes out, and the parent or teacher follows him to the sandbox without comment. If Billy spits again, the parent or teacher will promptly remove Billy to the bathroom *every* time. After only a few times, the spitting will stop.

A typical home problem focuses on television viewing. In a discussion with the children, parents decide which programs are suitable for watching. The parents and children agree that once these shows are over, the children are expected to turn off the set. One evening after a favorite show, Kevin's father says, "Time for your bath and a story." Kevin whines, wanting to keep the television on. Father again states that first Kevin must have a bath. Then he will be willing to read a story of Kevin's choice. Kevin starts to whine again. Father says, "Kevin, the decision is no more television. Come on, I'll help you run your bath if you need some help." He offers Kevin his hand and together they move toward the bathroom. Firm limits consistently maintained by parents help children.

Parents frequently have problems with following through on limits when guests are present. Children are quick to notice that parents are not paying full attention. The children sense that parents may not enforce limits. Before guests arrive, the wise parent helps the children plan what they will do to keep themselves occupied while guests are present.

1. State the limits positively in a short, clear statement. In the previous example, the adult said to Billy, "Stop spitting." If you say, "Stop it," or "Stop that," the child does not know what "it" or "that" refers to.

2. State the guidance in a manner and tone of voice that indicates you expect the child to comply. Use a firm voice, look directly at the child, and avoid being distracted by other children or other events. For example, adults in social situations often state limits to children. But then they forget about the stated limits as they return to their conversations with other adults. This distraction and lack of attention make the child feel that the guidance is less important.

3. Follow through on enforcing limits. Use firmness, not anger. Being unemotional helps keep the picture clearer for the child. Take the child by the hand, if necessary, to see that he or she follows the direction stated.

4. Stay close by the child. Adults who stay close to children are more likely to be listened to and have their guidance followed. Also, being close, the adult knows what is taking place and may be able to foresee problems and to give guidance before a crisis arises.

Guidance Appropriate for Age

Most 3-year-olds still need physical guidance, such as showing, helping, and leading. Of course, words are used along with physical guidance. As children become better able to understand language, verbal guidance becomes more effective. The teacher or parent must be sure the child listens, hears, and understands. Getting close to the child and stooping down helps a child know the directions are for her or him. Children nearly always ignore directions that are yelled across the room or play yard.

Remember to tell children when they are doing something you like. This is *affective guidance,* or positive feedback. For example, 4-year-old Kay was not playing with children. This worried parents and teachers. The teachers began giving Kay attention whenever she was playing with another child. They said, "I like the way you and Tom are sharing the book." Nothing was said to Kay when she played alone. Soon, Kay responded to this praise and became more social.

Misbehavior and Boredom

Planning and preparing the learning activities of the school and home are also a form of indirect guidance. Indirect guidance is the behind-the-scenes work of adults that sets the stage for the behavior desired in children. If there are many interesting things for children to do, they are more likely to play peacefully and productively. They will not have time to get into trouble.

Many of the suggestions you will read in Chapter 38 about activities for prekindergartners can be used at home. The best toys are those that can be used in a variety of ways, such as blocks, clay, and snap-together blocks. Although building blocks are expensive, they are worth the investment. They cost less in the long run than a lot of expensive toys that are used once and then forgotten.

Parents can help their children keep from becoming bored by rotating their toys and play materials from time to time, putting some away for a while.

Although a lot of research has been done on the effects of television on young children, experts still cannot agree. But, it seems that children who watch great amounts of television will not learn to entertain themselves as well as children who watch less. Parents will probably want to limit their prekindergartners' television time to a few hours per week. Parents should often watch programs with their children so they can watch children's reactions and determine whether the programs are of high quality. More discussion of television appears in Chapter 44.

Children with interesting things to do are less likely to test rules. Indirect guidance promotes positive behavior.

Tips for Guiding Children

"They never listen to anything I say . . ." In Chapter 34, you learned that short, clear statements work best when guiding children. Children accept guidance that is delivered with an unspoken attitude of: "I'm sure about what I want you to do and I'm certain you *will* do it." Here are 6 techniques that make this type of verbal guidance even more effective.

1 **Use positive phrases.** Tell the child what to do, instead of what not to do. Positive phrases help a child become self-directed.

Negative	Positive
"Don't spill your juice."	"Hold your glass straight, Ted."
"Don't interrupt me."	"You can ask a question when I'm finished talking to Mrs. Paterra.
"Don't walk on the wet floor."	"Step over here."

What positive statement would you use in the situation shown here?

2 **Put the "action" part of your statement first.**
Then the child knows what you want right away. For example, "Come here," is clear. However, "You're standing too close to that swinging door, so come here," is not immediately clear. The child must process too much information before she knows what to do.

What would you tell Nicole?

3 **Try to give 1 direction at a time.** If you must, give 2. More than 2 directions will cause the child to forget what he is supposed to do. For example, "Put on your sweater, find your umbrella, and bring me your boots so I can help put them on," will probably bring no results at all. The child should be given the second direction after he successfully completes the first one.

How would you help Kurt to clean up his paints?

322

5 **Adults can give too many directions and become bossy.** Constantly being told, "Do this," or "Do that," does not allow the child to become self-directed. Stop and watch. Prekindergartners may surprise you by the many situations they can handle by themselves.

Delora is climbing the jungle gym for the first time. What should you say?

4 **Give directions at the right time and place.** The child will not keep the directions in mind for long, so they must be given when they are needed or in the place where they will be needed. The best time to set limits about crossing the street is when you are holding the child's hand and about to step off the curb.

When should you tell Tracy how to behave during a wedding service? What should you tell her?

6 **Give reasons to back up your request.** The reasons should be accurate and easy to understand. If rules and limits do not have a good reason, perhaps they should not exist.

For example:

"Let's put your pajamas on." (Child protests.)

"I want you to go to bed early tonight because you have a cold. Extra sleep may help you feel better tomorrow."

"Turn off the television." (Child protests.)

"We turn off the television now because there are no more programs for children coming on."

How will you tell Eric that he must go to the store with you, even though he wants to stay home by himself and continue to play?

Children learn both positive and negative behavior by imitating adults.

Parents and Teachers

Parents and teachers can work to provide a good home and school situation for the child. This parent-teacher interaction is another form of indirect guidance. Teachers should remember that parents know their children better than anyone else does. If parents feel comfortable with teachers, they will share information that may help teachers understand their children better.

Also, teachers often see aspects of a child's personality that parents do not see. Teachers may often help parents see some positive aspects of a child's personality and growth. They may also be able to alert parents to problems.

A conscientious teacher will not hide problems from parents. But the tactful teacher knows timing is important. Greeting a tired parent with, "Joan has been whining all afternoon," will make the parent feel angry. "Joan seems to be having a tough time today. Is it okay if I call you at home to talk about it this evening?" is more diplomatic.

Guidance and Positive Self-concept

Guidance should be planned to help children feel good about themselves. Teaching children skills will help them feel more capable and self-confident.

Telling children they are "bad" only makes them feel guilty. A child who hears this repeatedly begins to believe it and behaves accordingly. Similarly, physical punishment often damages a child's positive self-concept. Punishment is also ineffective because it does not help the child know what to do. The lesson the child learns is not that certain behaviors are undesirable but that *getting caught* is undesirable. Then the child tries to avoid getting caught, rather than improving behavior.

❓ Decisions, Decisions

The children in your preschool group were playing a circle game. Four-year-old Kara made a mistake in the game and let out a loud curse word. Some of the children giggled. Others had no idea what she had said. How would you handle it?

Imitation

Being the kind of person you would like the child to become is an effective form of guidance. Children learn a lot by imitation. If you study families, you will find striking similarities in children's and their parents' voices, mannerisms, attitudes, and ways of responding to problems. Children get positive feedback when they copy a parent's behavior. They want to please their parents and to receive love from them. They fear loss of love. Therefore, they begin early to imitate those they love.

Children will also imitate their teachers. A teacher who captures their love can influence them a great deal. If parents and teachers model happy, generous, stable behaviors, children will copy these behaviors. On the other hand, if children see adults who are mean, bossy, or selfish, adults should not be surprised when children behave the same way.

Neither parents nor teachers can be perfect, however. All people—parents and children alike—have bad days. Children are very resilient. They would probably have an unrealistic view of the world if they never saw adults get angry or behave unreasonably. Dealing with a certain amount of frustration and inconsistency probably helps children learn to cope. However, parents, because they are older, should be expected to take a long-range view of problem situations. They can understand the harm that may come to the child if they let their anger match the child's. If a child or parent has a bad day, then parents must be mature enough to figure out at least a temporary solution to problems without harming the child physically or psychologically.

Saying, "I get upset when you throw your toys all around the living room" helps the child know what bothers the parent. The "I-message" lets the child know that it is the parent's problem. Saying, "You mess up the house with your toys" puts the blame on the child, who probably is not bothered at all about the messy house. "I-messages" get more positive responses from children than "You-messages."

Also, parents can apologize. No harm can be done by a parent or teacher who is willing to say, "I'm sorry I yelled at you. I'm really not feeling too well today, and what you did made me pretty angry—but I still shouldn't have yelled."

Adults should also recognize that most children exhibit totally unexplainable behavior occasionally. A 3-year-old will start behaving more like a 2-year-old. Some children go on crying for no apparent reason. Then they seem perfectly all right once they have gotten the crying out of their systems. If an adult and a child are having a bad day the same day, the situation can seem unbearable. Probably the best advice that can be given for such days is to try to keep a sense of humor and realize that the crisis will not last forever.

Concluding Comments

The guidance of prekindergartners follows the principles of guidance suggested in Chapters 18 and 25. Guidance is defined as everything adults do to influence children's behavior. Guidance is both direct and indirect. Indirect guidance means setting the stage for appropriate behavior. Arranging the environment, setting time schedules, planning learning activities, and cooperating with parents are all forms of indirect guidance.

Direct guidance can become more verbal as the child understands language better. Adults must state limits clearly and enforce them if these limits are to be effective.

Affective guidance is often called positive and negative feedback. Affective guidance lets children know what they are doing well and what behavior is displeasing. With adequate enforcement, parents can eliminate bad habits without punishment. Punishment is generally ineffective in teaching the desired behavior. Also, it may have undesirable side effects, such as damaging the child's self-concept.

Activities

1. Visit a preschool to observe a teacher interacting with 3- or 4-year-olds.
   a. Describe several examples of the teacher giving a child guidance.
   b. Include at least 1 example of affective guidance used with positive feedback.
   c. How effective was each guidance example in influencing behavior?
2. Ask the preschool teacher to describe a situation in which he or she discussed a child's guidance with the parents. Report orally or in writing.
3. Describe the indirect guidance carried out at the preschool.
4. Discuss how some of these indirect

guidance techniques can be used effectively in the home.
5. With parents' permission, care for a 3- or 4-year-old child for several hours. Practice some of the guidance techniques described in this chapter. Report the results in detail.
6. Ask the parents of 5 prekindergartners how many hours of television their children watch each week.
   a. Combine the results of your poll with your classmates'.
   b. Make a chart showing the percentage of children who watched TV less than 5 hours per week, 5 to 10 hours, 10 to 20, 20 to 30, and more than 30 hours per week.
   c. Discuss the results with your classmates.

Home Routines for Prekindergartners

Objectives

To describe how home routines change when the child becomes 3 or 4 years old.

To describe some routines that the child can now take care of independently.

To describe some routines where the child still needs adult help.

Susan and Rick, both 4-year-olds, are preparing a meal for their dolls. Using a low play table, each of the children has a doll propped up on boxes and pillows. They use a small set of dishes to serve the meal and they make the meal as authentic as they can. "The bread goes on this plate," says Rick. "We need coffee in these cups," Susan observes. "Rick, will your mommy give us some coffee?"

Rick goes to the kitchen and returns with some apple juice, which the children pretend is coffee. Finally, the preparations are complete. The children sit down to eat the meal and to feed the babies.

Home Routines Change

When the child becomes 3 or 4 years old, many home routines may probably have to be changed. These include furniture arrangement, afternoon and evening routines, bedtime routines, shopping routines, and visitors.

Arranging the House

Making the home comfortable for prekindergartners means arranging the space for children's imaginative play with friends, such as the role-playing of Rick and Susan in the opening story.

By the time the first child is 4 years old, some families have another baby. Consequently, the family cannot rearrange the house much to fit the first child because the new baby will be "into everything" before long. One important consideration is to protect the older child's things from harm by the infant. It is also essential to protect the infant from harmful objects—such as crayons or pins—that may be found in the older child's room.

Many families cannot provide separate rooms for each child. Sometimes a room divider will give the older child needed privacy. If this is not possible, parents can set off one corner for the 3- or 4-year-old, where special toys are out of the infant's reach.

Usually, 3- and 4-year-olds need space for vigorous, boisterous play. The yard and sidewalk near the house or apartment are usually used for wheel toys. Parents should be particularly concerned about safety, since children, especially 4-year-olds, want increased independence. This is the time when parents begin to appreciate the space and activities offered by a good nursery school.

Children of this age like having their own rooms or a place of their own for their toys, even though they often bring some toys to the room where most of the family congregates. Prekindergartners can help tidy up their own rooms. However, being asked to put away all the toys they have taken out during the day

How would you work with this child to clean up her messy room?

can be overwhelming. Children will need help from their parents to keep at the task. The parent might say, "I'll put away three blocks and you put away three." Or, "You pick up the red ones, and I'll pick up the blue ones."

Afternoon and Evening Routines

Late afternoon and early evening are often difficult times for both parents and children. Usually, the child's energy is beginning to fade. Both parents are probably tired, either from the long day at work outside the home or from the everyday household chores.

A parent who is trying to get supper on the table may feel short-tempered, because many children's demands increase at this time. Some parents find it helpful if one prepares the meal while the other plays with the child or helps with bathing and putting pajamas on.

Many prekindergartners love to stand on a stool or a chair and watch or help while a parent prepares the meal. Wearing a plastic bib or smock, a child can "wash dishes" while the parent works. Providing a small plastic pitcher, some cups, and a funnel will keep the child busy for half an hour or more. This is often a good time for conversation, too.

Other parents may not be comfortable having a child in the kitchen. If parents allow their child to watch a certain amount of television, this may be a good time for an approved program.

Bedtime Routines

Most parents move children to a regular bed at about age 3. Most 3-year-olds may still need an afternoon nap. However, most 4-year-olds will have stopped taking naps altogether.

Children of both ages should be well established in their bedtime routines by now. A bath, a bedtime story or two, a song, and a nightly ritual of tucking favorite toys into bed usually make bedtime peaceful and enjoyable.

There are problems in some families with television programs that these older children may wish to watch. Parents must decide on a policy to follow. Watching television after a certain hour may rob children of needed sleep. The next afternoon, the children may be unusually cranky with friends or family members. In such cases, parents should limit television viewing hours.

❓ Decisions, Decisions

Melba hates to have her hair washed or even combed. "There must be a way to make hair washing and combing pleasant," thought her Dad. Can you think of some ways?

Bathing and Dressing Routines

Both 3- and 4-year-olds enjoy a bath at bedtime to clean off the day's dust from their active play and to help them relax before bedtime. A 3- or 4-year-old still needs help while bathing and should never be left alone in the bathtub.

Children between the ages of 3 and 4 make great strides in self-dressing. With properly designed clothing, children can become completely independent in dressing. Children of this age are best able to handle pullover shirts and pants with elasticized waistbands. Zippered overalls, especially those with

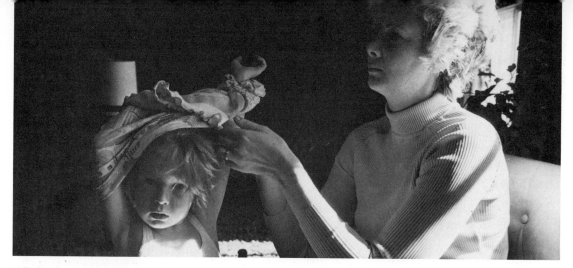

While prekindergartners are capable of dressing themselves, they still need help with certain clothes.

large rings, are also easy for young children to manage.

Although elasticized pants are easy to find for girls, many manufacturers of boys' clothing make dungarees with large, unwieldy snaps and wide belt loops. Few children this age are able to buckle belts or manage the snaps, which require a good deal of strength and coordination. Parents who want their children to be self-sufficient, rather than stylish, should look for clothing the 3- or 4-year-old can manage easily alone.

Shopping Routines

Claudia, a young mother, was shopping with her 3-year-old, Anne. Claudia had several purchases to make at the local drugstore, which also carried a full line of toys. Anne asked if she could look at toys while her mother shopped. Claudia answered, "Yes, you may look at them, but please don't take anything off the shelves." She knew Anne was able to follow such directions. Also, permitting Anne to look at the toys helped make shopping easier.

When Claudia had finished making her purchases, she walked back to the toy counter. There, Anne was staring at a row of toy dump trucks.

"It's time to go now, Anne," said Claudia. "Take one more look at the trucks, and let's go to the car."

"I want you to buy me the red dump truck, Mommy," said Anne.

"Not today, honey. Maybe we can build a dump truck with your blocks when we get home."

"I want the dump truck!" cried Anne, tears beginning to well up in her eyes.

"I know you do," said Claudia, "and I know it makes you sad to leave it here. But we can't buy it today. Come on now, it's time to go home."

"No!" shrieked Anne, and sat down on the floor, her lower lip stuck out.

"I'm going to the car now," said her mother. Claudia walked calmly toward the door of the store without looking back at Anne.

When her mother got to the door, Anne ran to Claudia, reaching her just as she opened the door to go out.

When they were on the sidewalk, Claudia said, "Look at that big, green garbage truck over there. What do you suppose it's doing?"

"Picking up the garbage," cried Anne gleefully. "Can I watch?"

Although guiding a 3-year-old may not always proceed so smoothly, the above example does demonstrate some sound principles. Claudia gave Anne as much freedom as she thought Anne could handle at her age. Then she let Anne know what was expected of her. She acknowledged Anne's feelings. But she refused to become involved in what could easily have turned into a tantrum.

Once the crisis passed, Claudia showed good judgment in not lecturing Anne on her behavior in the store. She allowed Anne to keep her dignity by changing the subject once outside.

Many 3-year-olds respond more like babies on shopping expeditions. They tire easily, demand their food on time, and are not easily distracted from their demands. However, most parents must take their children along, at least part of the time. The following suggestions may help make shopping a little easier.

1. If parents allow between-meal snacks, such as fruit or juice, they may bring these snacks along. Most child-rearing experts agree that food should not be used as a bribe.

2. A bag filled with a few toys will help entertain the child. Many children like to choose the toys they wish to take. Parents can expect to be asked to carry the bag part of the time.

3. The parent of a young child—especially a parent who works outside the home—will usually be pressed for time. But if parents try not to rush the child, the trip will be more enjoyable and less frustrating for both parent and child.

4. A simple shopping trip can turn into a learning experience. The parent might ask, "How many red things can you find in this window?" or "How many round things do you see on that corner?"

5. This is also a good time to practice simple concepts. A parent could say, "Show me how you can walk *behind* me, *in front of* me, *beside* me. Can you walk *under* me? *On top of* me?"

Most 4-year-olds generally enjoy the outing and can tolerate a delay in their time of eating or resting. However, they are occasionally demanding of their own wants. The child may press the parent to purchase a toy or other object that the parent would prefer not to buy. Parents must decide on a policy about such requests. For once the child is rewarded with a purchase, another request will certainly be made on the next shopping trip. Grocery stores can be especially difficult. They often have tempting displays of candy near the checkout counter, where parents and children must wait in line.

If the child is getting restless from waiting in the checkout line, the parent can begin counting objects, telling jokes or riddles, or playing games to while away the minutes. A guessing game describing objects in the shopping cart might be fun. For example, the parent can say, "I see something round and yellow that's made from milk. What is it?" The next turn is the child's.

Almost all 4-year-olds are particularly alert to television advertising. They can embarrass a parent with their persistent demands for things they see on television. Of course, this is just what televi-

Home routines may have special problems when parents work outside the home.

sion advertisers try to achieve. Parents generally want to make purchases only after full consideration of needs and resources. They can tell the child that they will discuss the purchase at home.

Parents Who Work Outside the Home

In more and more families today, both parents hold full-time or part-time jobs outside the home. This means that these parents must make special arrangements for the needs of their children.

By the time a child is 3 or 4 years old, some parents will want to try to find a full-time public or private prekinder-

garten program. Other parents may prefer the child to spend half a day in a prekindergarten program and the other half day with a baby-sitter or relative.

In any case, these parents, as well as single parents, face special problems. The morning is usually somewhat rushed. Everyone has to get dressed, have breakfast, and be ready to leave at a certain time. If the nursery school program does not begin until 9:00, and the parent or parents have to leave the home at 8:00 or 8:30, arrangements must be made for the child to stay with a neighbor, friend, or relative. This person might then take the child to school or put the child on the school bus.

One father says, "I always let Sara take her time on the way home, because I feel so bad about rushing her so much every morning."

Special problems may arise if the child is ill. Either parents must find a care-giving adult or one parent must stay home from work. Many employers are not sympathetic to such needs. The employer may take the days from a parent's valuable vacation time, rather than allowing a mother or father to take sick days or personal days to care for the child.

In spite of all these problems, more and more women are finding that they are happier working part time or full time outside the home than they would be staying at home with a child. Many say that they enjoy their children more than they did before and that the children also seem more content.

Of course, for many couples—and for almost all single parents—work is an economic necessity. Our system of child care is just beginning to take these needs into account. As more and more women enter the work force, we will need to develop creative ways of providing quality care and educational programs for young children.

Visitors

Both 3- and 4-year-olds will enjoy having a friend come to play in their home. Most 4-year-olds will get along quite well if there are only 2 children. But they will need an adult close by if there are more than 2. Many 4-year-olds will enjoy spending the night with a close friend.

Most 3- and 4-year-olds have problems with adult social occasions if the adults expect them to say the right thing, shake hands, keep quiet, and stay dressed up for an extended period of time. Parents should try to avoid taking children to such functions. If the child must be present, perhaps arrangements can be made for a special children's play area. If this is not possible, parents must realize that the child will probably get restless before too long. Some favorite toys may help. But a parent will probably have to interrupt his or her activity to give the child some attention.

Concluding Comments

A 3- or 4-year-old may be easier to live with than the 2-year-old was. Often the emotional storms have ended. The prekindergartner is usually more capable of holding a conversation, being a companion, and, in general, being a more reasonable human being.

The home routines discussed above are general suggestions. There are no hard-and-fast rules about family sched-

ules. Each family must work out its own routines, and the routines may change frequently. Although children like the security of schedules, they are very adaptable. Most children think that whatever their family does is "normal." If a family sits down to dinner together only twice a week, the 3- or 4-year-old will probably think that all families do this. As long as children's physical, emotional, and mental needs are met, the home routine is probably an acceptable one.

Each family works out its own way of completing household chores and allowing time together for parents and children.

1. Talk with the parents of a 3- or 4-year-old. Ask how their child helps at home. Or, ask your own parents how you helped them when you were that age. Report your findings to your class.

2. Check the clothes for 3- and 4-year-olds offered for sale at a department store, discount store, or specialty shop.
   a. Briefly describe at least 3 items for sale that would be easy for a child to put on without help.
   b. Describe at least 3 items that would make it hard for a small child to dress independently.

3. With parent's permission, take a 3- or 4-year-old shopping with you. Act as if you will be taking this child with you regularly when you shop— do not buy the child a gift or use other methods of keeping the child quiet that you would not want to continue doing each time.
   a. Describe the experience in detail.
   b. Play some learning games with the child sometime during the shopping trip.
   c. Include in your report a description of the games and the child's response.

4. Ask a working parent of a prekindergartner to describe a typical day for the child. This parent may be either single or a parent whose spouse also works outside the home.
   a. Get as detailed a schedule as possible.
   b. Do they have specific times they spend with their child?
   c. What time does the child go to bed?
   d. Describe the child's bedtime routine.

5. Discuss with a teacher of young children how expressions of jealousy are handled in the classroom. Report to your class.

Feeding Prekindergartners

Objectives

To describe mealtime and snacktime for prekindergartners.
To state factors that influence children's food choices.
To explain the importance of early nutrition for prekindergartners.

"I'd like milk for snack, please. I have cavities and I can't have drinks with sugar. They are bad for my teeth," Ellen reported to her teacher. She explained how the dentist had found five cavities and that he hurt her "a little" when he filled them. The dentist warned her that she will have more cavities to be filled if she does not stop drinking soft drinks.

Good Nutrition: The Goal

Good nutrition cannot wait. It must be provided for children every day or children's physical and mental health may suffer. During the early years, the responsibility for adequate nutrition rests largely with the parents, care givers, and teachers. They buy, prepare, and serve food to the children. Children's daily intake should include the Basic Four foods—milk and milk products; vegetables and fruits; meat, fish, poultry, and eggs; and bread and cereals, preferably whole-grain.

Children's acceptance or refusal of foods influences their nutrition considerably. According to various studies, prekindergartners have certain preferences in food.

1. They like variety in texture—some soft, some crisp, some chewy foods.
2. They like foods separate, rather than together in casseroles or mixed in salads.

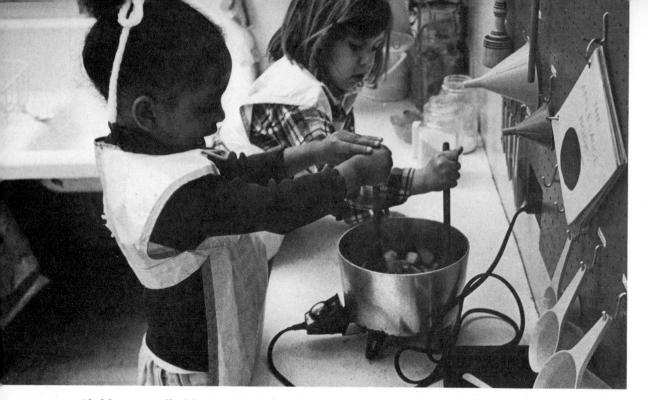
Children usually like any food they help to prepare.

3. They like color, selecting brightly colored foods when they are available.
4. They like mildly flavored foods and mildly spiced foods. Therefore, some vegetables are unpopular because of their strong flavor.
5. They like desserts. These should be planned as part of the child's needed nutrition and not used as a reward.
6. They will usually try new foods if they can decide how much of the new food to eat after tasting it.
7. They will usually like any food they have had a part in preparing.

These are general characteristics, and children will differ. For example, children may show cultural differences. Latin American children may acquire the taste for spicy foods. Chinese children may be accustomed to having foods mixed together and may dislike soft, overcooked vegetables. Some children may resist trying new foods, whether or not they have helped prepare them. Adults should respect these differences and should never force any food on a child. Forcing children to eat can cause weight problems later on.

? Decisions, Decisions

At age 4, Stuart is fat. "He just loves to eat," says his mother. "He always says he's hungry. What should I do? Put my 4-year-old on a diet?" What would you suggest to Stuart's mother?

Nutrition Education for Children

Prekindergartners can learn the rules for being well nourished. Informing children about nutrition can start with discussions at mealtime, snacktime, and during every food-preparation project. Adults can introduce children to nutritional facts by telling them that:

1. You need food such as bread and cereal to have energy to run, play, and learn. If you do not eat, you will be like a car without gas—you will not go.
2. You need milk and milk products to make your bones and teeth grow. Bones need to grow every day so you will get taller and stronger. Milk helps make strong teeth.
3. You need vegetables such as carrots and peas to keep your eyes bright and to help you grow.
4. You need fruits such as oranges, grapefruit, apples, and bananas to keep your skin and gums healthy.
5. You need meat, fish, chicken, or eggs every day. These help make your muscles grow strong.

Many of these rules can be explained to children as they are eating the foods listed. Eventually, adults can ask the child questions such as, "When you drink milk, which parts of your body will grow strong?"

Plenty of nutritious foods are available in the United States. Nevertheless, many people are ignorant of sound reasons for choosing one food over another. Nutritional concepts may be difficult to understand. But it now seems important to begin nutrition education in the early years, just as we do safety education. The positive approach of "what is good for you" may be useful for the child like Ellen who already has personal evidence of dental problems.

It is important for adults to help prekindergarten children learn to like a wide variety of foods. However, the available choices should provide all the required nutrients. Prekindergartners are usually willing to try foods at school if they see teachers and other children enjoying the food. One way children learn at this age is by imitation. But food prejudice can also be learned by imitation. The big sister who says she "hates milk" has a lot of influence on the prekindergarten brother or sister.

Food-preparation projects can interest prekindergartners in foods that they may dislike at home or that may be unfamiliar to them. They often go home demanding that their mother get the recipe from the teacher and make "some" immediately. One mother was puzzled as to why the prekindergarten apple sauce was so "special," according to her son. She called the teacher for the "secret recipe."

Mealtimes

Prekindergarten children usually eat better if they have a quiet period before mealtime. They vary in their food needs and eating habits, both at home and at school. One is a picky eater, "not eating enough to keep a bird alive," says his father. Another is on a "mashed potato binge." Another enjoys a little of everything and seconds on dessert. The task for parents and teachers is to attempt to adjust to such individual differences without making an issue of eating.

Goals for Prekindergartners at Mealtimes

1. *To eat a well-balanced meal.* All the foods available should be good for children. If children *taste* a little of everything and eat the foods they like best, they are likely to be well-nourished.

2. *To enjoy mealtime.* Mealtimes begin to be social occasions for 3- and 4-year-olds. They may enjoy sitting next to a special friend. Most prekindergartens and day-care centers plan special seating arrangements. They make sure that children who need help are close to an adult helper. Also, children with well-developed eating skills can be seated next to children who need to learn some of those skills.

Parents and teachers alike should avoid unpleasant topics, emotional disagreements, or criticisms at mealtime. Fear and anger interfere with digestion and bother adults as well as children.

3. *To taste and come to enjoy eating a wide variety of foods.* New foods should be presented along with favored foods to broaden children's tastes. New foods may be served in tiny servings, just big enough to encourage tasting. "Enough" and "too much" are very personal decisions that the child should make.

4. *To learn to feed themselves.* Children of prekindergarten age can help with setting and cleaning up the table. They can also usually handle eating utensils fairly well. They enjoy pouring their own milk from a small pitcher. There should be no more milk in the pitcher than will fit into the child's glass. Otherwise, the child may keep right on pouring after the glass is full.

5. *To sit at the table and develop acceptable table manners.* Some prekindergartners have a habit of getting up and down from their chairs at mealtime. When they come to prekindergarten, they need help to learn to sit up at the table and remain there during the meal. Most schools have children carry their used plates to a kitchen cart before picking up their dessert. This provides a little opportunity to move about and also fosters independence.

Parents' Participation at Mealtime or Snacktime

The recommendations in this chapter apply to both home and school. In addition, parents may have the chance to come to school to participate in snacktime or mealtime.

Parents, too, should avoid concentrating so heavily on the child's feeding that they neglect their own nutrition. Also, some parents develop the habit of nibbling scraps off the child's plate. This habit may lead to an unbalanced diet and an unwanted weight gain.

Concluding Comments

High-quality nutrition for prekindergartners is the responsibility of parents and teachers. Children should learn about nutrition early. Then they can make food decisions on the basis of sound information.

Meals, snacks, and food projects offer a number of opportunities for teachers and parents to provide nutritious foods. With an increase in poor nutrition among young children, even in the midst of plenty of food, adults should stress good nutrition early.

338

Mealtimes are learning times. Seated at the family table, children learn which foods to eat, which table manners to use, and how to talk to one another.

Activities

1. Find at least 3 recipes for foods suitable for prekindergartners. Choose recipes for items that a child could help you prepare.
2. Help 1 or more prekindergartners prepare 1 of these recipes. Report your experience to your class.
3. Plan, prepare, and serve a meal to one or more prekindergartners.
   a. Include the food the children helped you prepare.
   b. Be sure you include a food from each of the Basic Four food groups.
   c. Encourage children to help set and clean up the table.

d. Report your experience. Include your menu and a detailed description of the children's reactions to the meal.

4. List at least 5 nutritious snacks suitable for prekindergartners.
5. Talk with a parent of a 3- or 4-year-old child.
   a. Ask what foods the child likes.
   b. Ask if the child has had any special food problems.
   c. Ask if the child helps with meals in any way. How?
   d. Ask if the child helps get snacks alone when at home.
   e. Report to your class.

Schools for Prekindergartners

Objectives

To explain the differences in various prekindergarten programs.

To give guidelines to help parents choose a prekindergarten program.

To describe high-quality prekindergarten programs.

Terms to look for cooperative nursery school • free-play program • Head Start • laboratory nursery school • learning centers • Montessori method

Types of Prekindergarten Programs

Prekindergarten refers to programs for 3- and 4-year-old children. There are several prekindergarten programs throughout the United States. Some communities have several, while others have none. Rural communities may have difficulty setting up prekindergarten programs because of the problems involved in transporting children long distances.

Nursery Schools

Nursery schools have been used primarily by families not requiring full-day child care. Either the mother or the father does not work outside the home, or one of the parents works only part time, or the working parent or parents are able to arrange care for the part of the day when the child is not in nursery school. There are several types of schools that fall into this category.

1. *Private, Profit-making Nursery Schools.* Private, profit-making nursery schools are usually the most expensive.

They must cover the costs of rent or mortgage, insurance, equipment, food, and a paid staff. In addition, they must make a reasonable profit.

2. *Private, Nonprofit Nursery Schools.* The most common type of nonprofit nursery school is one located in or connected with a church, synagogue, or charitable organization. The church may often provide space for a very low rent and cover the cost of insurance. The nursery school usually has to pay for materials and teacher salaries out of tuition fees. Some of these nursery schools offer religious instruction. Some may have a snacktime prayer or weekly religious observation. Others have no religious element at all.

3. *Parent Cooperative Nursery Schools.* Parent cooperative nursery schools are organized by parents who want to provide a nursery school program for their children at low cost. In these schools, parents take turns acting as teacher assistants.

Parents who work outside the home may find that the cooperative nursery school, although low in cost, is not practical. They are unable to take time off from their jobs to work in the classroom. A parent who is interested in a particular cooperative nursery school might check to see if some other service (helping repair equipment at night or on weekends, typing newsletters, and so forth) could be substituted for classroom work.

4. *Laboratory Nursery Schools.* Laboratory nursery schools have been developed by high schools and colleges. They provide a laboratory in which students can learn child-development principles and ways to work with young children.

One of the benefits of a nursery school is that it broadens a child's world.

5. *Head Start.* Head Start is a program funded by the federal government for children of the poor who particularly need the advantages of a nursery school. Such children may not have developed important language skills and other learning skills. Giving these children a head start through a good nursery school program might help them avoid later school failures.

? Decisions, Decisions

During nursery school, four-year-old Angela decides to give her friend Patty a haircut. Before you discover what is happening, Angela has scissored off much of the hair on one side of Patty's head. What do you do?

341

Day Care

Day care has been the traditional program serving parents who work outside the home. Day-care centers are not new. Charitable organizations ran day-care centers as early as 1854 for the children of poor immigrants. Since women's participation in today's labor force is skyrocketing, many more day-care centers are now opening up to assist parents with child raising.

1. *Publicly Funded Group Day Care.* Children are enrolled in group day-care centers for 8 to 10 hours a day. Programs are generally operated Monday through Friday, although some operate 6 or 7 days a week. Some states permit overnight care.

Fees in public day-care centers are most often based on the parents' ability to pay and are subsidized by state and/or local governments. In many states, children are not eligible for this service if family income exceeds a certain figure.

Although many states require only that day-care centers meet certain physical and sanitary requirements, parents are increasingly requesting that day-care programs offer educational activities to their children. Some states and cities now require that centers have one licensed teacher in each classroom, in addition to one or more assistants.

2. *Profit-Making Day Care.* In addition to public day-care centers, an increasing number of profit-making day-care centers are in operation. Some of these are private businesses, just like private nursery schools. Some are franchises, in which the operator buys the business from the parent company. Others are chains, in which the operator is manager of one division.

3. *Family Day Care.* Family day care provides care for children in the home of the care giver, who is generally a mother or father caring for one or more of her or his own children. The educational equipment, materials, and curriculum can be minimal in family day care. But states and localities—often at the urging of parents—are requiring increasingly strict educational standards for these care givers.

At its best, family day care can offer a warm, homelike atmosphere for the young child. Many parents of 3-year-olds feel that their children are too young to spend as many as 10 hours a day in the day-care center. Family day care offers an alternative.

Educational Content in Prekindergarten

Children have qualities of mind and body the prekindergarten program can help bring out. No one knows what a child's talents might be. The teacher's challenge is to provide educational experiences that will develop each child's talents and enable the child to function effectively in today's world.

Young children learn by experimenting and exploring on their own with equipment and supplies. Children do not learn effectively when people only talk to them. They need things to do. For example, young children learning about apples learn more if the teacher lets them pick an apple, hold it, smell it, wash it, taste it, and cook it. Children need these hands-on experiences.

Parents used to send their children to nursery schools primarily to help the

Special visitors acquaint children with many different jobs.

children learn to get along with others and to give the parent some valuable time away from the child. Because research has indicated that 3- and 4-year-olds learn at a rapid rate, many theories of education are now in operation in prekindergarten centers.

The most common type of nursery school program is the "free play" approach. In free play, children choose their own materials and work with them in ways they wish. Teachers have chosen these materials with the interests of the children in mind.

Many nursery schools offer a more structured approach to early learning. An example would be the Montessori schools, based on teaching methods developed by Maria Montessori. In these schools, emphasis is placed on teaching children to perform tasks in a specific, orderly sequence. Children are still free

to choose their own materials and to work at their own rate. But they are expected to learn a specific, correct way of working with the materials. Each material must be put away in its place before the child selects another activity.

Because failures in reading and mathematics have increased in public schools in recent years, some prekindergarten programs teach academic skills, such as reading and writing. They try to teach children through drill and memorization. Such centers question the value of play. Such materials as blocks and dress-up clothes may not be found at all. Many educators criticize this approach. They feel that children learn best through play and that these centers fail to give children the opportunity to exercise their large muscles.

Some preschools have grouped children according to age. But other schools are now experimenting with having different age groups together for part of the school day. Many educators believe that children learn from each other. Having children of different ages together gives each child more freedom to progress at his or her own rate.

Choosing a Prekindergarten Program

The type of prekindergarten program a parent chooses depends on several factors. The following are some questions families and single parents might ask themselves before deciding.

1. Is a full-day program needed, or will the 3-hour nursery school be enough? Parents who work outside the home and who have a fairly high combined income or single parents with a high income may be able to afford a combination of private nursery school and child-care person. If one parent works outside the home only part time or not at all, the 3-hour nursery school may be enough. It can provide a needed break for the parent and give the child new kinds of experiences.

2. How will the child get to the program? Some prekindergarten centers will be located close enough to the child's home to allow the child and an escort to walk there together. Many private nursery schools provide bus service, but this can be quite expensive. Car pools are the answer for many parents. A parent who works outside the home may be able to take the child to school, then arrange for either bus service, the

In a high-quality prekindergarten, the teacher takes time to respond to children's comments and questions.

other parent, or a friend to bring the child home. Most public day-care centers are located within walking distance of the homes they serve. Private nursery schools sometimes serve a larger area, and transportation may be more of a problem.

3. What types of learning will the program offer? Different possible approaches were discussed earlier in this chapter.

4. Does the program offer religious instruction? Parents may want a child to receive such instruction. In this case, they should check to see if their church, synagogue, or other house of worship has a prekindergarten program.

5. What type of discipline is used? Parents will probably want this to be compatible with the type of guidance they use at home.

6. Are the teachers specially trained in early childhood education? Parents may want to check on the qualifications of the staff, because licensing requirements vary from state to state and from city to city.

7. What types of snacks or meals are served? Many parents are very concerned about good nutrition. They may want to make sure that few sugar-sweetened snacks are served. Full-day programs often post menus every week. This helps parents to plan their home meals accordingly.

8. Is television used? If so, how much? Although most prekindergarten centers probably do not use television, some do. Parents may want to see how it is used. Family day-care homes should have a policy on how much television children are allowed to watch.

9. How is the adjustment period handled? Centers vary widely on this subject. Some insist that the parents stay in the classroom, or at least on the premises, for as long as a week. Some allow parents to leave on the first day if the child seems happy. Many feel that this should be a decision left up to each individual parent.

10. What about the teacher? No matter what kind of program parents prefer, the teacher is the most important factor in any prekindergarten center. A warm, loving teacher who is genuinely interested in the development and welfare of each individual child is the most important factor in choosing a prekindergarten program.

What Is a High-quality Prekindergarten?

"Teacher, my kitty came home!" announced Juanita happily as she entered the Lolly Pop Nursery School one morning.

Her teacher remembered that this kitty was a source of great pleasure to Juanita. She said, "I'm so glad. Now you can take good care of it again."

Mrs. Cohen, Juanita's teacher, operates a small prekindergarten. She always tries to have everything ready when the children arrive. That way, she can take time to listen to children's stories about events. She had learned long before today that Juanita's kitty was very important to her. Mrs. Cohen knows that conversations with Juanita and with all Lolly Pop Nursery School children are important contributions to their mental, social, and emotional development.

What to Look for in a Day-care Center

You can ask the teacher of a day-care center about programs, schedules, and activities. But many times, what you see in a high-quality day-care center will speak for itself. A sound program and skilled teaching is usually present when you find:

- An adequate staff-child ratio. For 3- and 4-year-olds, one staff member is needed for every 10 children.

- Outdoor play area

- A place for books

- Places for solitary play

- Provisions for food and rest

- Storage and open shelves to keep order

- Colorful, interesting surroundings

- Materials for make-believe

- Places for group activities

- Learning centers or activity tables

Learning centers offer space and supplies for children to work alone. Here a child cares for his plant—a year-long project.

Daily Routines in the Prekindergarten

A high-quality prekindergarten program follows a routine every day to help children feel secure. Here is one schedule for a 3-hour nursery school program:

9:00–9:10 A.M. Teacher greets children and parents. Children choose materials for "free play" or "activity period." The teacher helps a child who is having difficulty making a decision.

9:10–10:00 A.M. Free-play period. Children work with materials they have chosen. They change activities often.

10:00–10:15 A.M. Clean-up time. Children and teacher put materials away. Children go to the bathroom and wash their hands for snack time.

10:15–10:30 A.M. Snack time. Children and teacher have juice and crackers or some other nutritious food.

10:30–10:55 A.M. Teacher and children have a group time, often called "circle time." The teacher may read a story or the teacher and children may discuss the morning's activities. They may sing some songs together or learn a special dance or other rhythmic movement.

10:55–11:00 A.M. Teacher and children prepare to go outside to the play yard or park.

11:00–11:45 A.M. Outdoor play time, if weather permits. If not, the children will probably do some indoor activity that exercises their large muscles.

11:45 A.M. The parents, care-giving adults, or the school bus arrives to take children home.

In the full-day program, lunch is served and is followed by a rest period. The afternoon usually consists of more free activities and more outdoor time.

The day-care child is often at the center for as long as 10 hours. Thus, the day-care teacher must be an especially warm, caring person. This teacher must be able to offer children substitute parenting for part of the time and also to provide educational experiences for them.

Learning Centers

Suppose you visit a high-quality prekindergarten for 3- and 4-year-olds today. You will probably see children busily engaged with a variety of materials from which they may design and construct according to their own ideas. Activities are selected that contribute to the four areas of development—physical, social, emotional, and mental.

The prekindergarten classroom is usually arranged in a number of *learning centers*. Each center contains room for a few children to work independently of other children or of teachers. Needed supplies are stored in each center.

Children are usually free to move in and out of these centers throughout their play time. They direct their own exploration within each center. For example, in the science center, they experiment with the weighing and measuring apparatus, trying various objects on the scales. Emphasis is on experimenting and exploring. Teachers may be close by to answer questions or to ask questions to help increase the children's learning. Most teachers are so busy helping so many children that such learning must depend on children's self-guided behavior. Otherwise, the school could never operate effectively.

Developing learning centers is an example of the teacher's indirect guidance. Indirect guidance, you will recall, is the teacher's behind-the-scenes activity that influences children's behavior. The teacher plans classroom materials with the skills and interests of these particular 3- and 4-year-olds in mind.

Children are seen creatively building with blocks, using art materials, dressing up in the housekeeping corner, or molding with sand. These are only a few of the many materials available in a high-quality school for children. These prekindergartners learn to be creative as they experiment with materials. They learn to share with the 12 to 18 other children present. Music and poetry provide other avenues for creative expression.

Laughter and friendly conversations predominate, though tears and anger are noted occasionally. Children are developing their social and emotional skills.

High climbing, hard running, and vigorous activities abound on the outdoor playground, where few limitations are put on children. The high-quality program offers a variety of equipment for developing large muscles. Except in very bad weather, children go outdoors for part of each day.

The language environment is rich with new words and new ideas. Books are highly valued, and story time is a favorite for almost everyone. Books are placed in various locations to encourage use. The staff uses every opportunity to extend children's vocabularies and to help them appreciate books.

If a prekindergarten center offers day care for 8 to 10 hours, then children must have nutritious food and a rest period to meet physical needs. Afternoon activities are usually relaxed. They give children worthwhile things to do until their parents arrive to take them home.

Parent Involvement

High-quality programs make efforts to involve parents in some way. Parents may belong to an organization that meets regularly or occasionally. Some schools have special parent rooms where parents who have time may come to have coffee and talk with other parents. In parent cooperatives and many day-care centers, parents are often involved in making decisions about school policy. Boards of directors of some prekindergarten centers have parents as either voting or nonvoting members.

Many teachers hold parent workshops once or twice a year. In such workshops, parents may come to children's classrooms and work with the children's materials. Teachers explain what kinds of learning they expect children to gain from these materials.

In addition to group parent meetings, most schools have teacher-parent conferences once or twice during the school term. Because parents and teachers often see different sides of a child's personality, such conferences may help both understand the child better.

In some prekindergarten programs, parents serve as classroom aides. Here, a parent-aide discusses the rest of the day's schedule with the teacher. At the same time, she is able to give special attention to one of the children.

Helping Children Enjoy the Prekindergarten

Parents can make their child's prekindergarten experience more enjoyable by showing a genuine interest in what the child is doing at school. But parents should not pump the child. Because children need privacy, most do not like to be asked, "What did you do in school today?" Some will answer, "Nothing." Some will say, "We just played." And still others may tell about something that happened several days ago or perhaps something that did not happen at all. Parents will learn quite a lot more if they relax and let things come out during the course of the day.

Parents will probably hear their children singing new songs when playing alone or taking a bath. A parent might say, "I really like that song. Will you teach me the words?" Some children will agree, but others might say, "Please don't talk to me (or look at me) when I'm singing." For some children, nursery school is a very private experience. Children have a right to their privacy, just as adults do.

Parents can put a special bulletin board or space on the wall for hanging children's drawings and paintings.

Children's prekindergarten experience will be even richer if parents enjoy and share it with them in these ways.

Concluding Comments

Most 3- and 4-year-olds can benefit from participating in a prekindergarten program. Many types of schools are available for prekindergartners. Parents should consider their own and their children's needs in choosing a prekindergarten program.

A high-quality prekindergarten program tries to meet the physical, emotional, and intellectual needs of young children. All-day programs must offer nutritious meals and an opportunity for children to rest if they want to.

The relationship between parents and teachers is very important. The child benefits when parents and teachers work cooperatively. Children enjoy their preschool experiences even more when parents show an interest in and appreciate what they do at school. Children feel proud when parents display their artwork or come to school for an occasional visit.

Activities

1. Learn about the prekindergarten programs available in your neighborhood.
   a. List as many available programs as you can.
   b. Call these programs. (One student should do this for the class.) Ask if they have waiting lists of children whose parents want them in the program. How long does it usually take to get a child into the program?
   c. Report the programs' answers to the class.
2. Visit a prekindergarten nursery school, Head Start class, or day-care center.
   a. Describe the daily schedule.
   b. Discuss opportunities for learning that are available to the participating children.
   c. Describe the children's general attitudes.
3. Talk to parents who have a child in a prekindergarten program. Ask:
   a. Do you think your child benefits from attending the prekindergarten program?
   b. What kinds of activities does the program offer? Which ones does your child enjoy?
   c. Are you happy with your child's teacher? How often do you talk with the teacher?
4. Talk to parents of a 3- or 4-year-old who have chosen to keep their child home. What are their reasons?

Activities for Prekindergartner Learning

Objective
To describe appropriate learning activities for prekindergartners.

"I like mine gooey," said Andrea as she squeezed the finger paint through her fingers and watched it drop in big globs on her paper.

"I like mine bluey," laughed Malcolm as he used both hands and swirled the blue paint in circular motions to cover the table in front of him.

"Gooey, bluey. Gooey, bluey," laughed Andrea. "We have a poem."

"Gooey, bluey, do-ey, gooey, bluey, do-ey. I said it, too. Do you like gooey, bluey, do-ey, Andrea?" asked Malcolm.

Malcolm and Andrea are two 4-year-olds attending a prekindergarten. Finger painting is one of their favorite activities. Here, they experiment with color, texture, and rhyming words. They enjoy a satisfying social experience as they share the paints and paper and work together in the art area.

Art Activities

The main point to remember about art activities is that the process, not the product, is important. Children try out creative ideas by drawing, painting, or modeling things important to them. It is wise not to press children to represent what the adult sees. Children may see something adults do not see.

Children need a lot of opportunity simply to experiment with colors, strokes, and shapes. They may not be trying to represent any object that would be familiar to an adult. Hence, adults should avoid asking children, "What are you making?" or "Is that a cow?" The child may not have named the object yet or may not even be making something with a name. A child who is making a horse or a mouse, not a cow, may be insulted or upset by the adult's question. Children need to feel free to explore, to put things together, and to try using different equipment.

Drawing and Painting

Scribbles are the first stage of drawing and painting. At first, the child simply scribbles all over the paper. Later on, between ages 2 and 3, the child may name the scribble, perhaps as "mommy," "baby," or "truck." The adult will not be able to recognize the figure. But the adult should still encourage these first attempts at representation by saying, "Oh, you used your red crayon to make the baby. Do you want to tell me about it?"

The second stage occurs between the ages of 3 and 4, when the child begins to connect a circle to make a human face. Usually, these early faces will have eyes, a mouth, and perhaps a nose. Eyebrows and ears rarely appear until later.

In the third stage, children begin to try to represent things they see around them. However, they may still like to scribble to fill in spaces. Or they may draw something with a paintbrush and then cover the whole paper. A child who covers the whole paper with black paint may explain, "It's night now." Adults may hate to see the first drawing disappear. But children paint for themselves, not for adults.

Scribbling, drawing, and finger painting provide important prewriting experience. A good background in drawing and painting helps the child learn to control the tools of expression. Writing with pencils will follow naturally.

Drawing Tools

Crayons are probably the most common art tool parents can provide at home. They are also one of the most popular tools at school. Thick crayons are the easiest for young children to handle. Removing the paper lets the child use the edges as well as the tips of crayons.

Water-washable, felt-tipped, colored markers are very popular with young children. The colors are vivid, and the markers are large and easy to grasp. Markers are expensive. But some of the newer ones last a long time and have tips that do not dry out, even when the cap is left off. Permanent-color markers are not recommended, because their dye often will not wash out of clothing.

"Pastels" are soft pieces of chalk. They are about 1 inch in diameter and 3 inches long and are used on wet Manila paper. The colors are intense. They glide onto the paper quickly, so children find them very satisfying. Children enjoy using them for making murals.

There are many types of drawing paper available. Newsprint is the cheapest, but it is also thin and tears easily. Most nursery schools and day-care centers use Manila paper for drawing. Parents can order this paper from school supply houses. Of course, parents can also purchase drawing paper in variety stores, stationery stores, or art-supply stores.

Clipboards can help young children who have a hard time holding the paper still as they draw. These boards are probably too expensive for schools to buy in quantity. But parents may want to buy a clipboard for their child to use at home.

Large rolls of brown wrapping paper

make good drawing paper, especially for watercolor markers and pastels. Teachers can roll out several feet of paper and tape it to the floor. Then they can let five or six children work together. Parents and baby-sitters may find this a good project for a rainy day, especially with more than one child at home.

Painting Tools

The most common type of paint for prekindergartners is *tempera* paint. It can be purchased from school-supply houses in either liquid or dry powdered form. Liquid starch can be added to extend the paint and give it a glossy appearance. Prekindergartners need large brushes and large sheets of paper. Newsprint is the most common type of paper used. Children can paint either at the easel or standing at a table.

All 3-year-olds should begin painting with only one color. If they have several colors, they will have them all mixed together. Then all the paint will turn brown. As children gain experience, they can use two, then three colors. Some teachers and parents like to teach children to wash the brush in water, then wipe it on a sponge before changing colors. Others prefer to give children a separate brush for each color. But, if children have several brushes, they will still mix colors together on the paper. So, eventually, each container will be filled with brown paint. If adults give children several brushes, they should be sure to use tiny amounts of paint.

Finger Painting

Colored tempera paints can be added to a starch mixture for use as finger paints. An easy finger paint can be made by adding color to paperhanger's paste

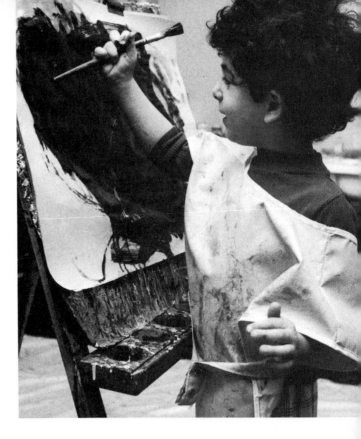

made with warm water. This paste is available at hardware stores. Children can paint on slick-surfaced paper and washable tables. If the children paint on tables, adults can help them press a piece of newsprint onto the finger painting to pick up the design. Most 3-year-olds may not care about keeping their design. They may enjoy the activity for its own sake. Most children enjoy the messiness of this type of painting. They will need smocks or aprons to protect their clothing.

Commercial finger paints are available. They are too costly for most prekindergartens, but parents may want to purchase them for home use. One mother lets her daughter finger paint in the bathtub. The child paints until she tires of the activity. Then both child and tub are easily washed.

Collage

Many recycled or "found" materials can be used for cutting and gluing projects, which are called *collage*. The 3-year-olds will be learning to use the scissors and may need help to prepare some materials. The 4-year-olds can easily cut most materials. The following items are good for cutting, gluing, sorting, and arranging into designs of the child's own choosing. The fun is in the novelty and individuality that each child brings to the activity.

1. Holiday and greeting cards.
2. Gift wrap and colorful shopping bags.
3. Magazines.
4. Fabric pieces and thread spools.
5. Wood scraps, shavings, and sawdust.
6. Packing materials, styrofoam, corrugated cardboard, excelsior.
7. Paper, such as computer paper, newsprint, and scraps from photocopy services.
8. Natural materials from outdoors, such as leaves, bark, twigs, seeds, cones, acorns, feathers, nutshells, and wheat straw.
9. Common household items, such as toothpicks, popsicle sticks, drinking straws cut in pieces, or cupcake or chocolate candy cups.

Collage materials should be stored in an orderly way so that they do not present a fire hazard. Each material needs its own box. Boxes can be stacked on shelves. They should be clearly labeled for quick identification.

White glue serves best for attaching materials in collages. This glue can be purchased economically in a large container. Then it can be transferred to smaller bottles for children's use. For some projects, the glue can be thinned with water and used with paste brushes.

Modeling

Modeling dough gives children a material to roll, pat, squeeze, and pound. Prekindergartners often make "cookies" as their parents do and rarely model figures such as people and animals. You can make modeling dough with a prekindergarten child or two. Watch how they enjoy learning to make and use it. Do not give them instructions on what to model. Instead, say, "Show me what you can do with the dough." Or, "I like that roll, how did you make it?" Listen to hear their ideas and their thinking.

Modeling Dough

Mix in a large bowl:
2 cups flour
1 cup salt
6 teaspoons alum (from drugstore)
2 tablespoons salad oil
2 cups water
colored tempera paint

If the dough seems too sticky, add a small amount of flour. Sprinkle each child's work space with flour. Children may want to pat a little flour on their hands, too.

Blocks

Building blocks are all-purpose learning materials. Using them, children learn concepts of size, space, and equality. They learn to sort and classify. They can make abstract designs or recognizable buildings. Blocks also contribute to the development of cooperative play.

Children who have never used blocks will usually carry them around in pocketbooks or trucks for a while. The next stage will be stacking. The children will pile the blocks on top of each other until the pile falls over. After stacking, children will begin to try making enclosures.

Observers who have studied children playing with blocks have found that almost all children go through all the stages with blocks. Thus, even the 5-year-old who has never used blocks will begin by carrying them around. Adults should not push children to build in the "right" way. They should let children take their time to experiment. Also, parents and teachers should not build *for* children. Children get discouraged when they see elaborate adult buildings.

The best building blocks are made of hardwood. Soft wood, such as pine, splinters and wears out easily. Hardwood blocks are expensive, so many parents feel they cannot buy them for home use. But most children will continue using blocks for several years. If a family has a 3-year-old and a baby, the blocks might well be in use for 8 years. Viewed in these terms, blocks do not seem so expensive. Block sets can be purchased a little at a time. Also, some parents have purchased used blocks at auctions or yard sales.

Clay

Most prekindergartens have a supply of regular potters' clay. Parents can purchase this for home use. It is relatively inexpensive and can be used and reused. If it dries out, it can be put into a plastic bag with a little water until it softens up again. For 3- and 4-year-olds, clay should be quite soft.

Many objects can be used as clay tools—wooden spoons, tongue depressors, cylindrical building blocks, and so forth. However, children should use only their hands at first. They will usually experiment by rolling, punching, and squeezing the clay. Later, they may make balls, "snakes," and little bowls.

Woodworking

A high-quality prekindergarten program should have a child-sized workbench. Woodworking gives children the opportunity to learn how to use tools such as hammers, saws, vises, screwdrivers, nails, and screws. The activity improves children's small motor coordination and offers them an outlet for creativity.

Books and Literature

The most important prereading experience children can have is to become thoroughly acquainted with books. They must be able to handle books and to look at them alone. And they need to have someone read books to them individually and in groups. From a book, a child can learn about people and places never seen directly. Information and expressions of emotion are found in books. If parents and teachers want children to develop mentally and do well in school, they will provide many, many books for them throughout the early years. Parents can emphasize the importance of books by buying books whenever it is gift-giving time.

In the prekindergarten program, a book corner with a weekly supply of different books should be available for 3- and 4-year-olds. Teachers and assistants will want to read each book before reading it to children. Only books that are well mended should be on the shelf.

Pillows and a washable rug can make the book corner more comfortable and inviting—at home or at school. Attractive posters and drawings may be put up to make the corner interesting.

A flannel board can be set up with a few flannel characters. Children can use these characters in telling their favorite stories and in making up stories.

Puppets may be made to accompany a story or a poem. A small paper bag with a face drawn toward the bottom end of the bag can be slipped over the hand to make a simple puppet. Also, figures may be made of felt and used on a flannel board to illustrate one or more characters in a story. At times, children

Children can do woodworking at home if parents have tools and a place to work. This is an activity that needs close supervision to be safe. In fact, generally only one child at a time should be allowed at the workbench.

Children should be allowed to choose what they want to make with wood. The 3-year-olds may be content just to hammer nails into a piece of wood. As they gain skills, they may decide they want to make a specific object, such as a boat or a radio. The idea of a boat or radio will not be the same as an adult's.

will enjoy acting out a story, using themselves as the main characters. Sometimes they may get distracted and think up entirely new lines for the character to say. Accept this as evidence of their creativity.

The public library, especially the children's room, is a delightful place for children to know. Children's librarians are especially patient and understanding persons. Children who get acquainted with the library at an early age have an excellent chance of becoming successful readers.

Dramatic Play

Dramatic play was discussed briefly in Chapter 31. By providing a few props, adults can help children engage in make-believe play for long periods of time. Hats of all kinds and other dress-up clothes are popular. Of course, a full-length, unbreakable mirror is desirable. With one, children can see how they look when they get all dressed up.

A housekeeping area should have a child's table and chairs. A couch or bed can be made from a back-seat cushion taken from an old car. Cardboard cartons and wooden packing boxes can be used for furnishings. Children are so skillful at make-believe that they do not need realistic equipment for dramatic play.

Dramatic play often spills over into the block area. Children make houses, beds, tables, and cars for their dolls and for themselves. For this reason, teachers should not make rigid rules about containing each activity in its own area.

Most 3- and 4-year-olds enjoy dramatic play at home, too. A parent or baby-sitter (with the parents' permis-

sion) may drape a blanket or sheet over a card table. The adult does not have to say anything to the child. Usually children will go right under the table and will say it is a house, truck, or tent. One boy made his own tent by propping up the lid to his blanket chest, then draping a blanket between the chest and two chairs.

Music Activity

You can continue to make your list of songs as suggested previously. Whether you are baby-sitting or working with a group, sing with children as often as you can. Share songs with your classmates and develop a handbook of songs. You will enjoy the fun of singing, and so will children you work with now and in the future.

Many good records for children are available. Children can be encouraged to listen and to respond to records. They will like to dance to a record or to accompany a song with rhythm instruments or clapping. Spontaneous as well as planned music experiences should be encouraged for the entire group. Records can help adults learn children's songs. For 3- and 4-year-olds, music is usually an active listening experience. They like to move, march, and dance to music. Most prekindergarten children can be taught to handle records carefully and to operate a record player.

Having a parent or teacher who plays the piano, guitar, banjo, or some other musical instrument can encourage children's interest in music. Most children of this age enjoy folk songs as well as traditional children's songs. If you play

an instrument, you will find your talent invaluable if you assist in a prekindergarten program or care for children in their homes.

Marching and Dancing

Marching and dancing to music are other forms of body movements that children enjoy. With a group of children, try various types of music and see how they respond to each type. As children hear the music, they will interpret it with their bodies, each in their own way.

Many prekindergarten programs invite parents with special musical talents to visit the children. The children can sing with these parents or can dance or beat rhythms to their music.

Food-Preparation Projects

Prekindergartners are very interested in food and in food-preparation projects. Even a hard-to-interest, aggressive child will generally respond to a call to help make ice cream or cookies. Children like to do part of the measuring, mixing, rolling, or turning. It is also often possible to involve them in picking apples or in buying food at the store. Purchasing helps children develop concepts of money.

An important rule in food preparation is that all involved should wash their hands before handling food. Dirt contains germs that can cause illness.

Scrambled Eggs

eggs (1 for each child and teacher)
2 tablespoons of milk for each egg
salt
2 tablespoons of butter or margarine
plate and fork for each child

Plan for enough scrambled eggs for each child and teacher. Even if some children do not want to help, they can still have scrambled eggs. Prepare the low work table with needed equipment: one large and one small mixing bowl, electric frying pan, 2 hand egg beaters, rubber spatula, set of measuring spoons, milk, eggs, and butter.

Help each child break an egg into a small mixing bowl. Use a spoon to help take out any eggshell that may fall in. Add 2 tablespoons of milk (count them with child) and beat the milk and egg using a hand beater. Pour each beaten egg into a larger bowl. As the child beats, talk about egg color.

Plan cooking time in order to have the eggs finished just at lunch or snacktime. Turn on the electric frying pan and add butter. Use low temperature for eggs. (High heat cooks the protein too hard.) Pour beaten eggs in the frying pan and sprinkle slightly with salt. Children can take turns stirring the eggs with a rubber spatula. (Talk about the change in consistency and color.) Stop cooking while eggs are still soft—do not dry them out.

Serve immediately on a small plate with a fork. Tell children that eggs make their skin, muscles, and hair grow. As they eat, have the children who cooked eggs review how they made the scrambled eggs. Ask children whether they know how we get our eggs.

Field Trips

Field trips increase children's knowledge and make them curious about their world. For 3-year-olds, short walking trips are best. These children are just beginning to feel secure at school. Longer trips may frighten them.

Most 4-year-olds are ready to move out to see the neighborhood. Extreme care must be taken when taking children on field trips for the children's safety. As you assist teachers with children on field trips, be sure to make their safety your responsibility both in cars or buses and wherever you are visiting.

Visiting Kindergarten

One important experience provided to prekindergarten children who will be moving to kindergarten is a visit to a kindergarten. Many of them feel fearful of what kindergarten will be like. The visit eases their fears. In some communities, visits are sponsored by local schools and include the children's parents. Even though the introduction takes place in the spring, some 3 months before the child starts kindergarten, the visit is important and helpful to the child.

Concluding Comments

Many learning activities for prekindergartners have been suggested that are useful for parents, teachers, and student assistants who want to help build a curriculum for 3- and 4-year-olds.

Adults should try out children's learning activities, themselves, in order to appreciate what the child might gain from the experience. By experimenting, adults will realize how a child might feel while trying an activity. For example, try working a new puzzle. Try a new book or record. Would you like people talking to you as you investigate? Would you want time to explore this activity on your own?

Activities

1. As a class project, collect and organize collage materials for a prekindergarten class.
   a. After reviewing the suggestions given in this chapter, discuss the project together. Each student should bring 1 type of material in quantity.
   b. Arrange materials in boxes that can be stacked on shelves.
   c. Clearly label each box.
   d. Donate the collection to a local prekindergarten program.
2. Make a batch of modeling dough with prekindergarten children. (See this chapter for the recipe.)
   a. Let children use dough on a flour-covered table. Record what they make *without* telling them what to make.
   b. How long did each child stay with the dough activity?
   c. Write a report and compare notes with your classmates.
3. Conduct a science "lesson" with several prekindergartners. Follow 1 or more of the suggestions given in this chapter or create your own.
   a. Describe what you did.
   b. Discuss the children's reactions.
   c. What do you think they learned from your lesson?

4. Read 2 picture books several times until you know them well. Choose books with a simple story for 2 or 3 prekindergarten children.
   a. Read the books to them in a quiet corner.
   b. Record each child's response.
   c. Record how long the children participated. Do not force them to stay.
   d. Write a full report and share it with your classmates.
5. Write and illustrate a child's story book. You may write a poem or a fiction or nonfiction book. Illustrate the book with your own drawings or with photos or magazine pictures.
   a. Read your book to two or three children. Record their reactions.
   b. Discuss the children's responses with classmates.
6. Plan and carry out a music activity with a group of prekindergartners.
   a. Teach them a song, encourage them to dance or clap to records, or choose some other music activity.
   b. Report results to your classmates. Include the amount of time the children wanted to spend on the activity.

Suggested readings for Part 5 may be found at the end of Part 6.

6

The Kindergartner

You will learn how
kindergartners grow and
develop physically, mentally,
socially, and emotionally during
the ages of 5 and 6. You will
learn how to care for, guide,
and teach kindergartners, and
what activities stimulate their
growth and development.

unit

14

The Growing and Developing Kindergartner

How Tall

The Kindergartner Grows Physically

Objectives

To describe some characteristics of physical growth for kindergarten children ages 5 and 6.

To explain the importance of physical activity for good health.

To explain how motor skills are assets.

To explain ways to help a less skilled child and a skilled child.

To describe some appropriate motor-skill activities for kindergartners.

Terms to look for   permanent teeth • self-concept • temporary teeth

"Mommy, do we have any relations who are midgets?" asked 5-year-old Sonia, as she ate a peanut butter sandwich and a glass of milk after school.

"No, dear," said Sonia's mother, puzzled by the question. "Why do you wonder about your relatives, Sonia?"

"The day we went to the fire station, we saw a little man on the street. The teacher said he was a midget and just didn't grow big. Today she told me I'm the littlest kid in my school. I think I'm never going to grow bigger. Probably I'll be a midget," concluded Sonia.

Growing big becomes increasingly important to children as they reach the kindergarten age. They now understand the ideas of biggest and littlest. They begin to want evidence that they will grow big like other children. Signs of growing, such as developing motor skills and getting permanent teeth, help a kindergartner develop an image of himself or herself, a *self-concept*.

Teeth Loss—A Sign Children Are Growing

"All I want for Christmas is my two front teeth," goes the old song. Surely the song refers to 5-year-old children. Most children are more anxious to have their teeth start coming out than to have them come in. Losing the first baby tooth is an important event for kindergarten children. They frequently loosen their front teeth deliberately, hoping to lose at least one. Kindergartners learn early that this event signals a coming of age, a readiness for "big school." Kindergarten is the average time for children to lose their first teeth. However, some children do not lose the first tooth until first grade. Others are even later than that. Such children should be reassured that late tooth loss does not mean that they are "little" or not ready to go to first grade.

When the temporary tooth is loosened naturally, the permanent tooth is usually close behind. Permanent teeth replace the 20 temporary teeth. More molars are added until there are 32 permanent teeth—12 more than in the temporary set.

Pretty teeth improve a child's appearance, which in turn improves the child's self-concept. Cavities and improperly aligned teeth interfere with eating and talking as well as with appearance. Dental care and proper nutrition are important in forming and keeping good teeth. The permanent teeth are the only ones the body will produce from now on. No other teeth will replace these if they rot or are broken off, except false teeth made by dentists. Teeth are well worth protecting.

The Kindergartner's Motor Skills

Exercise is necessary for a child if bones, muscles, and tissues are to grow and develop properly. Thus physical activity is very important for young children. Such activity must be a part of each day's routine for children.

Many children have little space to run and play. Many have little stimulation for the vigorous activity needed for good physical development. The following factors may prevent children's physical activity and development:

1. Small apartments and little or no yards hinder physical activity. Also, close neighbors may ask that parents keep children from being noisy.
2. Television encourages people to sit passively for many hours. Children "hooked on" television do not get enough exercise. Poor sitting positions cause poor posture and muscle tone.
3. There may be only a few or no other children in the family or neighborhood to share adventures outdoors. A child without playmates often lacks interest in physical activity.
4. An emphasis on toys for mental development may lead parents to neglect toys for physical development.
5. Busy parents who work outside the home find it hard to make time for physical games and outings.

Because of these home situations, schools need to provide opportunities for vigorous physical activity for all children. Vigorous exercise develops bones, muscles, and tissues. It prepares children for a long and healthy life.

Motor Skills—Part of Self-concept

A child's motor skills are related to acceptance by other children. The most popular children and the leaders are usually the most skillful. Motor-skill practice develops social goals.

Children decide how capable they are in motor skills. If they decide they are skillful, they enter groups with confidence. If they decide they are not capable, they avoid situations where they do not perform well. Therefore, motor-skill development must be a high priority among parents and teachers.

Failure is not likely, given the proper equipment, help, and expectations. For example, a father who expects his 5-year-old child to catch a regular-sized softball is setting up the child for failure and himself for disappointment. Failure makes the child less willing to practice catching another day.

Helping a Less Skilled Child

Because physical activity is so important, teachers should take the following steps if a child avoids doing vigorous activity.

1. Check the child's health and nutrition. Illness and lack of proper food causes a child to sit and watch others rather than to participate.

2. Develop an individualized plan for the child after an illness or a nutritional problem is corrected. Determine how well the child walks, runs, and climbs. A child that has some problems will refuse to participate if other children are competing. Focus attention on the skills the child does best.

3. Let a child who needs help be aware that you are interested in what he or she is doing. Show your interest by talking to the child and by recognizing what the child likes to do.

367

4. Give strong positive feedback or praise for "good running," "high climbing," "high jumping," and so on. Relate your praise to the child's previous record. Say, for example, "You ran faster than you did yesterday."

5. Help keep the child out of direct competition with others until the child starts that competition. A child who is ready for competition will refuse your hand for a jump, saying, "No, I can do it." This child knows that other children do the activity alone and wants to be like them.

6. Begin short practices to work on skills with which the child has problems. But do not identify the difficulties as problems. Make practicing fun and natural to do. Combine the child's skilled areas with the less developed skills. For example, have the child run independently. But allow the child to hold your finger while jumping from a high place, such as a platform or a box.

Helping a Skilled Child

Skilled children also need attention and challenges. They move fast and well. So they may be the ones you hear people tell "Don't climb so high," or "Not so fast." Parents and teachers should judge what the child is capable of doing safely by watching the child. They should stay nearby to help in case of a slip or a sudden fear reaction. Suppose children are up high on a jungle gym. The teacher can say, "Hold tight with both hands," rather than, "You might fall." Actually, most children will climb only as high as they feel safe, so all the talk is probably unnecessary.

Some kindergarten children were climbing in the trees of the kindergarten yard. They were far higher than any adult could reach. The teacher said only, "Hold tight. Remember, you don't have wings." Many of the children lived in new housing developments with only small new trees. The climbable kindergarten trees attracted them for this rea-

Often, the less-skilled child will start doing physical tasks for a special person who is warm and interested.

son. The teacher stayed nearby to be sure that children climbed the trees because they wanted to, not because they were overencouraged by a friend. The teacher also stopped any crowding that might have led to pushing. Nonskilled children fear pushing most of all.

Skilled children who can catch a big ball may be ready for a smaller ball. A child who can hit the wastebasket with a beach ball could be ready to try a basketball hoop placed at a low level. Jumping practice over higher or broader objects can be started for more skilled jumpers. As with nonskilled children, the adult's help should be individualized and noncompetitive. Avoid saying, "Jump farther than Chris." Instead say, "You jumped 3 feet yesterday and 3½ feet today."

Maturing Kindergarten Girls and Boys

Skeletal-age studies show girls are biologically more mature at a given age than boys. Adults should consider this fact when setting goals for children. Some people, who thinks girls are only weak, sweet, and demure, expect girls to perform poorly because they are girls. In fact, more boys fail in many school tasks than do girls.

Many failures of boys are believed to be closely related to their biological immaturity. Wise parents often keep an immature boy with younger children, where he can be a model and a leader. With an older group, he may be constantly put down and expected to follow. For example, an immature boy is often kept in a prekindergarten rather than sent on to kindergarten. This extra year can assure early successes in school tasks and in peer relations. Children are seldom aware of age differences, especially when the difference is only a matter of months. Later on, if the boy catches up, he can move himself along faster than usual in high school or college by taking extra courses or summer school. Such a child could reach the same graduation day as others in his age group. However, if the child needs the extra time, parents need to adjust their expectations to his individual developmental timetable.

Children can break the failure cycle—especially the psychological barrier—through excellent motor skills. Perhaps you know a high school student whose success on the basketball court is far superior to her or his success in algebra. The basketball skill gives the child a positive self-concept. This enables the child to cope with the less favorable self-image that comes from the poor algebra skill. The successful athletes in high school are often the students who mature early. Or they may be among the oldest in their class, owing to the month of their birth or to being held back a year. You can check the last part of this statement, yourself, by collecting the birth dates of the members of your school varsity teams.

? Decisions, Decisions

"I just don't understand," exclaimed the father who was attempting to teach his 5-year-old son to ride a two-wheeler. "Suzanne didn't have any trouble learning, but Joey doesn't even seem to try." What suggestions would you make to this father?

Skilled children need encouragement but not competition. Adults can emphasize *doing* rather than *winning*.

Games for Motor-Skill Practice

The games suggested in Chapter 38 are appropriate for kindergartners because children keep improving skills.

Skipping

Skipping is a skill that children learn during the kindergarten year. To skip, the child must be able to change the weight from one foot to the other. If skipping is difficult for a child, then the child needs more hopping and galloping practice. Time to practice away from their peers is also helpful. Most 5-year-old girls will more often be able to skip than boys because girls are biologically more mature. Adults should never criticize children for their poor showing. Adults should encourage them to practice hopping and galloping, which are preliminary skills to learning to skip.

Tumbling

Kindergartners enjoy learning tumbling. They can start with simple forward rolls on a tumbling mat. Then they can progress to backward rolls later on.

Some will enjoy trying to do a handstand and a cartwheel. But these skills take years to develop. A headstand is easier if you help the child locate three points in a triangle—one for each hand and one for the head. If all three are in a straight line, the base will be unstable and the headstand unsuccessful.

Hanging from Horizontal Bars

Kindergartners enjoy the challenge of swinging on a horizontal bar by their arms and legs. Some also like to go hand-over-hand along the bar or on trapeze rings hung in a row. These are advanced challenges that the late 5-year-olds and early 6-year-olds are often ready for.

370

Bicycle

The two-wheeled bicycle is the symbol of physical motor success for a 5-year-old. When children learn to ride the bike without training wheels, they are truly proud of themselves.

Many parents buy a bicycle too soon. Children may be discouraged if they take too many falls, and they may refuse to practice. Some children happily use training wheels (two small wheels attached to the back wheel). Other children refuse to use them because their peers refer to the training wheels as "baby wheels." Riding a two-wheeled bicycle without the training wheels is a big status symbol.

In all the skills mentioned above, keep in mind that the stated ages are *average*. Children vary widely in their abilities. The important thing for parents and teachers to remember is to give children encouragement and approval, whatever level of physical skill they have reached.

Concluding Comments

A child's physical growth and motor-skill development follow a predictable path from conception to maturity. You have, through several chapters, studied an important part of physical motor development—the first 6 years.

Parents and teachers can aid a child's physical development. They can observe the child closely and assist with the right kind of help when the child seems ready for it. Parents who help develop their children's bodies well at this early age help to ensure a lifetime of good health for them in the future.

Activities

1. Discuss what connection watching a lot of television has with the lack of development of motor skills.
2. Interview a kindergarten teacher.
   a. Ask the teacher to describe a student who is not able to perform motor activities as skillfully as expected.
   b. How is the teacher helping the child develop these skills?
   c. Does the child appear to have a good or a poor self-image?
3. Observe a kindergarten class during free play out of doors.
   a. How many played actively?
   b. How many children sat or stood quietly?
   c. Write a report and discuss with your class.
4. Help 2 kindergarten children perform the same motor skill.
   a. Describe how each one does the task.
   b. Explain how the children are the same or different.
   c. Find out the age in years and months of each child. Is age an important factor in motor performance?
   d. Compare your findings with those of your classmates.
5. Do you remember learning to ride a two-wheel bike? Write at least 1 page describing the experience. How did you *feel* about it?

The Kindergartner Develops Emotionally and Socially

Objectives

To explain in what way the kindergartner is socially advanced over younger children.

To explain aggressive behavior.

To discuss the influence of television on children's behavior.

Terms to look for   aggression • empathy

Beth showed Max how to make her doll talk. She brought the doll from home to show the kindergartners at "show-and-tell." Max gently guided Beth, who was less skilled than the other kindergartners. He invited her to sit down beside him. He then gently held the doll and carefully pulled the string. He appeared to enjoy the company of Beth and the talking doll for a half hour.

Max grabbed Mike's navy hat in a pestering way. Mike shouted, "That's mine! Give it back!"

Max started hitting and kicking Mike. He used an arm hold on Mike's neck and started to throw him to the floor.

An aide intervened. "Max, you'll hurt Mike. What's the problem here?" he asked.

Max, without a word, released Mike. The hat was on the floor, and he ignored it. Max's sudden burst of aggression seemed completely gone.

Kindergartners' Changing Behavior

Max is a husky kindergartner (age 6 years, 2 months). His interactions with Beth and Mike occurred on the same afternoon. Judging from the first situation, you would conclude that Max is a

372

kind, gentle, and helpful child. Then, looking at the second event, you might conclude that he is rather mean and hostile. Which is true? One conclusion you should make is never to judge a child on the basis of just one observation. If you just wait a minute, the child may change.

Most children have a wide range of social and emotional behaviors. These behaviors range from gentle to aggressive, from kind to cruel, and from quiet to noisy. However, most 5-year-old children are emotionally controlled, secure, and able to cope with new situations that arise. The independence that kindergartners can assume is striking when compared with the behavior of children a year or two younger. If 5-year-olds live within walking distance, they will carefully walk to school, staying on the sidewalks and stopping at street crossings. If they live farther from school, they can readily meet the bus or car pool at a set spot.

Socially, there is a rapid development of cooperative play after the fifth birthday. Dramatic play has become more sophisticated, with roles available for a large number of children. The increased language ability of 5-year-olds aids their social exchange.

Kindergartners show their feelings without any embarrassment. Here, a 5-year-old shows his nurturing side. Parents and care givers need to be aware that these feelings may change rapidly. For no apparent reason, the child may strike out at the baby.

? **Decisions, Decisions**

Bobby, age 5, is afraid to go outside whenever Brian and Timmy are out because they have threatened to "beat him up." How could Bobby's parents help him with this problem?

Influences on Behavior

The physical setting, the people involved, and the time of day all affect children's behavior. In the situation with Beth, Max's natural kindness and generosity is shown. Yet with Mike he seems aggressive. All people tend to

373

have both sides to their personality, though you might not see examples as close together as Max exhibited.

Years ago, the negative aspects of personality, such as aggression, hostility, meanness, and so on, were considered important. People believed that education and socialization were required to tame these negative aspects. Today, most people believe that babies are born with positive personalities. This belief makes a difference in the way children are taught. If the environment of home and school is supportive, according to this belief, the positive virtues will be emphasized.

Max at 6 years and 2 months is mature enough to begin to understand someone else's feelings. It could be that this maturity was expressed with Beth. Perhaps Max *empathized* with this child, who frequently expressed the desire for somebody to play with her. *Empathy* is an ability to imagine how others feel. This ability grows as children mature.

Aggression is marked by an attack on someone or something. Aggression was seen in the exchange between Mike and Max. Aggressiveness can have positive and negative sides. When we speak of an *aggressive* tennis player, for example, we mean a player who fights hard to win the game, not one who jumps over the net and punches the opponent.

Some people feel that some controlled aggressiveness is good. It is part of a person's drive to work hard and succeed.

Max's episode of aggression is of interest. Parents and teachers usually prefer to have aggression eliminated, or at least controlled. In studies of preprimary children, conflicts usually occur over toys or objects, such as the hat. Boys tend to be more aggressive than

Girls, as well as boys, need to find acceptable ways to release their aggressive feelings. Punching bags provide a safe and fun outlet.

girls, although researchers disagree about why this is so. Some feel that boys are naturally more aggressive. Others say that our culture expects more aggression from boys than from girls. They believe that we begin to stifle girls' aggressive behavior from infancy. For example, how many fathers tell their daughters to go punch the child next door in the nose?

Studies show that when parents or teachers permit aggression then children tend to act with aggression. Parents may encourage their child to act aggressively toward another child. But they will not permit their child to act aggressively toward them. This creates a problem for a young child who tries to discover the logic in the rule. When parents punish by striking the child, they are demonstrating aggression. There are more effective ways to control children, so physical punishment should be avoided. (See Chapter 18.)

Parents are naturally concerned that their children not be picked on or taken advantage of. They want their children to learn how to defend themselves. For this reason, parents often say, "If anyone hits you, you hit back." Unfortunately, this approach does not really work. For example, if Tony hits Laura and Laura hits back, Tony will not stop at that. He will hit Laura again. Laura will hit back again, and the result will be a fight. Adults might try telling Laura, "Don't let Tony hit you. Hold his hands, push him away, or go away from him." Or, "Tell Tony you don't like hitting, and it's against the rules." These approaches will not always work, but they do let children know that the adults in authority do not approve of physical aggression. They make it clear that in this home or kindergarten, aggression is not the way to solve problems.

It is also important for adults to accept the emotion (usually anger) behind aggression. It is all right for Tony to be angry with Laura but not to hit her. Some kindergartens keep a punching bag or inflatable pop-up figure. A child who is feeling angry can hit the punching bag. Parents can also use this approach. Pillows can serve the same purpose.

Television Violence

According to many studies, television is teaching children aggression. Violent programs give children the message that the way to "win" in life is to be bigger and stronger and to punch harder than other people. For this reason, certain programs are not permitted on the air during the times of day when children usually watch television. Parents and teachers should be very selective about their children's television. They should be especially careful if they allow their children to watch television beyond the "family hour" in the evening. After that time, more violent programs are aired. Adults should turn off the set when violent and frightening programs come on while children are watching.

Concluding Comments

Kindergarten children are considered the most charming and the easiest preprimary children to work with. They seem to realize their capabilities and enjoy living up to them. They like to learn the rules and to follow them. This makes kindergartners a joy to the teacher. Parents, too, generally have an easy time with kindergartners.

Helping Children Develop a Positive Self-Concept

Your self-concept is the mental image you have of yourself. A child who has a positive self-concept feels that she is worthwhile, that she can make choices for herself and can do certain things well. She is not overwhelmed by her feelings. She can both give and accept affection. A child who thinks of herself as lovable and capable truly has a head start on life. She can make the most of the experiences that come her way because she is secure from within. Here are 6 ways to help children develop a healthy image of themselves:

1 **Praise the child for achievements, even small ones.** Praise honest attempts, too. A quick hug, a smile, or a word is all that it takes.
"You did a good job folding those socks and washcloths. And I appreciate the way you let Jimmy help you."

2 **When you need to correct a child's behavior, object to the behavior, and not to the child.** Children can translate angry messages into rejection messages.
Do this:
"It makes me angry when you walk in the garden. The flowers won't grow if you keep stepping on them."
Not this:
"Get out of that flower garden! How many times have I told you to walk around it!"

3 **Talk about the feeling the child is expressing and give it a name.** This helps children understand their feelings.
"I know how sad you feel. You really wanted to stay outside."

5 Give children choices whenever you can. Make sure they really have a choice.
Do this:
"Would you like scrambled eggs or fried eggs for breakfast this morning?"
Not this:
"How about some eggs this morning?"
"No."

4 Keep competition to a minimum. Never compare children. Set individual goals for each child.
Do this:
"Before long, you'll be able to write your name."
Not this:
"Jason can write his name. Why don't you try it?"

6 Give children room to achieve and explore.
Do this:
"You try it."
Not this:
"Here, let me do that."

Activities

1. With parents' permission, observe a 5- or 6-year-old for several hours.
   a. Keep an anecdotal record of the child's behavior. (For an anecdotal record, describe as completely as possible whatever the child is doing.
   b. Write a report describing the different kinds of behavior shown by the child.
   c. Analyze your report. Did the child's behavior change?
   d. Can you identify any reasons for changing behavior?
2. Ask a kindergarten teacher how he or she handles students' aggressive acts. Report answers to your class.
3. Visit a group of kindergartners:
   a. Record the number of groups within the larger group.
   b. Record the number of boys and the number of girls in each of the smaller groups. Record each group's activity.
   c. Decide the type of play involved—solitary, parallel, or cooperative.
4. Continue observing the group.
   a. Record an instance of joy. What caused the joy?
   b. Record an instance of aggression. How did it start?
5. Discuss television viewing with the parents of a kindergarten child.
   a. Discuss the number and kinds of television programs the child watches.
   b. Ask the parents how they feel about television influencing the child's behavior.
   c. Write a report.

The Kindergartner Develops Mentally

Objectives

To explain the changes in mental ability that occur during the fifth and sixth years.

To explain the value of various early childhood education experiences for mental development.

To describe suitable learning activities for kindergartners.

"Why does an astronaut wear a helmet?" John, a 5-year-old kindergarten child, asked his teacher.

Before the teacher could answer, John's friend Maggie volunteered an answer, "So his head won't get hurt if he crashes on the moon."

John was using questions to enlarge his store of information. The question was prompted by a picture book showing the astronauts ready for a space shot.

Maggie answered from her current knowledge of helmets. She knew the use that football players make of helmets.

Within Maggie's brain is stored information awaiting use. She will need more information to answer the question accurately. At present, she is putting together the information she has.

Brain Development

During the years before kindergarten, the brain is becoming specialized. The left half specializes in reception (hearing), in language production (speaking), and in reading and counting.

The right half of the brain specializes in perceiving and interpreting space, for instance, in artwork, block play, and rhythm. By age 5, and during the school-age years, the two halves of the brain become better connected. This helps the child become coordinated.

This information about the brain helps you better understand why adults should present a broad range of learning

379

activities to children. Both brain halves must be stimulated. The information may also help you understand a person who has had a stroke, which damages a portion of the brain and interferes with certain motor or verbal functions.

Preoperational thought, as described in Chapter 32, continues during the fifth and sixth years. Children still need to handle real materials and to experiment. This helps to develop their thinking processes. Their thoughts are now less self-centered than earlier. However, it is still difficult for them to realize how others feel. For example, the teacher held a meeting of the five-year-olds because they were leaving a girl named Carmella out of their play group. The children were reinforcing each other's decision "not to play with Carmella."

The kindergarten teacher asked the children how they would feel if other children would not play with them. They answered that such children were "bad" or "naughty." They could not relate this conversation to their refusal to play with Carmella. Right and wrong were easy for the children to talk about. But they did not apply it to their actions. They all were very self-centered.

Language

Language skills continue to develop both in receptive language (what one hears and understands) and in productive language (what one can say).

Children continue to practice grammar by trial and error. Adults are useful as models. Children will pattern their

Dress-up play encourages children to assume other roles. It gives them a chance to use their language skills and to speak in front of others.

expressions after older brothers and sisters and after their parents and teachers. Adults should always encourage children's language efforts. Though some errors are humorous, it is unkind to laugh at children for language mistakes. Laughter may inhibit needed practice, because children fear ridicule.

Interestingly, if you analyze a child's language mistakes, many times you will find the child is logically correct. Nevertheless, the child must learn our illogical language traditions. Study this example. Little 5-year-old Jo Ellen ran into the house exclaiming excitedly to her mother, "My cat eated a big mouse, head and all!" Her mother corrected, "You mean ate." Jo Ellen responded, jumping up and down, her eyes as big as saucers, "Yes, ated a big mouse, every bit of it!"

Jo Ellen's brain was working. Her grammar was logically correct. Yet, Jo Ellen, and all English-speaking children around the world, will spend a good deal of parents' time and school time learning the irregular and illogical grammar that became part of our English language centuries ago.

A sense of humor blossoms during the sixth year. Most 5- and 6-year-olds are gaining a large enough vocabulary to understand some puns or plays on words. They now may appreciate the two meanings of a word or the different uses of a word. They will laugh about a "bare bear" or a "hoarse horse." Poems, songs, or stories that are slightly ridiculous delight this age group. With their increased vocabulary and wider experience, kindergartners are able to see the humor in situations. At 4, they took everything very literally and seriously. Now they can see the funny side.

? Decisions, Decisions

"What makes it rain?" asked 5-year-old Tony. How would you answer this question? If you do not know the answer to a child's question, how could you handle the situation in a positive way?

Adults Can Stimulate Mental Development

Kindergartners are ready to go far and wide to increase their knowledge of the world around them. Parents and teachers can use this curiosity to help kindergartners grow and develop mentally.

Songs, word games, and books contribute to language skills. A child who lives in a home where books and reading are part of everyday life is likely to be eager to learn to read. Dramatic play encourages role playing and the use of vocabulary. These activities combine listening and speaking skills.

Often, kindergartners seem to use older children as models—wanting to read, write, or do other things an older sibling or friend does. This is part of every child's desire to grow, and adults should encourage it. Of course, adults will want to know the older child well enough to be sure he or she is someone they want their child to imitate.

Parents and teachers need to be aware of the importance of children's using language and expressing their ideas.

Busy parents need to take time to sit down and listen to their children each day. This time together, started at an early age, helps build a strong parent-child relationship.

Adults can help by talking to children and listening to them as well. Adults should never punish children for speaking or for problems they may have in speaking.

More specific activities for guiding children's mental development will be discussed in Chapter 47.

Concluding Comments

Mental growth and development are important parts of human growth and development. Adults should provide continuous stimulation during these early years.

Parents and teachers are responsible for providing children with experiences to help them develop thinking skills, language skills, and prereading skills.

The kindergarten age is a period when children seem to be in tune with their world. They usually have outgrown health and personality problems that may have been troublesome earlier. Now they are delightfully bright, exciting to be around, and eager to learn more.

Activities

1. With parent's permission, observe a 5- or 6-year-old for at least an hour.
    a. Write down every question the child asks.
    b. Did the child ask many questions?
2. Listen to 5- and 6-year-olds talk.
    a. Record several examples of any grammatical errors
    b. Are the errors "logical"?
3. Visit the home of a kindergartner.

   a. Observe and record information about the child's toys. How do they contribute to mental development?
   b. Does the child have books?
   c. Ask if the child enjoys having the parents read stories aloud.
   d. What books and magazines do the parents have.
   e. Write a report of your visit. Discuss it with classmates.

42

Health and Safety for Kindergartners

Objectives
To list and define safety measures for kindergartners.
**To describe crises that can affect the kindergartner's mental
and emotional health.**

"Let's run," called Jennie to Clare, a kindergarten friend and neighbor. The girls, with papers and hats flying, ran toward home. They stopped at a street crossing, looked both ways, and crossed quickly. Seeing a can, they started kicking it. They enjoyed this game for most of the four blocks. Once, the can went into the street. They looked for cars before going after it. Then both ran to their houses to greet their parents and unload their school things.

Physical Health

Kindergarten children's world is enlarging. They may now walk to school without protection of an adult. Children require special teaching to be sure they understand the route to school and how to wait at crossings. Parents will caution their child. They will not want to make the child fearful—only safe.

One couple had taught their son to wait on the curb until there were "no cars in sight" before crossing. On a particularly snowy afternoon, the boy waited and waited as the cars slowly inched along on the slick, snowy street. His mother watched from the window. The boy waited on the curb across the street from home. Though the cars were driving very slowly, they were still in sight. The boy was having difficulty making an exception to the rule. Helping children to learn rules and to think about possible exceptions to the rules is part of a parent's responsibility.

Safety from Molesters

In addition to safety around traffic, children need to be protected from child molesters. Many people are rightly concerned about children who are abused in their own neighborhoods by adults and youths. Children must be cautioned against accepting rides with strangers.

Parents can maintain a delicate balance, making children cautious but not fearful. Children should be cautious enough to ignore strangers who try to get them to go for a ride. They should be taught to run home or to a neighbor's house to avoid danger. In some communities, a group of parents display a red hand in the window called a "helping hand." Children are taught that this sign means there is a mother or father there who will help them if they are ever lost, hurt, or frightened.

Fractures

With increased independence often comes an increased opportunity to climb up on things and to fall off things. Riding a two-wheeled bicycle may be the cause of a fall hard enough to break a bone. Most 5-year-olds like to climb up trees and climb over walls. Both are places from which children could fall and break a limb. A broken bone usually heals well in a young child, but pain and discomfort result from such accidents. However, children need to try all these things. Parents and teachers, while advising caution, should not make the children so fearful that they refuse to exercise.

Mental and Emotional Health

Children whose experiences so far have been primarily positive are generally mentally and emotionally stable at age 5. Their stability is shown in their cooperative nature and their increased independence.

Questions of Sexuality and Reproduction

Usually, 5-year-olds are curious about their femaleness and maleness. They want to hear about how babies are born. They notice pregnant women and adults with new babies. Children enjoy being close to new parents, hearing their per-

Children jump and climb on anything. They need a safe place with sturdy equipment.

sonal stories. They like to hear discussions of real family concerns. Children can get very positive feelings about such experiences. On the other hand, frightening discussions of difficult childbirth or overly detailed conversations about sex are probably unsuitable for 5-year-olds. Sound information adds to children's good feelings about themselves.

? Decisions, Decisions

Mrs. Allen is expecting a baby. Her 5-year-old daughter came home from kindergarten and asked her where babies come from. She told her daughter that she was going to the hospital so the stork could deliver the baby. How would you have answered this question?

Crises

Crises may damage the mental and emotional health of kindergarten children. Examples of such crises are rivalry with siblings; parents' marital problems, separation, or divorce; illness; and death of a loved one. Adults can help children through crises.

A certain amount of sibling rivalry is to be expected. Parents who deny its existence are generally kidding themselves. The closer children are in age, the more rivalry seems to exist. Many cases start with the birth of a new baby. Giving the older child extra attention at this time and allowing some more grown-up privileges usually helps.

As children grow older, adults should be careful not to make unfavorable comparisons between siblings. Saying, "When Erica was your age, she could

ride a two-wheeler," or "Jim was in my class last year, and I never saw him pushing other children," will only make a child resent the sibling more. Instead, adults should try to stress the positive parts of each child's development.

Marital problems, separation, and divorce are upsetting more and more American families. Children will often blame themselves for their parents' problems. A hostile atmosphere in the home, sharp words, and threats can leave emotional scars on a child.

Often, parents are so involved in their own problems that they are unaware of their children's feelings.

Sometimes parents think that if they argue behind closed doors or after children have gone to bed, children will not be aware that the marriage is in trouble. But children can sense problems in a relationship, even if they do not actually see or hear them. They often fear that one or both parents do not love them or that both will leave them. Parents should try to explain the situation on a level that the children can understand. "Mommy and I still love you very much, but we don't feel that we can live together any more. You are going to keep living here with me, and Mommy will come to see you as much as she can."

Divorce and marital problems are sensitive and difficult areas for families to deal with. Often, help from outside the home is necessary to help children cope well. There are family counselors available for this purpose. Also, several good books dealing with these subjects are currently in print.

Death in the family can cause mental upset for a young child. People frequently want to "protect" the child from hurt. Such action only leaves a child

Children need help in understanding and coping with family problems. Parents must explain over and over again that the child is not the cause of the problem.

Often a child returns to school after a family funeral or other crisis and goes about playing as usual. The child is glad to be back to the normal world. Adults are often surprised by this. They wonder if they should help the child speak about the death. Actually, the best approach seems to be to wait and to be open to talk when the child brings up the subject. For example, if Johnny says, "My mommy died," the teacher can calmly say, "Do you want to tell me about it, Johnny?" Johnny is now ready to talk about death. He should have a willing listener available.

Mental and Emotional Illness

Behavior problems and mental and emotional illnesses do arise with kindergarten and younger children for the above reasons and others. These children require special counselors, psychologists, and child psychiatrists who are trained to help them with such illnesses.

Services for children with emotional illnesses are available through public health facilities. Early treatment for any emotional illness will bring the best results. Teachers who know a child who appears to need help should recommend nearby services to the parents. Teachers, of course, cannot arrange treatment without parental cooperation. However, teachers may recognize problems before parents become aware of them. A kindergartner with problems may display some of the following symptoms.

with no one to talk to about the hurt or nowhere to get explanations. It is best to state frankly that a loved one has died. It is also wise to explain the cause of death. If people are not frank, the child will eventually learn anyway and will feel deceived.

A kindergarten child was told that a friend's mother died of "flu or something" when she actually died of cancer. The child worried for a long time because many people—even she—had been sick with flu. She worried she might die also.

1. The child is not toilet trained.
2. The child is aggressive, cruel, or

hostile for long periods.

3. The child is not talking or cannot be understood.
4. The child has unreasonable, lasting fears.
5. The child has developmental lag in one or more areas.
6. The child seems friendless or is usually isolated from the group.
7. The child is usually unhappy, whiny, or crying.
8. The child refuses to look at people or manipulates an object repeatedly.
9. The child usually breaks rules.
10. The child has a physical illness that treatment is not helping.

Concluding Comments

Children's safety and their physical, mental, and emotional health are all of concern to parents and teachers as they guide children and provide for their needs. By using positive guidance techniques, parents and care givers can teach children to handle their independence so they will not get into trouble when they make decisions. There is really no way to protect children from many hazards except for them to learn to protect themselves. For parents, letting go and letting children grow up may be scary. But parents must let go if children are not to be hampered in their full development.

Activities

1. Observe a group of children walking home from kindergarten. Follow along behind them for several blocks at a discrete distance.
   a. Do they comply with usual rules for safety?
   b. Do they talk about the rules they are expected to follow? Do they caution each other?
   c. Write a report and discuss it with your classmates.
2. What could a parent do to prevent sibling rivalry in these situations?
   a. An older child is allowed privileges that are not yet granted to a younger child.
   b. One child is skilled in athletics and the other is clumsy.
   c. Both children adore their grandmother and compete for her attention.
   d. One child looks like one parent. The other child does not resemble either parent.
   e. One child is outgoing and has many friends. The other child is quiet and has few friends.
3. Find out about public and private agencies in your community that help children with emotional problems.
   a. Are trained psychologists, psychiatrists, and social workers available?
   b. How can a family learn about these services?
   c. What are the costs of public services? Private services?

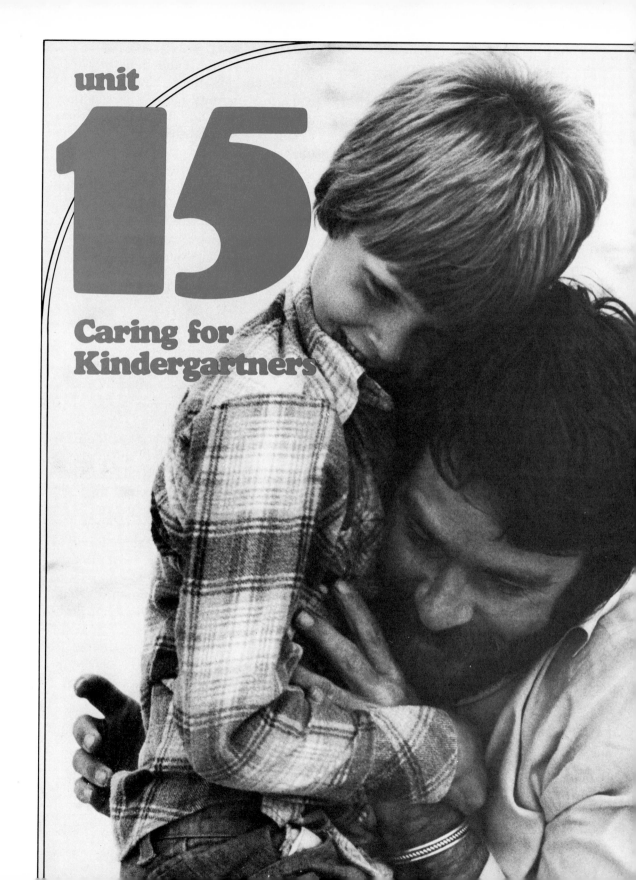

unit

15

Caring for Kindergartners

Guiding Kindergartners

Objectives
To explain how guidance principles apply to kindergartners.
To compare internal control with external control.

"You gotta share," demanded 5-year-old Pete. He had just arrived in the kindergarten and found the children hovering over three small white rabbits. Pete stood in the circle of children for a minute or two and repeated, "You gotta share. You guys are holding them too long. It's my turn now."

The children who had arrived before Pete wanted their turns. Pete waited while they held the rabbits. He attempted to interest himself in another activity, but returned. Finally his turn arrived. He settled himself comfortably with his back to the circle of children. He tried to tune out the requests of children who wanted their first turn. Finally, the teacher reminded Pete that other children wanted a turn, too. He gave up the rabbits unwillingly.

Pete is an example of a child who knows the rules and can state them yet has difficulty following them when they apply to him. Pete also confuses sharing and taking turns. You may wish to review the discussion of these terms in Chapter 31 in the section titled "Social Skills of Sharing and Taking Turns."

The principles of guidance in Chapters 18, 25, and 34 can apply to kindergartners as well. Kindergartners usually cooperate. If you recognize that kindergartners naturally have good motivations, you will succeed in bringing out desirable responses in them.

More Freedom for Kindergartners

For parents and teachers, guiding kindergarten children is somewhat different from guiding younger children. The

Kindergartners are able to carry out many tasks with very little guidance. Positive guidance at earlier ages has helped to build self-control.

5- and 6-year-olds are generally more self-directed than younger children. Also, having developed a longer interest span, kindergartners stay with each activity longer. Some become able to stay with and carry through projects of their own choosing even when other children encourage them to join in play. Such growing independence is a sign of increasing maturity. As children become more independent, they will need reminders about safety rules. Review Chapter 42, "Health and Safety for Kindergartners," for tips.

Awareness of Rules

Young children first become aware of rules through the continuous guidance of parents and teachers. As children become more familiar with the rules, they are able to repeat them. Children may even become "tattletales," reporting to parents and teachers when friends or siblings break rules. Usually, the children expect that the adult will do something about the misconduct. Being a tattletale means that the child has reached a level of being able to remember and to state the rules. Though many people do not like tattling, adults should praise rather than criticize the ability to repeat the rules. It is good to say, "You remembered the rules. That's good. Be sure you always follow them." Adults should avoid running directly to the child who has been told on. They should also avoid correcting a child only on the basis of another child's report.

Parents sometimes put older sisters and brothers in a position of reporting to them if a younger child fails to follow the rules. Parents will want to know when the younger child is doing something destructive or dangerous. However, parents should not encourage the older child to report every broken rule. The younger child is bound to become resentful. Guiding with praise for correct behavior, as described above, is likely to help parents handle tattling smoothly. Outside the family, a child who has developed the habit of reporting others' behavior to parents or teachers will find a cool response from peers.

? Decisions, Decisions

Janie, age 5, is always tattling on other children. How could her parents help her stop this?

Give Reasons for Rules

Parents and teachers who make a habit of explaining the "why" of rules give children a firm basis for decision making and self-direction. Children gradually become mature enough to understand the basis for the rules they have been hearing. Young children start out believing that rules are firm and unchanging. Then, during school age, they learn that flexibility may be appropriate in following some rules. At the kindergarten age, some children are just beginning to understand reasons beyond, "My teacher told me," or "My daddy told me." Children around 5 or 6 years old are beginning to recognize other people as persons like themselves. As children develop empathy, they can apply rules related to social give-and-take. They begin to see how another person feels if not treated well.

Children need to know why it is important to follow rules. When a rule is broken, it must be explained again. This type of guidance is far more effective than yelling or scolding.

Parents may sometimes have difficulty finding effective ways of guiding children at home. The classroom teacher has several advantages over parents. Teachers are usually in charge of many children. Children can remind one another of the rules and reinforce each other's behavior. A teacher also has the advantage of being able to go home in the afternoon. Parents are responsible for children's guidance full time, 7 days a week.

Perhaps the most important principle for parents is that of using guidance techniques which relate to the rules they want their children to follow. For example, if Dad asks Emily to put away her blocks and she refuses, he might say, kindly but firmly, "I see that you don't want to take care of your blocks. I'll put them away for a couple of days. When you are ready to take care of them, you may have them back." Or, if Mike sits down at the dinner table and pronounces each item "yukky" (occasionally, even the most cooperative 5-year-old may do this), parents can say, "You don't have to eat it, but saying it is "yukky" is impolite and spoils dinner for the rest of us. If you want to sit with us, you'll have to talk politely."

When parents use this type of language, children understand the reasons behind the rules. They also understand

These children are learning why the fence is there and why they must not climb over it. Once this is internalized, the parent will not need to accompany them to this site. How do parents know when it is time to trust their child's self-control?

the consequences of their rule breaking. Such techniques are far more effective than yelling, scolding, or lecturing.

Concluding Comments

Guidance is needed for children from birth to maturity. Little by little, parents and teachers release children to take over the decision making that controls behavior. The children at this age are nearing the goal of self-control. Rules become internalized, and children act on those rules. Rules have been explained. People have helped children understand how others feel if they break rules. When the rules are internalized, adults do not have to be present to enforce rules. Children follow the rules because they have learned self-control.

Parents and teachers who give children reasons for the rules help children develop control from within. Being controlled outwardly because of fear of punishment or fear that "people won't like you" is a very poor substitute for internalized self-control.

Activities

1. Visit a kindergarten class.
   a. Record 5 episodes of guidance. Use quotes from children and from the teacher.
   b. Analyze each episode. What type of guidance was used in each episode? Did the guidance influence the child's behavior in the way the teacher planned?
   c. Write a report and discuss it with your classmates.
2. Visit a kindergarten class.
   a. List and briefly describe each learning center.
   b. Explain how these learning centers are planned for indirect guidance of the children.
   c. Describe one child using a learning center. How was the child directed?
   d. Complete a report of your visit and share it with your class.

3. Talk with the parents of a kindergartner.
   a. Ask them to describe examples of their child's misbehavior.
   b. What do they do about this misbehavior?
   c. Ask them if their child is easier or harder to "manage" than the child was a year ago.
4. Can you remember a time when another child "tattled" to the teacher or a parent about your misbehavior? How did you feel? How can an adult handle the child who tattled and the child who misbehaved?
5. Give examples, real or imaginary, of using guidance techniques to guide kindergarten children's behavior at home. See examples on page 390. Then describe 3 different situations. Include guidance suggestions for each.

Home Routines for Kindergartners

Objectives
To describe how home routines change when the child becomes 5 years old.

To describe some routines that the kindergartner can now take care of independently.

To describe routines where the child still needs help.

Steve and Kent, both 5-year-olds, were playing at Steve's house. Steve told his father they were hungry. His father said, "Steve, you know where the peanut butter and milk are. You can make some sandwiches for you and Kent." The boys collected the ingredients in the kitchen. Before long, they were munching happily on their sandwiches, and drinking their glasses of milk.

Independence Is Key in Routines

Steve and Kent have learned to be independent in making their snack. They are also independent in many other aspects of living now that they are 5 years old and in kindergarten. The children play independently and without conflicts most of the time. Nevertheless, their parents still feel that at least one adult should be at home for emergencies.

Home and Yard

Steve and Kent consider the neighborhood their playground, as they ride their two-wheelers back and forth between their houses. They cross several streets to walk to kindergarten. Both children prefer outdoor to indoor play, even in cold weather.

Steve and Kent like to have several building or science projects in progress in their rooms or yards. They do not appreciate the younger visitors or neighbors who take things down, uproot plants they are growing, or rearrange the yard without consulting them.

Researchers and psychologists have traditionally said that 5-year-old boys prefer to play in groups of several boys, whereas 5-year-old girls tend to enjoy the company of one other girl at a time. However, many people now feel that such behavior is the result of training, not of genes or hormones. Our culture, television, and adults (consciously or unconsciously) all act to give 5-year-olds the idea that they should now begin "girl play" and "boy play." In fact, both girls and boys can enjoy boisterous group play. Both can enjoy a quiet afternoon with a friend of the same or opposite sex.

Bedtime Routines

After a busy day, many kindergartners are ready for bed by 8 o'clock. However, bedtimes vary from family to family. In families where one or both parents work late outside the home, children may stay up later so they can spend time with the parents. Also, although most 5-year-olds have given up the afternoon nap, those who spend a full day in a day-care center may need a rest period or nap during the day. Then, these children may not be sleepy until a later hour at night. Most 5-year-olds will probably follow an old routine of a bedtime bath, followed by stories. Occasionally, before retiring, children like to finish some activity in their rooms after they have said good night to their parents.

Five-year-olds love to be part of a group. Friends are becoming very important to them.

Cuddling before bedtime gives children a strong feeling of security at the end of a busy day. This quiet routine also lowers the resistance to bedtime.

Eating Routines

Kindergartners' eating habits are generally well established by now. They also enjoy helping prepare a meal or a snack. The usual pattern in this country is for 5-year-olds to have dinner with their parents. Nevertheless, parents have to work out routines that are best for their own family. For example, Bill's parents both work outside the home. His mother arrives home at 5:00 P.M.; his father, at 6:30 P.M. The parents found that getting dinner on the table before 7:00 was impossible. And by the time dinner was over, neither parent had much time to spend with the children before bedtime. In addition, Bill's 3-year-old brother, Sam, was so tired and hungry by 7:00 that he could not sit through the meal without becoming cranky and disruptive.

Bill's parents decided that the solution for them was to have the boys' babysitter prepare dinner for Bill and Sam. Dinner was ready for their mother to put on the table when she came home. While the boys ate dinner in the kitchen, their mother could sit and talk with them. Or, she could begin preparing the parents' meal. When the boys' father came home, one parent would bathe the boys while the other worked on dinner preparation. Then, both parents would have some special time with the boys for singing and storytelling. When the boys were in bed, their parents would sit down to a quiet dinner at 8:00.

These parents had learned to be flexible. They were able to work out a solution that took into account the needs of all members of the family. On weekends, they would try to have an early dinner with the boys. Both parents felt that learning to eat with others was important for the children.

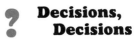

Decisions, Decisions

Six-year-old Curt has a difficult time getting ready for kindergarten. He complains about the clothes his mother has gotten out for him. He is very slow dressing. He complains about breakfast and often cannot find his shoes. By the time he finally goes out the door, his mother is exhausted. "He's just not a morning person," she tells herself. What suggestions could you make to ease this situation?

Toileting, Bathing, and Dressing

Kindergartners have the routines of toileting, bathing, and dressing down pat. They can handle the routines themselves with little help from their parents. They can usually tie their own shoes—a skill that took a lot of patience to develop. They like to choose what they will wear each day. They are beginning to want their clothing styles to be the same as their classmates'.

Responsibility

Along with their increased independence comes the increased ability of kindergartners to handle responsibility. Usually, 5-year-olds can learn to make their own beds. They can put their soiled clothes in the hamper and keep their rooms neat. Children should learn to regard such chores as part of regular family life and as a sign that they are becoming more grown-up. Parents should be careful to express approval for what their children are able to do. Parents should not redo tasks. Whether the bed is perfectly neat is less important than the fact that the child can and does make the bed. Parents can also encourage improvement with such statements as, "You missed only one little crumb when you wiped the table. You're really getting to be a good cleaner."

Parents can turn routine tasks into valuable learning activities. For example, parents can label shelves so that each toy or group of toys has a specific place. Most 5-year-olds are old enough to be consulted about where they want to put things. Cars and trucks can go in a cardboard box labeled "garage," blocks on a "block" shelf, "books" on a bookshelf, and so forth. The child's clothing can be separated into boxes in drawers. Each box can be labeled "shirts," "pants," "socks," and so forth. Such labeling can help children with sorting and classification, which are both prereading and premathematics skills. The labels also give children a few sight words. These labels help interest children in reading. Children of both sexes can be encouraged to do the routine chores of wiping up and putting away with both parents. By doing this, they learn that the entire family is responsible for housework.

Television

A 5-year-old told his teacher, "I like to turn things on and watch them. I don't want to make anything." This statement was quoted by Dorothy Cohen, of Bank Street College of Education, in a speech she gave at a meeting of the Midwest Association for the Education of Young Children. In the same speech, Ms. Cohen stated that experienced teachers have reported "a decrease in imaginative play and an increase in aimless running around, noninvestment in play materials, low frustration tolerance, poor persistence, and confusion about reality and fantasy."

These remarks emphasize how important it is for parents to supervise and limit their children's television viewing. Television is a fact of life. Few programs may be good for the social, emotional, and mental development of children. Parents should try to acquaint themselves with what are the best children's programs.

One serious problem about television is that it is passive. It requires children to sit and take in stimuli rather than to act on stimuli. Children simply do not learn well just by listening and watching. They need to get their hands on objects and to be with people in order to understand their world. Television gives children no opportunity to ask questions. It moves too fast to allow reflective thinking. A television kindergarten might be available now, but a real live kindergarten class is much better. The child can interact with others and learn in all respects: physically, mentally, and socially.

It is wise for parents to watch programs with young children in order to explain misunderstood concepts. By watching with the children, parents can soothe fears that arise. Parents can also share the experience with the children. Even programs with humanitarian objectives may frighten a child. One little girl was disturbed when, in a ranch story, a young colt was rescued by helicopter. The colt was hurt and the weather was snowy. But the child was apparently disturbed because the colt was being taken away from its mother. Her mother's presence comforted her.

Advertisements may be particularly persuasive to 5-year-olds and young 6-year-olds. Kindergartners frequently discuss a toy they see advertised on television. And they announce they expect to get one. The social pressure placed on their peers to get that toy is enormous. Parents and others should help children keep values in balance. Discussing whether to use money for an advertised toy or for another attractive item can help kindergartners learn to make decisions. Parents should require

What potential problems do you see in this picture?

that decisions to buy be made at home after serious discussion and not on the spot by impulse. This will ease the pressure to buy. Also, a similar demand is less likely on the next shopping trip.

Shopping Routines

Kindergartners can be pleasant company on shopping trips. They may helpfully remember items needed in the household. They usually will gracefully accept a "no" to a request to purchase a toy.

Shopping trips can also offer further opportunities for learning experiences. The 5-year-olds can practice following the rules, waiting for the green light, and so forth. A grocery store can help them practice their classification skills. A parent might say, "Where do you think we'll find the butter? What is butter made from? Where do you think the pork chops are? What about the grapefruit?"

One of the best ways to teach children is to know what interests them and to follow up on those interests. Kim, a 5-year-old, was crazy about trucks and cars. Her parents had borrowed from the library several books about trucks and cars. As she and her mother walked along the street, she would tell her mother what make each car was. "That's an Oldsmobile. There's a Mack truck." She first learned to distinguish the cars by their emblems, then by their shapes. At 5, her first sight words, after *Kim*, were *Ford* and *Dodge*. Her mother encouraged her interest. She turned shopping trips into learning trips.

Often, 5-year-olds will prefer to stay home and play in the neighborhood rather than go shopping, if supervision can be arranged for them. If parents

Shopping can be a learning experience when children are included in the process. What could you teach a 5-year-old in the supermarket?

have helped their children become accustomed to having other adults care for them, the children readily accept the supervision of a neighbor or baby-sitter.

Visitors

Kindergartners enjoy having a friend for companionship. They make plans at school for what they can do at home after school or on weekends. They enjoy "sleeping over" at each others' houses. They may even request the privilege of staying up a little longer on these occasions.

Adults can teach kindergartners to be polite to adult visitors. They remember polite phrases, such as "please," "thank you," and "excuse me." Kindergartners can now more easily remain quiet during religious services or other public gatherings than they could when they were younger.

Concluding Comments

Parents who do the best job with their children work themselves out of a job. You will readily agree with this statement if you have already read about home routines for infants, toddlers, and prekindergartners. You now see how independent children become when they are 5 years old and going on 6.

Most parents gladly turn routines over to children and go on to other activities, themselves. Perhaps there are other children in the family who require attention. Or perhaps the parents can turn to some long-neglected personal interests of their own. For it is certain that healthy kindergartners do not need their parents' help with many of their routines anymore. Of course, though, children continue to need their parents' care, love, nurturance, and guidance. In the remaining chapters, you will note where the influence of parents on their children is quite essential.

Activities

1. Talk to the parents of a kindergartner.
   a. How much and what kind of help does their child need with bathing and dressing?
   b. Does their child choose the clothes to wear each day?
   c. What is the child's time and routine for going to bed?
   d. Does the child make his or her own bed and put dirty clothes in the hamper?
   e. In what other ways does the child help take care of the home?
   f. How free is the child to come and go in the neighborhood?
2. Write an essay in which you react to Ms. Cohen's comments on the effect of television on children.
   a. Do you think she is right or wrong? Explain your answer.

   b. Should anything be "done" about it? If so, what?
   c. If you had a kindergarten child, would you set any limits on television viewing? Explain reasons for your answer.
3. Visit with a kindergartner. Observe and ask:
   a. How many friends do you have that you play with in the neighborhood?
   b. What do you like to do together?
   c. Do you like to help your mother and father around the house? What do you do?
   d. How do you feel about walking to school? What rules do you follow to be safe?
   e. Make a report of your discussion. Compare with your classmates.

Feeding Kindergartners

Objectives
To describe kindergartners' independence related to food.
To describe ways kindergartners can help with food.
To describe field trips that are related to food.

"What are we making, teacher? Can I help?" Shelly asked eagerly as she entered the kindergarten. She had noticed the electric frying pan sitting on the table usually reserved for food-preparation projects.

"Remember, we're making pancakes, Shelly. Yes, you can help. You can count the plates and forks to see if there are 16. That's enough for everyone in the class," concluded Ms. Rohrer, the kindergarten teacher.

"I want to help, too," volunteered David as he tossed his coat in the locker and joined Shelly and Ms. Rohrer.

"You can both wash your hands, and we'll get started," said Ms. Rohrer. "It takes a lot of time to let everyone make a pancake. How many of you help make pancakes at home?"

Thus begins an eventful kindergarten day. The children are eager to participate in the food-preparation project. While some of the children cook, others are involved with their usual activities. They are sufficiently self-directed so that the teacher can watch the pancake-making operation closely.

Food Needs of Kindergartners

Kindergartners typically have outgrown most eating problems that may have been troublesome in earlier years. There are fewer food demands on parents, because the child can now easily

Kindergartners are quite capable of preparing many nutritious snacks, themselves. Still, parents need to lend a hand with knives or ovens.

wait to eat with the family at mealtime. A child's growth rate is slow. However, the rate will increase again, usually after the child goes to the first grade.

Nutrition education for prekindergartners was discussed in detail in Chapter 36. The need for nutrition information applies also to kindergartners. Kindergartners become increasingly able to understand the nutritional facts that parents and teachers present. Providing a rich kindergarten curriculum that stresses the need for nutritious food is a worthwhile effort. Another avenue is to seek help from the kindergartners'

parents. They can continue to influence their child beyond school hours toward being well nourished and conscious of nutritional facts. At home, parents can talk about the importance of eating a balanced diet. They can encourage their child to eat foods from each of the Basic Four food groups every day.

Independent Food Decisions

Teachers and parents may have to take the initiative when their kindergartners have choices of snack foods to buy. The adults may need to help children choose nutritious snacks. They should help children develop an understanding of why some snacks are better choices than others.

? Decisions, Decisions

In Paul's kindergarten, the children are allowed to bring in snacks. Paul's mother fixes healthy snacks for him, but he keeps asking for junk food like the other children bring in. What might Paul's mother do to solve this problem?

Obligation to Serve Nutritious Snacks

In one school system, a sixth-grade class was selling doughnuts to raise money for a trip. Kindergartners began asking their teacher to be allowed to spend their milk money for doughnuts. The teacher asked the principal to rule against the practice. The teacher knew that doughnuts were less nutritious. He also knew that children would buy doughnuts with their money instead of the milk. The older children's project continued. The principal saw no problem with it.

Some children brought enough money for doughnuts and milk. Other children were hurt because their parents would not, or could not, afford the additional expense of doughnuts. Some children bought doughnuts instead of milk. Some bought a doughnut for one friend—leaving out their other friends. Worst of all, the teacher learned of a child stealing from family members at home and from a classmate in order to have money to buy the doughnuts. At this point, the teacher again approached the principal and reported what was happening. Based on the negative social results, the kindergarten teacher finally got the doughnut sale moved away from the school building.

In another kindergarten, the school system initially failed to take any leadership in regard to children's snacks. The school system told the parents that they could send canned juice and other foods, "if you want your child to have them for snacks." The school territory was composed of a poor neighborhood and a wealthy one. As might be expected, the wealthy children brought juice, soft drinks, and other snacks. The poor people had no snacks. A new teacher observed the social and nutritional results of this system. She won a case to begin the policy of purchasing milk with school funds. This milk was supplemented with foods made by the children in class. In this way, the teacher put the children on an equal footing and provided the nutritious foods needed by all.

Parents, teachers, and assistants should make sure that nutritious foods are served in meals and snacks at school. Good food practices support the effort to teach children about nutrition. If the school sets a good example, education on nutrition is more effective than if the school sets a poor one.

Combining Food Projects and Field Trips

Kindergartners are ready to move out beyond the school walls and investigate their community. A number of worthwhile trips can focus on how food is raised, processed, or purchased.

Apples

Apples are fruit that most children like. In the fall, a walk through an orchard for picking apples offers opportunities for learning many facts about apples as well as about the fall season. The children will like counting the apples they pick and discussing the color differences. They can help carry the "heavy" baskets back to school or home.

Back at the kindergarten, the boys and girls can help prepare apple sauce. They can wash, core, cut, and cook the apples slowly in an electric frying pan. The product becomes fragrant apple sauce. If the apples are tart, they can be sugared slightly. Sprinkling them with a touch of cinnamon adds to their flavor and aroma. There is no need to peel the apples. The skins add color, texture, and nutritional value to the sauce. An apple cutter is handy. This is a gadget that cores the apple and cuts it into six sections, all in one stroke. Children can easily stand and cut their own apples with this cutter. The cutter relieves the worry about knives that could hurt the children.

The apples can be used for a variety of recipes. Apple sauce, apple pancakes, and baked apples are just a few possibilities. While eating their apple dish, children can talk about their walk. They can also recall the steps involved in making the dish. This total experience gives the teacher or parent an opportunity to tell children that apples are good for them. They can explain that apples have many vitamins that help children grow and develop.

Apple sauce is also an easy dish for children to help prepare at home. Children will enjoy serving their dish to the whole family at mealtime.

Milk

Visiting a dairy and a milk-processing plant are two excellent field trips for kindergartners. Children like to see, hear, touch, and smell the cows. It may be difficult to take a class to a dairy at milking time. Milking may be done very early in the morning. It may start again in late afternoon, when children are usually not in kindergarten. This trip is a good one to recommend to parents for a family outing. However, with special assistance from parents, some teachers are able to arrange a trip to the dairy in the late afternoon, around 4:00 or 4:30 P.M. The children see dairy workers and the milking machines. Seeing the process in operation helps children gain valuable information about milk, a food they use very frequently.

As a follow-up to the dairy trip, the children can visit a milk-processing

Five-year-olds like to know where their food comes from. How food gets from its source to the market to the table is of real interest to children.

plant. Here they can see the bottling machines in operation, the pasteurization system, the ice cream-making and packaging process, and, perhaps, the cheese-making process. Each process provides more information about foods that are in the children's daily experience. Kindergartners frequently have many questions. This is especially true when they have been prepared through stories and discussions before taking the field trips.

Finally, children should have the chance to use dairy products in a recipe. Good possibilities include making yogurt or ice cream or making butter from cream.

Parents and Teachers Assist Each Other

Teachers can ask parents for assistance in planning and carrying out food projects that are a specialty of their ethnic group. Certain foods have a special significance in each culture. Kindergarten children and parents can share their own traditions about special foods and can try out the special foods of others. Those who do this are participating in a valuable learning experience. Such projects are carried out throughout a school year, as they fit in with other learning projects.

Helpers

Kindergartners are good helpers during food preparation. Their help can extend to regular mealtime help at home or at school. The kindergarten boy or girl can help set the table, peel vege-

Kindergarten children and their parents can share their special food customs with the class.

tables, make some salads and desserts. After the meal, the child can remove dishes from the table to the dishwasher or to the sink for washing. Of course, they are more likely to enjoy dishwashing if someone works along with them. An adult or older child can assist with the hard or heavy parts and can encourage the kindergartner's "good job."

Kindergartners can usually help themselves. They will do so if snack foods are stored where the kindergartner can reach and handle them. Parents can set aside a place in the refrigerator and cupboard where the child can expect to find foods approved for snacks. This sets limits that are helpful in the child's striving for independence. The child can learn to put away snack materials as well as to get them out.

Concluding Comments

Nutrition continues to be of great importance to kindergarten children. They are on the verge of their second growth spurt. They are beginning to have permanent teeth to care for. The kindergarten child's nutrition education must move forward, because the child is becoming increasingly independent.

Involving kindergarten children in food-preparation projects gives them concrete experience with food. This involvement can also help them relate nutritional information to their diets. From various ethnic groups can come suggestions for food projects that add to the total learning experience of the kindergarten.

Activities

1. Call or visit your local elementary school.
   a. Ask what snacks are available for children at the school.
   b. Do kindergartners have a choice of snack foods?
   c. Report on the nutritional value of the snacks available.
2. Plan a field trip for kindergartners to increase the children's understanding of food production and food processing.
   a. Plan the appropriate time, get permission, and make any other plans for the trip.
   b. With parents' permission, take one or more kindergartners on the field trip.
   c. Write a complete report of the trip. How did the children behave? What did they learn? Did they enjoy the trip?
3. Plan and carry out a follow-up project to the above trip. Either follow suggestions in this chapter or use

your own ideas. Report on the activity.
4. Visit a parent of a kindergartner.
   a. Ask how much independence the child has in food choices.
   b. Ask whether the child is able to get his or her own snacks.
   c. Ask whether the child helps with mealtime at home.
5. With parents' permission, plan a family meal the kindergartner could prepare. Include food from each of the Basic Four food groups.
   a. Discuss the meal with the kindergartner.
   b. Help the kindergartner prepare the meal for the family.
   c. How did the child feel about cooking "all alone"?
   d. How did the family react to the meal?
   e. Report the event to your class.
6. Help kindergartners develop a collage of magazine pictures showing the Basic Four food groups.

Schools for Kindergartners

Objectives

To describe 5-year-old and young 6-year-old children in kindergartens.
To describe a high-quality kindergarten.
To describe interaction with kindergartners.

"Hey, bring that big board over here—no, here," commands Angie as she and Tim build a "hideout" out of the blocks in the kindergarten. Tim hands the board to Angie and reaches for another. Other children arrive, notice the structure, and start helping by handing Angie the boards. She is using them to make a roof for the "hideout." Angie and Tim are leaders in the kindergarten. The other children enjoy their company.

The kindergarten teacher values the creative growth taking place, as the dramatic play unfolds. Social give-and-take is being practiced. Language is being used, and ideas are being expressed. The drama comes from the children's experience and knowledge. They decide how the props will be used.

Types of Kindergartens

There are several schools where you find late 4-year-olds, 5-year-olds, and young 6-year-olds in kindergartens.

Public School Kindergartens. Kindergartens have been part of the public schools in most Northern states for years. Recently, some Southern states have begun funding them.

Each state sets requirements for teachers and the number of children that one teacher can be responsible for. In most states, kindergarten is not compulsory. The age of compulsory attendance is usually 7 years.

Most elementary teachers believe kindergarten prepares children to succeed in upper school levels. Kindergarten teachers notice that children who have been to prekindergarten enter kindergarten activities more readily.

Parent Cooperative Kindergartens. Parent cooperative kindergartens are organized similar to the parent cooperative nursery schools described in Chapter 37. The southern United States had a widespread development in cooperative kindergartens before public kindergartens existed.

Private Kindergartens. Private kindergartens have served wealthier families who desire special schooling for their children. Many times, tuition costs eliminate families. Tuition covers costs of operation, unless endowments contribute to budgets. Some religious groups organize private kindergartens to promote their religious philosophy.

Head Start Kindergartens. When the federally funded Head Start program began in 1965, many groups of 5- to 6-year-olds were enrolled in Head Start, especially in states that did not have public school kindergartens.

Day-care Centers. Day-care centers were described in Chapter 37. Children whose families are eligible for full-day care send their children to day-care kindergartens rather than to half-day public kindergartens. Generally, these day-care kindergartens use the morning for the majority of the learning activities. The afternoon program follows lunch and a rest period.

Extended Day-Care Schools. Extended day care is the service provided by child-care centers for kindergarten children who attend kindergarten half the day. They need care for the other half day while their parents are at work. The children may attend kindergarten in the morning or they may attend in the afternoon. They usually eat lunch in the child-care center and may be transported by bus between the kindergarten and the child-care center.

These children pose a special challenge both to the kindergarten teacher and to the teachers at the child-care center. The children may be tired when the second teacher welcomes them. The children may be highly stimulated by the morning's activity. They may need to wind down during the afternoon. The afternoon teacher must accommodate the needs of each child. The teacher must not be disappointed in or critical of the tired child. Many activities are essential. The child should not become bored from doing the same kinds of activities in both schools.

Some cooperation between kindergarten and extended day-care teachers is certainly ideal. Children gain much more when cooperation, rather than unhealthy competition, exists between these two parts of their world.

Extended day care given in child-care centers allows kindergartners to do many activities. It also provides safety and protection for many children who might otherwise spend many hours alone unsupervised.

What Is a High-quality Kindergarten?

Many kindergarten teachers believe that, if 5-year-olds live active lives in kindergarten, they will be ready to con-

A kindergarten is a busy place, with many activities going on at the same time. This freedom of movement requires lots of advance planning on the part of the teacher.

front the tasks of elementary school. If you spent the morning in a high-quality kindergarten, what would you see?

Long Interest Spans. In a high-quality kindergarten, you would see children working in groups and alone. This solitary play in the kindergarten is different from that in the toddler group. Now children have skills for group play. But they work or play alone because they are able to concentrate on a project for a long period of time. For example, Ana Maria was making a train using cardboard boxes. She spent part of each day for a week on the project. Ana Maria knew how to play with others. She just wanted to finish her work.

Show-and-Tell. Toward the end of the day, the children often sit in a circle on the floor. They wait their turn to tell about what they brought from home to show their classmates. Their speaking and listening skills are developing.

Learning Centers. The teacher has put learning centers around the room. At these centers, children operate science equipment or slip into a painting apron and express creative urges by finger painting.

Things to Look At. The teacher has bulletin boards and cupboard shelves arranged with things to look at and wonder about. Books are prominently displayed. Reading stories aloud for fun is given high priority as an important prereading experience.

Experience charts on the wall may tell of a recent trip, project, or science experiment. The teacher has written what the children have dictated, so the stories are in the children's own words.

Children's drawings, paintings, collages, and other works are on the walls.

Writing Skills. Children use crayons, pencils, and felt markers to write their names. They enjoy reading their names

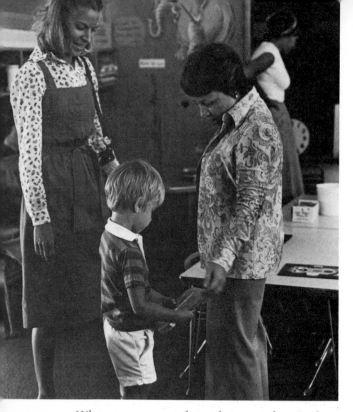

When parents and teachers work together toward the same goals, children do not become confused about what is expected of them.

from bulletin-board posters. If the kindergarten has a sand table, children use their fingers to write in the sand.

Parent Involvement. Parent involvement in the prekindergarten is discussed in Chapter 37. Many of these principles apply to kindergarten parents and teachers. Parents of kindergartners are generally cooperative in attending parent-teacher conferences and group meetings.

Effective teachers will want to learn what parents expect their children to gain from the kindergarten. Teachers may also discover that parents do a lot of teaching at home. When parents and teachers have good relationships, children gain extra benefits from the kindergarten experience.

Parents Can Help Children Enjoy Kindergarten. Many suggestions in Chapter 37 also apply here. Most 5-year-olds will be glad to share their experiences with parents.

At this point, parents may suddenly discover that they are in danger of being buried under the mountain of paintings, drawings, and collages that come home with their children. Some 5-year-olds may agree to discard some of their work. However, they should be allowed to choose what stays and what goes. A good way to keep the papers organized is to make books. Parents can get colored poster board to make covers for books. Two holes can be punched at the left edge of the poster board and of each drawing. The books can be fastened with yarn or shoelaces. Parents can help their child write "Richard's Drawings" or "Sally's Paintings" on the front and decorate the cover.

? **Decisions, Decisions**

The O'Briens have just moved to a new community. They have a 5-year-old son and need to find out what kinds of kindergartens are available. What advice would you give the O'Briens? Once they determine what is available, how would you suggest they make their selection?

Assisting in the Kindergarten

Assisting in the kindergarten may be the experience with young children that is easiest for you to arrange. There are usually several kindergarten classes available near your home or school. Many teachers welcome assistants.

In interacting with kindergartners, remember to let kindergartners do things for themselves. They can and will become independent if encouraged. Encourage them to button or zip their coats, to tie their shoes, and to put on their boots. Tell them you want to find out what *their* ideas are. Their development is the teacher's goal. Development for you is to learn how to foster the child's independence and self-confidence.

Remember, as an assistant, you are playing an adult role—not a 5-year-old role. The teacher, the children, and the parents will expect you to use your time fostering the children's growth, not playing with the children's toys.

Concluding Comments

Living and working with 5-year-olds seems to be more harmonious than it is for some other ages. True, this harmony may not prevail for one child all the time or for a few 5-year-olds who seldom seem to fit these characteristics. However, for the majority, this is a period of being in step with harmonious expectations.

Five-year-olds have developed longer interest spans and are able to solve many of their own problems. Their independence is growing steadily and they press parents and teachers to allow them to do more. The challenge to adults in kindergartners' lives is to have interesting things available for them to do. Interesting activities keep kindergartners happy.

Activities

1. Have 1 class member call the office of your Superintendent of Schools to ask the following questions:
   a. What kinds of kindergarten classes are available?
   b. Do most 5- and 6-year-olds attend kindergarten?
   c. By what age must a child attend school according to the law in your state?

2. If your community has more than 1 kind of kindergarten, choose a student to visit each kind: public, private, Head Start, day-care center, and extended day-care school. Each student should ask the following:
   a. Why do parents choose your class rather than in a different kind of kindergarten?
   b. Do the parents pay a fee for the kindergarten class?

   c. How are parents involved, if at all, in the kindergarten?
   d. Describe a typical day of activities in the class.
   e. What is the ratio of children per teacher? What is the ratio of children per all care givers?
   f. Compare the various centers. Discuss how the different classes are alike or different.

3. Volunteer to assist in a kindergarten for 1 or 2 hours a day for a week.
   a. What activities are available for the children?
   b. With what activities do the children need help?
   c. Which activities can the children do by themselves?

4. As you work in the kindergarten class, plan a project to help the children be more independent.

unit

16

Kindergartners Learning

Activities for Kindergartner Learning

Objective
To describe learning activities appropriate for kindergarten
children.

"I'm gonna go to your birthday party,
Nancy," says Ruth.

"I am too, Nancy," chimes in Jack.
Then, mysteriously, he adds, "Betcha
can't guess what I'm bringing you."

Nancy, glowing in response, smiles
and shows the spaces for missing teeth.
"My mommy made my birthday cake,"
she says. "It says, 'Nancy is 6 Years
Old.' I'm going to "big" school when
I'm 6. I won't be in this kindergarten
anymore," she concludes firmly.

For the kindergartners turning 6,
there is real excitement. Just like Nancy,
they are going to "big" school. Many
think that immediately after their sixth
birthday they will enter first grade,
never to return to the kindergarten. Parents and teachers must help kindergartners realize that their start in first grade
may be months away. Otherwise, they
may be in for a tremendous letdown.

Preparing for the Future

The future is an unknown that healthy
people look forward to with great anticipation. We plan, we save, and we prepare for "the future." Teachers and parents who help kindergartners live and
learn effectively today are helping them
prepare for the future.

The activities in this chapter are
meant for children who have had the
kind of rich prekindergarten experience
described in the previous section. If
children have not, then many prekindergarten experiences must become a
part of the kindergarten program. In any
case, children learn something new each
time activities are presented. So most
activities can profitably be repeated.

Planning Kindergarten Learning Activities

The kindergarten classroom should be decorated with interesting bulletin boards, science displays, bookshelves, and artifacts of the community. Teachers should encourage children to talk about what they see in the displays.

Show-and-Tell

Kindergarten teachers often have a session called "show-and-tell." This is a period each day when children plan something to tell or bring something to show their kindergarten friends. They develop ease in speaking alone. They also learn to tell a story in the order in which it happened.

Understanding-the-Self Projects

Developing children's ability to understand and care for themselves offers opportunities for class projects—health, hair, teeth, inoculations, and so on. Safety in the home, streets, school, and family car is important to teach.

Relationships with family members, including sibling rivalries, offer avenues for exploration and expression. Understanding what it is like to be a boy or a girl, breaking down sex-role stereotypes, and understanding the meaning of reproduction are all good for discussion and learning. Parents and teachers have the chance to broaden career possibilities concerning what young people can do with their lives. So they must be certain not to teach children that career doors are shut to them because they are girls, boys, or members of a minority group. The goal is to help children feel competent and to provide them with a good early education.

Understanding the Community

The community, its people, its institutions, and its festivals provide opportunities to teach kindergartners about the culture of their country. They may also be ready for learning about faraway culture, especially if someone they know comes from that country.

Kindergarten children often are taken on field trips to many places in the neighborhood. Here they become acquainted with many community workers in the fire station, the post office, the filling station, the grocery store, the health clinic, and the like. The class may develop a map of their neighborhood. On it, they can locate each other's homes as well as community facilities. This knowledge makes them more at ease as they are allowed to go out into the community on their own.

Parents should teach children their addresses and phone numbers. Teachers can help children practice reciting these and using the telephone. This will help a child who is lost. Some teachers teach children how to report a fire. However, teachers should teach children that calling in false alarms is unwise and dangerous.

Following Directions

Providing practice in following directions is part of a high-quality kindergarten program. Kindergartners can now remember two-step directions. For example, the teacher says, "Hang up your coats and get ready for story time." Or the teacher says, "Put the toys away now and get ready for snack time." Kindergartners are usually ready to follow two clearly stated directions.

The teacher plans transitions carefully and lets kindergartners know what they can expect to happen next. The children may feel confused when schedules are changed. But they can readily adjust if the teacher lets them know what is expected of them.

Caring for Themselves

Kindergarten children are expected to take care of their belongings and to store them in the locker as directed. They should be able to dress themselves from top to toe. When necessary, the teachers and parents teach children how to put the ends of a zipper together to get it started, how to tie shoes, and how to pull on boots.

Tying shoes may require some special help for a few children. They can be taught to tie shoes in these steps:

1. Cross the strings.
2. Make a loop with one string, "like a bunny ear."
3. Then, cross the second string over the loop. Pull the string through the hole made by the finger that is holding the first loop. This makes a second "bunny ear."
4. Finally, pull both "ears" firmly.

To demonstrate shoe tying, you may need to sit on the floor on your knees with the child's back toward you. The child sits in front of you. If you demonstrate while reaching around the child, the kindergartner can see the steps better than if you sit opposite.

Field trips in the community are a favorite kindergarten activity. Public places that adults take for granted are fascinating to 5-year-olds. Allow plenty of time for looking and questions.

Science Experiments

Many experiments can focus on children's natural curiosity and their inclination to explore. The emphasis should be on discovering facts, not on lecturing about facts.

Plant Projects. Kindergartners love to grow plants. Possibilities range from growing pots of beans or flowers to planting window boxes and making outdoor vegetable or flower gardens. In the fall, children can harvest a few fall crops, can notice leaves change color, and can pick reeds for dry bouquets. In the spring, they can learn by planting flowers and vegetables.

Sprouting seeds and beans is fun and gives fast results. Place alfalfa seeds or dried soybeans in a glass jar. Cover them with a little water. Put a piece of cheesecloth over the top. Then place the jar in a dark place. The children can look at the jar each day. With the teacher's help, they can draw and write about the changes that take place every day. In 3 to 5 days, the seeds will sprout. They can be rinsed off and eaten raw.

Animal Projects. Small animals can visit kindergarten for a day or two if there are suitable cages for them. Many good kindergartens keep gerbils or guinea pigs. Children learn how to be gentle with animals. They also learn what foods animals like to eat and how animals enjoy exercising.

Some toads, frogs, and fish can stay in terrariums and aquariums. Children can see other animals on field trips to zoos and farms. Kindergartners are interested in animals, such as cows and chickens, that give us food, such as milk and eggs.

Physical Forces Projects. Physical forces, such as air, wind, gravity, temperature, weather, speed, and distance, are concepts that can be explored through a number of avenues, both indoors and outdoors.

Air and Water Experiments. Kindergartners can conduct a simple experiment by soaking a sponge with water. Then they set the wet sponge on a table or windowsill. The next day, they will discover that it is dry. They can discuss what might have happened to the water. The teacher can record their responses on an experience chart.

Magnets. Magnets are fascinating to 5-year-olds. They may enjoy experimenting with several small objects to see

The day the chameleon came to school! Science for kindergartners is a matter of satisfying natural curiosity.

which ones the magnet will pick up. The teacher can help them record their observations.

Machine Projects

Kindergartners like to work machines and to watch machines work. If a street is being repaired, they learn as they watch the workers. If a building is under construction, they will watch from day to day with interest. They enjoy visits to airports, railroad stations, bus stations, or boat docks. Most 5-year-olds can use small machines, such as the mixer or the record player. Both girls and boys enjoy using hand tools such as saws, hammers, pliers, and screwdrivers.

Mathematics and Premathematics

Mathematical learning can be related to other projects. Children can keep their own height and weight charts. They can count the number of cartons of milk needed for a snack, the number of sandwiches needed for a picnic, and so forth. Numbers are related to the calendar, to the temperature, and to the time. Children's concepts of dates, temperature, and time are just developing. Parents and teachers must try to straighten out considerable confusion.

Blocks. Blocks help children discover mathematical relationships and equivalents. A teacher or aide might say, "Can you find two blocks that will fit exactly on top of this block?" Children will learn many of these concepts on their own. As they build, they must find just the right blocks to fit their structures.

Blocks can also be used for measuring. Instead of using rulers or yardsticks, children can count how many of a certain size block they must use to go from one end of the bookshelf to the other.

Coins. Children are first introduced to the names of coins. They then learn the number and kinds of coins needed to pay for such things as milk for snacks, a bus ride, or ice-cream ingredients. Handling coins, rather than simply talking about them, makes learning easier.

Writing

Writing skills begin in painting and drawing. But now, in kindergarten, the teacher shows children how to use manuscript writing for their names. This writing forms letters with lines and circles in lower and upper case. It is the form used by first-grade teachers.

The teacher shows children how to write their names, having them start in the left-hand corner of the page. This helps children learn that we read from left to right. It also has the advantage of leaving children plenty of room on the page for their names. If they start their names toward the right side, the children frequently run out of space. Then, they place the last few letters above or below the line. This ruins the "picture" their names make as they look at them.

Children's names are used on many classroom charts. This gives the children practice in reading their own names and those of their friends. Kindergartners are often heard asking how to write other words. Teachers and parents can help the children when they ask.

Many activities foster speaking and listening skills. Children are encouraged to relay information from school to home and from home to school. The teacher may say, "Your mother wanted to know when vacation starts. Tell her that vacation begins on Friday."

Prereading and Reading

During the early years, background information and many skills are accumulating. They form a firm base upon which reading skills will be learned.

Many activities develop prereading skills during these early years. For example:

1. Using many books for information and for fun makes the child highly motivated to learn to read.
2. Seeing words grouped as phrases or sentences on book pages begins training the eyes to read.
3. Relating pictures to the words on book pages helps children realize the relationship between the two.

In most communities, children can have their own public library cards as soon as they can write their first name. What can a 5-year-old learn from owning a library card?

4. Recognizing one's own name on pictures, name tags, and various lists is a first and very personal reading experience for the child.
5. Writing one's name on artwork, using the required manuscript letter forms and the left-to-right movement, begins developing a child's reading skills.
6. Telling experiences orally builds a speaking vocabulary that helps children understand the written vocabulary in stories.
7. Recognizing shapes, sizes, likenesses, and differences in art materials and in other kindergarten activities helps the children interpret a teacher's directions about written language. The teacher may point out words or letters that are large or small, curved or straight, the same or different, and so on.
8. Visiting numerous places and people serves as background information when the child later reads about these places or people.
9. Learning about librarians as helpful people, about the library as an exciting place to go, and about the appropriate care and respect for books helps children become interested in books.
10. Knowing parents, teachers, librarians, and friends who share a love of good books may be a significant outcome. The love of books is usually "caught" rather than "taught."

Fun with reading is an important emphasis in kindergarten. This emphasis is partly in response to the anticipation of learning to read in the first grade. However, books become important to kindergartners as sources of information and pleasure. The kindergarten teacher encourages children to use the kindergarten library. The teacher usually sets up a library loan system so children can borrow books from the classroom.

Dedicated parents and teachers will readily provide these important pre-reading and reading experiences during the early childhood years. Teaching the mechanics of reading is relatively easy for the first-grade teacher when children have had this type of background for reading.

Visiting First Grade

Visiting the first-grade classroom is a long-awaited opportunity for kindergartners. The teachers arrange the visit to ease any fear or concern the children may feel about their next step on the school ladder. Sometimes first graders themselves show the kindergartners around. They may let them try out their desks and help them locate the bathroom. Teachers stress the fun that first grade will be.

Kindergartners' parents are usually invited to meet with the first-grade teacher as a further step to help ease the transfer to first grade. Parents are advised against fostering fear of first grade in their children. They are advised to help children expect it to be a comfortable, happy place to work and learn.

During the summer, parents can help ease the transfer from kindergarten to first grade. They do this by helping the child feel ready for a new level of experiences. Compliments such as, "You can take care of your clothes, so I think you are ready to go to school," are good. Or parents can remind children that they are ready for school if they can remember to call on the telephone when they get to grandmother's house. Practice helps children keep telephone numbers in mind that were learned in kindergarten. Being able to phone parents often relieves fears a child may have.

Concluding Comments

Rich experiences through the years from birth to 6 are the best assurances that children will be ready for their primary school years. Development must proceed on all fronts. For example, sometimes the child's physical development is very fast. Then it may slow down while language skills catch up. Development and growth are not a lock-step process. Yet there are predictable trends.

Parents and teacher first have to recognize the strides children are making as they scale the ladder of maturity. Then they can provide opportunities that help the upward climb. If, for some reason, the child is not reaching the appropriate rungs on the developmental ladder, parents and teachers must promptly seek to understand why. There may be measures that can be taken to help the child. Nearly all these measures require that diagnosis and treatment of problems begin as early as possible.

Activities

1. Plan a bulletin board for a kindergarten room. Choose a theme that will help kindergartners learn.
   a. If the teacher approves, arrange the display you have planned.
   b. Describe your bulletin board display in detail or hand in a sketch that shows clearly what you did.
2. Teach a child to tie his or her shoes.
   a. Select a child who needs *and wants* to learn to tie his or her shoes.
   b. Demonstrate as suggested in this chapter.
   c. Write a report of the results.
3. Help kindergartners carry out a science experiment. Ideas for experiments are given in this chapter.

4. Ask a kindergarten child to tell you a story. Explain that you will write the story down for the child.
   a. Type the story, then read it back to the child.
   b. Display the story either at the child's home or in the kindergarten classroom.
   c. Explain to your class the learning that is encouraged through this process of writing down a child's story, then showing the results.
5. Take one or more kindergarten children to the public library.
   a. Introduce them to the children's librarian.
   b. Encourage them to browse among the books in the children's section of the library.

Suggested Readings for Parts 5 and 6

Part 5

Chess, Stella et al., *Your Child Is a Person: A Psychological Approach to Parenthood Without Guilt*. New York: Penquin Books, 1977.

Dreikurs, Rudolph and V. Stolz, *Children: The Challenge*. New York: Duell, Sloan, and Pearce, 1964.

Gordon, Thomas, *P.E.T. Parent Effectiveness Training*. New York: Peter H. Wyden, Inc., 1970.

Gordon, Thomas, *P.E.T. Parent Effectiveness Training*. New York: Peter H. Wyden, Inc., 1974.

Green, Martin I., *A Sigh of Relief: The First-Aid Handbook for Childhood Emergencies*. New York: Bantam Books, 1977.

Hildebrand, Verna, *Guiding Young Children*. New York: The Macmillan Company, 1975.

Hildebrand, Verna, *Introduction to Early Childhood Education*. New York: The Macmillan Company, 1976.

Hymes, James L., Jr., *Teaching the Child under Six*. Columbus, Ohio: Charles E. Merrill Publishing Co., 1974.

Landreth, Catherine, *Preschool Learning and Teaching*. New York: Harper & Row Publishers, 1972.

Larrick, Nancy, *A Parent's Guide to Children's Reading*. New York: Bantam Books, 1975.

Macht, Joel, *Teaching Our Children*. New York: John Wiley & Sons, 1975.

McCord, Ivalee, *Child Care*. Washington, DC: American Home Economics Association, 1975.

Seefeldt, Carol A. *A Curriculum for Child Care Centers*. Columbus, Ohio: Charles E. Merrill, 1974.

Sprung, Barbara, *Non-Sexist Education for Young Children: A Practical Guide*. New York: Citation Press, 1975.

Taylor, Barbara J., *A Child Goes Forth*. Provo, Utah: Brigham Young University Press, 1975.

Part 6

Clark, Kenneth B., *Prejudice and Your Child*. Boston: The Beacon Press, 1963.

Cooper, Elizabeth, *Science in Your Own Back Yard*. New York: Harcourt, Brace, and Company, 1958.

Harlan, Jean Durgin, *Science Experiences for the Early Childhood Years*. Columbus, Ohio: Charles E. Merrill Company, 1976.

Hildebrand, Verna, *Introduction to Early Childhood Education*. New York: The Macmillan Company, 1976.

Kappelman, Murray and Paul Ackerman, *Between Parent and School*. New York: Dial Press, 1977.

Leeper, Sarah et al., *Good Schools for Young Children*. NY: Macmillan Co., 1974.

McFadden, Michael, *Bachelor Fatherhood: How to Raise and Enjoy Your Children as a Single Parent*. New York: Grosset and Dunlap, 1975.

McGovern, Ann, *Arrow Book of Poetry*. New York: Scholastic Magazines, 1965.

Salk, Lee, *What Every Child Would Like His Parents to Know*. New York: Warner Books, 1973.

Glossary

Page or chapter reference given after every entry.

affective guidance Adult guidance of infant behavior, by expressing appreciation of good behavior or disapproval of undesired behavior. (pp. 177–178, 249–250)

aggression An act marked by an attack on someone or something. (p. 374)

ambivalence The condition of being drawn both toward and away from something. (p. 66)

amniocentesis A technique that tests whether a fetus has abnormal chromosomes that could cause disease or mental retardation. (p. 66)

anemia Tiredness that occurs when the blood does not contain enough iron. (p. 84)

antibodies Substances that fight against bodily infection. (p. 143)

attachment behavior A baby's affection for a person who regularly attends to the child's needs. (pp. 125–126)

autonomy The ability to act freely and independently. (p. 244)

babble A baby's playful use of lips and vocal cords in repeating sounds. (p. 136)

babyproofing Making the home and other places free from hazards that might threaten the child's safety. (pp. 168–169)

baby teeth A baby's first teeth, which begin to appear approximately at age 6 months. (p. 121)

Basic Four The four food groups that provide the essential nutrients for life and growth. (p. 83)

bonding Establishment of a healthy, affectionate attachment between child and parent. (p. 165)

Braxton-Hicks contractions Occasional, irregular painless contractions felt by many women during the course of their pregnancy. (p. 76).

breech position The positioning of a baby in the uterus so that the baby moves down the birth canal buttocks first, instead of head first. (p. 190)

carbohydrates Natural sugars found in fruits, milk, bread, sweets, and vegetables. (p. 83)

care giver A person who earns a wage by taking care of children. (pp. 18, 32)

cervix The channel through which a baby passes to emerge from the woman's body. (p. 104)

cesarean section An operation in which a doctor removes a baby from the uterus through a cut made in the woman's abdominal wall. (p. 109)

child-care aide A person who assists a teacher in a child-care center, where care is provided for children all or part of the day. (p. 32)

child-care career A job or profession that involves caring for children. (ch. 1)

chromosomes Threadlike particles within a cell nucleus that carry the cell's genes. (p. 64)

circumcision The surgical operation that removes a portion of the skin covering the head of the penis. This portion of skin is called the *foreskin*. (p.166)

colic A pain or cramp in the baby's stomach, caused by the formation of gas. (p. 150)

complication Any danger to the mother's life or to the life of the fetus during childbirth. (p. 73)

conception The union of the male and female sex cells within the woman's body. (p. 47)

conditioning Repeated experiences that affect attitudes and actions for a lifetime. (p. 21)

contraction The tightening and relaxing of the muscles surrounding the uterus during childbirth. (p. 105)

cooperative nursery school A school organized by parents who want to provide a nursery school program for their children at low cost. (p. 341)

cooperative play A type of play in which children, about 4 years old, have enough social maturity to play *with* each other. (p. 299)

cradle cap A patch of scaly crust on an infant's scalp, usually prevented by daily washing and massaging of the scalp. (p. 149)

crib death Sudden death of an infant during the night. (p.172)

"custodian concept" The definition of parenting that suggests that parents are caretakers of another life. (p. 49)

day care 8 to 10 hours of care for toddlers, outside the home. (p. 274)

deciduous teeth Teeth of infants, toddlers, and preschool children. See *Baby teeth* (p. 206)

development A baby's increased physical, mental, emotional, and social skills. (p. 118)

diarrhea A condition marked by severe looseness of the bowels, which may be caused by eating particular foods or by an infection. (p. 166)

dilation Enlargement of the cervix, especially during childbirth. (p. 104) diphtheria A contagious bacterial infection, with symptoms of high fever, difficulty in breathing, and general weakness. (p. 167)

direct guidance Adults' actions and verbal instructions that guide very young children toward desired forms of behavior. (p. 177; ch. 25)

discipline Positive teaching designed to bring about acceptable behavior. (pp. 175–176)

dominant genes Genes that are strong in relation to other genes. When a dominant gene is paired with a recessive one, the characteristic of the dominant gene becomes visible, while the characteristic of the recessive gene is hidden. (p. 64)

dramatic play Spontaneous play in which children pretend to be people or animals and take part in events that they know about. (p. 301)

egocentric Self-centered. (p. 224)

emotion A strong feeling that seems to arise spontaneously in a person. (ch. 13)

emotional development A child's progress in being able to express feelings, such as love, joy, or unhappiness. (p. 128)

emotional problems A child's frequent unhappiness as opposed to occasional outbursts of undesirable emotion. (pp. 217–218)

empathy The ability to imagine how others feel. (p. 374)

episiotomy A small cut in the opening of woman's vagina, made during childbirth, to make it easier for the baby's head to come out. (p. 109)

family day-care home A home in which an adult provides care for other children, while also caring for his or her own children. (p. 185)

fats Chemical substances found in plant and animal tissue. (p. 84)

fetal alcohol syndrome (FAS) A set of serious birth defects sometimes found in babies born to women who drank large amounts of alcohol during their pregnancy. (p. 91)

fetal monitor A device used to record a woman's contractions and the fetal heartbeat during childbirth. (p. 105)

fetus The name applied to unborn young from the end of the eighth week after conception until the moment of birth. (ch. 7)

"finger foods" Foods that a baby can hold alone and eat as an introduction to self-feeding. Examples are toast sticks and crackers. (pp. 161–162)

folic acid A chemical substance necessary for proper bone development. (p. 85)

fontanel The area at the top of a baby's head between the four skull bones where the bones have not yet joined. Also called the "soft spot." (p. 119)

foreskin The loose fold of skin that covers the head of the penis. See circumcision. (p. 166)

formula The combination of milk, water, and sugar (or corn syrup) that is mixed as food for the bottle-fed infant. (pp. 144–145)

fraternal twins Twins that are produced when two ova are released by a woman's ovary and each is fertilized by a different sperm. (p. 66)

free-play program A program where children may choose their own materials and play with them as they wish. (p. 347)

general practitioners Doctors who provide overall health care and a wide range of medical services. (p. 71)

genetics The study of heredity. (p. 63)

glucose Sugar water, usually given intravenously to pregnant women in labor to maintain energy and a high blood-sugar level. (p. 107)

grasp reflex A baby's involuntary (automatic) response to an object that touches the palm of the hand. (p. 121)

gynecologist A doctor whose specialty is the health of the female reproductive organs. (p. 70)

Head Start A prekindergarten program funded by the federal government for children of poor families. (p. 341)

head-to-toe direction The direction of physical development in babies. Development occurs first in the head region, then in the trunk, and last in the legs and feet. (p. 118)

health protections Measures taken to safeguard a baby's health. (pp. 164–165)

hidden curriculum Games and educational toys used as learning activities for toddlers. (p. 281)

identical twins Twins that are produced when a single fertilized ovum splits into two identical cells. (p. 66)

incisors A baby's first 6 teeth, the 2 lower middle teeth and the 4 upper front teeth. (p. 121)

indirect guidance Any method of guiding children toward desired behavior that sets the stage for the child to act properly, instead of using direct communication. (p. 177; ch. 25)

infant-care center A place where infants are cared for while parents work. (ch. 19)

infectious Able to cause infection. (ch. 24)

inheritance The set of characteristics established the moment the sex cells combine. (p. 63)

inoculations Injections or vaccinations given by physicians to protect against diseases such as diphtheria, pertussis (whooping cough), tetanus, polio, measles, and mumps. (pp. 166–167)

jealousy An emotion that combines anger, fear, insecurity, and anxiety. It stems from a real or imagined loss of love. (p. 303)

laboratory nursery school A school, developed by high schools and colleges, that provides a laboratory where students learn child-development principles and care-giver skills. (p. 341)

LaMaze method of childbirth preparation A program of breathing exercises, developed by Dr. Frederick LaMaze, that helps pregnant women take an active part in labor and childbirth. (p. 97)

large motor-coordination toys Toys and equipment used to stimulate the toddler's motor skills. These skills include climbing, walking, jumping, and throwing and catching. (p. 282)

large motor skills Skills such as walking, running, jumping, galloping, hopping, and pedaling that children can practice to develop strong, healthy bodies. (p. 293)

lead teacher The trained person in charge of a group of children in a child-care center. (p. 38)

learning centers Sections of the prekindergarten classroom with room for a few children to work independently of others. (p. 349)

limits Guidelines set by parents and teachers for protection of the child, of other children, and of the environment. (p. 319)

low birth weight Below-normal birth weight, caused by inadequate nutrition during pregnancy. One of the most hazardous risks of children born to teenage mothers. (p. 58)

mainstreaming Placing disabled children in regular classrooms to keep them in the mainstream of life. Educators agree that disabled children develop their potential more fully if they can learn with children who are not disabled. (p. 295)

malnourished Being in poor health. (pp. 81–82)

maturation Total growth and development—physical, emotional, mental, social. (p. 122)

maturity The ability to think and act in a way that is reasonable, responsible, reliable, and independent. (p. 48)

mental development in infancy Growth of the thinking and knowing processes of the brain. (p. 222)

milk substitute Formulas made primarily from soybean powder for babies who are allergic to cow's milk. (p. 146)

milk teeth See *baby teeth.* (p. 206)

minerals Natural substances, found in certain foods, that are necessary to good health. (ch. 8)

minerals in milk Calcium and phosphorus, needed to build strong bones and teeth. (p. 157)

miscarriage Spontaneous abortion of a fetus. (p. 93)

Montessori method A highly structured teaching method, developed by Maria Montessori, that teaches children to perform tasks in a specific, orderly sequence. (p. 347)

motor development Development of a baby's ability to move the body and to use the arms and legs. (p. 133)

motor skills Physical skills that help children develop their muscles and coordination. (pp. 293–294)

negative feedback Disapproval an adult shows to a child whenever the child oversteps limits. (p. 319)

negative self-concept Feelings of inferiority that cause a child to think he or she is bad, weak, incapable of coping with the world, and unloved. (p. 213)

negativism The tendency of toddlers to say "no" frequently. Such behavior is related to a child's urge to become independent. (p. 244)

nurse-midwife A registered nurse, trained in obstetrics and prenatal care, who is able to perform normal deliveries of babies. (p. 71)

nutrient A chemical substance, present in foods, that nourishes the body. The basic nutrients are minerals, proteins, vitamins, carbohydrates, water, and roughage. (p. 156)

object permanency The knowledge that objects continue to exist, even when they are out of sight. (p. 223)

obstetrician A doctor who specializes in delivering babies and caring for pregnant women before, during, and after childbirth. (p. 71)

oral poliovirus A vaccine, given through the mouth, that protects against polio (poliomyelitis). Polio is a very serious viral disease that can cause paralysis, destruction of muscle tissue, and deformity of the body. (p. 238) pacifier   A toy, resembling a nipple, on which a baby sucks. (p. 150)

pap smear   A medical test in which a sample of secretions from the cervix or vagina is examined to detect cancer at an early stage. (p. 75)

parent helper   A person who baby-sits or takes care of a child or children. (p. 40)

parenting role   The functions performed by a person who has the prime responsibility for raising a child or children. (ch. 1)

paternity leave   An employer's grant of permission for a father to be temporarily absent from work so that he can take care of his young child or children at home. (p. 185)

parallel play   Recreational activity in which toddlers play independently in the same area and notice each other. (p. 220)

pediatrician   A doctor who specializes in the care of infants and children (pp. 164–165)

pelvic examination   A physical examination of the uterus and vagina. (p. 75)

perception   The act of becoming aware of something through the senses, especially through sight or hearing. (ch. 23)

permanent teeth   The teeth that appear after age 5 or 6 and replace baby teeth. (p. 121)

personality   The sum of the qualities that make a person what she or he is. (ch. 22)

pertussis, or whooping cough   A childhood disease caused by bacterial infection of the lungs and breathing passages. (p. 167)

physical development in infancy   The steady increase in an infant's ability to use and control the body. (p. 193)

physical guidance   A form of direct guidance in which the adult helps the child toward a desired goal by giving physical assistance, such as by extending the arms to beckon the child toward the adult. (pp. 178, 249)

play school   A low-cost school organized by mothers and fathers who want some group play experience for their toddlers. (p. 274)

positive feedback   An adult's positive response to a child's action. Positive feedback encourages desired behavior. (pp. 137, 225)

positive reinforcement   The act of rewarding a child for desired behavior. (p. 180)

positive self-concept   The good feeling that comes from knowing you are worthy of being loved and wanted. (pp. 125, 213)

postpartum depression   Extreme melancholy and periods of crying that may affect a mother shortly after the birth of a child. (p. 153)

premature   Born after a shorter than usual period of development in the uterus. (p. 58)

prenatal care   Care of a mother and fetus before birth. (p. 71)

prenatal health hazard   Any practice or activity by which a pregnant woman may harm the fetus. (p. 88)

preoperational thinker   A child who is past the sensorimotor stage and can put evidence together to form new conclusions. (p. 307)

primary attachment   A strong tie of affection between an infant and an adult. (p. 189)

productive language   Language that the child uses to speak, as distinguished from language spoken by another and received by the child. See *receptive language.* (p. 228)

professional role   An adult's proper behavior in coping with a baby's show of anger. It consists of avoiding anger and giving as little attention to the outburst as possible. (pp. 127–128)

protein foods   Foods rich in proteins, for example, meat, eggs, fish, poultry, beans, and milk. (p. 158)

proteins   Nutrients essential in building the body's muscle tissue. (p. 84)

random   Unplanned. (p. 64)

recall   The ability to remember information or experience that is stored in the brain. (p. 223)

receptive language   "Understood language." Language spoken by another person and received by a child. (p. 228)

recessive genes   Genes that are weak in relation to other genes. The characteristic carried by a recessive gene will recede, or not be physically visible, when a recessive gene is paired with a dominant gene. (p. 64)

Rh factor   A substance present in the blood of most people. Blood that does not contain this substance is called *Rh negative.* Both types of blood are healthy. (p. 92)

Rhogam   A medication that can be given to mothers with Rh negative blood to avoid childbirth complications. (p. 92)

rubella   German measles. (p. 92)

self-absorbing stitches   Surgical stitches made with thread that dissolves naturally, instead of having to be removed later. (p. 109)

self-concept   A developing image of oneself. Signs such as mental, physical, and emotional development, a good appearance, and the like help improve a child's self-concept. (p. 365)

self-demand schedule A flexible routine that fulfills a baby's needs, rather than a fixed schedule. (p. 142)

senses The five sense organs: sight, hearing, taste, smell, and touch. (p. 136)

sensorimotor stage The stage of intellectual development during the first two years of life that focuses on using the fives senses and on the physical handling of objects. (p. 223)

sensory Having to do with the senses. See *senses*. (ch. 23)

sex-role stereotyping Dramatic play in which children take on stereotypic roles, according to their gender. Parents and teachers should encourage equality of the sexes. (p. 303)

sibling rivalry Competition among brothers and sisters for their parents' attention. (p. 303)

small motor-coordination toys Puzzles, writing utensils, bath toys, or similar small articles that stimulate the toddler's motor skills. (p. 283)

small motor skills Skills, such as independent dressing and playing with crayons, puzzles, and small blocks, practiced by children in the pre-primary years. (p. 294)

social development The gradual process of forming relationships with other people and learning expected social behavior. (p. 125)

social interaction The process of affecting others and being affected by others. (pp. 218–219)

socialization The process by which children learn and use skills that enable them to get along in society. (p. 175)

"solids" So-called solid foods for a baby, especially strained cereal and fruit, as distinguished from liquids, such as milk. (pp. 159–160)

solitary play Recreational play in which young toddlers ignore other children instead of becoming part of the activity of a group. (p. 220)

speculum An instrument that opens the walls of the vagina during a pelvic examination. (p. 75)

staff-child ratio In a center that provides group care for infants, the number of adult care givers per number of children. (pp. 186, 189)

stages of labor The three parts of the childbirth process: (1) dilation of the cervix, (2) birth of the baby, and (3) expulsion of the placenta and other tissues. (pp. 105–109)

sterilization of formula The process of boiling the milk mixture used in bottle feeding to kill any harmful bacteria. (p. 146)

stimulating environment An environment that encourages infants to develop mentally by using their five senses. (p. 136)

stimulus Something that is received by one of the five senses and transmitted as information to the brain. (pp. 222–223)

substitute care giver A person, other than the mother or father, who provides care for a young child, usually on a day-long basis. (p. 184)

sucking reflex A baby's automatic sucking action, present from birth. (p. 120)

sudden infant death syndrome See *crib death*. (p. 172)

temper tantrum A fit of bad temper that may be either a child's early striving for independence or an act for attention getting. (p. 214)

temporary teeth A child's first teeth, also called *milk teeth*. (p. 366)

"terrible two's" A term that describes the peak stage when toddlers strive for independence and display a trait called *negativism*. (p. 244)

tetanus A bacterial disease that most often enters the body through an open wound. (p. 167)

time line A graph of how you will spend the years of your life. (p. 15)

toddlerproofed Arranged in a way that ensures freedom of movement and safety for a toddler, while protecting adult valuables. (pp. 245–246)

toxemia A condition often suffered by pregnant women, probably caused by malnutrition. (p. 92)

transition An uncomfortable period of rapid, irregular contractions that occurs between the first and second stages of childbirth. (p. 107)

verbal guidance A form of direct guidance of child behavior. An adult speaks to the child to bring about desired behavior. (pp. 178, 249)

Vitamin foods Foods rich in vitamins necessary for normal life functions: milk, egg yolk, green and yellow vegetables, cereals, meats, dairy products, and citrus fruits. (p. 158)

vocabulary The total number of words that a person uses or is capable of using. (pp. 136–137)

wage-earning role The set of functions performed by a person to earn money. (ch. 1)

well-nourished Being in good health. (pp. 81–82)

woman's personal preparation for childbirth Activities that prepare a person mentally and physically for the birth of a child, including visits to the doctor, book reading, classes, and exercise. (pp. 95–98)

X and Y chromosomes The hereditary material in a cell nucleus that determines sex. (p. 65)

Index